CHINESE IN THE WOODS

Chinese in the Woods

*Logging and Lumbering
in the American West*

SUE FAWN CHUNG

UNIVERSITY OF ILLINOIS PRESS
URBANA, CHICAGO, AND SPRINGFIELD

Library of Congress Cataloging-in-Publication Data
Chung, Sue Fawn
Chinese in the woods : logging and lumbering in the American West /
Sue Fawn Chung.
pages   cm. — (The Asian American experience)
Includes bibliographical references and index.
ISBN 978-0-252-03944-7 (hardcover : acid-free paper) —
ISBN 978-0-252-09755-3 (e-book)
1. Foreign workers, Chinese—West (U.S.)—History—19th century.
2. Loggers—West (U.S.)—History—19th century. 3. Lumbermen—
West (U.S.)—History—19th century. 4. Chinese—West (U.S.)—
History—19th century. 5. Immigrants—West (U.S.)—History—19th
century. 6. Working class—West (U.S.)—History—19th century.
7. Lumber trade—Social aspects—West (U.S.)—History—19th century.
8. West (U.S.)—Economic conditions—19th century. 9. West (U.S.)—
Ethnic relations—History—19th century. I. Title.
HD8081.C5C47   2015
331.6'251097809034—dc23   2015006371

For Alan Solomon, my invaluable helper

CONTENTS

ACKNOWLEDGMENTS

The story of the Chinese in logging would not have been told except for the archaeological work that revealed much about the lifestyle of these men who left no written record. The United States Department of Agriculture Forest Service, Humboldt-Toiyabe Division, especially archaeologists Fred Frampton and Terry Birk working in conjunction with University of Nevada, Reno, Professor Emeritus of Anthropology Donald Hardesty and his graduate students, particularly Kelly Dixon, Ralph Giles, Jane Lee, and Theresa Solury, have augmented our knowledge. Former Olympic Forest Service Supervisor Dale Hom assisted in obtaining grants for the projects. The volunteers in the Passport in Time program lent invaluable assistance in uncovering material artifacts. Much has yet to be discovered and hopefully more work in the field will be forthcoming. Other archaeologists, especially Penny Rucks, Clifford Shaw, Carrie E. Smith, Susan Lindstrom, Priscilla Wegars, Barbara Voss, Paul Chace, Robert Morrill, and Mary Rusco were among the many who guided me in studying archaeology. Alexander and Alan Solomon joined me at the pit sites while I served as historical consultant.

The written records were also fragmentary. Professor Emeritus Roger Daniels introduced me to the importance and use of census data and other primary sources. Marian Smith, Immigration and Naturalization (INS) historian, showed me valuable INS resources. National Archives and Records Administration (NARA) staff members at Seattle, Riverside (Perris), Washington, D.C., and San Francisco (San Bruno), especially Marisa Louie and volunteer Vincent Chin, were very helpful. Wuyi University sponsored a tour of several Siyi counties in Guangdong under the leadership of Jinhua Selia Tan; the tours demonstrated what occurred in the home regions of the Chinese Americans. The staff members of the Nevada State Historic Preservation Office (especially Ronald James), Nevada State Museum (especially Robert Nylen), Nevada State Railroad Museum (especially Wendell Huffman), Nevada Historical Society (especially Lee Brumbaugh), Nevada State Archives and Library (especially Guy Rocha), Storey County Courthouse, Washoe County Recorder's Office, Ormsby County Recorder's Office, Douglas County government offices, Truckee Historical Society (especially Gordon Richards), California State Railroad Museum in Sacramento (especially Stephen Drew), California State Archives, Shanghai University Library (especially Luxia You), Shanghai Public Library, Huntington Library, Bancroft

Library, Ethnic Library at the University of California, Berkeley (especially Wei-Chi Poon of the Asian American Division), Special Collections at the University of California (San Diego and Los Angeles), Special Collections Divisions at the University of Nevada (Reno and Las Vegas, especially Su Kim Chung and Christine Wiatrowski), and the University of Washington, Seattle, all allowed me generous access to numerous archival materials. The University of Nevada, Las Vegas, and especially the History Department and Dean of the College of Liberal Arts, have been very supportive of this endeavor. Oral interviews with the late Professor Elmer Rusco of the University of Nevada, Reno, the late Frank Chang of Lovelock, the late Shirlaine Kee Baldwin of Berkeley, the late John Fulton of Tahoe City, the late Anna Kwock of San Francisco, former Forest Service Ranger Clifford Shaw, Ray Walmsley of Dayton, Robert Morrill of San Francisco, Andrea Yee of Berkeley, Landon Quan of Santa Rosa, John Fong of Carlin, the late Henry Yup of Reno and Lovelock, Rowena Chow of Los Altos Hills, Dennis Wong of San Marino, and Ynez Lisa Lai Chan Jung of San Rafael added insights into this project. I am indebted to Nicholas Menzies, James Rawls, Yong Chen, and Evelyn Hu-Dehart for their comments. University of Nevada Reno graduate student Ralph Giles was extremely helpful with Carson Tahoe Lumber and Fluming Company documents. Several of my graduate students at the University of Nevada Las Vegas, especially Philip Lockett and John J. Crandall, also uncovered information for this project. Special thanks go to Annette Amdal, UNLV History Department administrator, and the editorial staff at the University of Illinois Press, especially Laurie Matheson, Thomas R. Ringo II, and Julie Gay for their invaluable assistance.

Roger Daniels, who introduced me to Asian American history, contributed the title for the book. Alan Moss Solomon drove me to many sites throughout the American West and British Columbia so that I could do the research, and he helped in editing the first rough draft. For all of his efforts and support, I have dedicated this book to him.

Chinese names can be complicated. In China the family name, being the most important, was stated first, followed by the first name, usually composed of two characters, hence two words. A few Chinese surnames, such as Ouyang (Cantonese Owyang) and Sima (Cantonese Seeto), are polysyllabic. The formal name often indicated generation and birth order for males. Males also had a familiar first name. Other names, such as a nickname, school name, birth order name (such as Li San—Li "number three") or studio name, might be adopted. "Ah" was a term of address, not a name, but the general American public was unaware of this and mistakenly believed it was a Chinese first or last name.

In general, if the Chinese characters are known, the last name is given in pinyin Romanization (officially adopted in China in 1949) first (in Chinese tradition), often with the Cantonese pronunciation or American version in parenthesis with the exception of well-known people such as Sun Yatsen. The last name of individuals can be variously spelled so that, for example, Wu in American documents could be Ng, Ang, Ung, Ong, and Eng, or Chen can be Chan, Chin, Chinn, Chen, Chung, but the pinyin permits uniformity. The exception is the Yu/Yi clan in Nevada, where the common American Yee is used, since the characters for all of the names were not available. If only the transliteration is known from English language sources, the name is given as written and usually with the first name first and family name last. There are one hundred common family names in China. Kee is not one but comes from immigration officials and often is seen in government records. Most names on the census were distortions or adaptations of formal Chinese names. Consequently, it has been difficult to trace individuals for two or three census periods. The census takers randomly spelled the name as they heard them. Complications arise when American government officials reversed the names, so that Joe Shoong (Zhou Song in pinyin, 1879–1961), one of the early Chinese American millionaires in California, got the family name of Shoong (his Chinese first name). A few Chinese took American first names. An even smaller number adopted American first and last names, either because they worked primarily with Euro-Americans or took the first step in "American-ization." Jim Humbold and William Poor were examples of men who adopted American names and lived in the boarding house with other Chinese who worked in logging in Virginia City, Nevada (Census 1870). Jim King, a Central Pacific Railroad (CPRR) foreman and labor contractor of Locke, California, originally from Zhongshan, and Billy Ford, a railroad supervisor in Sparks, Nevada, origi-nally from Kaiping, were known by their American names and had adopted an American lifestyle for themselves and their families. Men also became known by the name of their business. Dr. Wing Lee of Portland and Salem, Oregon, was a Chinese doctor who arrived in 1862 or 1864 with the family name of Zhang (in pinyin; variously transliterated in Cantonese-English as Chang, Chung, Jung, Cheung, Chiang, and other spellings) and the full name of Zhang Liang Rong Li (Liang was his first name, Rong Li was his mother's name), using the traditional order of names with last name first, but known to Oregonians as Dr. Wing Lee.

When known, birth, death, and immigration dates are given as a temporal context for the individual. The census takers were often inaccurate and erred on undercounting the Chinese men and especially women. One reason was a (foreign) language problem but the other also might have been the fact that poll taxes were levied against the Chinese using census data. Individuals found in the newspapers often were not in the census even though the individual, like vegetable peddler Sam Lee Melarkey, lived in Winnemucca, Nevada, for over forty years.

Upon first mention, association names are given in pinyin with the Cantonese or commonly spelled name in parenthesis, thus allowing for the uniformity in transliteration. Place names and terms referring to China are usually rendered in pinyin, but Cantonese is used for the people who originate in the vicinity of Guangzhou (Canton). In some instances the pinyin/Cantonese rendition is used.

The term Euro-American is used because it is more precise than the com-monly used "white" and Caucasian. It designates peoples of European ancestry in the United States and therefore does not include peoples of Central and South American or Asian Indian ancestry.

NVSHPO, formerly known as "Find People," is used to designate the Nevada State Historical Preservation Office's online census database (1860–1920), which was compiled from the National Archives *Census Manuscripts* (Population Sched-ules of the Bureau of Census, usually referred to simply as "census") issued every decade except in 1890, when the schedules for the western states were accidentally destroyed by fire. The database and census were used for numerous individuals in this study, but NVSHPO discontinued the database around September 2013.

ABBREVIATIONS

BBRR	Bodie and Benton Railroad
CCBA	Chinese Consolidated Benevolent Association (Chinese Six Companies)
CCRR	Carson and Colorado Railroad
CPRR	Central Pacific Railroad
CTLFC	Carson Tahoe Lumber and Flume Company
EDWFC	El Dorado Wood and Fluming Company
PMSC	Pacific Mail Steamship Company
PLWC	Pacific Lumber and Wood Company
PWLC	Pacific Wood and Lumber Company
PWLFC	Pacific Wood and Lumber Fluming Company
SNWLC	Sierra Nevada Wood and Lumber Company
SPRR	Southern Pacific Railroad
SVRR	Sacramento Valley Railroad
SWLFC	Sierra Wood and Lumber Fluming Company
TLC	Truckee Lumber Company
UPRR	Union Pacific Railroad
VLC	Verdi Lumber Company
VTRR	Virginia and Truckee Railroad

INTRODUCTION

Little is known about the Chinese working in the woods, a crucial but ephemeral occupation in the history of the American West, because the men and their employers wrote little or nothing about what transpired. A closer look at the Chinese men in the woods, with a focus on the Sierra Nevada in the 1870s to 1890s, reveals that these men often constituted 90 percent of the workers, performed a variety of tasks, had limited upward mobility, sometimes earned more than the one dollar per day salary generalization (and even surpassed non-Chinese workers in wages earned), interacted with the larger community while maintaining close contact with their fellow countrymen, and left the occupation around the turn of the twentieth century for reasons beyond their control. Like the railroad employers, influential lumbermen like Richard Henry Alexander (1844–1915) of the prestigious Hastings Sawmill in British Columbia erroneously asserted that the Chinese were physically incapable of working in the woods (Canada, Parliament 1902, 367). The Chinese often found their jobs through regional and/or family associations, labor contractors, or friends as a part of chain migration. This is exemplified by examining the Yee (pinyin Yu) clan network that enabled them to get jobs, obtain familiar goods, and maintain ties with their native place and fellow regionals in Nevada. While their experiences and lifestyles were somewhat unique to each location, there were generalizations that emerged that demonstrated the challenges they faced and contradicted popular stereotypes of Chinese workers as docile, cheap laborers. Emerging Euro-American lumber barons, such as Duane L. Bliss and Henry M. Yerington, were willing to hire them and support them during economic downturns and anti-Chinese movements. Both the Chinese and lumber barons were able to prosper as lumber companies transformed from small entrepreneurial concerns in the pre-1870s to larger and growing enterprises prior to 1900. Chinese successes and the emerging union leadership contributed to the expanding anti-Chinese sentiment that led to their expulsion from logging towns, first in the late 1870s and then in the mid-1880s. Carson City and Truckee, with a brief look at other towns, illustrated the differences in the development and outcomes of the anti-Chinese activities. Racial tensions and multiethnic interactions played important roles in working conditions.

This study demonstrates Chinese workers' heretofore unrecognized contribution to the building of the American West by examining their migration, their

communities and lifestyles, transnationalism, their work in relationship to mining and railroad construction, the timber barons and companies that employed
them, the anti-Chinese movements, and their departure from the Sierra Nevada
forests. Without their labor the communities in the West would not have been
settled as quickly in the last half of the nineteenth century.

This study focuses on the Sierra Nevada (Spanish for "snow-covered mountains") with its spur, the Carson Range, which straddles the central California and
northern Nevada borders, yet similar situations could be found in other western
forests (J. James 1995; Scott 1975). The pristine forests of the Sierra Nevada, ranging four hundred miles long and forty to eighty miles wide from Tehachapi Pass
(near Bakersfield) in the south to the Susan River near Lassen Peak in the north,
along the borders of California and Nevada, provided the majority of the wood
for the regional mines, including the famous underground Comstock mines: ties,
cars, fuel, and bridges for railroads, particularly the transcontinental railroad and
Nevada's intrastate lines, and building materials for the new booming communities in the West and overseas in Hawai'i, Japan, and China.

In the 1850s to 1860s farming, ranching, and mining were the major attractions for the new western settlers. The forests often satisfied the innumerable
needs of the new communities with wood products and opened the doors to
more widespread mining and railroad construction. In 1849 Sutter's sawmill,
near Coloma, California, was the site of the discovery of gold that started the
gold rush to the West. Houses, buildings, barns, fences, sidewalks, barns, wagons,
bridges, firewood, and equipment were matched by the miners' need for fuel for
the mills, long toms and other equipment, underground mining supports, machinery, wheels, and numerous other items. The small timber owners generally
could hire only new immigrants who were eager to do any type of job to work in
the woods. Among them, Chinese immigrants were drawn to the work because
many had some experience in China in logging; because discriminatory laws
and local policies did not allow them to mine and kept them from other desirable jobs; and because this occupation afforded them a good living as well as the
opportunity to work away from anti-Chinese agitators.

As the West developed, employment opportunities were plentiful, and many
adventurers made fortunes from both mining and lumbering. Alvinza Hayward
of the Sierra Flume and Lumber Company of California exemplified many early
timber barons whose firms thrived between 1875 and 1878 (Hutchinson 1973). Often,
money made from mining funded endeavors in logging. Hayward first made his
fortune through the Crown Point Mine on the Comstock Lode beginning in 1870.
He expanded into logging and bought timberland in California's Plumas, Lassen,
and Tehama Counties, totaling one hundred thousand acres for $516,000—worth
$1.5 million in cash by 1877. He owned two hundred thousand acres of forest land,
ten sawmills, twenty-three miles of logging tramway, 156 miles of lumber flume,
three planing and molding mills, two sash/door/blind factories, three lumberyards,

a telegraph line, and a main office and export agency in San Francisco. Like other timber barons with extensive holdings, Hayward probably hired many Chinese workers who worked in the woods in these counties (Census 1880).

Hiring workers was often difficult for early timber ranchers because they had to compete with mine owners for employees. The Chinese were often available because many Euro-American gold prospectors, who believed that they could get rich quickly, did not want to work in logging. The Chinese were responsive to any call for employment, and logging was a familiar occupation: cutting timber for fuel and construction was a common occupation in every South China village. They carried out a wide range of duties in the woods and, as was the custom, were paid according to the type of work they performed. Chinese played a major role in several forests in the West from the 1870s to the early 1900s, a period when the industry experienced its greatest growth. Between the 1870s and 1880s Chinese workers—an unofficial estimate sets their population at approximately three thousand—represented from 80 percent to 90 percent of the workers in the Sierra Nevada. They lived in temporary tents or log cabins in the mountains or in boardinghouses in the nearby Chinatowns or at wood camps. Because of their isolation in the mountains, these workers found that Chinese goods were often unavailable, so they had to adapt to American culture and foods, as seen in archaeological evidence. In some cases they were integrated with other groups of men in logging; but when the crew was managed or the company owned by East Coast men, they remained in segregated work groups (see chapter 2).

Like the non-Chinese loggers, between 1850 and 1900 they transitioned from a relatively young, predominantly single, male workforce to an older one. By 1920 there were only a handful of Chinese woodcutters scattered throughout the West, including one on the border of Nevada and California, China Tom, who was married and living with his wife and children. At this time Euro-Americans in the woods also brought their wives and children into wood camps and logging towns, and the loggers' lifestyles became more family oriented. By the 1920s, the majority of Chinese moved from logging into other, less physically strenuous occupations.

Concern among the Chinese about forest management had a long history. Nicholas K. Menzies (1994b), who studied the history of forestry and deforestation in China, especially southeastern China, discovered that the Chinese already wrote about forest management in the Shang Dynasty (ca. 1700–1027 B.C.). Even the famous Confucian philosopher Mencius (372–289 B.C.) of the Zhou Dynasty (1027–221 B.C.) wrote, "If the axes . . . enter the hills and forests only at the proper time, the wood will be more than can be used" (Mengzi 1923, 3:130). "Forest farmers" planted crops between the rows of trees for greater productivity (Menzies 1988b). Religious temples raised trees to earn money to support the temples. Wood charcoal was produced for fuel as well, and the soot from charcoal kilns was the main ingredient in Chinese ink.

Sawing wood in China was a labor-intensive job. These two men, using a hand saw, cut wood for themselves and people in their village.

The process of logging was similar in South China and the American West. In China, timber farmers specialized in forest management because it was vital to their business. Often, certain clans dominated the timber trade (Zurndorfer 1985). Various segments of society played a role in the timber market, and each "shared in the financial risk, the peril of [transporting logs down] the river, and the profit promised at the point of sale" (Songster 2003, 455). Workers began by felling the timber and then bringing the wood from the mountain to the river. Timber owners designated the trees to be cut. The fellers, called *linhu* ("forest households"), were hired laborers working for lumber companies or private landlords. Using different types of axes and, eventually, different types of saws, they harvested the fir or pine trees at about ten to fifteen meters high for fast cash returns; new trees were planted and matured in about twenty years. Men hauled the logs on skid roads or on their backs to the waterways or market towns. These transient workers had to rely on mountain brokers (*shanke*), who also were transient, to introduce them to river merchants who moved the logs on the river to the timber mills, often using slipways, forerunners of the flume system (Totman 1995; "Dollar Steamship Company"). Roads had to be constructed, and this often involved cutting, filling, and bridging ravines and rice paddies to create the proper gradient for moving the logs to the streams (Songster 2003). Some bridges for log transportation were fifteen hundred feet long and forty feet high from ground level (Cannon 1925, 49). The descent from the mountains could be treacherous and rapid. Men and wood were at risk. From the river, the timber often went directly to the marketplace and was sold by specialized merchants domestically or internationally. Native banks supplied loans for the commercial exchanges. Many villages had a shop that specialized in selling wood products.

In South China, logging practices changed. By the late eighteenth century, clear cutting and the destruction of the forests left many Chinese woodsmen without a job. Trade with the West and the increased demand for tea led to deforestation as the land was cleared for growing tea and other crops for overseas sales. Bandit and rebel groups, including the Taiping rebels (1850–1864), Red Turban, and Black Flag groups in neighboring Guangxi, were just a few of the troublemakers responding to the social and economic disruptions in South China. Some of the Cantonese[1] Taiping leaders were forced to flee to the United States, which often was noted in their American obituaries. These disruptions led to the government's policy of burning forests where rebels traditionally hid. The destruction of forestlands and temples was compounded by natural disasters such as floods, droughts, and fires in South China.[2] In 1852 one of the most powerful Chinese officials, Zeng Guofan (1811–1872), reported that the price of silver had doubled in relation to the value of the copper coins, which the common people used, so the resulting inflation was especially hard on the farmers and the general populace because it meant that they paid a 20 percent increase in taxes (Chen and Zhang 1994, 523). Poverty-stricken farmers harvested the remaining trees in order to survive. By 1854 the tall fir trees on Baiyun ("White Cloud") Mountain near Guangzhou, for example, had been ruthlessly cut. Chinese loggers looked to new areas to continue their livelihood, and the American West looked promising.

Mining was the first attraction for Chinese immigrants new to North America, but when they met with resistance and opposition from miners, they turned to other work, such as logging. In 1859 the Gold Hill, Nevada, miners prohibited the Chinese from working there. Virginia City and other mining communities throughout the American West adopted the policy. In the 1870s, when the Great Western Mine in California needed men for timbering work (a highly skilled and better-paying job), Chinese workers were hired (Johnston 2004, 25). Many other mine owners and timber ranchers looked to the Chinese to help them provide wood for the mines. The connection between mining and logging, especially for the Comstock Lode in Nevada, was great in the 1860s to 1890s (see chapter 3).

Railroad construction required tremendous amounts of wood. Train cars, fuel, ties, bridges and trestles, snow sheds, and other facilities all used wood. Logging trains opened new forests. The West could no longer be dependent on the East, so men began to harvest the western forests, especially those near rivers, lakes, and the Pacific Ocean, to make transportation easy. Railroad companies hired thousands of Chinese to do the work, defending the right to use them as workers. Later, large corporations took over smaller logging concerns and continued to hire Chinese workers (see chapter 4).

Many local, state, and federal laws discriminated against the Chinese and helped shape American legal history (Cole and Chin 1999). In 1866, when Congress passed the first federal mining law, the Chinese were effectively excluded from filing mining claims because only citizens were allowed to file. Since the enactment of the 1790 Naturalization Law, the Chinese were barred from becoming citizens because they were not "free white" persons (Gold 2012). The Page Law of 1875 was ostensibly designed to stop the immigration of prostitutes but effectively was used to keep out Chinese women, who, in the 1870s, were widely regarded by Americans as prostitutes (Peffer 1999; Abrams 2005). This created an unnatural, male-only society for most Chinese. On May 7, 1879, California adopted Article 19 for the state constitution, prohibiting corporations from employing (directly or indirectly) any Chinese and allowing the legislature to pass laws to enforce this provision, which it did as early as 1880 (Johnston 2004). Other states followed suit, but often the laws were ignored or struck down by the courts. All of these discriminatory statutes culminated in the passage of the 1882 Chinese Exclusion Act, which made the Chinese the first population not welcomed to immigrate into the United States and set a precedent for Canada and Mexico to follow suit (Chan 1991a; Hing 1993, epilogue; Zhu 2013).

As additional restrictive laws were passed, the Chinese labor pool shrank. Beginning in the 1890s, the influx of Japanese immigrants replaced the Chinese in logging, railroad maintenance, and other jobs until they, too, were excluded from immigrating in 1924 (Dubrow 2002). The 1924 National Origins Quota Immigration Act essentially closed the "golden door" for Asians.

Chinese workers were seldom noted in the history of the West, in accounts of lumber companies and their activities, or in biographies of the lumber barons; occasionally, they were mentioned in passing in a few written works. Such information is so fragmented that some assumptions must be made regarding their experiences in one location as being similar to what occurred elsewhere. In the era of virulent anti-Chinese movements, timber owners and other employers usually tried to hide the fact that they had hired Chinese workers. Very few documents acknowledge any type of leadership or managerial role by the Chinese, but payroll records indicated otherwise. Moreover, independent Chinese companies contracted to supply wood for the Central Pacific Railroad and other entities. The contributions of the Chinese immigrants in the lumber industry provided the bridge between the booming mining and railroad industries and the development of the communities in the West. In this way the Chinese contributed to the building of the American West (chapters 4 and 5).

This study will try to dispel some of the popular stereotypes that developed during this period of emerging unionism. It will also question the validity of the assumption of "cheap Chinese labor" that has been a cornerstone of interpreting the Chinese experience in late-nineteenth-century America (Tam 2002, 124–39): Chinese workers held a variety of positions in logging and were not paid the lower wages portrayed in popular literature. District court records demonstrated that Chinese lumber contractors received the same amount of money for the same amount of wood as non-Asian lumber contractors such that there was equality in earned income. Chinese workers were also not the docile workers they were often portrayed to be. For example, in April 1873 the Chinese called for a strike against James Lemon, the contract grader on the Collins Summit, California, project who wanted to increase the workday for his seventy-five-member Chinese crew from ten to eleven hours; Lemon was forced to recant (MacGregor 2003, 89). As Lucy Salyer (1995) and Charles McClain (1994) have demonstrated, the Chinese were also not hesitant to go to court. Washoe County (Nevada) district court records reveal that this trend was regional. In many of the pre-1882 cases, the Chinese won their lawsuits in matters of employment. As well, the employers of Chinese often protected their workers from anti-Chinese agitators (chapter 5). In return, Chinese workers helped many companies achieve financial success.

Using a combination of archaeological reports, government documents, immigration papers, theses and dissertations, newspaper articles, court records, lumber company records, census data, railroad records, oral histories, memoirs, letters, and other archival materials, as well as secondary sources in Chinese and English, a picture of the Chinese experiences in the lumber industry emerges. Visits to many of the former logging sites augmented this study. Although consideration is given to studies in geography, environmental studies, and economics, this work uses theories and information from the fields of history, sociology, anthropology, and archaeology, and it considers, too, the objectivity and prejudices of the various authors (Chan, 1996a, 8–17; Chan 1996b, 363–99). Studies about Chinese Americans have shaped interpretations of the past, and from the nineteenth century to early twentieth century, almost all of the literature cast them in a negative light. Post–civil rights era scholarship has changed the assessment of Chinese American history as scholars reevaluated situations and individuals instead of making generalized statements based on false assumptions. After 1980 American and Australian archaeologists contributed to the field with their assessments of material culture's relationship to ethnic identification and cultural changes. Their work allowed new insights into the lifestyles of Chinese immigrants who left no early written record (Voss 2005; Ross 2013). For example, the diversity of ceramic pieces found among more expensive tableware indicated a rise from a low station to higher level in the segmented labor market. An analysis of specific locations and local/regional experiences provided greater insights into the Chinese American experience.

Local and regional racism, economic competition, religious hostility, and nativism were also part of the growing national discrimination against the Chinese.

The popularity of pseudoscientific concepts about the superiority of the Euro-American or white race and inferiority of colored peoples—Chinese (Mongolians), American Indians, and African Americans—fed into the racism of the nineteenth and early twentieth centuries (A. Chan 1981, xvi; Anderson 1991). Abolitionists raised the issue of color, and the Civil War highlighted the American racial consciousness. The interrelationship between the different ethnic groups was a factor in the plight of the Chinese and the evolution of American racism. The need to solve the post–Civil War problems surrounding the position of African Americans affected the position of the Chinese in American society and intensified racism toward people of color (Aarim-Heriot 2003). An American "color conscious" developed: African Americans were labeled "black," American Indians "red," and Asians "Chinese" or "Mongolian" or "yellow." These perceived differences were reflected in the census, attitudes, politics, and literature of the time.

Influential historian Hubert Howe Bancroft (1832–1918), in his *History of California* (1890, vol. 7), reflected the popular description of the Chinese: "The color of their skin, the repulsiveness of their features, their undersize figure, their incomprehensible language, strange customs and heathen religion . . . conspire to set them apart." Clearly physical and cultural differences separated the Chinese from the majority population.

The rapid growth of foreign-born Chinese in California between 1850 and 1870 added to the awareness of these strangers in the midst of Californians. The Chinese were the most numerous foreign-born group in 1860 (34,935) and 1870 (48,790), compared with the Irish in 1860 (33,147) and 1870 (54,421), who were the other large contingent of immigrants and in this early period often regarded as "black Irish" when they had black hair. The visibility of the Chinese contributed to the growing awareness of ethnic and cultural differences and helped foster American nativism (the fear of and hatred toward foreigners) (Chan 2000, 44–85).

In the late 1860s, as a result of Reconstruction efforts, many Republicans tried to adopt an antiracist stance, but Democrats were quick to adopt the anti-Chinese banner and spread this propaganda. Beginning in 1877, political support from emerging labor union leaders, especially Denis Kearney and his local, which was then national Workingmen's association, popularized the rallying cry to get rid of Chinese laborers, resulting in the 1882 and 1892 national Chinese Exclusion Acts. The new and growing field of popular magazines, especially the *Illustrated WASP* and *Harper's*, AFL labor leader Samuel Gompers's famous speech, "Meat vs. Rice: American Manhood against Asiatic Coolieism; Which Shall Survive?" (1902), and songs like "Ching Ching Chinaman" (1923) popularized powerful derogatory imagery that fanned the flames of the anti-Chinese movements from the 1870s to the 1920s. Pulp fiction also added to the negative images of the Chinese. The fear of "yellow peril" that originated with the Mongol attempt to conquer Europe and Asia in the thirteenth century was revived as Chinese workers, noted for their reputed cheap labor, "swarmed" into the West. Irishman Sax Rohmer (Arthur H. S. War, 1883–1959) began his fictional Fu Manchu series in 1912, and many readers believed the power-hungry scientist who wanted to control the world exhibited a "genetic" trait of the Chinese. Combined with economic competition, depressions, and the lack of political power of the Chinese, anti-Chinese activities were extremely popular and successful beginning in the 1870s, especially among politicians and labor organizers who gained mass support by taking an anti-Chinese stance.

Relations between China and the United States also complicated the development of racist perceptions. Stuart Creighton Miller (1969), among several other scholars, traced the resulting negative images of the Chinese in China and of Chinese Americans, both of which were intertwined, and concluded that these images reinforced racial discrimination. Many Chinese stereotypes developed through the writings of nineteenth-century American diplomats, traders, and missionaries to China, and their attitudes were often quite deprecating.

Sociologist Howard Winant (2001, 19) has argued that race is a "constitutive element, an organizational principle, a praxis and structure that has constructed and reconstructed world society since the emergence of modernity." Race involved cultural and economic systems that created hierarchical divisions between communities. Late-nineteenth-century writers and scholars used racism as a reason to not be concerned with the condition of these inferior peoples in their midst, so groups were often ignored or cast in a negative light. This added fuel to the American nativist movement to keep the United States "Anglo-Saxon" and Christian.

Most Chinese could emotionally endure these deprecations because they firmly believed that their two-thousand-year-old continuous Chinese civilization was superior to all other cultures. Their cultural values emphasized community harmony, benevolence, and compromise. Their lack of knowledge about American society discouraged them from fighting back except in critical court cases. Living in relatively isolated ethnic communities (called Chinatowns), they created a survival pattern that was not unlike other American immigrant groups. When they interacted with the larger community, they often encountered hostility and discrimination. This called into question whether American culture and society should be emulated (Arkush 1989, ch. 2). Nor did they have the option of "passing" or "melting" into the majority community, as some immigrant groups could.

Racism influenced the interpretations of the history of the Chinese in America; therefore, it is important to understand the developing trends in order to attempt to reconstruct aspects of their experiences in the American West. Late-nineteenth-century American literature focused on several criticisms of the Chinese: their physical and cultural differences; their inability to assimilate or acculturate—and, conversely, their adherence to their traditions, customs, and beliefs, especially non-Christian values and beliefs (they were therefore called "heathens"); their reputation as "coolie" or "slave labor" working at the direction of labor bosses under adverse conditions or terms, all in an era of freedom for slaves; their reputation as cheap labor, which led to their displacing Euro-Americans (first and later generations whose ancestors came from Europe) from jobs and fueling the rallying cries of newly formed labor unions; their inability to settle in the United States and become residents or immigrants instead of sojourners; their remittances to China, thus hurting the American economy by not spending their earnings in the United States; and their addiction to smoking opium, a habit that spread to the Euro-American population along with other "communicable" health conditions (on labor, Cloud and Galenson, 1987; on health, Shah 2001). Many of these charges were similar to those made against past and contemporary immigrant groups alike, but specifically for the Chinese, federal and state laws and local ordinances that reinforced racism were passed.

One of the main issues was assimilation, often called the "melting pot" and the "melting pot mistake," dominated popular and scholarly writings of between 1900 and 1970. Any attempt to acculturate (assimilate culturally) or assimilate (to merge with the larger community with the implication of becoming nearly indistinguishable) into a host society is a two-way street: the immigrant must want to do it, and the host society must be willing to accept the immigrant. The Chinese made attempts, but racism and discrimination hindered acceptance and assimilation. Scholars and writers traditionally have ignored discernible attempts to acculturate until recently. Instead of helping them merge into the American society, prejudices kept the Chinese separate and isolated.

This phenomenon interested scholars. Sociologists and historians from the 1920s until the 1960s examined the race-relations cycle, a concept developed in the 1920s by Robert E. Park at the University of Chicago. Park theorized that all immigrants, with the exception of African Americans and Asian Americans, passed through four stages of interaction with the host society: contact, competition, accommodation, and assimilation. The Chicago School popularized the fallacious belief that the Chinese were sojourners, men who longed to return to the land of their birth and therefore did not need to adjust to their new social environment. Statistics from the U.S. Secretary of Commerce office, based on the records of the Bureau of Immigration for 1906, showed that many Chinese returned to the United States: in 1901, 2,785 Chinese departed from the United States and 2,280 returned; in 1903, 1,995 departed and 1,459 returned. This indicated that most were not sojourners. With the stricter enforcement of immigration laws in 1905, only 500 departed and 623 returned (House Report 1906, 76). Federal controls against Chinese immigration seemed to be working.

Park's disciple, Rose Hum Lee, focused on the Chinese American experience and demonstrated that the Chinese had not assimilated (Yu 2001). These ideas stemmed from "The Stranger," an essay by Park's mentor, sociologist Georg Simmel (1858–1918) who theorized that when newcomers bring customs and values that differ from those of the indigenous population, the majority community regards them as perpetuators of old ways, unable to change and merge into the new society (Simmel 1955a and 1955b). The belief that the Chinese were strangers, only temporary residents (sojourners) who sent their money back to China instead of investing in America, compounded the criticisms against them.[3] (Yu 2001; Yang 2002, 235–58) Until the mid-twentieth century, there was little academic acknowledgement that sojourning among first-generation immigrants was a universal historical phenomenon for many ethnic groups. Even though Euro-Americans viewed Chinese immigrants as tradition bound and unchanging—unable to assimilate, or "melt"—government records demonstrated that the ratio of those who returned to those who departed was greater, suggesting that the public ignored the reality of the situation.

Land ownership signified the immigrant's desire to be a permanent resident, but most Americans erroneously believed that the Chinese did not own land. The California Legislature tried to prohibit "non-whites" from land ownership, but the court overturned the laws until the 1913 Alien Land Law was passed. Nevada discouraged Asians from owning land, but Article 1 of the state's constitution allowed *resident aliens* to buy and sell real estate. As a result, the Chinese did buy, own, and sell land in Nevada. This included the ownership of timberland and was reasserted in a famous lawsuit initiated by Fook Ling (discussed in chapter 2).

Writings in the 1920s to the 1960s ignored subtle changes of adaptation and accommodation and reinforced the image of the "alien" Chinese. Scholars believed that because of the conflict and antagonism the Chinese experienced, they remained separate and isolated; others writers felt that the Chinese wanted to stay in the comfort zone of their ethnic enclaves. A few saw some integration that laid the foundation for acculturation and assimilation. Historian Oscar Handlin (1951) argued that new immigrants were uprooted from their homeland and felt alienated in their new country. Because nineteenth-century immigrants from Europe could not always be distinguished physically from earlier immigrants, they had an easier time adjusting and assimilating. Based on Handlin's notion of the uprooted immigrant, Gunther Barth (1964) took the concept of assimilation and applied it to the early Chinese immigrant experience, but he encountered inconsistencies because the Chinese, with their cultural distinctiveness, different social organization, and absence of families to ease them into the American society, did not fit into the uprooted and assimilation models. In his opinion, the reason the Chinese did not change was that they were sojourners and resisted assimilation despite efforts by Christian Euro-Americans. Living in ethnic communities, they could preserve their traditions and separate identity. Barth erroneously concluded that the Chinese were primarily at fault for their failure to become Americanized. He did not consider the fact that Americans needed to accept the Chinese as well.

Beginning in the 1960s Asian American studies became more sophisticated as scholars freed themselves from earlier biases. Roger Daniels (1988) called for a reexamination of the plight of Asian Americans, and Robert McClelland (1971) pointed out that the earlier negative images of the Chinese were not realistic and were based on the "private needs" of Euro-Americans. Ethnicity (communal solidarities, cultural attributes, and historical memories) instead of race became a key concept in analyzing immigrant adaptation, and ethnic movements made it acceptable to retain group identity and solidarity. The acknowledgement of multiculturalism as a positive factor in American life made the preservation of traditional customs acceptable. Rapid transportation and instant communication systems made the world seem smaller, and issues such as transnationalism and the Chinese diaspora broadened knowledge about Chinese Americans.

Chinese Americans began to analyze their own history, and more primary sources, especially those written in Chinese, were uncovered, released, and incorporated into published academic works. The careful scrutiny of documents led to new directions in scholarship. In the 1980s historian Yuen-fong Woon (1983–84) proposed that racism and discrimination played a major role in preventing the Chinese from acculturating and assimilating at the same rate as European immigrants. Recently, the controversy has arisen over whether Chinese Americans preserved their culture and bonds with China or adapted their institutions and lifestyles to their new environment (Huang 1993; Chan 1986, 369). As Shehong Chen (2002) and Him Mark Lai (2003) have pointed out, Chinese American organizations, newspapers, families, and elites played an important role in promoting acculturation as more permanent Chinese American urban communities began to evolve in the years between 1916 and 1924. On the other hand, Anthony B. Chan (1981) concluded that the Chinese did not assimilate: they had no political empowerment, were excluded from better-paying occupations, and were segregated in public schools in urban settings like San Francisco. Looking at transnationalism and utilizing both Chinese and English sources, historian Madeline Hsu (2000a) demonstrated the maintenance of connections between the immigrants and their birthplace in Taishan, Guangdong province, in the late nineteenth century through family ties, magazines, government and association efforts, and financial obligations. Like other American immigrants, the Chinese did not ignore the land of their birth, and the Chinese government and Chinese regional and clan associations wooed their support, especially financially (Lai 2003). Numerous other scholars, including many from China, presented new insights from Chinese language sources. Studies about women, men, families, and Chinese interactions with other ethnic groups resulted in a greater understanding of the Chinese American experience.

In 1985 historian John Bodnar proposed the coexistence of two immigrant Americas: one of workers with menial jobs and one, much smaller, of those achieving personal gain and leadership. Most of the Chinese workers were in the first category, but those in the second have been neglected in American history. In the late nineteenth century, Chinese merchants and labor contractors, intermediaries between the Chinese laborers and the larger society, formed part of the elite of the Chinese community and often accomplished this status through the traditional system of kinship ties. The networking allowed those in menial jobs to buy into business partnerships and elevate themselves to the status of "merchants" or laborers who have outstanding debts of one thousand dollars or more or substantial property ownership, which allowed them to visit relatives in China. Chinese Exclusion Act files in the National Archives and Records Administration in Seattle, Washington, have thousands of records showing that Chinese laborers utilized the debt loophole to reenter the United States between 1903 and 1920. As these records demonstrate, only a few Chinese immigrants could visit China, often staying the maximum period of one year allowed by the federal government, but most could do so only once—if at all—after their initial arrival in the United States.

As numerous case studies have shown, there were some who had adjusted to the American lifestyle to such a degree that living in China was regarded as "too backward" and undesirable. Others created ties with family members in China for business, educational, and/or marriage purposes, as demonstrated in several family histories, including Haiming Liu's (2005) study on the Chang clan based in Los Angeles, California. Contrary to the idea that few Chinese entered during the exclusionary era (1882 to 1943), historian Erika Lee (2006, 1) has shown that an estimated 300,955 Chinese—more than the preexclusionary era number of 258,210—entered the United States for the first time, or as returnees, or as American-born citizens or children of men already here.

Sociologists Alejandro Portes and Jozsef Borocz's (1989) segmented assimilation framework argued that various factors, such as the nature of immigration and the reception of the immigrants, led to differing degrees of assimilation. K. Bruce Newbold (2004) added spatial considerations, including the type of employment available, the economic and social strength and size of the ethnic community, the long- or short-term settlement process, and personal attributes, especially the ability to speak English, as contributing factors in assimilation.

In the 1990s archaeologists added to the growing body of scholarship about Asian Americans (Ross 2013). Archaeological investigations of Chinese American sites have provided new insights. In recent decades several U.S. Department of Agriculture Forest Service archaeological projects centering on Chinese sites on federal lands have contributed to the growing knowledge about Chinese Americans and their experiences. The volunteer "Passport in Time" projects (guided by Donald Hardesty and his students at the University of Nevada–Reno, working in the late 1990s with Forest Service archaeologists Fred Frampton and Terry Birk) have attracted many participants to the digs, which have yielded much information and have made the present study possible. Archaeological investigations at Chinese wood camps, such as those in Spooner Summit and Verdi, provided the basis for a great deal of graduate and postgraduate scholarship, such as the works of Leslie Kibler Hill (1987), David Valentine (1999), Theresa Solury (2004), and Jane Lee (2008). The archaeological evidence demonstrated, for example, that the Chinese in the woods could afford better dishware than the miners and railroad workers and in some cases may have had better living quarters and, contrary to popular literature, were involved in all stages of lumbering, from felling the trees to transporting logs to sawmills. Some U.S. Forest Service survey reports are available online, most notably those regarding Genoa Peak Road; Spooner Summit vicinity; Douglas County, Nevada; Slaughterhouse Canyon Railroad Grade; east shore of Lake Tahoe; and Carson City, Carson City County, Nevada (see "Genoa Peak Road and Slaughterhouse Canyon").

Archaeological evidence, discussed later, shows limited aspects of integration. Mary K. Rusco (1981a; 1981b), Donald Hardesty, and Eugene Hattori pioneered archaeological studies of the Chinese in Nevada and demonstrated how the life and experiences of Chinese Americans can be revealed through artifacts. Susan Lindstrom, Frederic F. Petersen, Robert R. Kautz, Danielle Risse, and other professional archaeologists have explored the Tahoe region and its Chinese camps, Carson City, and the Virginia and Truckee Railroad sites. Unfortunately, most of their reports are unpublished and difficult to access, but some are available in the UNLV Lied Library Special Collections. Barbara L. Voss of Stanford University has led many archaeologists to reevaluate their findings regarding the Chinese. Finally, Forest Service archaeologist Carrie E. Smith and Penny Rucks, Kelly Dixon of the University of Montana, and Priscilla Wegars of the University of Idaho have uncovered more information to add to a growing body of knowledge.

Robert Kautz and Danielle Risse (2006, ch. 9), who studied Carson City's "China Town," felt that archaeologists have two conflicting paradigms for interpreting their data: the conflict model that derives from a generalized Marxian hypothesis and a structural-functionalist bias that emphasizes symmetry and interdependence of social units. They concluded that both paradigms are useful, given the passage of time, as greater accommodation and more interaction takes place. The present study will demonstrate this but in the context of a faster time frame than most archaeologists have accepted.

Archaeologists have indicated that there were varying degrees of modification in the lifestyles of the Chinese as they adopted some American practices and artifacts. Peter B. Mires and Margaret E. Bullock (1995) surveyed a Chinese residence (dated from approximately 1885 to 1900) occupied by one or two males and found that the numbers of Euro-American canned goods nearly equaled the number of Chinese food storage containers. The dilemma presented was to consider whether the use of non-Chinese artifacts was a result of nonavailability of traditional products or a conscious adoption of the host society's goods, or as simply an economic factor. Cultural beliefs and practices are by their nature dynamic and multidimensional, and one can never say with certainty that the use of an American-made teapot at a Chinese site was part of the household wares of the Chinese individual, a gift from a non-Chinese, or the household wares of a later or earlier non-Chinese resident at the site. The Chinese also may have developed a preference for some American foods, such as Vermont maple syrup (much tastier than its Chinese equivalent), as found in Island Mountain, Elko County, Nevada (Chung 2011). A focus on food and the remnants of food products should not be emphasized because dietary habits are one of the last things discarded in steps toward assimilation. The cost of imported goods was a major factor in purchasing decisions, but often Asian goods were less expensive because ships carrying logs to Asia needed goods to bring back to America, so Chinese merchants in Hong Kong loaded the return ships with all sorts of products, regardless of weight.

These studies occurred in tandem with the burgeoning interest in African American sites, a product of the mid-1960s civil rights movement. Archaeologist Charles E. Orser Jr. (2004, 86) suggested that "racism played some role in the archaeologists' general failure to investigate sites associated with Asians." Orser accepted the prevailing opinion that "Chinese immigrants tended to create and maintain their ethnic boundaries, only manipulating their limits when they chose to do so," while archaeologist Barbara L. Voss argues otherwise. Voss (2005) discarded the old paradigm of the marginality of Chinese as conceptualized through the interpretation of acculturation and assimilation, advocating instead for insights acquired through closer community-based studies, such as the interaction of the Chinese with the larger society.

Changes within the Chinese communities in the 1920s and 1930s were significant. Some Chinese had achieved a modicum of financial success, and most were no longer involved with physically labor-intensive jobs such as lumbering and construction. The second and third generations were coming of age, and influencing the character of Chinatowns, and moving in the direction of acculturation and assimilation, as seen, for example, in the growth of the Chinese American Citizens Alliance, founded in 1895 (Chung 1998). These American-born Chinese wanted to exercise their political and social rights and were not as passive as the first generation. As a result of the traditional Chinese emphasis on education, many became college graduates, professionals, and white-collar workers.

Racism, discrimination, prejudice, hatred, and the inability to move higher on the economic ladder also were important deterrents to a better integration into American society for the Chinese. The presence of a large European immigrant population, the power of the capitalist leaders of the community, and the influence of newspapers and the popular press helped to shape the response of Euro-Americans to the Chinese. The patterns and practices established in the Sierra Nevada were repeated in other lumbering regions, particularly in northern California, Oregon, Washington, Idaho, and British Columbia. Once the Sierra forests were depleted, the lumbermen, both Euro-Americans and Chinese, moved to other forests. Although most literature gave a deprecating Euro-American attitude toward the Chinese, a closer examination of the population of Carson City, Nevada, and Truckee, California, for example, reveals important differences in the people's reactions to the Chinese, thus challenging prevailing stereotypes of race relations (see chapter 5).

This study will focus on the Chinese who worked in the woods, their experiences, and their relations with the larger community. It will begin with early contact between Chinese and Americans, the trade in lumber, the Chinese immigration to the American West, the recruitment of workers to North America, chain migration, and the importance of early Chinese organizations. The number of workers, the types of jobs they performed, and their lived experiences will be the focus of chapter 2. They established Chinatowns broadly across the Northwest, and Carson City and Truckee are just two of many examples that illustrate the experiences of the Chinese and their interactions with the larger community, especially in an era of anti-Chinese activities. Chapter 4 explores the link between mining and logging, as many of the mine owners needed wood products to support their endeavors. This was closely connected to the construction of railroads that used Chinese workers to cut trees in order to clear the roads, make ties, and provide fuel for the trains, discussed in chapter 5. Finally, the Conclusion reveals that by 1920 the Chinese eventually depart from their involvement in lumbering and turn to less physically demanding jobs for a variety of complex reasons, such as the emerging forest conservation movement, technological improvements in logging, decreased demand, and the establishment of large corporations that drove the smaller lumber firms out of business.

CHAPTER 1

Early Contact and Migration

Contact between China and the West Coast perhaps began centuries ago, but after the discovery of gold in 1848 and the construction of western railway lines beginning in the late 1850s, many Chinese immigrated to the United States. Mining and railroad construction required large quantities of wood, and the abundance of virgin forests, with huge trees often in rough mountainous areas near and along the Pacific Coast, fulfilled this need. Although immigrants from many countries were hired to work in the lumber industry, the contributions of one group—the Chinese—have usually been ignored or forgotten, yet they were a major presence in the forests. Why and how did the Chinese first come to the American West? What kinds of organizations did they establish? How were they recruited for work? What did they contribute to the building of the new frontier?

Several interesting legends recorded early Chinese contacts with North America. Chinese history books recount the travels of the Buddhist monk Huishen to the "land of Fusang" in 499. Some believe that Fusang was somewhere on the West Coast of North America because trees and plants indigenous to China are present in the area (Leland 1975; Steiner 1979). In the 1880s the prevailing belief in the Monterey Peninsula and among some Asian Buddhists was that the Monterey cypress (*Cupressus macrocarpa*) was a tree brought to the new world by Huishen. Ming dynasty (1368–1644) artifacts have been found on sunken ships in coastal areas of the continental North America, suggesting that some trading may have occurred during this later era of Chinese maritime exploration. In 1571 Chinese skilled workers were employed in lower California (Reimers 2005, 37). In 1774 Spanish explorer Juan Bautista de Anza visited Carmel Bay and observed "an oriental boat" (Lydon 1985, 15). Some Chinese junks were known to have successfully sailed across the Pacific to North America prior to 1860.

The presence of Chinese sojourners was reported in the late eighteenth century to early nineteenth century. In 1781 a Chinese man resided in Los Angeles when it was founded. From 1785 to 1786 three Chinese sailors lived in Baltimore, Maryland. Chinese shipbuilders also were found on the West Coast around that time (Reimers 2005, 37). Crews consisting of Chinese sailors manned many of the Spanish galleons sailing along the Pacific coast. In 1788 Captain John Meares began a trade in lumber between Macao and the Pacific Northwest; he brought approximately fifty Chinese laborers who felled trees and shaped them into spars and ship's timbers (Cox 1974, 5; MacKay 1978, 227). This first group of Chinese "professional" loggers in the Pacific Northwest were based on Vancouver Island. In his diary, Meares noted that one of the Chinese seamen, Acchon Aching, fell to his death from a tree and was subsequently buried on the shore. Bad weather discouraged Meares from future attempts to return to Asia, but other trading vessels arrived with Chinese on board as the years passed.

The Hudson's Bay Company established a small mill at Fort Victoria (present-day Victoria, B.C.) to ship lumber eventually to San Francisco and from there to other locations in the West, Hawai'i, and Asia. They built a two-story house surrounded by a stockade; this is also the location where the initial Chinese crews assisted in the building the first ship constructed in that location, a forty-ton schooner named the *Northwest America*, the first of such vessels crafted in the region. The ship operated along the coast between September 1788 and June 1789 (Quimby 1948, 249–50; Hildebrand 1977, 3). Other trading ships brought more Chinese in the hopes of establishing a timber trade. Captain James Colnett, who arrived in 1789, brought a crew that included Chinese carpenters, blacksmiths, bricklayers and masons, tailors, shoemakers, seamen, and a cook (Quimby 1948, 249). In 1790 Colnett brought a Chinese carpenter and a Chinese armorer from San Francisco to Vancouver Island. No one knows how many of these Chinese workers eventually settled in the area, although we do know that six deserted Colnett's ship when it landed in Mexico.

Other individuals became interested and engaged in the lumber trade between the Pacific states, Hawai'i, China, and Macao through the early nineteenth century. In Monterey Bay, the first documented Chinese resident, Annam (d. 1817), who came from Macao, was a cook for Governor Pablo Sola of Alta California and in 1815 was baptized as Antonio Maria de Jesus (Lyndon 1985, 15). By 1816 the ship spar trade increased as vessels took spars from the Pacific coast to China (Ficken 1987, 12). Wooden junks, primarily fishing boats, dotted the California coast from the mid-nineteenth to mid-twentieth century. In 1853 Chinese fishermen and their families settled in Point Alones, Pacific Grove, California, until their village was burned to the ground in 1906. They were forbidden from reestablishing their community there (Williams 2011). The homes and junks were made from local wood.

These early encounters were not well documented, but there is evidence of Chinese immigrants' presence in the region: they liked to plant trees that were cultivated for fruit and for medicinal purposes, such as the persimmon, lychee, loquat, ginko, and the *Ailanthus altissima* (known as Tree of Heaven), which were found throughout California and in places where the Chinese settled in the nineteenth century (Anon. 2000). A favorite fruit-bearing shrub, *Ziziphus jujube* (the jujube), rose bushes, and camellias also were planted.

Between 1810 and 1900 the American West changed from a rural society to a more commercial, industrial, and urban one that utilized large quantities of wood. This was a golden age for wood products. The first sawmill in the Pacific Northwest was built in 1827; by 1833 Oregon timber was sent to China because so much of China's coastal forests had been denuded ("History of Logging in Oregon"). By the 1850s American lumber was marketed in China, the Hawaiian Islands (purchased by Chinese, who in 1900 were 80 percent of the lumber dealers and building contractors), Japan, and other foreign ports.[1] By 1853 the Seattle and Puget Sound regions in Washington were actively logging, with some of their products destined for Asia. In the 1860s British Columbia also entered into the China market but was much slower in developing its lumber industry and overseas trade (Hak 2000, 28).

Trade between the West Coast and China's eastern coastal cities also developed. With the opening of new treaty port cities in China after the end of the Opium War (1839–1844), new Western style buildings, requiring large quantities of wood, increased the transpacific lumber trade. Frequent fires in China's port cities led to greater demands for reconstruction. The freighters carried lumber to the port cities because it was cheaper to buy the lumber from the West Coast than to develop the lumbering industry in China's interior regions, which had no transportation support system. This trade, during times of North American depression or the downward fluctuation of lumber prices, helped to balance the books for American and Canadian companies, which built offices and lumberyards in Chinese port cities. According to historian Thomas Cox (1974, 133), this brought "an increased degree of stability to this high-risk industry by broadening the market base of the cargo mills." Technological improvements in ship transportation cut the time of travel to one month when the weather was good. There is no evidence that the droghers (single-decked schooners designed to hold lumber) returning to the Pacific coast brought Chinese workers, but they often brought back Chinese goods with little regard for the weight of the goods, since the shipments were never as heavy as the logs and lumber that had been shipped to Asia (Cox 1974, 146–50). The trade declined after the 1890s but gradually increased after World War I with China's new modernization program. The purchase of timber and wood made up 6.4 percent of China's total imports from the United States (May and Fairbanks 1986, 257). From the 1870s on, businessmen, especially those based in San Francisco, tried to be cognizant of the possibilities of trade between China and the United States as the "dream of the China market" and its potential profits. As Earl Pomeroy (2003) argued, San Francisco was the catalyst, banker, and base of operations for the regions west of the Rocky Mountains, especially with respect to trade with China.

The discovery of gold in California increased the China trade as merchants, such as John Heard (1825–1894), realized they could make profits from 75 percent to 200 percent on each item brought from Hong Kong in 1850 compared with goods shipped from New York. Makee, Anton, and Company on California Street,

San Francisco, subsequently brought over luxury items, candles, spices, chairs, tables, wooden trunks, lacquer boxes, silks and satins, tiles, tea, sugar, and food products (San Francisco Maritime Museum exhibit, 2012). The famous William C. Hoff Store in San Francisco carried items such as underglazed blue porcelain toiletry sets and fancy Chinese ware (Delgado 2009, 102–3). Busy transoceanic trade developed between China and California and allowed San Francisco to become a major commercial hub in the maritime market beginning in 1848.

When a San Francisco city ordinance banned tent housing, Chinese carpenters and "China houses," which used no nails, became popular. The enterprising Jacob Primer Leese (1809–1892), working for John Heard and family, decided to send prefabricated wooden houses from Hong Kong to the new boomtown of San Francisco in 1849; along with the shipments were fifteen Chinese carpenters to construct the homes (Layton 2002, 179–87). Leese paid $125 for each carpenter to sail on the *Mary*. This was much more than the usual $50 transpacific fee, so they presumably traveled in a better class than most Chinese immigrants. Rough boards sold for $500 or more per thousand board feet, so the prefabricated wooden houses, which had doors and windows and could include funnels, fireplaces, window glass, and paint, were a good solution (Cox 1970, 17). Bayard Taylor (1988, 85, 153, 155) noted in the fall of 1849 that at least seventy-five houses had been imported from Guangzhou to San Francisco and built by Chinese carpenters. Colonel John Fremont's home was a "China house" as well as the Double Springs Courthouse in Calaveras County, California. The frame and exterior covering sold for $1,500 in 1849 (Layton 2002, 179–87; Peterson 1965, 321).[2] In the July 12, 1849, edition of the *San Francisco Alta*, J. C. Anton advertised the sale of houses, bricks, and iron chests, as well as the services of carpenters like Ah Ting, who constructed thirty frame houses of different sizes for his clients. Like Chinese furniture of the time, these houses fit together "like a puzzle" and had no nails except for the roof (Fremont 1878, 96). One of the early shipments, which included doors and windows for the houses, was on the *Frolic*. The ship sank but was salvaged decades later, thus demonstrating items transported and the constant danger of transpacific shipping. "China houses" were popular throughout the American West until the late nineteenth century.

Undoubtedly, the Chinese carpenters remained in San Francisco because there was a great economic incentive and their skills were in demand. The 1880 census listed fifty-one Chinese carpenters, or 1.4 percent of San Francisco's 3,865 Chinese (Stephens 1976). The Chinese also were well known for making other wood products, including furniture (chairs and tables), altars, and chests, exported to the United States as part of the transpacific trade or built in the American West (Defebaugh 1906, 1:559). On July 31, 1858, the *San Joaquin Republican* noted that a Chinese carpenter had built an impressive eighteen-foot boat, capable of holding sixteen people, to sail on the San Joaquin River.[3] When California achieved statehood in 1850, two visitors to San Francisco noted that much of the furniture in the renowned J. L. Riddle and Company office building had been imported from

China (Chen 1997, 520–46). Carpenters from Zhongshan and Shunde Counties were renowned for their craftsmanship in furniture making and undoubtedly a few were recruited to work in the United States.

Chinese lumbermen and carpenters realized that there was an opportunity to earn more money in these fields in the United States, especially if placer mining was not to their liking. Their presence was threatening enough to Euro-American carpenters that in June 1867 the two House Carpenters' Eight-Hour Leagues in San Francisco took a stance against Chinese workers in their field and hoped that the eight-hour limitation would discourage the Chinese from this occupation (Saxton 1971, 69). Certainly in 1870 San Francisco the carpenter Ah Mow, age twenty-nine, was prosperous enough to have his wife, Ah Hing, age twenty-five, a cook, living with him and provided housing for Ah Quosu, age thirty-seven, a cook, and his wife, He Leen, who worked in a shoe factory (Census 1870). In all probability these two couples were related. The crowded living conditions were not uncommon as workers tried to economize and because neighborhoods, like San Francisco's Chinatown, had strict residential restrictions.

Throughout the decades of the 1870s to early 1900s, Chinese carpenters tended to live together and probably worked together on projects. In the 1870s and 1880s, according to the census takers in Nevada, all of the Chinese carpenters—eight total in Virginia City, Eureka, Battle Mountain, and Carson City—could read and write and therefore could meet the demands of their American customers as well as their Chinese customers (NVSHPO 1870, 1880). This was surprising, since the census takers were prejudiced against the Chinese but still credited them with the ability to read and write.

Chinese merchants realized that Chinese goods were needed in the West, so they established branch companies and trading systems that often were regionally based: *Sanyi* customers were generally loyal to *Sanyi* suppliers, for example.[4] The business acumen of the Guangzhou (Canton) traders was well known among Americans working in South China, so it was no surprise that they recognized the possibility of overseas business expansion. Economic dislocation as new treaty ports opened away from the former foreign trade capital of Guangzhou motivated Hong Kong and Guangzhou merchants to seriously consider overseas trade (Liu 2002; Daniels 1988; Barth 1964). A networking system was established between the hometown supplier and the overseas stores.

Some Chinese merchants, especially in Hong Kong, contracted with ships to carry Asian merchandise and passengers on return trips. Hop Kee and Company of Hong Kong was among the prominent firms sending laborers and goods (Cox 1974, 150–51). Although rice and tea were main trade products, ceramic bowls, rattan chairs, camphor-wood chests, wooden statues, elaborately carved altar tables, clothing, curios, large ceramic jugs of soy sauce, heavy jars of pickled vegetables, and even tar paper for roofing were shipped from China to the United States (Valentine 1999). Many of these merchants also acted as brokers for remittances from overseas Chinese to relatives in home villages, towns, and cities, and they made a profit from the exchange rates, interest charges, transfer fees, and other payments, while the families received the remainder. In many cases, these families relied on the funds to provide for 80 percent of their living expenses (Chen 1923; Chen 1940). In addition, wealthy Chinese merchants donated money for projects to improve their hometowns, including schools, railroads, and other community institutions and festivals (Hsu 2000a). The ties to China weakened only with the passage of time and the passing of the first and second generations.

The political and economic conditions in South China spurred thousands to seek new opportunities abroad at the same time the California gold rush changed the nature of Chinese–Pacific coast trade and immigration. The peoples of South China, because of their proximity to Hong Kong and American traders, diplomats, and missionaries, learned about the increasing demand for labor in the United States and the discovery of gold—instant wealth—that lured them overseas in the last half of the nineteenth century (Chen 1997, 540–46). Word reached Guangdong residents that fortunes could be made, so many sought the fresh opportunities in this new land not only in mining but also in other occupations. Fellow villagers who had left poor and returned wealthy motivated many to leave their homes. The presence of fashionable overseas Chinese "communities," often with Western-style homes and guarded twenty-four hours a day from potential bandit raids, reminded neighbors of the prosperity of the overseas Chinese and added fuel to the desire either to go abroad or, for the women, to marry a "Gold Mountain Man." Like many others, the father of Henry Yup (Chinese family name Hu/Woo) of Lovelock and Reno, Nevada, built two three-story side-by-side houses

Many of the homes of Chinese Americans in Kaiping, Guangdong, a poor rural area, looked like the Quan family home. The modern, multistoried structure inspired others in the county to go overseas in search of riches for the family. (Photograph by Landon Quan)

in his home village, one for his wife and children and the other for his brother's family (oral interview, 2010). Contract labor companies also spread propaganda to attract workers. Such stories and influences motivated the emigrants.

In the mid- to late nineteenth century, the Chinese in the United States came from a small area in southeastern China: from western Guangdong, a rural area composed of the *Siyi* (Cantonese, Szeyup, meaning "four counties or districts") of Xinhui (Sunwui), Taishan/Xinning (Toishan [prior to 1914]/Sunning), Kaiping (Hoiping), and Yanping (later Hoshan County was added to make it the present Wuyi,"five counties"); from the Pearl River Delta, a more urban and commercial center composed of the *Sanyi* (Samyup, meaning "three counties or districts") of Nanhai (Namhoi), Panyu (Punyu), and Shunde (Shun Duck), and also Zhongshan/Xiangshan (prior to 1925, Heungshan, renamed Zhongshan) County; and from eastern Guangdong and southern Fujian, an area inhabited by minorities whose speech, diet, and customs differed considerably from the first two groups and often were "lumped" together under the category of *Kejia* (Hakka, "guest people/families")(Leong 1997; Cohen 1996, 36–79). Within these counties, there were several mutually unintelligible spoken subdialects, but most could read the same written language. Prior to the mid-nineteenth century the Pearl River Delta was central to regional and international trade. Artisans and laborers traversed between counties for employment, so some quickly realized the need to be conversant in both Siyi and Sanyi as well as the approximately twelve subdialects.

Sociologist Da Chen (1923; 1940) studied Chinese migrations in the 1920s and 1930s and concluded that Chinese migration from Guangdong, Fujian, Shandong, and Zhili fell into three stages: informal emigration via junk, brokered emigration through an emigration company or contract labor agency, and government-sponsored migration because of overpopulation, famine, natural disasters, and the ease of overseas migration from coastal areas. Informal emigration was seen in the travels of Lim Lip Hong (1843–1920), also known as Lim Yuk Pon, Wing Dai, Lim Dai, Lim Tye, Lim Tie, Wing Tai, and Lim Lip Pong, who left Kaiping, Guangdong and sailed for six months to America on a junk with a dozen relatives in 1855. He eventually worked on the construction of the Central Pacific Railroad (CPRR), lived in Virginia City, Carson City, and Deadwood, and finally settled in San Francisco in the 1880s, where he lived until his death.[5]

There were other factors in the "push and pull" theory of migration. Yong Chen's study (1997) of the internal origins of the Chinese suggests that chain migration played a major role in the establishment and growth of Chinese American communities. Many of Nevada's Chinese of the late nineteenth century were born in Taishan (an estimated 60 percent in 1868 growing to an estimated 82 percent from 1876 to 1926/1928), one of the Siyi counties in Guangdong. Their Yee, Wong, Lee, and Chan impressive family association headquarters in San Francisco symbolized the wealth and power of clans (Chew and Liu 2004, 73). This permitted the Yee clan from this region to rise to prominence in Carson City and other parts

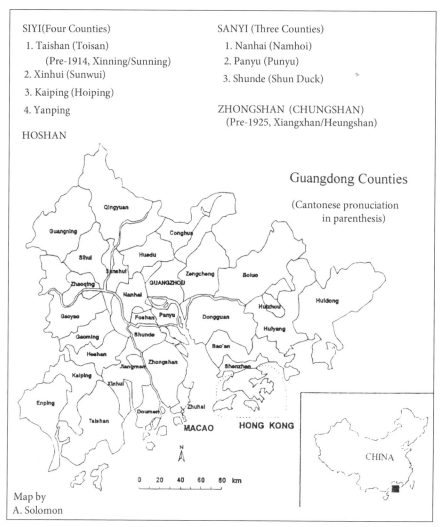

SIYI(Four Counties)

1. Taishan (Toisan)
   (Pre-1914, Xinning/Sunning)
2. Xinhui (Sunwui)
3. Kaiping (Hoiping)
4. Yanping

HOSHAN

SANYI (Three Counties)

1. Nanhai (Namhoi)
2. Panyu (Punyu)
3. Shunde (Shun Duck)

ZHONGSHAN (CHUNGSHAN)
(Pre-1925, Xiangxhan/Heungshan)

Guangdong Counties

(Cantonese pronuciation in parenthesis)

Map by A. Solomon

In the mid- and late nineteenth century, most of the Chinese came from these counties in Guangdong province.

of Nevada. As news of the discovery of gold and "instant wealth" spread, a few Chinese from central and northern China also migrated to the United States.

Primarily, transportation across the Pacific Ocean was by ship. The Pacific Mail Steamship Company (PMSC), established in New York in 1848 to transport passengers between the East Coast and San Francisco, was the major carrier. In 1867 the PMSC with its Chinese crews had regular service between Hong Kong and San Francisco via Yokohama and Shanghai, which could take up to six months between October and March, or a shorter seventy-five days between April and

September (PMSC 1867; Schwendinger 1988, 210; Barde and Bobonis 2006; "Dollar"). Greater than 50 percent of the traffic between Asia and San Francisco from 1913 to 1915 used the PMSC. Passenger lists included Chinese workers. Between 1875 and 1882, for example, the Big Four, as they were called—dry goods merchant Charles Crocker, grocer Leland Stanford, and hardware-company partners Collis Huntington and Mark Hopkins—leased at least two of the PMSC ships to transport Chinese workers for their various projects. The three thousand Chinese who built the Tehachapi Railroad, with its famous 2 percent grade and numerous bridges, as well as the four thousand workers James Harvey Strobridge required for the Mohave line traveled on PMSC ships leased by the Big Four (Crocker to Huntington correspondence, December 1881). Between 1893 and 1915 the Southern Pacific Railroad (SPRR), which owned the Central Pacific Railroad (CPRR) relied on Chinese workers recruited in South China to work on various other projects. One of the PMSC sheds in San Francisco served as the Bureau of Immigration's interrogation center for Chinese immigrants prior to the opening of Angel Island's Immigration Station in 1910.

The other major carrier was the Occidental and Oriental Steamship Company, which sailed under a British flag but was owned by Leland Stanford beginning in 1878 so that goods from Asia could be transported on the CPRR. The rivalry between the two lines ended in 1908, when the Occidental and Oriental went broke yielding to the dominance of the PMSC (Tutorow 1971). The crews on both lines usually were predominantly Chinese (Schwendinger 1978; Grider 2010, 478–81). Between 1876 and 1906 approximately eighty thousand Chinese seamen, boatswains, firemen, coal passers, cooks, and other workmen under the direction of Euro-American officers served these companies and were known as the "invisible merchant marine." The presence of Chinese crewmen undoubtedly made the passage across the Pacific a little more tolerable for Chinese immigrants. In 1925 lumber and shipping magnate Robert Dollar took over the PMSC line, and eventually the Dollar Steamship Company dominated the transpacific trade, including the transportation of passengers (see "Dollar").

The population in the American West grew rapidly, and the Chinese population also increased. Chinese migrated overseas in several important ways. Many went as "coolie laborers." In 1845 the coolie trade in cheap human labor began to the West Indies and quickly expanded to other locations, including the United States. Under this system, the Chinese worker was obligated to work for a prescribed number of years, provided with food and housing, but received little pay or none at all. This method declined after 1874 because the Qing government protested the treatment of her citizens overseas.

Others migrated as contract laborers, which was the most popular practice. The contract-labor system in China dated back to the late Ming Dynasty (1368–1644), when it was advantageous for male workers in groups of ten, twenty, or more to live and work together and be hired out to employers as a unit for a specific period to complete a specific task, often away from home (Rowe 1990, 256–59). In this way, they established so-called "employment families." Once the work was done, the men returned to their families living elsewhere. The head of the group, called the *futou* or *baotou*, negotiated the employment terms and took a percentage of the wages, sometimes working with a labor broker (*fuhang*), who guaranteed good faith on the part of both parties. Good faith and honesty in financial matters were an integral part of the system, and if one party reneged, community pressure was brought to bear on the dishonest individual until the situation was rectified.

A modified "contract labor" system based on this practice was carried to the United States. American companies preferred the use of a labor contractor and his foreman (commonly called a "headman") because employers did not have to deal with individual workers, only the foreman, who usually guaranteed that a set number of workers would show up for work (Johnston 2004, 26). When Virginia and Truckee Railroad (VTRR) Superintendent Henry M. Yerington (b. 1828 or 1830 in Canada, d. 1910) needed Chinese workers to finish the VTRR from Carson City to Reno, where it met the CPRR, he searched for a competent "boss man" to supervise about five hundred Chinese workers from 1868 to 1872 (David Alman Bender to Yerington, July 21, 1872, Yerington UCB; Yerington to Mills, July 21, 1875, Yerington UNR). J. Cutter and Sam Thayer, who worked for labor contractors Sisson and Wallace, were recommended by David Alman Bender of the VTRR Reno office. Eventually, the Chinese headmen agreed to provide 125 workers for one dollar per day, less than half of what Euro-American workers would have received, according to anti-Chinese advocates. The low-cost labor enabled the VTRR to be completed quickly—but not without resistance from anti-Chinese forces in Virginia City for the last section of the track laying (James 1998). The VTRR connected the Comstock ore-producing mines to the quartz-reduction mills and brought needed lumber, mining timbers, and cord wood for fuel to the Comstock. Most of the Chinese working on the VTRR also worked for the Carson Tahoe Lumber and Fluming Company (CTLFC), cycling back and forth between these two affiliates of the Bank of California that were headed by Yerington and Duane L. Bliss (Chester 2009, 162). Local merchants also filled job requests by using their networking (*guanxi*) system, a common practice in South China.

The third system within the migration process was a credit-ticket method in which the emigrants relied heavily on their families, clan, villages, towns, or employers to pay the passage and startup expenses in the new location. Repayments might be made at high interest rates, but often the assistance of the clan or fellow villagers made finding and keeping a job easier. This probably was the most common way for Chinese migrants to pay for their passage. According to Jinhua Selia Tan of Wuyi University, clan leaders encouraged members to go abroad in order to contribute to the clan's general funds, which could be used to purchase land from destitute neighboring clans, thus enriching the clan coffers. This was an important factor in sending young men abroad (Oral interview, 2014).

Finally, a small percentage of Chinese emigrants paid their own way. This was common among mercantile families who wanted to expand their businesses overseas and among those who came from a higher socioeconomic class. Self-financing was also popular among generational immigrants as one generation brought the next generation over in succession, as seen in historian Erika Lee's family ("Preface," in Yung and Lee, 2010). Emigration brokers or agents, often connected to a merchandising firm in Hong Kong, arranged rooms for the emigrants in cities prior to departure, tried to arrange jobs abroad, and forwarded mail and money to their families back home.

The plight of the newly arrived Chinese immigrant was expressed in this poem:

> After considering and planning to satisfy my longing for a long time, I traveled to America. After much suffering from wind and storms, I reached my destination. I left my poor old home behind and came to this country. . . . At home my parents are longing for me without condolence from anyone. On the ship I went through hardships and in the detention shed I suffered. At the wharf I could not meet my kinsmen. The idea of being sent back did not enter my mind. The detention shed was a gloomy place in which to be confined. There I played my musical instrument, sang and played, trying to forget my troubles. Every day I was prostrated on my bunk with grief. My clothes were wet with tears. Poverty drove me eastward and with much reluctance I left home. I have traveled thousands of miles without thinking that I would be confined in a detention shed cage.[6]

China's emigration policies and American immigration laws hindered Chinese migration. The Manchu government in China was not supportive of their overseas emigrants. In 1644 the Sincized Manchu nomads from the northeast invaded China proper and established the Qing Dynasty (1644–1911). The Manchu emperors passed harsh edicts against overseas travel because of a fear of revolution that could be based beyond China's borders. Returnees were subject to immediate arrest and execution. After China's defeat in the Opium War, the growing economic problems in southeastern China and the advent of the news of new economic opportunities in places like the American West forced the Qing government to change its position (Mei 1979). In 1859 the governor of Guangdong independently legalized overseas emigration in an attempt to control the increasing "coolie" labor trade, yet by 1868 these circumstances changed with the signing of the Burlingame Treaty, which stated that the United States and China

> recognize the inherent and inalienable right of man to change his home and allegiance, and also the mutual advantage of the free migration and emigration of their citizens and subjects, respectively, from one country to the other, for purposes of curiosity, of trade, or as permanent residents . . . and [that] Chinese

subjects visiting or residing in the United States shall enjoy the same privileges, immunities, and exemptions in respect to travel or residence, as may there be enjoyed by the citizens or subjects of the most favored nation. (Quoted in Hing 1993, 201–2)

Although it was not very effective, the privileges and immunities provision was aimed at protecting Chinese in the United States against discrimination, exploitation, and violence. The treaty opened the door for increased recruitment of Chinese workers and encouraged more to go abroad. The dream of instant wealth and ability to return to China without any penalty were the biggest reasons for emigration to the United States.

At first the number of newly arrived Chinese was small. In 1830 the first census was taken: three Chinese were listed. The records of the U.S. Immigration Commission listed eleven Chinese arriving between 1820 and 1840 (Lee 2003). In 1848 three Chinese, two men and one woman, arrived in San Francisco aboard the American brig *Eagle*. The woman became a servant in a minister's household; the two men went to work at John Augustus Sutter, who had recognized the importance of lumber and as early as 1843 had hired men to saw wood, produce charcoal, and manufacture items needed at Sutter's Fort. His sawmill near Coloma, California, just north of San Francisco where John Marshall discovered gold in January 1848, attracted hundreds of gold seekers.[7]

News about the new wealth increased the desire to travel abroad. A news report in the *San Francisco Alta* (August 1, 1850) described how Chinese miners just outside San Francisco were robbed of the substantial sum of $3,000. This was compounded by the report in San Francisco's *Weekly Pacific Miner* (February 15, 1851) of a Chinese miner digging up gold worth $20,000 at Chinese Diggings. Other similar tales were reported. The San Francisco Customs Office estimated arrivals from China as 325 in 1849, 450 in 1850, and 2,700 in 1851 (Chiu 1963). By 1852 there were at least 20,000 Chinese in California, and the population continued to skyrocket. In 1867 only 4,283 Chinese left Hong Kong, but by 1875 more than ten times that number had left the primary port of departure for the Chinese (quoted in Cox 1974, 140). According to historian Sucheng Chan (2000, 73–74), "gold was such a lodestar for the Chinese that persisted in mining longer than any other ethnic group" and constituted a large percentage of the California miners between 1860 and 1880. The 1868 Burlingame Treaty was a victory for American capitalists who needed Chinese laborers on projects like the building of railroads and for the Chinese who wanted to emigrate during the second wave of departures.

Arrival was often unpleasant for the Chinese immigrant without a regional association, relatives, or friends. In one of the files for a duplicate certificate of residence was a beautifully written essay in Chinese dated March 1897, on the advantages and disadvantages being in America. Huang Heyun (Cantonese, Wong

Hock Won), originally from Xiangang Village, Kaiping District, Guangdong Province, expressed feelings shared by many others:

> After years of planning and trading [in America], property [in China] would be regained, hundreds of [acres of] farmland would be acquired, and a mansion for the use of my wife and myself would be built. I would clothe myself in the finest of fur garments and mount a fat horse. Upon bended knees I could care for my parents and freely provide for my family. All these were my desires! Hearing these, hundreds [of my countrymen] exclaimed, "We have the same desire."
>
> So we came to America. Outside the gates there stood [American immigration] men of great cruelty—and believe these words for they are true. At the shore before one may enter, all must be clean. These [officials] strip all [Chinese immigrants] to nakedness and lead them to be steamed [in quarantine], after which, in scanty garments, the [immigrants] go to the place of detention and are told, "You will stay here." Although this may be ruinous to one's health, there must be no complaint. All say, "This is terrible." I gave one look and it was enough. Entering [the detention shed] I looked to the right and to the left and saw only bunks and a few benches. "You stay here, you stay here," is all the [officials] say. Here a person is cramped and doomed never to stretch. If one complains that the shed leaks, they say, "Why should you care? You will be here only a day." No words can express the misery [experienced here]. Deep in my heart there is a wounded spot. These barbarians [Americans] have neither mercy nor compassion and are like lions and tigers.
>
> . . . [The 4th century B.C. Chinese philosopher] Confucius has said, "For the good things which we will have, we must undergo many hardships." Why should you feel hurt? You suffer these torments for your wife and others. There is an old saying, "First of all be patient and enduring," and this is true [in the United States]. It is the nature of people to possess great things, but for me, I have failed in this. Although I am ever watchful for it, I have not found the road [to success] nor am I sure that there is such a road.[8]

Contrary to the prevailing stereotype of the illiterate Chinese immigrant, Huang's essay and the numerous poems on the walls of Angel Island's detention shed demonstrate that some early immigrants were literate, perceptive, and unhappy (Lai, Lim, and Yung 1991). Huang summarized the "American dream" held by most Chinese immigrants—that in America there was the possibility of success but at home there was little hope. They were willing to take the risk and endure the numerous hardships—from being locked in the wooden shed on the PMSC wharf in San Francisco prior to 1910, to being victimized in anti-Chinese riots—in order to fulfill their dream of achieving prosperity.

New immigrants were greeted by overseas regional and family associations, often called *huiguan* (literally, "meeting halls"; benevolent associations) or *gongsi/gongsuo* ("clan halls" or companies), which were under the general umbrella of the Chinese Consolidated Benevolent Association (CCBA, *Zhonghua huiguan*, or

Chinese Six Companies). The organization frequently provided temporary housing. David Chuenyan Lai (2010) studied the huiguan in depth in Victoria, Canada,
and its practices applied to the organizations in the American West. Regional or
lineage identity was reinforced in the organizational structure of overseas Chinese
communities. The huiguan had begun in commercially developed cities in China
as far back as the Southern Song Dynasty (eleventh century) to provide services
such as helping the poor, sponsoring festivals, providing medical care and buri-
als and offering consumer credit, interest-free loans, and joint business venture
opportunities (Rowe 1990). By the Qing Dynasty (1644–1911) regional huiguan
were influential commercial and merchant organizations that promoted business
and trade as well as legal aid, charitable activities, maintenance of religious rites
and an altar or temple, ownership of cemetery site with provisions for reburials
in the home village or town, housing, and employment for their migrant members (Armentrout-Ma 1984; Chung and Wegars 2005). In late Qing China, the
huiguan had a headquarters building that contained a hostel and temple with a
primary deity of that region and a recreation area. For this reason many of their
association buildings in the American West were called "joss houses,"[9] with the
altar and deity on the top story of a two-story building (closest to heaven).

Overseas Chinese communities followed the same general pattern of services,
but merchants instead of scholars provided the leadership of the organizations
until the association could afford to hire a scholar from China. Many of the Chinese merchants of the 1850s and 1860s were born in the Sanyi and Zhongshan
regions, but they yielded to the growing number of Siyi immigrants by the 1870s
and 1880s. Some of the early merchants in the American West actually were connected with merchandising companies owned by kinsmen in their birthplace or
in Hong Kong. The connections helped increase the power and prestige of Hong
Kong firms (Sinn 2013).

The huiguan in the American West also provided protection from outsiders, remittance services for families in China, legal services with well-known
Euro-American attorneys, mediation between the Chinese and non-Chinese
community, and criminal and civil trials for its members (obviating the need
for the western judicial system). In some cases, they helped in monopolizing
certain trades and crafts for the group "against strangers" (Sinn 1997, 375). They
encouraged special construction projects such as building railroads and educational institutions in the home county. Many Americans in the late nineteenth
century mistakenly believed that the CCBA recruited the laborers, but a careful
examination of sources indicate that this was not among its functions (McClain
1990; process of recruiting by labor contractor Wan Fook is noted in Bancroft
Scraps). Most family associations and some regional associations recruited workers, often under the directions of Euro-American employers. Multi-surname,
nonlocalized lineage organizations also existed, such as the Four Surname Association, or Longgang Qinyi Gongsuo (Zhang/Chung, Liu/Lew, Guan/Quan,

and Zhao/Chew families), based on the four clans swearing allegiance during the Three Kingdoms Period (220–280 A.D.), but most family associations were single-lineage organizations that reinforced kinship ties.

Migration networks reduced the cost of travel, providing information about job availability and housing in their destinations, and preferring the recently arrived to live with relatives or friends in the new location overseas (Liang 2008, 709). Toward this end they formed gongsi (also spelled *kongsi* and *gongsuo,* an enlarged partnership and brotherhood for economic gains), a type of huiguan for business partnerships and financial assistance (Wang Tai Peng 1994). The gongsi, more prominent in Southeast Asia, resembled the English guild and often regulated business practices to the advantage of its members and provided legal aid and burial services, and supported charitable activities (in which case it might be called a *shantung*) for its members and fellow regionals. In 1880, for example, Young King, Kan Tong, To Shing, and Long Bow established a Chinese Carpenters Mutual Protective Association in San Francisco, with branches in other parts of California and in Nevada, in an attempt to establish a minimum wage standard of two dollars per day, to buy and sell real estate, to regulate the conditions and terms of apprenticeships, to protect and assist its members, especially in cases of sickness or distress, to support the aged and infirm members, and to assist those who want to return to China.[10] Each member contributed seventy-five dollars for the cost of filing the articles of incorporation and starting their operations. Eight years later, they raised the current wage of $2.50 to $3 per day for a ten-hour workday. For those in San Francisco, the Chinese carpenters did much of the interior finishing of houses everywhere in the city as well as in buildings in Chinatown.

Almost all of the early Chinese immigrants were members of an association, and as the numbers grew in a given area, the members often split from the older association. The huiguan built their membership base by hiring people from the same region or villages within that region through a networking system (*guanxi*) and directing them to new job opportunities, thus enhancing their the power and prestige (Ng 1992). The huiguan was also a source of contact between the emigrant and one's native place. Emigrants from the same locality frequently shared information about home, ate the same types of food prepared in the same way, and enjoyed the same art, customs, and festivals in the same manner. They provided some level of comfort and security in a strange land.

In South China the family, clan, and village ties bonded individuals in economic, social, and political relationships. These continued in the United States but became expanded as the laborers' self-identification became broader—an identification as "Chinese" instead of "Taishanese," for example. As Francis K. Hsu pointed out (1967; 1970), the importance of such kinship ties was in sharp contrast to the concept of American individualism. Eventually one adopted a Chinese provincial and national identity along with a broader American identity. As Eric Wolf (1982, 381) stated in studying labor immigration under capitalism,

"Ethnicities rarely coincided with the initial self-identification of the industrial recruits, who first thought of themselves as Hanoverians or Bavarians rather than as Germans." Siyi and Sanyi local and regional identifications similarly broke down with the passage of time in the United States. Like many immigrants with a strong cultural heritage, the Chinese worked to preserve their culture but had to adapt to the host society by making changes. The influence of merchants, labor bosses, living conditions, and environmental factors all played a major role in the adjustment of the workers. Close kinship ties helped continue some Chinese traditions; the necessity to work alongside or live with Euro-Americans necessitated some changes, but the Chinese could nevertheless hold onto some of their regional traditions.

The counties of origin changed as the decades passed. A news article in the *Oriental* (January 25, 1854) showed that the Chinese of the Yanghe Association (people from Zhongshan who were urbanites and merchants, with some agriculturalists) had 16,900 arrivals, 2,500 departures, and 400 deaths, with a total of population of 14,000. The two more rural areas were *the* Siyi Association with 16,650 arrivals, 3,700 departures, 300 deaths, leaving a total of 9,200, while Ningyang Association (people from Xinning or Taishan, part of the four counties) had 4,899 arrivals, 1,269 departures, 173 deaths, with a total of 6,907. The higher percentage of immigrant deaths from Zhongshan and the higher percentage of departures of immigrants from Siyi has never been explained. Although there is very little concrete information to indicate this, two figures (collected ten years apart) from the district associations and revealed by the CCBA showed the rapid growth and eventual domination of Chinese immigrants from the Siyi of Ningyang, Hehe, and Gangzhou (in Cantonese, Sze Yup, Ning Yung, Hop Wo, and Kong Chow), while the more urban Sanyi of Sanyi, Yanghe, and Renhe (in Cantonese, Sam Yup, Young Wo, and Yan Wo) sent fewer people: the increasing number of Siyi immigrants meant greater political power within the Chinese community, and between 1876 and 1972 the Ningyang immigrants and their descendants were the most powerful in American Chinatowns.

Table 1–1. Changes in Places of Origin in Guangdong*

District Association	1866	1876
Ningyang (Ning Yung)	15,000	75,000
Yanghe (Young Wo)	11,500	12,000
Sanyi (Sam Yup)	10,500	11,000
Siyi or Gangzhou (Sze Yup or Kong Chow)	9,000	15,000
Hehe (Hop Wo)	8,500	34,000
Renhe (Yan Wo)	3,800	4,300
TOTALS:	58,300	151,300

*[Washoe City] Eastern Slope, July 14, 1866; Lorraine Barker Hildebrand, *Straw Hats, Sandals, and Steel: The Chinese in Washington State* (Tacoma: Washington State American Revolution Bicentennial Commission, 1977), 7.

After 1870 a large percentage of the Chinese were from Taishan, a district that "enjoyed neither the rich alluvial soils nor the readily traveled waterways that produced such wealth so close by. . . . Taishanese primarily assumed the roles of laborers, farmers, and petty entrepreneurs" (Hsu 2000b, 309). Historian Madeline Hsu (2000a) studied the flow of communication between Taishan and Chinese Americans in the late nineteenth century and demonstrated the close connection between those abroad and those at home. People of Siyi had begun to specialize in the sale of particular goods and brought these skills with them to the United States (Chen 2000, ch. 1). Many of the merchants linked the sale of goods to labor contracting, which provided a ready market for their products.

The transplantation from South China to the United States of clan and community involvement in lumbering is important to this study. Clans and associations often held land collectively. Land was more than property; it was a means of livelihood, so individuals and clans placed a high value on the ownership of land. In China they used the resources from timberland toward the protection of important ritual sites, such as ancestral graveyards and ancestral halls, or to raise funds for community activities, including supporting educational activities and providing for public works for the benefit of the clan or community. Maurice Freedman theorized that the clan organizations originally served as support and protection groups, particularly during the Tang (618–907 A.D.) and Song (960–1279 A.D.) dynasties (Freedman 1966). Dou Jiliang (1943, 1) theorized that native place consciousness was the spiritual power supporting the formation of regional institutions (huiguan and gongsi) abroad and acted as the focus for social, cultural, religious, and economic activities for fellow regionals (*tongxiang*) (see also Sinn 1997; Lai 2003, pt. 2). Overseas Chinese organizations provided a center for familiar cultural and recreational activities, including the worshipping of popular deities associated with southeastern China; hence, these centers often were mistakenly identified as religious joss houses (Ng 1992, 472).

In China, a director and two clerks, one for finances and the other for provisions, generally headed the community organizations. The additional task of labor recruiting and contracting was simply an outgrowth of the organization's entrepreneurial activities. These activities were re-created in overseas Chinese communities. Boardinghouses permitted the establishment of "employment families" that replaced the traditional kinship system in China. The tradition of establishing fictitious kinship ties evolved so that senior managerial members were called "uncle" or, in rare cases, "auntie," and therefore the Confucian filial piety practices were operative (Cochran 2000, 61–62).

Those who rejected the regional bonds because of disagreements within the group and those whose members were from small localities joined brotherhoods, often called *tang* ("meeting hall," or tong), which differed from open membership associations, also called *tang*. In some cases, the employment relationship was established through these secret societies, or brotherhoods, and the relationship of master and disciple was common. In the latter case, the disciples gave the master gifts during major festivals and celebrations, which in the Western world were regarded as bribes. The most prominent tang to rival the CCBA in power in some communities was the Zhigongtang (Chee Kong Tong, or "Chinese Free Masons"), a secret brotherhood that originally had the political aim of overthrowing the Manchu regime and reestablishing Chinese rule in China, and its splinter organization, the Binggongtang (Bing Kong Tong), which was involved in illegal activities with less emphasis on political goals (Chung 2006). The activities of the tang varied from place to place, depending on its location and its leadership; in some locations, the memberships overlapped. Like the CCBA, these organizations frequently encouraged relations with their homeland, sponsored traditional festivals to maintain their cultural heritage, settled disputes among their members, provided mutual aid services like burial insurance, protection, recreation, and employment opportunities. The headquarters had a hostel, recreational room, kitchen, and altar, usually dedicated to Guan Yu (also called Guan Gong or Guandi), the "God of War, a protector" also known as the "God of Literature." Secret brotherhoods gave no consideration to the person's regional identity or birthplace or family name and had to be nominated for membership by a member in good standing. Like the CCBA, the main purpose was protection of its members from within the community and from outsiders. The secret society tangs that became famous via coverage in American newspapers were those involved in illegal activities, especially gambling, opium trade, and prostitution. These activities had evolved from the early-nineteenth-century banditry in Guangdong, which had caused some of the economic dislocations (Antony 1989). Some tangs in the United States were legitimate and were primarily involved in the welfare of their members, but many were engaged in criminal activities; still others were involved in both legitimate and criminal activities.

Arrival in America meant immediate adjustments. One of the first and most common Western-style article of clothing the Chinese adopted soon after arriving was American boots, as the Chinese cloth shoes were unsuitable for work in the West.[11] This often was the first "cultural adaptation" the new arrivals had to make. Chinese merchants were quick to stock this item and saw new opportunities in selling supplies to their countrymen. Eventually, sturdy stone Chinese stores, one of which still stands, were built at Sutter's Mill and elsewhere to provide goods to Chinese miners and other workers in the region (Heizer 1947, 144, 152). When goods could not be obtained from China or a Chinese American store, the Chinese adopted American-made products, as revealed in archaeological sites in Spooner Summit, Verdi, and elsewhere, where western foodstuffs, teapots, and other objects were found (Solury 2004; Lee 2008). They also purchased goods from American merchants like Kasper Kubli (1830–1897) in Jacksonville, Oregon. Gradually, a small number adopted partial or complete western-style dress, as seen in a photograph from the 1870s in Lisa See's *On Gold Mountain* of railroad-worker-turned-merchant Fong See (1857–1957, who immigrated in 1871).

Some, like Billy Ford (aka Min Chung) and Sam Gibson (aka Non Chong Yee), took American names. The process and degree of acculturation varied with the individuals, their age, their occupation, and their environment.

As the Chinese began to arrive in increasing numbers, resentment against them swelled. In 1850 California was the first of several western states to pass the Foreign Miners Tax, which eventually was paid primarily by Chinese miners until it was declared illegal. More direct steps were taken, such as the prohibition of hiring Chinese miners in 1852 in Tuolumne County, California, and in 1855 in Shasta County, California (Chiu 1963, 18). The discrimination targeted the wage-earning miners, and the popular press publicized the "cheap Chinese labor," thus fomenting greater support for the anti-Chinese activities. As these miners moved to other mining locations, they carried their prejudice against the Chinese with them, and local anti-Chinese laws were passed. The Chinese lacked political clout because of the 1790 Naturalization Act that prohibited them from becoming naturalized citizens and enjoying rights accorded to other immigrant groups; this gave aspiring American politicians an easy scapegoat in their election campaigns and helped newspapers and magazines to sell more copies by carrying sensationalized stories about the Chinese. Economist Mark Kanazawa (2005) examined the impetus given to the exclusion laws by the depressed labor market conditions and the increased tendency for Chinese to compete directly with firms owned by Euro-Americans or occupations dominated by Euro-American. Some Chinese turned to other occupations, including working on timber ranches and in the logging industry because those areas provided employment opportunities and supportive employers. Since many rural South China farmers harvested and chopped their own wood, their experience helped them find jobs in the logging industry.

Unlike the situation in China, there were few married men and even fewer families in the American West. The 1875 Page Law essentially made it difficult for Chinese women to immigrate and thus created a bachelor-like society for the Chinese until the 1943 Repeal of the Chinese Exclusion Act. The 1882 Chinese Exclusion Act prohibited the entry of Chinese laborers for ten years and defined Chinese women/wives as laborers, creating a male-dominated immigrant community. The 1860 male-to-female ratio of 19:1 widened to 27:1 by 1890. The anti-Chinese agitators regarded the 1882 act as ineffectual and turned to statistics such as those published by the *San Francisco Bulletin*, which claimed that Chinese immigrant arrivals tripled in number between 1883 and 1885 (reprinted in *CDI* January 29, 1886). This led to further agitation for more stringent laws. The 1888 Scott Act prohibited the entry of all Chinese laborers, including those who had left temporarily with valid return certificates. Many Chinese laborers were thus stranded and could not return to the United States despite having documents that should have allowed them to return. The 1892 Geary Act extended the 1882 act and redefined "laborers" to include doctors and priests. It also required all Chinese, including those born in the United States, to register with the federal government so that those found without their "certificate of residence" and/or "certificate of identity" were subject to immediate deportation. These laws discouraged the Chinese from leaving the United States unless they intended never to return. Such exclusionary measures reduced the pool of workers for labor contractors. The 1894 treaty between China and the United States substantiated the terms of the Chinese exclusion acts with the modification that Chinese laborers who had a wife, child, or parent in the United States or property valued at $1,000 (which could be debts) could reenter the United States if they had the proper reentry papers (Irick 1982; Tsai 1979; Godley 1975; Yen 1981). Lost papers meant that the Chinese had to apply for a duplicate certificate through a very complicated immigration system that usually involved expensive legal assistance.

The exclusion laws became harsher. In 1904 Congress extended Chinese exclusion indefinitely, and the 1924 Immigration Act, creating a quota system based on early-nineteenth-century immigrant figures, essentially closed the door to Chinese immigrants. There were exceptions for immigrants creative enough to find another way to enter. The Chinese devised the paper son–paper daughter system as well as illegal entryways (Lau 2006); a particularly common method was purchasing "merchant status" by investing in a company as a silent partner. These harsher laws had the effect of increasing the male-female ratio in Chinese America until 1970 (when it was approximately 1:1) and contributed to the sojourner and transnational mentality of the Chinese, who traditionally revered family as an important component of life. Until 1943 older Chinese men outnumbered younger ones, and in an occupation where youth was important, woodcutters and sawyers disappeared from the scene partially because of the discriminatory legislation and the lack of new workers. The drastic decline in the Chinese American population was a result of the American immigration policies and the weakness of the Qing and Republican governments in China to support the overseas Chinese.

*   *   *

Sutter's Mill set the precedent for the connection between mining and lumber. For example, remnants of the traditional Chinese wooden waterwheels, used for agricultural irrigation in South China, as well as other wooden artifacts were found at placer mining sites throughout the West. A small sawmill in Bodega Bay, California, was built in 1835, but it could not meet the need for wood for the booming western mining communities after 1848. Residential and industrial needs contributed to the fluctuating prices of timber. Amador County, California, for example, had the rich timberland on the west side of the Sierra Nevada, and Euro-American lumbermen, many from Maine and Canada, worked these forests in the 1860s through the1880s.[12] Farmers often cut trees during the slack season, and it was said that in the late nineteenth century, "a farmer could use a bundle of shingles to buy goods in a store, acquire livestock, or even pay taxes" (Judd

1984, 61). Few Chinese were involved in the timber industry at the time because most preferred to try their hand at mining in the early years. This was the case in Volcano in Amador County, California, where the Chinese began mining in 1858 but did not get involved in lumbering until later, if census records are to be believed.[13] The 1870 census manuscript for Volcano listed only two Chinese, Ah Hong (b. 1830) and Ah Chew (b. 1835), working with four Euro-Americans at a sawmill owned by Ethan Philbrook, formerly of Maine. This multiracial crew typically characterized these early sawmill workers (Census 1870). The situation changed in 1880, when Ione City, Amador County, which had no Chinese working in lumbering in the previous decade, had ten Chinese woodchoppers living in three groups (3–3–4), with the eldest age fifty and the youngest age twenty (Census 1880). Workers in lumbering were transient and often had multiple names, so it was not surprising that the names did not repeat themselves in subsequent federal census manuscripts.

The gold rush expanded to other western regions and increased the need for wood, the nineteenth century's universal building material. Chinese immigrants answered the call for workers in the woods as the population grew. In 1846, for example, California's population was estimated at 8,000 to 12,000 but by the 1860 census it had exploded to 380,000 because of the discovery of gold. The Chinese population in California increased dramatically from 2,716 in 1851 to 20,026 in 1852 (Coolidge 1909, 498). Other western territories also saw an increase. Chinese miners and workers traveled to Marysville, California, by boat and then headed across the Sierra Nevada to the North Yuba River town that became known as Downieville. Both Marysville and Downieville had large Chinatowns that attracted miners during the offseason and break times. From there the Chinese probably traveled into the Carson Valley, Utah Territory. This was the route that James Fenimore, who named Virginia City, William Morris Stewart, the first state senator of Nevada, John Mackay ("Bonanza King, owner of the Consolidated Virginia Mine"), and Mark Twain took. By 1860 some twenty-one Chinese had moved into the Carson Valley. Their visibility—different appearance, dress, and customs—led to the phenomenon described by sociologist George Simmel (1955) as the reaction to the "stranger": fear, hostility, and conflict.

In 1860 there were 34,933 Chinese in the United States, the majority in the West; in 1890 the number reached 107,488, but with the enforcement of federal Chinese exclusion laws, the Chinese population dropped to 105,312 in 1894.[14] Oregon, Washington, Idaho, and Nevada saw dramatic population increases between 1870 and 1890 as new mining areas, which needed lumber, opened.

The earlier rush into mining and railroad construction eventually gave way to other occupations. According to a local Nevada newspaper, the *Reese River Reville* (July 26, 1866), in 1866 the CCBA reported that of the fifty-eight thousand Chinese registered with them, 25 percent worked for the CPRR. By 1876 more than one-sixth of the Chinese were in California and employed by the CPRR or

Table 1–2. Chinese Population by Location and as Percent of Total Population, 1860–1890

Location	1860	1870	1880	1890
United States	34,933* (0.1%)	63,199 (0.2%)	105,465 (0.2%)	107,488 (0.2%)
California	34,933 (9.2%)	49,277 (8.8%)	75,132 (9.8%)	72,472 (6.0%)
Nevada	33 (0.5%)	3,162 (7.4%)	5,416 (8.7%)	2,833 (6%)
Oregon		3,330 (3.7%)	9,510 (5.8%)	9,450 (1.9%)
Idaho		4,274 (28.5%)	3,379 (11.6%)	2,007 (2.4%)
Washington		234 (0.1%)	3,186 (4.7%)	3,260 (0.9%)

Source: U.S. Census, 1860–1890.
*Figure from Census Bureau undercounted.

other public improvement projects, while more than one-half were in manufacturing, woolen goods, cigar making, and other types of work. Approximately ten thousand were in the laundry business. Agricultural work was the other early occupation.

Because of the absence of women and distance from China, "employment families" evolved: men lived, ate, worked, and spent recreational time together. Those who could read the newspapers or letters kept others abreast of events in their native place and in their new environment.[15] Merchants, who often were labor contractors, sometimes were also the heads of the "families." Not all Chinese merchants and labor contractors were the same, however; most had to have basic literacy (ability to read, write, and do calculations). Some had knowledge of the Confucian classics, evident in the poem in chapter 2. Others had enough knowledge to express their feelings in poems (written from 1910 to 1940) on the walls of Angel Island, California, where many Chinese immigrants were detained.

This brand of literacy differed from the Qing Dynasty (1644–1911) Chinese concept that required a mastery of the Confucian classics and its commentaries and an ability to compose poetry in order to be regarded as a learned scholar (zhuren and jinshi). Some Chinese immigrants had a basic knowledge of the language and could read and write but not in the erudite manner and depth of the "scholar." In the late nineteenth century, Chinese merchants in urban Chinatowns sometimes turned to Chinese scholars from China to assist them in informal governance. This was seen in the leadership of the CCBA because the original charter was composed of six associations whose main purposes were to fight discrimination, raise funds, adjudicate and maintain peace and order within the Chinese communities, provide housing and meals during periods of unemployment or while en route to another job, enforce payment of debts, administer hospitals, cemeteries, schools, and other social services, sponsor programs to preserve Chinese culture, regulate economic competition among various businesses, and provide employment opportunities whenever possible (Douglas 2006; Qin 2009; Lai 2003, ch. 3). A literate Chinese secretary kept records for the organization. According to Otis Gibson (1826–1889), a Methodist minister in San Francisco's Chinatown, and others who were in positions to have such knowledge, the CCBA had recruiting agents in Hong Kong who loaned the workers money to travel to the United States, often under contract at the rate of two-thirds their monthly salary until the debt was paid. But the CCBA was not the only labor recruiter. Although inconclusive at this point, it is probable that the regional organizations, not the CCBA, were a major labor recruiter, since many of the Chinese workers came from the same region or district (county) or village, or were clan members themselves.

Labor contractors and employment agencies played an important role in the recruitment of workers in China and in the American West. For example, J. Nicholson, who operated the Chinese Labor Office on Sacramento Street, San Francisco in the 1870s, sought cooks, waiters, laundrymen, field workers, wood-choppers, railroad men, and miners.[16] Chinese-owned employment offices also existed. The Quong Sing Company of Truckee advertised for Chinese workers in the forests. Euro-American agents represented themselves as a company or agents of firms like the CPRR. The Tong Hua Company in Los Angeles's Chinatown hired Chinese and Korean workers at the turn of the twentieth century.

Chinese merchants based outside of San Francisco and Sacramento also participated in the recruitment of Chinese workers. For example, Lee Lung of Portland, Oregon, was a merchant who had stores in Portland, New York, and Baltimore, but he found that working as an agent for the North Pacific Steamship Company was also profitable.[17] When he tried to bring his wife and daughter to Portland, he was able to put up a bond of $2,000 in gold coins so that the women could live outside of the detention compound while their case and subsequent appeal, which was denied, was heard. Both Euro-American and Chinese American labor contractors apparently profited from the trade, but their influence with government officials was limited.

Many Chinese American merchants became labor contractors because they could sell goods to the men they helped to hire. One of the early records of the labor contracting system was revealed in the *San Joaquin Republican* (August 1, 1857) when a labor contractor hired two thousand Chinese at twenty-five dollars per month per person to dig a ditch on the south fork of the Merced River. For centuries Chinese farmers in South China had dug irrigation ditches, so this type of work was very familiar. The system of working together with fellow regionals was also familiar. Unlike the contractors for European immigrants and East Coast newcomers, who levied a set fee on the salaries of the men they recruited for lumber companies or charged a flat rate as an employment agency whenever a worker was placed in a job, the Chinese labor contractors, if they were storeowners, often did not take a percentage of salary but had the right to sell goods to the workers.

A few labor contractors did take a fee. In 1876 a Chinese contractor charged a commission of fifty cents per person, furnished transportation to the site, had the right to board the workers for eight to ten dollars per person per month, and provided a cook for every twenty-five workers, with the food and provisions purchased from the merchant's store (Chiu 1963, 127). Lee Ting, a railroad contractor at Carlin, Nevada, in the late nineteenth century, was also one of four partners, each investing $1,000 in Wah Hing and Company in Wadsworth and Cortez, Nevada, in this vein.[18] Some merchants, like Non Chong Yee of Carson City, served as labor contractor and recruiter to employers in the lumbering and railroad industries as well as a boardinghouse operator (in the name of his wife) and supplied goods to the "men in the mountains" handling the logging activities. He became very prosperous as a result of his activities. Dr. Ah Kee of Carson City found himself in the same prosperous position as he recruited workers for the construction of the VTRR.[19]

Chinese and Euro-Americans differed in fees to labor contractors and whether room and board were included. During the construction of the CPRR, room and board were included for Euro-American workers but not for the Chinese. The situation was similar for logging, but Euro-Americans paid fees prior to employment. In 1914 the Commission on Industrial Relations hired Peter Speek to investigate the living and working conditions of migratory Euro-American laborers, especially new immigrants (Woirol 2011a). In the Northwest he concentrated on lumber and railroad camps and discovered that the labor contractor (called an interpreter) charged each immigrant worker $13 ($9.75 for the employment agency, $2 for the interpreter, and $1.25 for negotiation expenses) to get the job. Unscrupulous contractors worked with unscrupulous employers in imposing poor working conditions so that the workers would quit after a short while; the contractor/interpreter could then earn more money by hiring another group of immigrants.

Speek reported that the workers often faced deplorable, unsanitary living conditions and terrible food at the logging camps, did not have good medical care for them (even though many paid a fee to their employers for doctor visits and hospital care), earned wages that fluctuated with the market conditions, and had more steady employment in mill work than in logging camps and railroad construction camps. In light of Speek's report, perhaps the Chinese workers were more fortunate because their room and board expenses were not part of their hourly wage but instead part of their contract (written or verbal) with the labor contractor or headman, who purchased provisions from Chinese merchants. They probably did not have to pay any substantial fees to get a job because the labor contractor, who often was a merchant, made his profit from the sale of supplies.

Contract laborers were used for railroad construction, mining, and agricultural work beginning in the 1860s. Workers were routinely indentured for a number of years in order to repay their passage, food, and lodging, but they received some wages, which most scholars believe were nevertheless lower than the prevailing rates for the job. Often the contract included medical care and funeral services, if needed. Theoretically there was some accountability, but in many cases a contract laborer was not much better than a European indentured servant of the era. The Wells Fargo Museum in San Francisco has a blank 1849 contract from a British firm in Shanghai offering local Chinese employment in California with an advance of the passage money of $125 to be deducted from the anticipated wages on a monthly basis in an agreement with the employer (Huang 2006; 2010). Anti-Chinese advocates quickly seized on the idea that this was the main method of employment of the Chinese; in the post–Civil War era, this kind of servitude was strongly opposed.

Labor contractors varied from being honest and honorable to unscrupulous and harsh. The labor contractor often spoke the same dialect as the men working for him or knew several local dialects in order to communicate with everyone. There were several occasions, noted in the newspapers, about labor contractors who provided dreadful food, treated the men poorly, or failed to pay their workers. The workers rebelled to the extreme of attempting to kill or successfully killing the disreputable labor contractor/headman. Such was the case in 1859, when a labor contractor failed to pay the 150 Chinese railroad workers, who then attacked the contractor's clerk.[20] The clerk escaped from the mob and took refuge at the station house, then tried to retaliate, wielding a large knife against some of his attackers until the police arrived. This contradicts the docile image of the Chinese workman and was a story frequently retold among Chinese workers.

According to payroll records at the California Railroad Museum in Sacramento, the CPRR hired many workers through Chinese labor contracting companies for work that included blasting trees to clear the roads, and chopping and transporting wood. Although the CPRR payroll records are incomplete, it was obvious that contractors rather than individuals were being paid. Only three men were listed in the fragmentary record as being involved in lumbering: Ah Foo—wood chopper; Ah Ting and Ah Tong—packers (W. Chew 2004, 70). Like Hung Wah, one of the earliest Chinese CPRR contractors, these probably were names of labor contractors themselves rather than individuals because of the large number of choppers and packers needed to provide the wood required.

As with the CPRR, the Chinese workers in lumbering were hired through an employment agency such as a Chinese district association, labor contractor, or mercantile company, assigned a Chinese "headman" (boss), and then contracted work with Euro-American lumber companies. The contractor could be Chinese, as in the case of Wa Kee, who hired one hundred Chinese workers for the Oregon-California Railway Company and worked with the attorney J. F. McCoy, who held the power of attorney for all of the Chinese labor in Oregon in the 1870s, or he could simply work independently, as in the case of George Chew, who in 1913 was the railroad contractor in Spokane, Washington (Currier 1942, 32; *Polk's*, 374).

Employers liked the contract system because the number of workers requested was reliable. If a worker was sick, the contractor simply hired another man for the job. The salaries were given to one responsible individual, who in turn usually deducted a fee and any room and board charges. The headman often arranged for food and lodging, thus freeing the non-Chinese company of that responsibility. Payment often went to the Chinese headman or contractor, who, in turn, paid the workers. Records of the names, number of workers, and salaries were kept in Chinese. An estimate of monthly income and expenses for CPRR workers on a monthly salary of thirty dollar had the following expenses:

The Chinese contractor often operated a boardinghouse and store, from which he also made his profit. In some cases, he might charge a fee or pay an accountant, whose salary came from a charge to the workers. The general system used in the lumber camps was to have a subcontractor manage up to twenty separate wood camps and provide food, supplies, and tools to the camps (Lindstrom and Hall 1994, 90).

Only a few of the non-Chinese labor contractors were well known. General Albert W. Sisson (1827–1888), Colonel William. H. Wallace (d. 1882) established Sisson, Wallace, and Company in 1857 in Sacramento as a general merchandising store that eventually sold goods to the CPRR. Beginning in 1872 the company owned patents connected with the CPRR, which were still in its possession in 1921 (Nevada County Deed Book 62 (1872), 48; 71 (1888), 327; 84 (1896), 628; see also Ficklin 1997, 13). In 1866 the firm began recruiting Chinese workers for the CPRR and had offices in Hong Kong, San Francisco, Truckee, and towns along the CPRR route. Labor recruiters used tempting posters promising instant wealth in a land where the streets were paved with gold. Sisson, Wallace, and Company hired men in groups of twenty-five to thirty; a bookkeeper maintained the accounts and worked with the gangs—and was probably the only person who knew their names.

Sisson and Wallace became one of the major firms employing Chinese, and their methods illustrate "the system" well. Payment was made for each gang, and

Table 1–3. Estimated Expenses for Central Pacific Railroad Workers

Steamship transportation:	$1.66	($40 amortized for two years)
Interest for loan at 4 percent:	0.14	($3.20 amortized for two years)
Share for food purchases	6.00	
Herbal medicine	1.50	
Headman fee	2.00	
Association fee	1.00	(probably includes burial expenses)
Letter writer fee	.50	
Equipment (shovel, $1.50)	.20	(amortized one year)
Total Expenses:	$13.00	
Net income:	$17.00	

Source: William F. Chew, *Nameless Builders of the Transcontinental: The Chinese Workers of the Central Pacific Railroad* (Victoria, B.C.: Trafford), 53.

the bookkeeper then paid the individuals. Sisson and Wallace owned a flume in the Martis Valley that eventually connected with the Richardson flume, about five-and-a-half miles long, that brought logs to the Martis Creek lumberyard (Coates). When building the California and Oregon Railroad, the company opened a Chinese supply store at Chico, California, for their workers.[21] In 1872 Sisson and Wallace employed more than 350 Chinese to cut timber and make wood charcoal (used for smelters and locomotives) near Truckee, and they hired additional Chinese to cut cordwood in the Crystal Peak and Verdi areas for both the CPRR and mines in Nevada and Utah (Elston and Hardesty 1981, 94–95). Sisson and Wallace were the largest operators in the Truckee River Basin in the 1870s; they shipped, for example, one thousand to two thousand bushels of wood charcoal weekly to Virginia City for smelters in 1874 (Knowles 1942, 28). They also had orders for eight thousand bushels of charcoal per day day from mines in Utah (Knowles 1942, 23).

In June 1874 Major Clark Crocker, younger brother of Charles Crocker (one of the Big Four), joined the firm of Sisson, Wallace, and (now) Crocker, which had become a major West Coast dealer in groceries, charcoal, wood, timber, lumber, and property; they also constructed and operated flumes, recruited Chinese workers, and imported Chinese goods directly from China. They even had their teas packed in China, thus eliminating the expenses of the middleman. Their advertisement in the Truckee newspapers indicated that their store there sold "a full assortment of China goods" as well as American products and groceries, dealt in wood and charcoal, and provided Chinese labor, even on short notice. They were also agents for Wells Fargo, and beginning in 1878, they owned the steamship *SS John L. Stephens*, formerly part of the PMSC fleet. When the SPRR was in the planning stages, Sisson, Wallace, and Crocker recruited Chinese laborers for its construction as well as the construction of other rail lines. They also were partners in the North Pacific Packing and Trading Company, incorporated in California, and owned a salmon canning and marketing firm in Alaska that employed many Chinese workers. They marketed Truckee cheese and butter in the 1880s because of they owned valuable dairy land in the Prosser Creek settlement.

According to Nevada City's *Daily Transcript* (January 21, 1886), Sisson, Wallace, and Crocker brought more Chinese "to the Pacific Coast than other and all white firms combined." The same newspaper on January 1, 1886, noted that in 1885 the firm had Chinese workers cutting thirty thousand cords of wood annually for the railroad company, employed in "teaming," and providing services in restaurants, boardinghouses, hotels, and laundries. Sisson, acting as the Wells Fargo agent, also was a partner in the Sisson, Egbert, and Company stable in Truckee (Selected Nevada County Property Records). This gave him an inroad into wagon freight transportation. The *Los Angeles Times* (September 9,1882) reported that Sisson, Wallace, and Crocker had extensive land holdings in Tulare, Nevada, Placer,

Sierra, and Los Angeles Counties in California; Benson in Cochise County, Arizona Territory; Carlin (Elko County), Reno (Washoe County), and Winnemucca (Humboldt County), Nevada; Evanston, Wyoming Territory; and all the SPRR line in Arizona, New Mexico, and Texas. The company sold property to Chinese, in Truckee and elsewhere. As a labor contractor, Sisson became a wealthy man. When he died in November 1888, he left an estate worth $616,000 that included stocks in Sisson, Crocker, and Company, Oregon Stock and Butchering Company, and a house worth $38,000.[22] The firm declined after his death.[23]

Another major Euro-American recruiter was Cornelius Koopmanschap, a Dutch immigrant who originally imported Chinese goods to San Francisco in 1850. Beginning in 1861 he became a labor contractor for thirty thousand Chinese, many of whom worked for the railroad companies throughout the West (Sinn 2013, 224–28, 123–27, 153; Barth 1965, 191–96).[24] Koopmanschap worked with a partner in Hong Kong, and together they had a thriving business in the recruitment and transportation of merchandise, including lumber and firecrackers, and Chinese workers on ships leased from the PMSC and from the Oriental Steamship Company, an auxiliary of the CPRR (Senate Report 689, 1877). Koopmanschap had business relations with Sisson and Wallace, but he operated differently. At first he paid forty-five dollars per individual for the transpacific crossing and guaranteed farm workers eight dollars in gold or ten dollars in currency per month, at least two new suits per year, twenty-six working days per month, water-tight housing, and good treatment. Chinese railroad workers, however, received fifteen dollars in gold per month. He supplied railroad workers to the CPRR, UPRR, Memphis and El Paso Railroad, to name a few. According to the September 29, 1869, *Columbus Daily Enquirer*, Koopmanschap brought thousands of voluntary Chinese workers for the CPRR "with the full knowledge and consent of the [local] Chinese authorities" to the United States. In 1870 he expanded his activities to the South, persuading the Texas Land Company to hire five thousand Chinese workers, the government in Georgia to hire thirteen hundred to work on roads, and the Louisiana farmers to hire several thousand more in rice and sugar production under the direction of Tye Cim Arr, a native of Hong Kong who was educated in England. Koopmanschap's efforts at getting the Chinese to replace African Americans in the southern cotton fields failed, but by 1875 he looked to Brazil to hire thirty-five hundred Chinese in the coffee and pepper regions at ten dollars per month with board, free passage, and guaranteed employment for three years.[25] Like Sisson, Crocker, and other Euro-American labor contractors, he visited China often. Just before the passage of the 1882 Chinese Exclusion Act, he brought several thousand to work on the Southern and Northern Pacific railroads under a contract for one and two years at twenty-five dollars to thirty dollars per month with future expectations of working on the Canadian Pacific Railroad. In late September 1882 Koopmanschap died aboard the *Rio de Janeiro* and was hailed as a man "who has had more to do than any other man with the importation of coolies for railroad work."[26]

The CPRR and the SPRR also recruited Chinese workers directly and had three steamships (part of the Oriental Steamship Company fleet) to transport the Chinese to the United States. Recognizing that the passage of the 1882 Chinese Exclusion Act would hinder their ability to get workers, in 1881 railroad companies also leased ships from the PMSC to bring railroad workers to their projects (Crocker to Huntington, December 1881).

Eventually other Euro-Americans found labor contracting profitable. The tremendous amount of money involved is exemplified by the Mills and Onderdonk Company, which, according to the *San Francisco Examiner* (April 11, 1882), had two contracts totaling $20 million to hire Chinese workers for road construction for the Canadian Pacific Railroad in 1882. The agents of the firm offered twenty-eight dollars per month with free passage across the Pacific, including meals, for unskilled Chinese workers with an increase of $1.25 per day after three months' work. For their recruiting efforts, labor contractors received approximately one dollar per person. This undoubtedly was adding fuel the fire of Chinese exclusion.

Like the CPRR, the used labor contractors to hire Chinese workers. Archaeologist C. Lynn Rogers discovered that the firm of Bell and Burke was one of the contractors for the original construction. (Rogers n.d.) The VTRR also utilized Chinese labor contractors for recruitment. One of the most notorious was Ah Jack. In 1880 Ah Jack (b. 1837) lived and worked in Truckee Meadows but sent workers to Carson City and other locations. He was regarded as the official interpreter for the VTRR (Wurm 1983, 84). From court records more has been revealed about Ah Jack. In 1881 Stephen Cornsen, who contracted with Ah Jack for labor services, owed Ah Jack $940.67 for approximately thirty-one men working thirty days at the rate of thirty dollars per month. Ah Chung and four Euro-Americans testified in court, and Ah Jack was awarded $964.16, which included court costs.[27] Because testimony from Chinese did not have to be accepted in court, it was important that Euro-Americans supported Ah Jack's position. Ah Jack provided laborers in California as well. In June 1882 he contracted workers for a land reclamation project for the Tide Land Reclamation Company based in San Francisco and was sued for false and fraudulent estimates of work.[28]

Ah Jack lost the case. By 1885 his fortunes had apparently declined: that year A. Lindley and Company sued him for goods purchased and delivered, totaling $1,706.72.[29] Unable to pay, Ah Jack's First National Bank account of $940 was attached.

Another important Chinese labor contractor was Ah Quong (b. 1847), who lived in Reno, spoke and read English, and was fluent in several Chinese dialects. This was important for communicating with Americans and Chinese workers. He often worked with Sam Thayer, who was also Chinese and worked for the CPRR, and who had been the Chinese labor contractor during the construction of the CCRR. Neither Ah Quong nor Sam Thayer had the financial success and stability that some Chinese and several Euro-American labor contractors had. Poor business practices, gambling, and speculation on the stock market contributed to their financial downfall.

Another labor contractor was the Pacific Chinese Employment Company, King and Merritt, proprietors, which serviced the interior towns along the Pacific Coast with workers of all kinds prior to 1877, when they stopped advertising in the local newspapers (Chiu 1963, 127). These employment agencies and contract labor companies made thousands of dollars by providing Chinese workers for various projects in the West and often leased ships or owned ships to provide the transportation required, but not all of them were successful. Part of their success came from having a monopoly on providing goods for the workers.

In the 1880 census manuscript for San Francisco, there were two Chinese employment agencies with a total of five officers and five employees (Chiu 1963, 128). Among the most renowned individual Chinese contractors was Chin Chun Hock (b. 1844), who arrived in the Seattle area in 1860 and within eight years had organized the Wah Chong Company, first located on Mill Street and later in an impressive brick building on Third and Washington. The firm manufactured cigars, offered tailoring services, and imported and exported goods. Chin became a labor contractor for a variety of occupations from railroad construction to lumber camps, including ones in Port Gamble. Later, he partnered with Chin Quong, who arrived in Seattle at age 11, and Chin Gee Hee, who arrived in Seattle in 1875 after working in the California placer mines and on railroad construction in Nevada (Hildebrand 1977, 23). Some Chinese labor contractors were more specialized, however; in the 1913 Polk's Spokane City Directory, George Chew, at 606 Hyde Building, advertised that he was a railroad contractor. Others, both Chinese and non-Chinese, often could be found in several city directories.

Railroad owners used the contractors and employment agencies in hiring for the construction of several rail lines. Edward Reed of Reno, for example, was noted in the *Carson City Morning Appeal* (December 22, 1880) among the contractors for Chinese labor for the construction of the CCRR. In 1880 the *Virginia Evening Chronicle* (August 4) reported that five hundred or more Chinese worked on the CCRR. Unfortunately, few of the Chinese or Euro-American labor contractors left sufficient records to determine which groups were the most active and successful, but certainly Sisson, Wallace, and Crocker, and also Koopmanschap were wealthy entrepreneurs as labor contractors.

What becomes evident is the importance of understanding the place from which the Chinese immigrants came. A greater understanding of economic, political, and social interaction between the host country and minority group can be best understood by examining the Chinese immigrants' institutional (organizational, business, and occupational) practices in Guangdong, the fragmentary information about the transplantation and adaptation of these practices, and the emerging Euro-American business activities. The process of integration was more difficult for the Chinese because of their predominately single-male society, artificially created by American laws regarding entry requirements for Chinese women (Ling 2012). The absence of family life worked against greater integration. Early-twentieth-century Japanese American families had made accommodations (adjustment to American lifestyle and adoption of American values and practices while retaining some features from the culture of origin) because of English-speaking leaders in the community (the result of the Meiji Emperor's educational reforms) and the English language education of the children. Immigration restrictions meant that Chinese Americans had "incomplete families of parent (father) and children" or employment families that often were based on kinship ties or multi-male households living together in boardinghouses (Wong 1998). The lack of a true family life was compounded by the fact that the Chinese were ineligible to be naturalized citizens and therefore could not vote. This excluded them from local, regional, and national political activities until the second generation reached their majority. The fact that many of the early Chinese working in logging had wives and families in China (in some locations the rate was as high as 50 percent) meant that conditions in China were meaningful to their lives and therefore they maintained the "sojourner" mentality. This was reflected in the popularity of the Chinese-language newspapers and magazines that carried stories about their native places but reported relatively little on the events in the United States.

The ties to the land of their birth were strong, especially if wives and children remained behind, but the ties in the United States often were equally compelling. Estimates indicate that about one-third of the early Chinese were married and living apart from their wives. As this study will demonstrate, there were cases of Chinese who retired and returned to China, but there also were cases of those who came to settle with a hope of returning at least once to visit parents, wives, children, and siblings left behind; most, however, remained in the American West until their deaths, probably because they were too poor to return to China or because they had adjusted to the American lifestyle and were no longer comfortable in a traditional Chinese milieu. There were also numerous cases of men sending for their sons, who were born in China, and turning over their businesses to them. When the sons reached their majority, they went to China to marry and start a family; they then returned to the United States to repeat the pattern. Wealthier Chinese often sent their children born in the United States to China for an education for several years, and these children (both male and female) tended to live in two worlds: one American, one Chinese-American.

Because of the shortage of women, Chinese American men went to China to marry if they could afford the journey. Lee Gee, who was born in San Francisco on September 15, 1877, and whose father was a carpenter in San Francisco, was an example of an American citizen who went to China to marry.[30] As a result of the Scott Act of 1888, prohibiting the immigration or return of Chinese laborers to the United States unless they had assets worth at least $1,000, Lee Gee (despite his American citizenship) was denied reentry in June 1898, even though he had the required "return certificate" (McClain 1994). This meant that those laborers leaving the United States after 1888 had little chance of being able to return to the United States. Some twenty thousand Chinese laborers were caught in this awkward situation and denied reentry, and the Supreme Court upheld the government's position.[31] Chinese laborers quickly learned about this risk and had to give serious consideration regarding a trip to China, which, for most, was inadvisable.

This undoubtedly discouraged Chinese in the timber industry from return migration unless it was permanent. In general, most lumbermen had to earn sufficient funds to be considered "wealthy" before they could return to China; many could not achieve this level of financial prominence, so they never left their adopted homeland. Most transient laborers, like those in search of green gold, fell into this latter category. The eventual solution was to earn and save enough money to achieve "merchant status" by buying into a partnership of a store, but even then there might not be enough money to make the trip to and from China, especially when the return fare was $100 by the 1890s. The other danger was the enforcement of the Chinese exclusion laws, which prevented, for example, the former woodchopper-turned-merchant Low Ching from reentering the United States in 1900 because his firm had failed while he was abroad.[32] Despite Ching's possession of documents allowing his return, the strict stance of the immigration officials rejected his application for readmission. It was risky to leave the United States for a temporary visit because one's return was not guaranteed. This became common knowledge in the Chinese American communities.

Although the Chinese working in the forests often lived and ate together, many had to interact with the larger community and this relationship aided in their acculturation (adopting values and practices of the host society). Foods and tableware that could not be obtained from China via merchants in San Francisco and Sacramento forced them to purchase American-made products. For some, the American lifestyle was their choice, and beginning in the 1850s, some indicated this preference by adopting American names like Billy Ford (aka Min Chung) and Sam Gibson (aka Non Chong Yee) of Nevada (Louie 1991; Louie 1985–1986). Life in remote areas created economic interdependence that sometimes resulted in greater social interaction and cultural adaptation among all ethnic groups. One's occupation requiring interaction with the larger community led to wearing Western clothing or decorating one's living quarters in American styles. Another critical factor was the purchase of land, and despite the scant records and informal land transfers in the mid-to late nineteenth century, this study will show that the Chinese made land purchases and other investments in America, thus giving them a sense of "belonging."

Like all immigrants, the Chinese focused on the practicalities of everyday life, and the foundation of that life was rooted in their heritage. What they could not do was to merge into the host society as immigrants from Europe voluntarily could do. Physical appearance, the need for protection within their own community against the host society, the absence of a family life that would have helped them integrate better, language and value differences, and the inability to achieve political power because they could not become naturalized citizens were all factors working against their acculturation and assimilation. Their plight challenged the drive for Americanization and "melting pot myth" and contributed to the "crisis of ethnic relations," as historian John Higham (1981) called it, in the 1890s to 1920s.

Although documents from the anti-Chinese era of the 1870s through 1890s implied that the Chinese workers were "slave laborers" or similar to "indentured servants," recent scholarship indicates that many came voluntarily, with some borrowing funds from relatives and friends, regional associations, and other organizations in order to seek new economic opportunities and to escape the conditions in their native place. Some were desperate enough to travel by Chinese junks; others paid for passage on one of the transpacific shipping lines. When they arrived, their huiguan and other Chinese organizational leaders greeted them and helped them with housing, clothing, and job opportunities in the early decades. As the conditions in China grew worse in some areas, especially in the Siyi counties of Guangdong, the organizations changed, and the Siyi emigrants represented a majority of Chinese immigrants. Chinese and non-Chinese labor contractors recruited thousands of Chinese workers until the passage of the 1882 Chinese Exclusion Act; when the public felt that the law was not stringent enough, other anti-Chinese legislation was passed, resulting in a decline by 1900 of the available Chinese labor pool. At the same time, the Chinese were adapting to their American environment, and the few children who reached their majority by the late nineteenth century began to have an influence within the community and turned away from the hard physical labor of construction work and logging.

CHAPTER 2

Work and Workers

Competing with other immigrants, especially French Canadians and lumbermen from Maine, the Chinese, some of whom were experienced, entered into the logging industry usually as unskilled laborers; eventually, however, a few worked their way up to more prestigious positions. Their ability to rise in the occupational hierarchy depended on their skills, personalities, and positive recognition from the Euro-American timber farmers and, later, lumber barons. Few newcomers wanted to do the hard manual labor of cutting trees and transporting logs. Timber ranchers nevertheless found one group who often were banned from mining to work for them in the mountains. From the 1860s to the 1890s the Chinese constituted 70 percent to 100 percent of the workers in some parts of the forests of the American West performing a variety of tasks and having some upward mobility. They provided the necessary labor, while Euro-Americans and others went into mining, ranching, and farming. Some earned more than miners and railroad workers. When injustices occurred, the Chinese were not hesitant to use the American judicial system if they could afford it. Working in the woods was a transient occupation and probably not appealing to many Chinese whose ancestors lived in the same locality for generations, but some found the work and pay to their liking in a rapidly changing western frontier.

From 1810 to 1860 the United States transformed from a rural society into a more commercial, industrial, and urban one that utilized large quantities of wood. At the same time, the frontier began to be settled and industrialized. Mining, railroad construction, and community development expanded the need for wood products in the West and led to a growth of the lumber industry between the 1850s and early 1900s. The abundance of trees near the Pacific Coast and in the Sierra Nevada meant that the lumberman's axe could cut the finest quality of straight, giant trees.[1] The average trees in the West yielded two twenty-foot lengths, each length twelve inches square, and so were larger than trees in the East and Midwest and required different skills of loggers.[2] Some of the trees in China were as tall and wide as those found in the American West, so some men were experienced in felling giant trees. In the seventeenth century the famous author Tan Qian noted in his 1935 *Miscellaneous Offerings from Date Grove* (*Zaolin zazu*) that ninety percent of the trees "of a circumference so great that several must join hands to encircle them" fell victim to the woodcutters (quoted in Brook, 2010, 130; Menzies 1994b, 575).

Three acts contributed to the rapid growth of logging. The Preemption Act of 1841 (27th Cong., Ch. 16; 5 Stat. 453) allowed for the sale of public lands and granted preemption rights to individuals already living on federal lands. The Pacific Railway Act of 1862 (US Statutes at Large, vol. 12, 489+) gave the western railroad companies the right to timber on public land for two hundred feet in width on each side of the tracks in a checkerboard fashion. The Timber and Stone Act of 1878 (45th Cong., Sess. 2, Ch. 151, 20 Stat. 89) sold western timberland (at first limited to California, Oregon, Washington, and Nevada) for $2.50 per acre in 160-acre blocks, as long as the land was unfit for cultivation, but trees and stones could be harvested. Ownership was possible within sixty days. Western lumber companies were actually able to obtain title for as many as twenty thousand acres. Fraudulent ownership and trespassing on government lands also was common. Millions of acres went into private hands during this time. This meant that workers had to be hired to log the trees (LaLande 1979, 20).

At first lumber was shipped from the East to the West, but with the abundance of forests in the West, it did not take long before individuals and industrial leaders harvested the "green gold," as lumber was called, not only for the American West but also for countries across the Pacific Ocean. Lumber barons emerged as economic, political, and social leaders in their communities. Many of their company headquarters in the greater San Francisco Bay Area became international business centers and influenced local, state, and national politics. Lumber companies hired predominantly low-paid immigrants, including the Chinese, who moved from site to site as the forests were depleted. These workers played a critical role in the emerging western lumber industry that reached its height in the 1870s through early 1900s.

The employment of Chinese in logging production varied. Each region had unique or different characteristics such that many of the broad, sweeping generalizations that have been perpetuated did not take into account the realities of the local situation. Historian Frederick Jackson Turner emphasized the role of the "empty land" in stripping away the hierarchical structures of the old world while creating open, egalitarian societies in the new. The Chinese workers in logging experienced some of this equal treatment, but prejudice and the rise of labor unions contributed to efforts to drive them out of logging, especially when mining in the region declined. The Euro-American employer often set the tone for the community acceptance of the Chinese, and sometimes the fact that they were involved in trade to China, Hong Kong, and the Hawaiian Islands contributed to their employment of the Chinese and familiarity with Chinese customs, thus challenging anti-Chinese movements.

Many communities and states followed California's lead in passing a foreign miners' tax that was aimed at Chinese miners, and the poll or "head" tax on people "ineligible for citizenship." In some mining communities, such as Tuolumne, California, in 1852, Shasta, California, in 1855, and Gold Hill, Nevada, in 1859, the Chinese were banned from participating in mining, and federal law prohibited them from filing original mining claims (but they could own claims sold by the initial claimant or be co-owners of claims with Euro-Americans or file preemption claims with the county recorder). In states that followed California's 1878 constitutional precedent (Article 19, sections 2–4) until it was struck down by the court for violating the 1868 Burlingame Treaty, corporations were not allowed to hire Chinese workers directly or indirectly or to allow them to work on public projects, so the Chinese turned to lumbering, a field in which some had experience and jobs were available. In the early years, the Chinese were successful in this occupation.

The effects of the Chinese exclusion acts of May 6, 1882 (22 Stat. L. 58), July 5, 1884 (23 Stat. L. 115), September 13, 1888 (22 Stat. L. 476), October 1, 1888 (25 Stat. L. 504), May 5, 1892 (27 Stat. L. 25), November 3, 1893 (28 Stat. L. 7), and others decreased the Chinese labor pool and drove a large percentage of the Chinese back to China or into work that was not as physically demanding. This continued until the Immigration Act of 1924 (43 Stat. 155; 44 Stat. 812, 45 Stat. 1009, 46 Stat. 854, 47 Stat. 656; 8 U.S.C. 204) established a quota of one hundred Chinese immigrants per year. The exclusion acts meant that timber barons had to look elsewhere for workers. At the turn of the twentieth century Japanese arrivals replaced the Chinese working in the woods (Dubrow 2002). The denuding of the forests from clear-cutting and natural disasters meant that fewer workers were needed and that the Chinese no longer worked in the forests in large numbers.

The effects of the exclusion laws in Nevada reflected the trends developing in the American West. In the Sierra Nevada, the boom years of lumbering were in the 1870s and 1890s and corresponded with the Comstock's mining boom years of 1863, 1872, and 1874, with a revival in 1886 to 1894, despite a recession. The frenetic railroad-construction era between 1863 and the 1910s added to the hiring of Chinese workers.

The number of Chinese in Nevada initially grew between 1870 and 1890 and then dropped 40 percent in the next four years. According to the 1870 federal census, the Chinese represented 7.4 percent (3,162) of Nevada's total population (42,491) and increased to 8.7 percent (5,416 of 62,266) by 1880. In 1890 they constituted only 6.0 percent (2,833 of 47,355) of the population, then four years later dropped to an estimated 1,143 while the non-Chinese population grew (NVSHPO).[3] The Chinese population declined drastically thereafter until the late twentieth century.

Archaeologist Leslie K. Hill discovered that in the 1870s Canadians dominated the lumber industry in Nevada's Carson Range, constituting 45 percent of the workforce, but the Chinese made up 49 percent of the woodchoppers in the

Table 2–1. Population of Chinese in the United States and Nevada, 1860–1920

	Total Population in Nevada	Total Chinese Population in U.S.	Chinese Population in Nevada	Percent of Chinese in Nevada	Chinese Males in Nevada	Chinese Females in Nevada	Ratio of Chinese Males to Females
1860	6,057	34,933	23	0.3	—	—	—
1870	42,491	63,199	3,162	7.4	2,817	306	1:9
1880	62,266	105,465	5,416	8.7	5,102	314	1:16
1890	47,355	107,488	2,833	6.0	2,749	84	1:33
1900	42,335	89,863	1,352	3.2	1,283	69	1:19
1910	81,875	71,531	927	1.1	876	51	1:17
1920	77,407	61,639	689	0.9	630	59	1:11

Source: Census, 1860–1920

Nevada counties of Storey, Lyon, Ormsby, Douglas, and Washoe, all supplying wood for the trains and the mines, especially the Comstock, and were located near or in the Sierra Nevada and Lake Tahoe Basin (NVSHPO 1870). The Chinese numbered twenty-six in Virginia City, Storey County; sixteen in Truckee Meadows, Washoe County, at the base of the Sierra Nevada; eight in Crystal Peak/ Verdi, also in Washoe County; five in Washoe, Peavine, and Long Valley, also in Washoe County; five in Eureka County; three in Esmeralda County; and two each in Carson City, Ormsby County, and Island Mountain, Elko County. In the same year, in Elko County (northeastern Nevada), which had been opened by the CPRR, the Chinese constituted 97 percent (35 out of 36) of the woodchoppers.

By 1880 Chinese workers made up 82 percent of the total logging workforce (Hill 1987, 34–35). The *Virginia Evening Chronicle* (October 16, 1880) reported that three thousand Chinese were working in the forests surrounding Lake Tahoe, but the census recorded smaller figures. It is probable that the census taker did not want to venture into the mountains to conduct the count. According to the 1880 census Chinese woodchoppers were more dispersed: in Ormsby County, with a total Chinese population of 988, forty-five of the seventy-two woodchoppers (62 percent) were Chinese; twenty-four Chinese woodchoppers lived in Tuscarora (Elko), eight in Franktown (Washoe), five in Eureka (Eureka), three in Mill City (Elko), two in Island Mountain (Elko), and one each in Spring Valley (Humboldt), Battle Mountain (Lander), Treasure Hill (White Pine), and Dayton (Lyon) (NVSHPO 1880). In Franktown, Washoe County, there were thirty-one Chinese wood loaders. The decades of 1880 and 1890 probably represented the greatest presence of the Chinese labor force in the woods in this region.

By 1900 loggers moved to new forests in Washington, Oregon, and other locations. In Nevada the Chinese woodchoppers diminished to two in Dayton and one each in Lovelock and Como Mining District (NVSHPO). In 1910 there were two in Esmeralda, one in Virginia City, and five in Ormsby County. The small number of Chinese in the woods indicated that they no longer worked in teams but rather as individuals in a multi-ethnic mosaic of lumbermen. This meant that they had to adapt to American ways and American culture. Boarding house

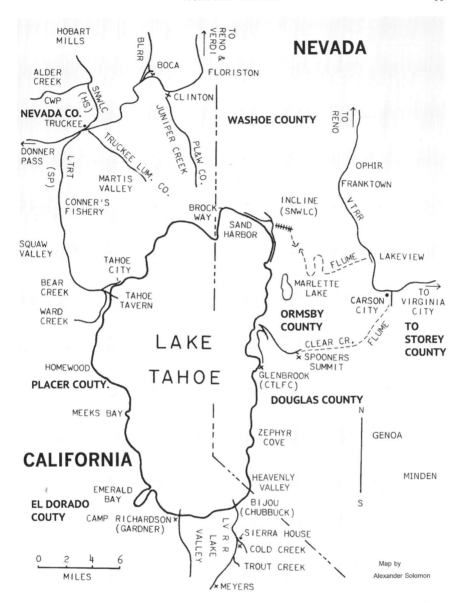

Sierra Nevada ("snow covered mountains") and its spur, the Carson Range, covered
eastern California and west-central Nevada and were heavily logged prior to 1900.

and camp cooks in the early twentieth century probably cooked only American
dishes, so a major dietary change occurred. Without the support of members of
their clan and fellow countrymen, they undoubtedly did not preserve as many of
the Chinese cultural traditions as earlier Chinese workers had. By 1920 there was
only one Chinese woodchopper, China Tom, who lived in Sweetwater, Mineral
County, near Table Mountain and Bodie, California. China Tom was age sixty-six

Table 2–2. Total Woodchoppers in Nevada Counties, with Chinese Wood Choppers as a Part of the Total

Year:	1870		1880		1900		1910		1920	
County	T	Ch	T	Ch	T	Ch	T	Ch	T	Ch
Storey	30	26	1	0	1	0	1	1	1	0
Lyon	5	0	0	2	1	12	3	0	0	0
Ormsby	3	2	72	45	17	0	10	5	0	0
Douglas	0	0	0	0	9	0	4	0	0	0
Washoe	177	29	9	8	7	0	11	0	0	0
Humboldt	8	0	13	1	2	1	0	0	0	0
Pershing	0	0	0	0	0	1	0	0	0	0
Churchill	0	0	0	0	0	0	1	0	3	0
Mineral	0	0	0	0	0	0	0	0	0	1
Esmeralda	55	3	16	0	9	0	13	2	2	0
Lander	10	0	23	1	9	0	0	0	1	0
Nye	3	0	30	0	30	0	13	0	14	0
Eureka	0	5	75	5	17	0	0	0	4	0
Elko	0	35	36	35	5	0	1	0	0	0
White Pine	138	0	15	1	17	0	4	0	0	0
Lincoln	4	0	25	0	7	0	0	0	0	0

T = Total wood choppers in county

Ch = Chinese wood choppers in county

Statistics taken from NVSHPO and do not include wood dealers and others involved in lumbering. "Wood-chopper" is a census designation.

in 1920, was either born in California or immigrated in 1871 (census data differs), delivered wood to Bodie and other mining towns, and lived with his wife, Ida Tom, age thirty-four, who was born in Nevada (Shaw 2013). The difficulty of counting men "in the mountains" due to accessibility and language problems meant that many Chinese in lumbering were not included in these census figures or were counted as "laborers."

Logging was basically the same throughout the world; it involved felling (or cutting down) and bucking (cutting off branches, sawing the logs into proper lengths, preparing for transport) of trees; herding or skidding (moving the logs to a central collection point); decking (piling the logs); loading (sorting and then loading the logs to be taken to a mill); fluming or transporting (moving the logs via flumes, rivers, or ponds to the mill for processing or to a railroad station for shipping to another location); and unloading at the mill (Clark 2002). Wood-cutting also required the clearing of a trail, making a place for the tree to fall, accurately estimating the direction of the fall so that no one would be injured, and then cutting up the fallen tree and its limbs. At first, trees were felled with axes, often with a double-bitted axe with a long narrow blade, made razor sharp by a whetstone (Drushka 1992, 32–42; Jager 1999; on camp life, Mackie 2000). At least one axe, discovered in 2003, was embedded in a large tree trunk at a Chinese camp in Heavenly Valley on the border between Nevada and California. In the late 1870s more efficient saws came into use. The early six- or seven-foot saw yielded to ten- to eighteen-foot crosscut saws for felling the mighty Douglas firs, redwoods, and sequoias. The new saws had antibinding edges so that they could sink quickly into the tree trunks (Williams 1989, 92–93). The "misery whipsaw" used by loggers in the 1870s was found in a Chinese wood-camp site in the Lake Tahoe area ("Archaeologists Find," 2003). With the exception of transporting logs by trains, the procedure was similar that used in China (Stoddard 1978, 165–66; Menzies 1988a)

Nevertheless, there were differences between the experiences of the Chinese in the lumber industry in China and what they faced in the American West. The process of bringing the timber to market in the United States was more favorable in the West because of better marketing, technology, industrialization, and transportation systems, especially with the use of trains. The fellers and sawyers operated in both countries in much the same way. Teamsters, who were in charge of the animal teams—oxen or horses—performed similar tasks in both sites, but in China, it was human labor that transported the wood (Menzies 1988a), whereas in the American West, horse chutes, log chutes, flumes, slick skid roads, and gravity chutes and/or logging trains commonly moved the logs to bodies of water and/or to mill sites.

Early fellers worked in pairs using crosscut saws, double-cut saws, and axes, while buckers worked alone with crosscut saws to cut off limbs and section the logs into specified sizes (Rajala 1989, 169). Around 1900 the raker-teeth saw was invented and used (Drushka 1992, 32–33). Fragments of these types of saws and the refashioned cans holding saw oil as well as files for sharpening saws were found in Chinese sites throughout the Sierras. The felling ax, which had a longer and narrower blade than Eastern axes, had a longer handle to reach into trees that were eight feet in diameter. Other equipment included a sledgehammer, wedges, a bottle of oil, and two springboards. The prime section of a log was cut into sixteen- to forty-foot lengths to become saw logs. Peelers stripped off the bark from the felled trees that had been sawed into lengths. Under unusual conditions, it was possible to cut forty-five logs into saw logs in half a day, but usually the handwork involved meant that it took several hours to fell a single tree (Moore 2005, 23; Rajala 1993, 81). The big trees normally were not cut in the winter months because of the deep snow, but cordwood cutting, the job of many Chinese in the woods, was a year-round job. Chinese fellers usually left a stump about three feet high (the sawing height of short men).

Hundreds of Chinese worked in the isolated mountains and performed a variety of tasks needed to supply the high-demand wood products in the rapidly developing frontier towns despite ethnic rivalries. They left no written records, and because of this, their work has been forgotten or, in some cases, ignored. Literature from the 1860s never acknowledged that the Chinese felled the trees, presuming instead that they performed only menial, unskilled tasks of trimming the branches off the felled logs, cutting the smaller logs into cordwood for fuel, preparing the roads for skidding or moving the logs, loading the logs, and transporting the logs, usually using waterways such as rivers, manmade lakes, chutes, and flumes. Men worked as "river hogs" to free jammed logs along the riverbanks. Pond men were in charge of floating log rafts to transportation centers or sawmills, which were often built next to waterways and where the Chinese also loaded and unloaded the lumber. They were known for removing stumps for cordwood by blasting the stump with black powder, a substance they used in railroad construction. They collected roots and stumps for fuel in homes, train engines, smelters, and mills. They also peddled the firewood in towns like Virginia City and San Francisco (Magnaghi 2001, 126).

But remnants of cross-cut saws and a variety of axes, for example, reveal that the Chinese indeed felled trees, a task often performed by French Canadians and Maine lumberjacks, who regarded their positions as the top of the logging occupational scale (Young and Budy 1979, 114). In general, Euro-American loggers were content to have the Chinese perform the unskilled tasks but were angered if the Chinese performed "skilled" jobs.

In most cases, the census manuscripts designated Chinese workers as "laborers," but if they lived and worked in a predominantly logging area, they undoubtedly performed tasks related to logging. Other tasks included cutting cordwood,

Similar piles of cordwood could be found in areas where the Chinese cut wood in the 1860s through the 1890s. This stack, one of many, is more than a century old. Some five thousand Chinese resided nearby at China Camp, Tuolumne County ("Yosemite Gold Country") . (Author's photograph, 2012)

tending flumes, making charcoal, loading and unloading logs, constructing train routes, roads, flumes, and bridges, riding log trains, and acting as wood dealers, teamsters, and maintenance men. Some also cooked in the logging camps. Although prejudice permitted only a few Chinese to rise to supervisory positions, some were able to make equal or better than equal wages when compared with Euro-Americans working in similar capacities—as camp cooks and watchmen, for example. A few headed teams of workers to fill lumber contracts. Logging required much teamwork, and in some cases the Chinese worked alongside each other or with other ethnic groups, as seen in a photograph of Chubbuck's Sierra House, log ranch in the Tahoe Basin (South Lake Tahoe Historical Society).

Their main work involved cordwood (chopped firewood stacked in a unit four feet wide, eight feet long, and four feet high, or 128 cubic feet). The census term "woodchopper" implied that they were cutting cordwood. Cordwood, cut with crosscut saws and axes, was used as firewood and fuel (Petersen, Seldomridge, and Stearns, 1994, 22). It generally was piled on the backs of mules (or on sleds in winter) for transportation to the mill. Cordwood crews were of a lower occupational status than lumberjacks and often were recent immigrants. During my fieldwork I observed forty or more huge, neatly stacked piles of cordwood still remaining in the Lake Tahoe Spooner Summit area where the Chinese cordwood cutters lived and worked until they were driven out in an anti-Chinese movement between 1876 and 1886. I found another, smaller group of similarly stacked cordwood on Cordwood Ridge, near the mining town of Bennettville (formerly Bennett City and Tioga), California, which thrived from the 1870s until 1884 just off the Tioga Road near Yosemite National Park. Several archaeologists have told me about similar piles of neatly stacked cordwood on other Chinese sites. Chinese also handled timber (uncut trees, logs, or other large pieces of wood with bark intact) and lumber (wood that has been milled, measured, and cut, usually in board feet twelve inches long, twelve inches wide, and one inch thick). Although it is not known how prosperous woodchoppers could be, and few were ever mentioned in local newspapers, on May 17, 1879 Carson City's *Nevada Appeal* noted the elaborate funeral parade of a local Chinese woodchopper, with firecrackers and traditional practices, so a few of these men probably acquired a modicum of wealth and prestige.

One of logging's most dangerous jobs was working the flumes. First, the Chinese built a dam to create a ready cache of water. The flume could descend forty-two hundred feet, as it did in the Kings River Canyon, covering sixty-two miles to Sanger, California (Zimmerman 1998). Wooden trestles or bridges, usually built in a week, assisted the route of the flume. The first such structures to be built were U-flumes, four feet wide at the bottom, five feet wide at the top, and thirty-two inches deep. The shape did not work well for lumber because the logs jammed easily. By 1869 the U-shaped flume yielded to the more efficient V-flume (shaped like the letter "V"), a three-sided wooden structure with two boards joined at a ninety-degree angle, twelve inches wide at the bottom, with thirty-inch sloping sides and forty-eight to sixty inches of water width, built in sixteen-foot sections and placed on a grade with a fall of about twenty-seven feet to a mile. The V-flume revolutionized the industry because it was more efficient, could transport logs from the summit of mountains with a relatively small amount of water as the lubricant, and jammed less frequently because the force of the water pushed the logs along before they could became stuck. The V-flume could move the logs at speeds of at least fifty to sixty miles per hour down the mountains (Petersen, Seldomridge, and Stearns 1994, 24–25; Koeber n.d.; McDonald and Lahore 1984, 25; Johnston 1984, chap. 5). Headgates regulated the amount and velocity of water so that the logs could be unjammed with a short-handled, curved pickaroon, and it was the job of the flume herder, who was often Chinese in the Sierra Nevada above Lake Tahoe, to do this dangerous job. He also sorted the wood by two sizes, one for twenty-four-inch firewood and other for cordwood (four to six feet), sending the types down different flumes. Flume herders, walking on narrow planks of wood that might be sixty feet or higher above the ground, had to unjam the fast-moving logs traveling down the chutes or flumes. Oncoming logs presented a variety of dangers.

Logs and cordwood were transported from the forest to the mill by an intricate network of roads, skid trails, chutes, and flumes (both dry and wet) that snaked around the mountain slopes. Log chutes were usually made of Douglas fir and other straight timber as the artificial channel for moving the cordwood and other types of logs to a body of water and eventually to the sawmill. Heavy wagons, often built on site, carried the logs, sometimes over great distances. In the early decades, mules, oxen, and/or horses hauled the wood on roads, dry flumes, or log chutes (Davis 1996, 14–18).

The Chinese constructed several notable flumes. In 1859 they built the Big Gap Flume, a wooden suspension flume twenty-two hundred feet long, with eleven towers, as a link in the Golden Rock Ditch System, which conveyed water from the south fork of the Tuolumne River to mining areas of present-day Groveland (Garrote), near Big Oak Flat, California. Made of sugar pine, the flume crashed in 1868 and was eventually replaced with a pipe. One of the most dramatic flumes they built was in Incline, Nevada; it started at a high point near Mount Rose and descended twenty-three miles. There were others the Chinese may have built or helped to build, including the Sugar Pine Lumber Company's three flumes (more than fifty miles long) in the 1870s in Fresno, California. The Kings River Lumber Company had a flume sixty-two miles long that began on the Kings River and ended in Sanger, near Fresno (Andrews 1954, 40).

Chinese flume herders worked many of the flumes in Nevada, as evidenced by the scattered Chinese artifacts in the areas surrounding the flumes. The 1870 "Report of the Surveyor-General to the Nevada Senate" highlighted three flumes in Ormsby County: the H. M. Yerington and Company flume two miles west of Carson City at the railroad station to the top of the mountain, four miles up; the Chamberlain and Company flume, beginning in the same location and also going four miles to the summit of the mountain; and the Summit Flume Company flume, beginning in the mountains at the headwaters of Clear Creek and ending 1.5 miles south of Carson City (quoted in State of Nevada, "Report," 1871, 9). The latter transported wood from Douglas County and was twelve miles long when completed. The longest Sierra flume covered twenty-five miles. By 1879 there were ten flumes in the Sierras, totaling eighty miles ("Dare to Shoot").

The Clear Creek Flume exemplified the work of Chinese flume herders who had to unjam the logs that traveled at high speeds down the flume. In 1872 the Carson Tahoe Lumber and Flume Company (CTLFC), a major employer of Chinese workers, bought the Clear Creek V-flume in 1875 and extended it another twelve miles, with a drop of three thousand feet. There were numerous branches and feeders. Skid roads and gravity roads connected with the flumes for ease in transportation. This facilitated floating the lumber and cordwood from Spooner Summit to Carson City, thus ending the wagon hauling over the Lake Bigler Toll Road (Kings Canyon Road). In 1873 Yerington, Bliss, and Company, a subsidiary

The Clear Creek Flume, eventually part of the CTLFC complex, began in Spooner Summit and ended at the CTLFC lumberyard (now the site of the Nevada State Railroad Museum) in Carson City. The Chinese flume tender probably occupied the cabin. (Source: Nevada Historical Society)

of the CTLFC, sent thirty-five thousand cords of wood from Spooner Summit down to Carson City, a substantial increase from the seven hundred cords of wood (a half-million feet of lumber) of an earlier period.[4] Most of the wood was then sent to the Comstock to use for mining and fuel.

Archaeological evidence and observations I made during my fieldwork along the complex of flumes indicate that the Chinese lived in cabins that were fairly regularly spaced along the flumes and near logging or skid roads. Life was probably very lonely, since only one or two men lived in the single cabins. Flumes and transportation roads covered the Sierra Nevada and Carson Range. Chinese sites have been found along this and other flume systems, suggesting that the Chinese worked as flume herders at several major flume operations.

*   *   *

Wood ranch owners, like those in China, marked the trees that were to be cut. A *Virginia Evening Chronicle* (September 25, 1883) reporter described the operations at the Marlette and Folsom Company operations at Crystal Bay in the Carson Range: The Company employed 375 men who worked from Spooner Summit to Lake Tahoe on the three thousand acres of heavily wooded land under their control. Of these men, 225 were Chinese woodchoppers and 150 were French Canadian lumberjacks (Scott 1957, 317). The French Canadians received higher wages and were regarded as skilled laborers who performed the initial felling of the big trees. As with many companies, especially those with East Coast roots, work gangs were segregated by ethnicities, and racial antagonisms often arose. Consequently, the popular belief at this time was that the hostility toward the Chinese originated with the French Canadians, but this does not take into consideration that several Canadians, including Michele Spooner and Henry Yerington, for example, were employers of many Chinese in the woods.

From 1880 to 1883, Marlette and Folsom took out three million feet of timber and 130,000 cords of wood. During the winter and spring they cut four hundred cords of wood daily. The trees were felled, cut into four-foot lengths, and rolled either on wet or dry flumes or on roads down the canyon, where they were split, measured, and transported. In one area, a stream was dammed to provide water for the wet flumes that moved the logs for twenty miles down the V-flume. One flume was four thousand feet long with a rise of thirteen hundred feet. An engine house ran the shafts and operated with wire cables eight thousand feet long and one-and-a-half inches in diameter to pull the cars carrying the wood to the top of the incline, where the wood was dumped, loaded, then transported to Lakeview, eight miles from the summit. From Lakeview the logs were shipped to the Sierra Wood and Lumber Fluming Company (SWLFC) for distribution. Even at this early date of 1880 the local newspapers expressed a public concern for the intense cutting of the forests and the dangers of fire, flood, and soil erosion that resulted.

Another significant occupation was charcoal production. The Chinese had centuries of experience in charcoal production for fuel in the production of bronze and iron in the Shang (ca. 1600–1050 B.C.) and Zhou (1046–256 B.C.) dynasties. In addition to the Han Chinese, the Kejas (Hakkas), a minority group in southeastern China, were famous for their employment in coal mining and charcoal making (Cohen 1968, 237–42; Leong 1997). Kejas migrated to the Pacific Coast during the second wave of Chinese emigration, many in response to the promise of railroad employment.

In charcoal production, the wood was harvested, cut to the appropriate dimensions, and transported to the kiln site. They used pine, oak, tamarack, and fir, as well as refuse timber. Charcoal, a black, porous form of carbon, is prepared by charring wood in a kiln (for example) from which all but a small amount of air was excluded so that the wood is converted to a product with a 96 percent pure carbon content. Charcoal burns more slowly than wood and creates the tremendous heat needed to run train engines and mine smelters. The wood was tightly stacked in the traditional Chinese rectangular shaped kiln with a near-semicircle cover, as opposed to the Italian-style beehive dome kilns. Small holes might be left for air intake during the firing process. An earthen layer was added to the outside of the woodpile to keep a second, outermost earthen covering from falling through any cracks and proving a tight seal to reduce oxygen. The first step was to burn the kindling that would reach three hundred degrees Celsius. After the tightly stacked wood was loaded, the access port was sealed to reduce the air intake. It took three to four weeks to fully char one hundred cords of wood. The collier, or kiln monitor, had to tend the kiln constantly, so he usually lived in a house or cabin nearby. At one site, a watch cabin was located near the kilns; a more permanent residence was about twelve miles away (Reno 1996, 19–21; Conner Prairie). One cord of wood could yield about thirty bushels of charcoal, and a typical mill used between twenty thousand and forty thousand bushels per year (Hattori, Thompson, and McLane 1987, 5–6). The *Truckee Republican* (March 23, 1872) stated that charcoal making "requires great amount of skill, but it needs care and patience; and these are traits that the Chinese possess to an eminent degree."

In 1868 the CPRR could burn some coal that had been discovered in Dog Creek Canyon in 1864, but its low grade made wood charcoal a more preferable fuel source (Goodwin 1960, 12). Between 1872 and 1874 Sisson, Wallace, and Company had more than 350 Chinese traditional-style, rectangular, wood-charcoal kilns built at the "Old Greenwood" site near Truckee, which were tended by more than three hundred Chinese colliers (Knowles 1942, 21–23).[5] Archaeologists Susan Lindstrom and Jeffrey T. Hall (1994), who excavated 150 kilns, believed that this was the highest density of charcoal kilns in the United States at that time.[6] In 1874 the company shipped between one thousand and eight thousand bushels of charcoal weekly to Virginia City; in April 1874, Utah ordered eight thousand

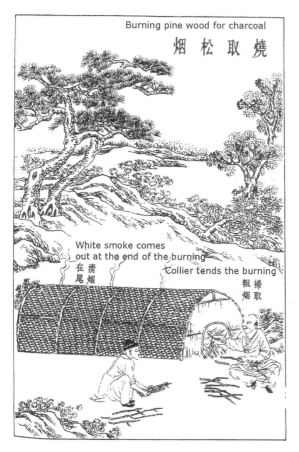

Burning pine wood for charcoal

烟 松 取 烧

White smoke comes out at the end of the burning
在清 尾烟

Collier tends the burning
粗掃 烟取

A traditional Chinese charcoal kiln, seen in the above illustration from an eighteenth-century manual, was rectangular instead of beehive-shaped like those in the American West. Archaeologists found 350 rectangular foundations of charcoal kilns near Truckee, California, that resembled the traditional-style kiln. (Source: *Sung Ying-Hsing, T'ien-kung k'ai-wu: Chinese Technology in the Seventeenth Century*, Chung Hua Tshung Shu edition, Taipei, 1955, p. 412)

bushels per day (Knowles 1942, 25). Later, fifty-eight thousand bushels of charcoal were produced weekly for Virginia City and the CPRR operations in Utah and for fuel for the trains (Elston and Hardesty 1981, 96–97; Whatford 2000). The *Truckee Republican* (June 1, 1872) reported that the Chinese, with their horses and wagons, also hauled the charcoal to the railroad stations to be shipped elsewhere.

Sometimes there was trouble between the Italian and Chinese charcoal burners. When the Italians clashed with mine owners in Eureka in 1871, they wanted to dominate the trade. In 1879 they went on strike in order to stabilize charcoal prices. The Truckee charcoal producers anticipated expanding their enterprise by hiring six hundred men or more (usually Chinese) for each of the Eureka furnaces they supplied. By 1880 the violent resistance in Eureka ended, and Truckee had to sell its overproduced charcoal elsewhere (Straka 2008, 3–8; Zeier 1987; Reno 1996).

In 1877 Sisson, Wallace, and Company expanded their operations and built three "beehive" kilns near the confluence of the Truckee River and Martis Creek, but it is unknown if the Chinese worked on these kilns as they had at the Truckee kilns, Ward kilns near Ely, Wildrose kilns in Death Valley, platform charcoal kilns in the Cortez Mining District, Eureka kilns, and the Wilderness Pass kilns in the Spring Mountains near Las Vegas. In the 1880s Pine Nut Hills in Douglas County, Nevada, had seventeen Chinese charcoal tenders (out of a population of 160 Chinese in the county) working to supply the nearby mills, especially on the Comstock (NVSHPO 1880; Douglas County Book of Deeds). Other, smaller clusters of earthen charcoal kilns with Chinese surface artifacts have been noted in the surrounding area, such as in the "Boca Sierra Development," but the "Old Greenwood" site near Truckee was the largest. The Chinese were not the only ethnic minority group to work on wood charcoal production, but in the 1870s to 1890s they played a significant role in making wood charcoal, an essential commodity.

*   *   *

Wage usually depended on the employer, location, and type of job. The employer hired a gang of twenty-five to thirty men from a labor contractor, often one based in San Francisco, and paid the salary for the group to the contractor or headman. A bookkeeper or accountant received the wages and divided the money among the workers. According to the *San Francisco Bulletin* (June 8, 1875), the wages for Euro-American workers in Mendocino, California, in 1875 were as follows: a chopper received $55 to $70 per month with board; a sawyer, $50 per month; swampers who cleared paths and cut brushes, $50 per month; and a road "water packer" who watered or greased the road for easy transport of the logs, $30 to $40 per month. Drivers, especially those working with oxen, got $75 to $85 per month with board. Chinese often performed the tasks at a lesser rate. The monthly wages in 1879 and 1887 Puget Sound's logging camps were slightly different: superintendents, $150; fellers $50 to $125; skid greasers, $30; swampers, barkers, and hook tenders (working the flumes), $40; skidders, $50; teamsters, $60 to $125; cooks, $40 to $100 (depending on crew size); head sawyers, $100 to $125; other sawyers, $60 to $65; filers, $80; millworkers, $30 to $40.[7] The Chinese seldom could attain the higher-paying positions, and news articles of the time estimated their monthly pay at $30, but this was not the case in all circumstances.

There were few "long time" loggers. A study of the payroll records of all sawmill employees from 1862 to 1876 in Clinton, Iowa, showed that in any one year the labor force that stayed the following year did not exceed 63 percent (Sieber 1971, 789). Although there were some companies with long-time Chinese employees, this generalization (as we will see later) probably held true for most of the Chinese in the woods.

Ideally, each Chinese subcontractor in the Lake Tahoe region may have managed up to twenty separate wood camps (Lindstrom and Hall 1994, 90, 145–48). Chinese goods were purchased from merchants in the nearby Chinatowns in Truckee, Reno, or Carson City, and these stores received their imported goods from Chinese mail-order companies in San Francisco or Sacramento, depending on the native region and relatives in the import/export business. This merchandising network system has yet to be studied in detail, but the late Anna Kwock, whose family operated a grocery and import business starting in the late nineteenth century, said that their customers throughout the American West were primarily from their home county of Zhongshan (oral interview in San Francisco, 1970).

Chinese camp cooks were highly prized for their preparation of good food. Workers of all ethnicities wanted to work where the food was tasty. As a result, Chinese cooks were rewarded with salaries comparable to and sometimes higher than non-Asian cooks in many parts of the American West.[8] According to George Kephart, a worker at a pulpwood camp, the common belief at lumber camps was that "the camp's ability to attract and hold men rested primarily on the cook's reputation" (quoted in Colin 1979, 177). If the diner disliked the food, he complained to the boss, and the cook often was fired; in most cases, however, Chinese cooks were retained.

Loggers worked up a healthy appetite, and western loggers ate more nutritious food than loggers in the Midwest, for example. Loggers also ate much better fare than cowboys and often better than miners (Colin 1989, 128–31). Several steaks or pork chops, potatoes, bread, and dessert were common for the hearty eater at dinner. Chinese cooks had the reputation of serving good food and were famous for their pies. In 1885, in response to an anti-Chinese mob demanding the firing

Ty Sing (d. 1918), standing by cords of wood, was a well-known chef in Yosemite for more than twenty-eight years. Stephen Mather (1867–1930), first director of the National Park Service, honored his favorite chef in 1899 by naming Sing Peak, at an elevation of more than ten thousand feet located just outside the boundary of Yosemite National Park, in Ty Sing's honor.

of Chinese cooks at Talbot and Pope's Port Gamble, Washington, camp, Cyrus Walker, a partner in the Puget Mill Company, capitulated, fired his Chinese cooks, but told them not to leave town, then hired a group of Euro-American cooks and told them to make one hundred pies daily in addition to the regular meals. The Euro-American cooks could not meet the demand, and by the end of the week, they had all left. Walker rehired his Chinese cooks, who easily made the required one hundred pies daily—and regular meals (Colin 1979, 182). He also admired their diligent work ethic and employed them in various other capacities in the Washington lumber camps (Ficken 1987, 73). In 1925 Pope and Talbot's Puget Mill Company in Washington compiled a list of employees working for ten or years or longer. Among their long-time employees were Chee Tuck, who worked for twenty-nine years as first cook; Ah Ling, who worked for twenty-five years as second cook; Ah Yen, who worked for eleven years as the baker; and Tong, who served as the chef in the company hotel for ten years (Coman and Gibbs 1968, 376–77).

Cooks sometimes moved around and could make good money. Some lumber companies, like the CTLFC, provided basic food, supplies, and tools to the subcontractors who were in charge of the Chinese and non-Chinese workers. Some labor crews at the CTLFC used a slightly different system. The company issued meal tickets to labor crew chiefs, who received their supplies from a centralized camp or Spooner Station facilities (Lindstrom and Hall 1994, 90, 145–48). In 1876 the CTLFC payroll record (box 5, "Sing") indicated that Chinese workers received one dollar per day for their work, while other Chinese cooks received fourteen dollars for twelve days of work. In 1878 Ah Gee cooked for a month and received forty dollars, while Ah Sam, another cook, only received thirty dollars in the same pay period. This was the same pay range for non-Chinese cooks. By 1890 the Chinese cooks received from thirty dollars to fifty dollars per month (CLTFC payroll, box 6), which, compared with Euro-American cooks, who were paid thirty dollars to forty dollars per month in the 1890s, was higher at the upper range. Presumably, the Chinese were better cooks. Even today, Cantonese cooks are noted for their culinary skills throughout China.

A Chinese cook at a wood camp probably made less than a cook in businesses such as the Glenbrook House near Lake Tahoe. In the late 1860s the Chinese cook at Glenbrook House earned twelve dollars per week; Chinese laundry service was paid $7.55. But at the nearby Markleeville Flume Company, cook China Charley, for example, was paid $44.28 ($1.43 per day) in December 1873, $28 in February 1874, and $44.28 in March 1874 (Markleeville Flume Company, NC 120, file 3/5; Glenbrook House, NC 1190). China Charley was paid by the day and in February probably took several vacation days to celebrate the Chinese New Year.

According to the *Truckee Republican* (January 17, 1883), Ah Soon, or Ah Sume, age forty-four in 1883, saved enough money working as a cook in boardinghouses and wood camps in the Truckee area such that he could send $4,000 to his wife and child in China. He had immigrated in 1869 and spoke English "tolerably well." Ah Soon was probably typical of a significant percentage of cooks in this area, and most Chinese immigrants, because of the Page Law of 1875 and Chinese custom, left their wives and children in China.

From these CTFLC payroll records and newspaper reports, one can discern that the Chinese cooks succeeded in part because they purchased goods from Chinese fishermen, who fished in nearby lakes and rivers and sold their catch to the wood-camp cooks (as seen in several payroll records), and from Chinese whose side occupation as farmers allowed them to grow herbs, fruits, and vegetables for themselves and for cooks working in Chinese restaurants, hotels, boardinghouses, and work camps.

Most cooks signed their names in Chinese on the payroll sheets (CLTFC payroll, boxes 5–6). One man, Ah Sam, signed his name in Chinese as Yee and therefore belonged to the same clan as Sam Gibson (aka Non Chong Yee), the labor boss in Carson City. Although many of the Chinese on the CTLFC payroll signed their names in English (for example, Charley Tong in 1882) or in Chinese, to match their given American name (such as Ah Sam in 1878), many of the cooks and workers signed in their real Chinese name: Ah Charley, who worked on the Summit Flume in the 1890s making fifty dollars a month, signed (in pinyin) Yu Ci (Cantonese pronunciation of last name Yee, first name probably Gee). Throughout this period, many Chinese were members of the Yee clan, which was indicated in Chinese only: Ah Sam (1879), Ah Joe and Ah Jean (1891), Ah Ling, Ah Charley, China helper (1890s).

Eating regular meals was an attraction to the Chinese workers, some of whom had been starving in China because of floods, famine, inflation, and banditry. Artifacts at campsites indicated that traditional menus were favored for Chinese work crews. Camp cooks used iron woks (Chinese frying pan) from China as their main cooking pot. One campsite on the VTRR route measured six hundred feet north/south by nine hundred feet east/west and had a possible cooking site measuring ten by twelve feet, which contained scattered remains of a cast iron wok, brass opium box, green Swatow ware, square nails, barrel hoops, a shovel blade, and refashioned tin cans (Drews and Mathiesen 1996, 18). Perhaps the most interesting artifacts on Chinese sites were the modified tin cans. Euro-American cans for fruits, vegetables, tea, and cooking oil, for example, would have holes punched in them or handles soldered onto one side in order to reuse the can as strainers, steamers, and containers, for example. Although other immigrant groups reused and modified cans, especially miners, who used refashioned cans for lunch pails, no one did this to the same degree as the Chinese in the late nineteenth century. The cooking and dining area probably also was the primary recreational area for telling stories, playing music, and playing games of chance. Opium smoking could or would take place away from the central area (Rogers 1997, 37).

Chinese cooks appealed to the courts if they were not paid. In 1871 Jack Gho, a cook hired by Charley Julles, a Snohomish Indian in Washington Territory, did not received his contracted salary while working in a logging camp (Wunder 1983, 194). Gho sued and won a lower court decision, which Julles appealed to the territorial supreme court on the basis that as a Snohomish, the court had no jurisdiction over him: he claimed that an 1847 congressional act declared void all contracts made by Indians. The justices disagreed, and Gho won.

Some Chinese cooks worked for a long time for one employer. An Chung, for example, worked in a wood camp in Diamond Valley, eighteen miles north of Eureka, Nevada, knew English, and had been a cook for mill superintendent David M. Brown and his family in Lyon County in the early 1870s. When the family moved, he moved with them and settled in Diamond Valley in the mid-1870s, but when Brown relocated to Ormsby County to work in another mill, Chung did not go because he had been seriously injured.[9] Unfortunately, he appeared in no other Nevada census records, but cooks and servants often moved around with families they liked.

Some Chinese in the West were able to own lumber companies and lumber-yards themselves, but there are few records with any details. One exception was Wen He (1836–1901) Born in Taishan, Guangdong, Wen He immigrated in 1864, recognized the market for wood, and opened a successful lumber company, Wo Kee Lumber and Timber Company, based on Pacific Street in San Francisco, with a timber ranch in Oregon (Wen, 1995, 13–17). Lured by the discovery of gold, Wen He and a group of Chinese miners with several Euro-Americans worked in California's Mother Lode, eventually ending up in Portland, Oregon, in 1868. There, Wen He and Jake Hoyt became interested in dressing and selling the much-needed wood in San Francisco and linked up with a supplier, Joseph Ark, in Oregon. Every month, Wen He brought the timber from Oregon to San Francisco until his death in 1901. When he had enough money, Wen He paid for Hoyt to attend law school, and this solidified their relationship. Eventually Wen He married a woman from his hometown in 1878 and they had six children. After he died, he left one-fourth of his business to his Chinese employees, one-fourth to Hoyt, and one-half to his family. He also had lumber/timber concerns in Hawai'i and Nicaragua. If his son, Wen Zhengde, had not known his father's story and told it, the history of this company would have been lost.

A partnership with a non-Chinese, as Wen He discovered, was helpful in establishing a new business. Such was the case with Kun Ai Chung (known as C. K. Ai), who arrived in Hawai'i in 1879 at age fourteen and eventually worked with James Dowsett (d. 1898), one of the leading lumber importers and plantation owner. In Hawai'i in 1829 Chinese carpenters, who learned their trade in China, began building wooden structures. They continued in the trade so that by 1884, out of the 264 carpenters in Hawai'i, fifteen were Chinese (Glick 1980, 86–87; "About City Mill"). They were the primary purchasers of American lumber in Hawai'i. Ai recognized this interest in wood products and sought to enlist the assistance of Dowsett, who helped Ai start his own import business that became City Mill, a large company that imported lumber, sold building materials, and milled rice; the company remains in the hands of the Ai family today.

A very impressive lumbering operation existed in Nicaragua around the turn of the twentieth century. John Wright (aka Jun Lai), leader of the Chinatown in Bluefields (a municipality in Nicaragua), specialized in harvesting and selling redwood to the United States.[10] When Wright, his wife, and their eight children relocated to the United States in 1941, he left the management of the company to relatives from China and made certain that his children retained a financial share in the business. There were other Chinese-owned and -operated lumber companies outside the continental United States, but none of those in the United States were as long lasting and prosperous as those outside the United States. Chinese logging owners were also found in Southeast Asia and other parts of the Chinese diaspora.

Wood ranchers, wood dealers, and wood packers earned more money and enjoyed a higher status. In 1870 the wood rancher Wo Cheng, age twenty-nine, lived in the mining town of Treasure City, White Pine County, owned real estate valued at $700, and had a personal estate of $200. Other wood ranchers in Treasure City were Yuen Sin (age thirty), Yee Yun (age thirty-four), and Hop Sang (age twenty-seven) (Census 1870 to 1910). In 1880 there were nine wood dealers and one carpenter living in Eureka, a mining town with many Chinese involved in charcoal production. In Carson City, there were two wood dealers, Tern Ching (age twenty-four and a single) and Hing Luck (age forty, married). Both lived in Chinatown and were able to read. In 1910 Ormsby County had one wood packer, Kowan (b. 1870, immigrated 1899), who lived near the woodchopper Dong Fee in Chinatown. Although few in number, these men represented upward mobility in the occupation achieved at a relatively young age.

Several others who were designated "laborers" could have been involved in logging. The 1880 census manuscript listed thirty-eight Chinese living in the logging community of Glenbrook, on the east shore of Lake Tahoe in Douglas County, Nevada: ten cooks, six laundrymen, one gardener, one sheepherder, and twenty laborers who lived in a boardinghouse next to wood contractor Michele Spooner and his family and obviously worked in lumbering (Census 1880; Wrobleski, 1996). The sheepherder lived in a Euro-American neighborhood. Glenbrook, the CTLFC headquarters, had four sawmills, a company-owned general store, two hotels, and a number of houses. Nearby was a "Chinese garden," where Ah Fung (b. ca. 1855) grew and harvested fresh produce to feed the workers. The 1880 federal census for Douglas County also listed fifty-two Chinese laborers in the mountains. In this group, the ages ranged from sixteen to sixty-five. According to the census taker, all were able to read English. For men doing this type of manual labor, the ability to read among the entire group seems highly unlikely, but if this was true, it meant that literacy was found among Chinese in lumbering. This was probably the group working in the mountains above Genoa and

In 1892 this group of Chinese woodchoppers posed for a photograph with W. H. Keyser (right), brother-in-law of Superintendent George D. Oliver, at George Chubbuck's Sierra House timber ranch. They worked in South Lake Tahoe. (Courtesy of South Lake Tahoe Historical Society and Museum)

South Lake Tahoe or in the Spooner Summit area for CTLFC. A photograph in the South Lake Tahoe Historical Society shows a group of Chinese lumbermen working under the supervisor, Oliver, at Chubbuck's Sierra House Ranch in 1892. No Euro-Americans were recorded in the same area, so it is highly probable that the Chinese were the only ones cutting wood at that particular location. Archaeological evidence indicated that the Chinese might have started their own lumbering operation at Slaughterhouse Canyon, near Glenbrook, that included a mill and flume. Rumors told of the deaths of several Chinese, including the mill supervisors or managers, who died in a boating tragedy on Lake Tahoe.[11] This ended the Chinese-owned operations at Glenbrook. It is likely that some of the "men in the mountains" could have been working for this Chinese operation.

By comparison, census records for locations in the Mother Lode, California, area indicated only a small number of Chinese were involved in the lumber industry (Chan 1984, 300–305). In 1860 Sacramento City had nine Chinese woodmen; the figure dropped to two by the next decade. The rest of Sacramento County in 1870 had twenty-three Chinese, and the number remained the same in 1880.

Marysville, with its large Chinatown, had five Chinese in 1870 and dropped to one in 1880. The rest of Yuba County had four in 1870, then three in 1880. Stockton City had three in 1880, and the rest of San Joaquin County, where rich forests were found, had eight-two Chinese in 1880. Sacramento County had one Chinese carpenter in 1880, Marysville had nine (including a wood carver), and San Joaquin County had two. The South Chinese were noted for their work in carpentry, so it was not surprising that many carpenters migrated to the American West. These are only a sampling of areas in central California, and the figures suggest that lumbering was not a significant Chinese occupation there, probably because farming was more attractive to them.

In 1880 in a predominantly logging area like Table Mountain, California, that served the mining communities of Aurora and Bodie, there were thirty-one Chinese men—twenty-three of whom were laborers (19 percent of total population; 30 percent of all laborers). Undoubtedly these twenty-three men worked in the woods (Shaw 2013). Table Mountain had a total population of 124 residents in thirty-two households with three Euro-American wood packers and two Euro-American teamsters. Like many sites in the mountains, neatly stacked cordwood piles that are more than a century old still can be seen. This orderly stacking, as opposed to Euro-American random stacking, was the result of cooperative efforts of the Chinese. Surface scatter of Chinese artifacts and remnants of cabins also still exist (Shaw 2013). Isolated wooded areas probably allowed the Chinese to participate in lumbering and to dominate the occupation.

Lumber and wood yards were also important. According to the Wells Fargo Company's "Directory of Chinese Business Houses" in 1882, San Francisco's Chinatown had two carpenters and seven wood yards. Fook Chan, carpenter, worked at 752 Washington Street; Quong Tong On, another carpenter, was at 123½ Waverly Place. The wood yards were: Chung Sing, 646 Pacific Street; Hop Lung, 721 Pacific Street; Sam Foo, 728 Pacific Street; Shoon Lee, 727 Pacific Street; Wing Hing, 922 Stockton Street (entered in directory twice); and Wing Hop and Company, 732 Jackson Street. Sanborn maps showed that most wood yards were accessed through narrow alleys in Chinatown. Nearby San Jose had two wood yards and Los Angeles had one yard.

Some information was available about these wood yards and lumberyards. Chinese Business Partnership records indicated that Woo Fook Kee and Company (823 Clay Street), Tie Hing and Company (839 Clay Street, near Stockton and Commercial Streets), and Ty Lee and Company (837½ Jackson Street) were three large firms specializing in lumber in the 1890s.[12] Seven of the eight partners of Woo Fook Kee were surnamed Woo (pinyin, Hu), with a capitalization of $4,500 in 1897; eighteen of the twenty-one partners of Tie Hing were surnamed Tom (Tan) with a capitalization of $20,000 in 1893. Like the Nicaragua company, these were clan businesses. According to the *Northwestern Lumberman* (August 4, 1888), Tie Hing (also called Tie Hong) was a hardware store, brickyard, wood yard, lumberyard, and planing mill. The company kept one hundred thousand feet of lumber on hand and supplied most of San Francisco's Chinatown with building materials. Chin Wo and his relatives Chin Sing and Chin Dy controlled Ty Lee and Company, dealers in wood and charcoal, with a capitalization of $2,500 in 1896.[13] Although their main customer base was probably Chinese, they also sold to members of the larger community.

While visiting San Francisco's Chinatown, a Euro-American observer for the *Northwestern Lumbermen* (August 4, 1888) noted:

> At one side of the lumber yard there is an engine and boiler, which furnish power to run a planer, saws, and a machine for splitting firewood. It takes six men to work the latter. The cordwood is made into the required length by means of a cutoff saw, and then fed to the guillotine-shaped splitter, which is run at full speed all day. About 30 heathens [Chinese] are required to keep the establishment going, and they have all the work they can do to fill their orders.

When the observer inquired about the price, the clerk at the desk told him that the price of lumber was the same as that at Pacific Pine Lumber Company, owned by E. M. Denick—that is, competitive.[14]

The Chinese recognized that they did not have much political power, but they went to court when they could afford the expenses in order to correct some wrongs. They tried to buy timberland in order to take advantage of the growing need for wood products, but their efforts were sometimes thwarted, and they sought legal remedies. The most famous case involved Fook Ling (discussed later in this chapter), but Chinese also went to civil court for protection in smaller matters.

Buying timberland was often very profitable, but few Chinese individuals had the financial resources to afford it. Unlike California, the Nevada Constitution, Article 1, Section 16, gave resident aliens the same rights as citizens regarding possession, enjoyment, and inheritance of property. This was reinforced by the state's Bill of Rights, which stated, "All men are by Nature free and equal and have certain inalienable rights among which are those of enjoying and defending life and liberty; Acquiring, Possessing and Protecting property and pursuing and obtaining safety and happiness." The 1868 Burlingame Treaty also gave the Chinese the right to own property.

By tradition, the Chinese placed great value on landownership, so they bought, traded, and sold land when they could. Early Nevada land deeds do not show these transactions because they were executed informally, but there were scattered accounts. One of the few on record was the purchase of 320 acres of Indian-owned land in the Pine Nut region of Douglas County in 1872 in order to provide more charcoal for Virginia City by the Hexingtang (Hop Sing Tong), a secret society based in San Francisco with a branch in Virginia City (Douglas County, Book of Deeds, Book D [A10]; Reno 1996). The Hexingtang paid taxes on the land in

1873 and 1874, and then abandoned the land some time later, probably because the forest had been denuded. It is highly likely that their entire crew in the woods consisted of Chinese workers. The practice of purchasing land and taking all of the big trees was common in this era. This fraternal brotherhood was involved in many of the "*tang* wars" of the late nineteenth century, most of them centered on issues related to prostitution and gambling. By the end of the twentieth century, this powerful and wealthy organization owned approximately one-third of the land on which San Francisco's Chinatown is located. Buying timberland could be quite profitable.

Lyon County, Nevada, had a Chinese wood rancher. In October 1879 Jacob Gugger of Sutro, Nevada, sold Hop Lee and Company of Dayton, Lyon County, a wood ranch, known as the Joe Williams Ranch, formerly owned by Richard Henderson, which included two hundred acres of land, a cabin, a store, and all furnishings in the buildings (Douglas County, Book of Deeds, Book F [A12]). Merchant Hop Lee owned the store called Quong Lee in Dayton.[15] Hop Lee's store was connected with Quong Hi Lung and Company at 304 I Street in Sacramento, probably a major mail-order supply store for Siyi merchants in rural areas like Dayton. Fortunately, there is more information about Hop Lee because of his efforts to bring his Dayton-born son (b. 1880), who was educated in Canton, back to Dayton in 1899. In his immigration papers, Hop Lee revealed that his son's name was Mee Wat Yee and his real Chinese name was Get Jung Yee; he was, therefore, a member of the powerful Yee clan in Nevada. Members of the same clan living in the same vicinity and in the same occupation knew each other, so Hop Lee undoubtedly had connections in the nearby towns, such as Carson City. Hop Lee, who had lived in Dayton since June 1869 (but was not in the 1870 census), probably used the clan connections and Chinese tradition of *guanxi* (personal relations) to do business (Sangren 1984, 405). It also was significant that James P. Haynes of Dayton testified on behalf of Hop Lee and his son and gave Haynes's occupation as a carpenter in Dayton since 1869. As was the case with many Chinese merchants, relationships with the local constable or sheriff were regarded as important, so another supporter of Mee Wat Yee's application for reentry into the United States was Morton W. Stiles, a former constable and deputy sheriff who gave a deposition in the case,. Although his store was very small, Hop Lee, who sold goods to the majority community as well as to the Chinese, made enough money to remarry after his first wife and mother of Yee Mee Wat died in Canton in 1892. The timber rancher Andrew Walmsley was a friend of Hop Lee's and had a photograph of Hop Lee and his wife, which he left to his descendants. Hop Lee was an easy name for Americans to say, but it did not indicate one's real Chinese name or the informal clan networks that existed.

The Nevada legislature tried unsuccessfully to stop Chinese land ownership by passing an act that exempted "subjects of the Chinese Empire" from Article 1, Section 16 (9th Sess., 1879, C, 73). This was part of a growing national trend to stop Chinese immigration and to drive those who were in the United States back to China. The issue of Chinese landownership in Nevada became significant after the United States Congress passed an act on June 16, 1880, offering public land for sale at a minimum of $1.25 per acre (Miller 1926, 385). Nevada Surveyor General C. S. Preble was in charge of the sale of the nonmineral land, known as the "Two Million Acre Grant," that the federal government was returning to the state. The *San Francisco Bulletin* of September 22, 1887, reported that Preble himself invested in nonmineral lands and in 1887 spent $140,000 for two thousand acres in the Feather River area. Fook Ling (aka Ah Lay), who lived in Dayton, applied to purchase forty acres of land at $1.25 per acre, but Preble denied him the right on the basis that he was "not a *person* entitled to apply." The case, *State ex rel. Fook Ling v. C. S. Preble*, addressed the question of whether Fook Ling was a person, defined in legal terminology as "a person free from any legal disability"[16] Since Chinese immigrants could not become naturalized citizens or vote, the respondent (Preble) reasoned that Fook Ling was not "a person entitled to apply" and did not fall "under the head of foreigner as is mentioned in section 16, article 1" of the state's constitution. The anti-Chinese movements of the late 1870s and 1880s and the issues of African American rights and the federal exclusion of Chinese immigrants had raised the question. Preble, whose views were obviously in the anti-Chinese camp, felt he was complying with the 1879 state law and did not want land to go to anyone who was Chinese. Preble asserted in court that three Chinese had applied to buy land after Fook Ling filed his lawsuit against him, and if the court granted Fook Ling the right to buy the land, this opened the door to other Chinese.

In the 1883 landmark decision *State ex rel. Fook Ling v. C. S. Preble*, Supreme Court 0123, case 1169, dated February 6, 1883, the court ruled that Fook Ling was entitled to purchase the land, stating: "The constitution gives to all foreigners who are *bona fide* residents of this state certain rights . . . guaranteed by the constitution" (Appendix of the Journal of the Senate and Assembly, 12th sess., 1885). The court further cited the Burlingame Treaty between China and the United States, which stated, "Chinese laborers who are now in the United States shall be accorded all the rights and privileges . . . accorded to its citizens and subjects of the most favored nation." This case allowed other Chinese to buy public land in Nevada, including timberland; this was evident, for example, in Mineral County at the turn of the twentieth century, when Ah Chew, Ah Poe, Ah Ark, Ah Sam, Sam Sing, Ah Yen, and Ah Joe each owned forty acres of timberland, and Ah Sing, Ah Wen, Ah Wing, and Ah Toy each owned eighty acres (Silver 2012). The largest property owner in the late nineteenth century in Mineral County, Nevada, was Quong Yea, with 160 acres of land.

The 1870 and 1880 census manuscripts do not list a Fook Ling or Ling Fook, but the local press referred to the person in question as Ah Lay.[17] The only Ah Lay in Lyon County in 1880 was a thirty-seven-year-old railroad laborer who could read English. He probably was the Ah Lay in the 1870 census who was age twenty-eight and a laborer who could read English, living in Virginia City. The one-year difference in age could be related to his birthdate and the date of the census taking. If this was the case, how could a railroad laborer have sufficient funds to buy a substantial piece of land? The answer was that it was a joint venture with his association, fellow regionals, or some group that pooled money under his name. He received funds from a rotating credit system that was common among overseas Chinese. The fact that the case went to court further suggests financial assistance from a Chinese organization because legal fees were expensive.

The Chinese found some protection in civil courts. Several early lawsuits filed in Washoe District Court provided more insight into the problems Chinese workers encountered. In 1879 the Reno Savings Bank sued Wing Hing Sung and Company (Ah Wow, Ah Hong, and Yek Font) for $1,045, payable by the following goods: 125 shovels, 125 picks, 4 sledges, 12 hand hammers, 6 drills, 600 feet of lumber, 25 mats, and Chinese merchandise, including rice and groceries.[18] In 1880 in Franktown, Ah Shue (b. 1850) cooked for the wood contractor Duncan McRae and probably acted as an intermediary for the other Chinese workers. McRae, a Canadian immigrant who arrived in Carson City in 1870, worked for the Sierra Wood and Lumber Company in the 1880s and supervised the cutting of wood at $1.50 per cord (Quong Hing and Company in Carson City was getting $1.80 per cord). In December 1880, McRae owed his creditors more than $10,000 for back pay, supplies, and other costs. Among the eighty-seven workers who sued him in Washoe District Court were two Chinese, See Wah[19] and Ahu (China Water), who were being paid at the same rate as the other men: approximately $1,879.90 as back pay.[20] McRae lost. By 1894 McRae had moved to Canada, where he died.[21] The Chinese, working under Hi Wah, a Chinese contracting company in Carson City, hired a team of six Chinese (Ty Hing, Sing Foy, We Duck, Ah Lung, Lun Foy, and Ah Neo) to cut wood at the same rate. McRae's workers cut 9,948 cords of wood; the Chinese cut 1,500. When Hi Wah (the individual was given the company's name) realized that his workers were not getting the same pay rate, he sued the SWLC in Ormsby District Court and was awarded equal wage rate on February 19, 1881.[22] The court awarded Hi Wah $2,198.32. This important case demonstrated that there was equal pay for equal work. There was one major difference, however: according to Chinese American tradition, the contractor usually provided at least lunch and tea to his work crew and took a percentage of the gross salary. Apparently, Hi Wah cheated some of his workers, and in December 1882 some of Hi Wah's men killed him. The *Morning Appeal* (December 27, 1882) commented, "The APPEAL always believed that this slippery Mongolian rascal would come to a bad end."

The Chinese were not hesitant about using the American judicial system to protect their interests. In another case on June 6, 1883, in Washoe County's District Court, Ah Lue of Franktown sued M. Hogan for $378 that was owed to him; Hogan was ordered to pay.[23] On the other hand, the Chinese also were themselves sued in court and could lose, as seen in Ah Jack's case (ch. 1).

*   *   *

Working in the woods, the Chinese also gained a reputation for being good road construction workers. From 1874 into 1875, for four and a half months they built the Wawona Road, twenty-three miles long with a four-thousand-foot elevation; in the winter of 1882–83 they built Tioga Road, fifty-six miles long at an elevation of ten thousand feet, in four and a half months using only hand tools and blasting powder in present-day Yosemite National Park area (Chan 2011). Despite the ban on Chinese workers employed in public projects, like road construction, employers were able to circumvent the law by hiring subcontractors who then hired the Chinese.

With their knowledge and work in irrigation systems and dam construction in China and the American West, the Chinese probably created some of the waterways and ponds for the transportation of logs. So with the exception of supervisory positions, the Chinese participated in all logging activities to some degree or another. They usually worked from 5:30 A.M. until 6 P.M. with a half-hour lunch break at noon, and dinner at 6:30 P.M. In northern Nevada, some Chinese woodchoppers cut wood and transported the wood to the mines for the smelters in the winter and early spring because of the mild weather. Men working in Pine Nut Hills, Douglas County, often resided permanently in Dayton, Lyon County, Nevada, to work in other jobs offseason (Dayton Historical Society).

Around the end of the nineteenth century technological improvements began to change lumbering. "Steam donkeys" transported the logs by cables over longer distances to logging trains and reduced the number of manual laborers needed, particularly swampers, barkers, and snipers, and made the industry less seasonal in nature. The steam-powered donkey engine with its steel cable running through a pulley near the top of the tree could remove five thousand tons of logs in eight hours and put them on narrow gauge railways designed specifically to haul logs out of remote places. Remnants of these cables still can be seen on many of the trunks of the Sierra Nevada and Carson Range trees. Winches, pulling chains wrapped around the trunks of standing trees, also were used to maneuver the logs, and their marks can still be seen on trees. Chinese and other campsites have been found in areas where the trees still bear the scars of the cabling, so they may have worked even as technology reduced the manual labor force. Each landscape was different, and the workmen had to figure out the best way to fell the trees and move the logs down the steep Sierra Nevada. This was not an easy task, and there were many inherent dangers that could be fatal or cause permanent damage. Advances in machinery and technology obviated the need for large numbers of workers. By 1882 this coincided with the beginning of the decrease in the avail-ability of Chinese workers due to the Chinese exclusion acts, but new types of tasks arose as the Chinese transitioned into other jobs.

In the 1880s the logging industry bean to employ tractors, eliminating the need for horses, oxen, and mules to pull the logs (Clark 2002). Narrow-gauge logging trains allowed lumbermen to go deeper into the forests and move the logs more easily. The Chinese built many of these logging and narrow-gauge lines and then returned to logging tasks. There are no figures available indicating how many loggers worked along these railroad lines in Nevada and California; however, records from the Simpson Logging Company, a subsidiary of Port Blakely Mill Company in Washington in 1899, had five hundred loggers employed along the eighty miles of railroad it owned (Rajala 1989, 169). In several locations, the Chinese manned these trains, loading them in the forest and unloading the logs at the mill or transportation center.

                              *   *   *

Like other workers in the mountains, the Chinese lived in wood camps. Some camps were located near sawmills; others were high in the mountains, often located near a flume. As in China, many of the early Euro-American lumbermen were primarily farmers or ranchers who logged on a part-time, seasonal basis. There were two major types of wood camps in the forest: those that were ethnically separated and those that were integrated. Owners who were from the East Coast and who usually were not on site felt that separating ethnic groups created a more productive atmosphere than if groups were integrated. Although the men might eat together, they usually were separated into groups for work. In 1870 a reporter visiting a camp in Washoe, Nevada, noted that the Chinese wood camp was on one side of the ravine and the "white wood camp" was on the other ("Winter Night's Ride" 1870). I observed the same situation existed in the Daggett Creek area (near present-day Heavenly Valley at the south end of Lake Tahoe) with the separation of two camps, one Chinese and one Italian, across the ravine from each other. Although Gregory Woirol's (2011b, 32–45) account of a lumber camp in the Sierra Nevada focused on the 1914 non-Asian experience, the principles were the same for large-scale production: a division of work by nationality; the skilled workers involved in felling and other tasks at the top of the occupational ladder and often returning annually; the unskilled workers, who represented about 30 percent of the workforce, performing tasks such as bucking, grading, and construction, and sometimes not returning to work for the company. Chinese workers usually re-turned to work with the same employer and in this way often differed from their Euro-American counterparts in unskilled jobs.

Wood camps moved from place to place in order to be close to the trees desig-nated for cutting. However, it often was seasonal work, so when the snows came, work opportunities declined except for woodchoppers, who cut cordwood for

Around 1880 to 1890 a wood camp in the mountains would have looked like this. The bunkhouse is on the left. Horses or mules were used to transport the cordwood. The trees on the nearby hillside have been clear-cut. (Source: Courtesy of the National Forest Service)

fuel, and flume herders in the Sierras, who worked during the winter months because wood could be sent down the frozen waterways. Woodchoppers could then move to camps in the Tahoe basin and Sierras in the late spring to early fall and thus avoid the snow. This type of seasonal labor required mobility, and their permanent residence could be far away from the work location.

A special correspondent for the *San Francisco Bulletin* (November 13, 1878) described his visit to the Sierra Flume and Lumber Company in the forests of the Sierra in Northern California as being typical of many contemporary wood camps:

> A logging camp is a little village of itself. The principal structure in it . . . is the saw mill. . . . Each camp employs from thirty to forty white men and perhaps ten or twelve Chinamen, with two Chinese cooks . . . and take their meals at the boarding-house. . . . The wages paid include board, except in the case of the Chinese.

The prejudice of the reporter is revealed when he points out that while the Euro-American wages included board, the Chinese wages did not, implying that because Chinese cooks were employed, the cooks managed to sequester food to their countrymen. He observed that the Chinese piled and trucked the lumber and worked under the direction of a Chinese "boss." When the superintendent of the camp tried to work without a Chinese headman, he was so frustrated because of the language problems, thereafter he always used a Chinese boss. From this report one can assume that the Chinese crews usually had a Chinese supervisor over the workers.

In the 1870s wood camps featured temporary wooden dormitories or boarding houses in the mountains, which generally held from ten to fifty men and resembled the dormitories for miners, with one large door and a few windows strategically placed near the roof to keep out the snow and wind (Rajala 1989, 168; boardinghouse at Bennettville, California). The windows provided some ventilation for the odors of dirty shirts and socks, smoke from wood burning in the cast-iron stove, and fumes from kerosene lanterns. Sometimes Chinese and non-Chinese lived together (Hill 1987, 35–36). Some dormitories were located near tallow stations, flumes, haul roads, or skid trails (Lindstrom and Hall 1994).

Private or semi-private cabins also existed. Some workers lived one to five men in a cabin. With the abundance of wood in the forests, it usually took as little as one day to construct a cabin. As one observer noted, "The Chinese carpenter and ourselves speedily felled some young saplings, and driving two strong posts in the ground, we fixed a long spar longitudinally; on this spar rested the saplings and branches in inclined position; then placing turf at the bottom, our bush-hut was finished that night" (Lindstrom and Hall 1994, 34). The boards of abandoned flumes also were used for the siding of cabins. In Northeast, the Euro-American loggers lived in "crude one-room shanties . . . roofed over with split poles, marsh hay, and earth" (Hidy 1963, 150–51). Some Chinese cabins in the American West could be described in the same way. Sometimes the men working in the forests lived in simple, A-frame, canvas tents that were useful for short-term, migratory living (Rohe 2002). Some cabins and bunkhouses were on skids or wheels and could be moved on rails; this was evident in Nevada Historical Society photographs of wood camps in Verdi. The more permanent wood camp had the cookhouse and maintenance shop or blacksmith shop to maintain tools, and perhaps an animal pen if oxen and/or horses were used.

The interiors in these temporary lodgings were sparsely furnished. Sometimes the Chinese transported their cast-iron stoves and heaters by splitting them in two and using a traditional carrying pole to haul them from site to site; others managed to have elaborate stoves designed for wok cooking.[24] Still others ate at a dining hall away from the sleeping quarters.

The crowded conditions at the wood camp were relieved when the men lodged at the boardinghouses in nearby Chinatowns. Sometimes, as can be seen in some male-dominated rooms in San Francisco's Chinatown, they rotated in and out of a boarding house or hotel because they had more than one "residence": one for work, one (which might be just a bunk in an association-owned structure) for "recreation."

Living patterns in the 1920s did not change much from those in the 1870s. In the 1920s at Joe Kerrone's camp on Mount Sicker, British Columbia, Kerrone provided the bunkhouse for his men. He also provided the Chinese workers with hot lunches and wanted to have more facilities at the camp so that the Chinese would stay and spend their money at the camp stores and recreation areas and not in town on the weekends (Drushka 1992, 150). This practice probably occurred in Heavenly Valley and Verdi as well.

As a general rule, the Chinese lived separately from the other workers at the large camps. In 1883 one observer at a California wood camp noted that the workforce numbered sixty or more, and half of these were Chinese (Ingersoll 1883, 207). He went on to say:

> John Chinaman is in force here, as everywhere, for all help-work. His slight, wiry frame, with its shoulder under the lever, shows as much tough strength as that of his burly white neighbor, and he grinds all day at the feed-cutter, or totes kegs of water, balanced across his neck, up and down the rough declivities from morning till night, without seeming to tire out or ever thinking of a holiday. His it is to manage the kitchen of the camp.

Workmen of all European nationalities could be found at wood camps, so the Chinese had to learn to interact to some degree with non-Asians. Because of the transitory nature of the occupation, close friendships between members of different ethnic groups seldom occurred. As one observer wrote, "Many of these men did not know the names of their mates beyond a Sam or Jake to call them by; and they had no especial curiosity to know, this atmosphere making a man tender about asking his neighbor personal questions" (Ingersoll 1883, 208). There were exceptions to this generalization, and some friendships, as we will see, developed between Chinese and non-Chinese workers. There were cases, such as in Verdi, where the Chinese workers followed their non-Chinese supervisor to Oregon to work after the Verdi company closed. For the Chinese who worked under the direction of a Chinese labor boss, this probably was not valid, since a labor contractor often put together the work team of men who came from the same village or region in China.

Chinese archaeological sites are distinguishable from Euro-American sites because of the imported material culture from China that was found. The practice of recycling materials (such as flattened kerosene cans for shingles, perforated cans for strainers, reshaped cans for pouring oil for frying) and the small amount of refuse made clear the presence of the Chinese (Dixon et al. 1995, 189) The Chinese imported many foodstuffs, both dried and in cans or pottery jars, as well as rice in cloth sacks and specially shaped Chinese "wine/whiskey" bottles, such as for Ng Gai Pei. Alcoholic beverages were used for cooking soups, especially in the winter, for recreational drinking, as an analgesic, and to speed up the healing process for bruises by rubbing Ng Gai Pei or a high-content alcohol liquor along with a hard-boiled egg on the bruise or wound. Small bottles for medicines, especially to aid in curing diarrhea and digestion problems, also were commonly found with the pills inside; these were often mistakenly identified by archaeologists as opium bottles, however.

Unlike Euro-American lumbermen, who ate lots of canned foods, the Chinese enjoyed freshly killed meats, as seen in the remains of animal bones at archaeological sites; whenever possible, their diet included fresh fruits and vegetables. When they cooked Chinese food in the wok, they often set the wok on stones or bricks outside so that the high fire required would not burn down the cabin or building. Stone stoves often were accessible from inside or outside a cabin.

Almost all sites had opium-smoking paraphernalia—tins, pipe bowl fragments, lamp parts. Surface scatter of Chinese artifacts have been found throughout the Carson Range and Sierra Nevada, but only recently have researchers engaged in archaeological studies and inventoried artifacts. Near the Spooner Summit cabin, there were 109 opium can fragments with three can lids embossed with the "Beautiful Origin" brand name along with four opium lamp fragments (Solury 2004, 60). "Beautiful Origin" was a more expensive brand of opium, and the ability to spend money for this product and the pale green "Winter Melon" bowls (often mistakenly identified as "celadon") suggests that these men were not in the lower economic echelons of their community. At a VTRR graders' campsite near present-day Western Nevada College north of Carson City, it was apparent that opium smoking did not occur where cooking, eating, and game playing took place (Rogers 1997, 37).

Opium smoking in opium dens was banned in San Francisco in 1875 and in Virginia City in 1876, but the hue and cry against opium smoking arose because Euro-Americans had adopted the habit. Other local and state laws banning opium smoking were passed shortly thereafter. In 1887 a federal law prohibited the importation of opium by the Chinese, and tariffs were added, since opium was used in American medications. Federal controls against opium were enacted in 1909. The Harrison Narcotic Act of 1914 had very broad provisions. Many of these laws were ignored or not enforced, and even in 1930 "opium dens could be found in almost any American city" (Anslinger and Tompkins 1953, 54; Brecher and Editors 1972). In a study of Port Townsend's Chinese colony, the value of the opium seized from individual Chinese was worth less than one hundred dollars in the majority of cases, while opium seized from Euro-Americans frequently was worth three times that amount (Liestman 1994). Evidence suggested that the Euro-Americans were the big sellers and buyers of opium, not the Chinese, who used it in small quantities.

Opium, originally unregulated, was often used as an analgesic. Smoking chandul, a purified and concentrated solution of poppy sap and water, had few harmful effects on the human body (Mark 1995). Chinese opium smokers were not all miserable and emaciated but cheerful and healthy, if small quantities were used. This was especially relevant in the case of tree fellers and flume herders, who had to be alert during the working hours because of the dangers inherent in their jobs. Low doses were used to alleviate pain from the hard, physical labor. As far back as the tenth century, the Chinese knew that if used in small quantities, a dose of opium acted as an analgesic, especially helpful for rheumatism, neuralgia, toothache, muscle ache, and diseases like dysentery, cholera, and other bowel disorders. In the Chinese cemetery in Carlin, Elko County, Nevada, all of the thirteen men buried there around the turn of the twentieth century had major or minor bone fractures (some treated, some not), so the need for analgesics was not surprising (Schmidt 2006). If the job were boring or involved strenuous physical exertion, such as flume herding, opium could be used for relaxation and pain relief. However, one had to be very alert and agile when the logs jammed in the flume, so the doses were probably low. Almost every archaeological site had Chinese Ng Gai Pei (whiskey) bottles and opium tins. For the most part these were normal activities, not deviant, for many Chinese at the turn of the twentieth century. Christian missionaries and philanthropic anti-opium organizations distorted much of the information about the Chinese use of opium and gave credence to the American popular image of the Chinese "opium eater" (Newman, 1995). These crusaders seldom labeled the Chinese as alcoholics.

Fragments of the containers for foodstuffs included brown-glazed utilitarian wares, such as spouted soy sauce jars and wide-mouth food jars, and six types of tableware: the most expensive, pale green "Winter Melon;" a cruder version of the pale green ware; bamboo ware, a grey porcelain stoneware with underglazed blue to grey-green painted floral/bamboo motifs on the exterior and a thin blue, black, or dark green band near the bowl rim; the Four Seasons design with enamel floral decoration; Double Happiness, a porcelain with underglazed blue painted swirl pattern and the Chinese character for double happiness; and Sweet Pea, a blue-on-white porcelain with painted cobalt blue leaf-and-vine decoration, usually on spouted pots (Sando n.d., based on Kwong Tai Company books). The pale green bowls and cups were found at the Spooner Summit flume herder's cabin, indicating that he made enough money to purchase some expensive tableware. This more expensive type of ware usually was not found in any great abundance. In the 1870s these bowls and cups had the wholesale price tag of six-and-a-half cents to nearly nine cents each. Archaeologist C. Lynn Rogers theorized that crew bosses, translators, or important visitors, or friends used the more expensive wares because of a person's elevated status or during special occasions (Rogers 1999, 46–47). The Four Seasons design was the next most expensive, and the others were relatively inexpensive wares. The bamboo pattern was the most common found at Chinese sites. Spoons, small teacups, wine cups, and regular-size teacups could be found in these design patterns. Fragments of these were found in wood camps, mining sites, and residences.

The Chinese were able to import relatively heavy items, such as ceramic soy sauce jars from Asia, because American trading ships, especially those transporting logs, would have returned to the United States empty, and therefore at a loss, if the ship owners had not contracted with Chinese merchants, especially those in Hong Kong, to fill the returning ship with Asian merchandise (Cox 1974, ch. 3). These products enabled the Chinese to preserve some of their eating habits and cultural traditions while living on the American frontier.

During such excavations, fragments of American- or European-made products also were discovered. The Chinese could have used a Western-style teapot that was uncovered at the Spooner Summit site, or it may have been left by Euro-American woodcutters. Most likely, it was for sale by the traveling merchant and easier to obtain than one from China. As well, it was more difficult to transport products from nearby towns like Genoa and Carson City up the steep Kingsbury Grade, a nine-mile mountain road with several switchbacks from the Carson Valley until it reached Daggett Pass at 7,344 feet before descending to the Lake Tahoe basin. Moreover, in the Daggett Creek area the Chinese wood camps were close to Euro-American camps; assuming they existed at the same time, the supply wagons probably brought more goods for the common usage of all groups. Heavy ceramic items may also have been too difficult to transport on the steep Kingsbury Grade. Western liquor bottles and bottles containing Western liquids and foods were among the many broken fragments at the campsites. Some of these items were consumed, but others may have been left as the result of the Chinese tendency to reuse bottles and other similar items. In addition, some alcoholic beverages were used for medicinal purposes. When shipments of Chinese or Japanese goods did not arrive, the Chinese made substitutions with American products. Eventually, some Western foodstuffs were preferred over similar Chinese products, which was the case with evaporated milk and maple syrup.

The Chinese lumbermen in Heavenly Valley, in contrast, did not have this luxury. In my fieldwork, I observed only a small amount of traditional Chinese foodstuffs, cookware, and tableware in those archaeological sites. American spoons and forks, as opposed to Chinese table implements, were more abundant than in the sites at Crystal Peak and Verdi. In a ten-by-fifteen-foot cabin of mixed log/stone construction, there were pieces of Swatow ware, four leather shoe fragments, Dutch oven fragments, shards of black bottle glass and of two champagne bottles, a lard bucket fragment, and other artifacts (Petersen, Seldomridge, and Stearns 1994, 1:11). Parts of saws, axes, and other tools, as well as studded boots, were found on sites. These were typical of many of the Chinese wood camps.

Archaeologists Susan Lindstrom and Jeffrey Hall (1994, 245–46) noticed that the Chinese working in Lake Valley, South Lake Tahoe, ate more American foods than their countrymen in Spooner Summit at the top of the Carson Range. They speculated that the Chinese substituted American alternatives because the Chinese supply networks may have weakened, making traditional foodstuffs not readily available. "As Chinese workers became more independent, like the wood contractors working in the Lake Valley Railroad operations, the need for the organization capacities and supply facilities once offered by Chinese companies may have declined. In this event, supply networks for overseas goods targeting hinterland logging camps, may have weakened" (245). They concluded that the workers' adoption of readily available canned foods, fresh foods from local suppliers, and standardized woodworking tools indicated participation in the regional economy and adoption of some American food habits by the mid-1890s.

American-made boots with pointed metal calks for loggers also were common at Chinese sites. At a Spooner Summit site there were five shoes or boots, basically of two different but general types: the rubber, slip-on work boot with a hardened rubber sole, and the leather shoe or boot with punched holes and/or metal eyelets for lacing. At Verdi, there also were American-made boots pieces with calks (Solury 2004; Lee 2008). Like the Chinese miner, the Chinese lumberman quickly learned about the superiority of Western footwear for his type of work.

Camps yielded other items as well. Chinese coins are often found at camps. A Spooner Summit site had five coins from the Qing dynasty (1644–1911) (Solury 2004). The coins probably were used for gambling, for decoration, as good-luck charms, or for folk beliefs (such as keeping evil spirits away) (Akin, Bard, and Weisz, 2015). Of these, gambling was probably the major reason for coins' presence. The earliest datable coin came from the Kangxi reign (1662–1772), the most recent from the Xuanzong reign (1820–1850). The coins clearly were not used as a medium of exchange. A Chinese brass key for a traditional style lock, a brass game piece, and part of a placer pan (suggesting that mining was combined with lumbering) were among artifacts discovered (Lee 2008). Work items found included black-powder cans, nails, lard buckets (used as lunch pails), and tools, including two-man saws and axes. In general, the Chinese used American tools but sometimes found use for traditional Chinese implements, such as Chinese-style pumps (Elston and Hardesty 1981, 20; LaLande 1979, 101, 104–6).

In the late 1990s U.S. Forest Archaeologist Penny Rucks rediscovered a site on Spooner Summit that had several cabins, evidenced by the foundations, and a large building that had served either as a meeting hall, a community hall, or a dining commons. A grove of willow trees grew near the cabin sites that had a picturesque view of Lake Tahoe. The Chinese were familiar with the properties of willow trees and often established camps near willow groves. In China, willow trees were used to make roofs, fences, furniture, and other objects, or they were used as fuel. This site, like many others scattered throughout the Tahoe Basin, was obviously Chinese because of the large number of Chinese artifacts mixed in with fragments of non-Chinese items. Nearby were numerous stacks of cut and organized cordwood dating from 1876.[25] There is no historical evidence to explain why these lumbermen left without transporting the site's cordwood to market, but it was probably related to either an anti-Chinese attack or the business failure of the contractor.

When the Chinese immigrated to the American West, some found jobs in the logging industry. Employment agents or labor contractors hired the Chinese to work in the woods, or the Chinese signed up for the jobs they saw in newspaper advertisements. In some areas, Chinese constituted the majority of men working in the woods prior to 1890. Sometimes they worked with only Chinese; other times, they worked—and perhaps lived—with Euro-Americans in the occupation. They performed many jobs, including as flume herders and cooks. They were not hesitant about seeking justice from the American courts when they could. They lived in logging camps or dormitories or boardinghouses, often apart from the general population. Their experiences can be illustrated by looking closely at their situation in Carson City and Truckee when anti-Chinese movements tried to drive them out of logging.

CHAPTER 3

Carson City and Truckee: Anti-Chinese Activities

Social theorist Joe R. Feagin (2014) has noted that systematic racism beginning with African Americans and extending to other peoples of color has characterized much of American history. In the case of the Chinese, anti-Chinese movements began as soon as Euro-Americans viewed the Chinese as threats to American jobs, economy, culture, and white supremacy. Between 1850 and 1908 there were 153 recorded violent anti-Chinese actions resulting in 143 deaths and 10,525 displaced from their homes and businesses (Jew 2003). Anti-Chinese activities intensified in the 1870s in preparation for immigration restrictions that led to the federal Chinese exclusion acts passed between 1882 and 1892. Andrew Gyory (1998) and Martin Gold (2012) have described this process on the national level. The economic recession and then depression of the late 1870s, which affected mining and lumbering towns, combined with the rise of unionism, the burgeoning media, and ambitious politicians rallying the public to support the cause, led to violence and the drastic decline in the Chinese population and the Chinatowns.

A closer look at the Chinese communities in Carson City, Nevada, and Truckee, California, demonstrate two approaches to solving the problem of ousting the Chinese. Both towns had prosperous Chinatowns with wealthy Chinese merchants who were involved in the logging industry as contractors for laborers and merchandising. Clan networking was evident in Carson City. Euro-American timber ranchers prospered from the use of Chinese labor, and the transition to larger enterprises took place at this time. Some resisted the demands of the anti-Chinese agitators but eventually acquiesced. The violence influenced other towns, including Marysville, Yuba County, California; the logging towns of Eureka and Arcata, Humboldt County, California, and Tacoma, Washington; the mining and logging towns around Portland, Oregon, and Seattle, Washington, as well as Bellingham, Whatcom County, Washington, to name but a few. Port Townsend, Jefferson County, Washington, exemplified the communities that rejected the movement because of the close relationship between logging companies and the town's Chinese leaders, especially Jim Boyd, aka Ng Shee Gim. But while the

Chinese population prospered briefly through the 1880s and 1890s, the effects of the 1882 and 1892 Chinese exclusion laws, the failure in the 1890s of the railroad to connect Port Townsend to Seattle and other large towns, and the faltering local economy of the 1890s contributed to the drastic reduction of its Chinese population by the turn of the twentieth century. A closer examination of the events and aftereffects provide greater insight into interethnic relations, the growth of early logging companies, Chinese clan networking, racism, political machinations, and the influence of the media.

Although there were other incidents, the first major anti-Chinese riot that set a precedent for later events throughout the region occurred in Unionville, near the California-Nevada border, on January 10, 1869 (Rusco 2001, 91–155). There unemployed Euro-American lumbermen joined with miners in acts of violence. Sixty armed members of the Anti-Chinese League of Unionville marched into Chinatown and demanded that the Chinese leave. According to a *Gold Hill News* correspondent, Unionville had always exhibited "a feeling of bitter hatred" toward the Chinese. They forcefully escorted thirty-five Chinese to the train station in protest against the twenty-four Chinese whom John C. Fall of the Arizona Mining Company had hired to work at his stamp mill. Fall took advantage of the cheaper Chinese labor to make money out of a mining site that had been considered unprofitable. Later the League's members justified their actions by stating that they had settled Unionville when it was a wilderness, fought the Indians for the land, and suffered greatly from unemployment or underemployment, so they were unwilling to be supplanted by the Chinese.[1] While members of the Anti-Chinese League were not punished for their role in this incident, their two leaders and co-founders of the league—W. S. Bonnifield and L. F. Dunn—were charged with violating the Burlingame Treaty of 1868. However, Bonnifield's older brother, McKaskia Stearns Bonnifield (1833–1913), an attorney and Nevada State senator at the time, was successful at having the charges dropped while pointing out that mob action was not the solution to the "Chinese problem." In February 1869 he proposed to the Nevada state legislature a law banning Chinese laborers from Nevada altogether.[2] However, with the ongoing construction of the CPRR, his proposal was doomed to fail. A decade later the Bonnifields and Dunn learned to be more tolerant of the Chinese and even bought property from and leased and sold property to them in Humboldt County (Valentine 1999). Their change in attitude was more evident in 1902, when M. S. Bonnifield, by that time a judge and devout Methodist Episcopalian, officiated at the marriage of a Chinese American couple in his home in Winnemucca, Nevada, and Dunn was a guest.[3] A few Chinese eventually returned to Unionville, but it was never the same. The transformation from hostility to acceptance was an important component in the acculturation of the Chinese into Nevada society.

Shortly after the Unionville incident, several bills were proposed in the Nevada legislature and those in other states to protect Chinese laborers from mob violence. For example, one bill proposed to make it a felony for two or more persons to prevent by force or show of force or by threats or intimidation anyone from being hired or hiring; however, this bill, like the others, was defeated, allowing mob violence against the Chinese to continue for the next four decades with little or no risk of punishment (Wunder 1986).

Anti-Chinese hostility increased with the campaign to pass Chinese exclusion legislation. Forceful expulsion of Chinese occurred in Roseville, Rocklin, and Garberville, California, in 1880. That year fires destroyed Chinatowns in Dutch Flat and Auburn, California, setting precedents for similar acts in 1882 in Diamondville and in 1885 in Susanville. When Congress passed the 1882 Chinese Exclusion Act, agitators were convinced that the law was not strict enough, so they continued their violence in 1884–1885 in Eureka, Arcata, Seattle, and Tacoma, as well as numerous other western towns. The 1885 murder of Chinese miners in Rock Springs, Wyoming, sparked more violence and eventually resulted in the only instance of federal reparations to the Chinese (House Report 1886). Numerous local, state, and federal laws discriminating against the Chinese were passed. Against this background, anti-Chinese violence erupted in Carson City and Truckee, which led to the decline of their Chinatowns.

Carson City, Ormsby County (formerly Carson County), was the commercial and transportation center that connected the rich forests of the Sierra Nevada to the west with the Comstock mines to the east and the major CPRR station in Reno to the northwest. Carson City was settled around 1851 as Eagle Valley, a trading post catering to emigrants traveling west into California, and attracted ranchers and farmers. The town site was platted and renamed Carson City, the territorial capital of the newly created Nevada Territory, in 1861, and then state capital in 1864. It was 125 miles from Placerville, California, and 275 miles from San Francisco. Ormsby County was covered with pine and fir trees; the nearby Pine Nut Range, on the east, had a heavy growth of piñon pine that was used for fuel (Straka 2010; Kersten 1964, 501). The first sawmill, which was steam powered, in Ormsby County was constructed in the fall of 1859 on Mill Creek, three miles west of present-day Carson City; by 1861 there were three mills employing more than one hundred men (Thompson and West 1958, 541–42). The town's strategic location made it a stopover to and from mining boomtowns and a center for shipping lumber and other goods. When the VTRR linked Carson City to the Comstock and later to the CPRR in Reno, the town's prosperity grew, and the Chinese established a thriving Chinatown that served as the "home base" for the men working in the nearby mountains.

The Chinese began to settle there in the 1850s—at first because of the mining opportunities, but after the placer gold had been depleted in the surrounding area or because they had been banned from mining by discriminatory legislation or local policies, they branched out into other occupations, including logging. Early lumbering efforts in the Sierra Nevada were complicated by expensive transportation to the Comstock until the construction of the VTRR. By the 1860s and 1870s, after the CPRR, VTRR, and CCRR lines had been completed, more Chinese found work in the area, accounting for the large percentage of male laborers (560, or 80 percent of the total Chinese male population) in the 1870 census manuscript who worked primarily for the railroads and the logging companies. The popular estimate of Carson City's population was two thousand, with another eight hundred in the mountains (Smith, 2000, 103). Anti-coolie clubs, linked to the San Francisco organizations, became prominent in April and May 1876 as part of the Kearney unionism efforts in a period of economic depression. Anti-Chinese agitators resented the employment of "cheap Chinese labor" when they could do the job themselves.

Out of the 2,032 residents of Carson City in 1870, 1,606 were foreign-born; of these, 697 were Chinese (US Compendium, 1870, table 9, 256). Almost half of the city's population came from a foreign country, so the nativism characteristic of California had not become an issue yet. The 1870 census indicated that Chinese men worked in a variety of occupations: twenty-six were domestic servants (4 percent), nineteen cooks (3 percent), twelve laundrymen (2 percent), eleven farmers (2 percent), six doctors (1 percent), and three merchants. Wood dealers were considered merchants in general, but most others connected with the lumber industry were regarded as laborers. In 1870 only three men—Hi Sonee (age thirty-two), Su Su (age thirty-five), and Ah Hin (age twenty-five)—were listed in Carson City as woodchoppers. That year the only Chinese death listed in the Ormsby County records was thirty-five-year-old Woo Hing, who was killed by a "sawed log" in April. From their background in China, the Chinese were very aware of the dangers of working in the woods. The Bureau of Immigration (later Immigration and Naturalization Service) required Chinese wood dealers and others in business to have papers such as the one issued for Chin Wo.

Carson City's Chinese community grew between 1870 and 1880, then declined thereafter. A *New York Times* (September 14, 1876) reporter remarked, "The number of Chinamen seen on the streets, neatly dressed in black, blue, or white calico blouses, is remarkable." By 1880 the occupations of the 802 resident Chinese varied from laborers (159), cooks (161), and laundrymen (103) to woodchoppers (45), servants (38), farmers or gardeners (24), merchants (14), hairdressers (4), jeweler (1), mason (1), watchmakers (2), painters (3), doctors (6), carpenters (2), wood dealers (2), wood packer (1), lumberman (1), dentist (1), druggist (1), and teachers (3) (Census 1880). The number of male laborers dropped twenty percent while the number of cooks increased by twenty percent. This change suggests that there was an upward mobility within the ethnic community from hard physical labor to cooking and service.

By 1880 the Chinese workers dominated regional logging operations. Most of the Chinese woodchoppers and those involved in logging lived in Ormsby County—forty-five out of ninety in the state (Census 1880). They were listed in

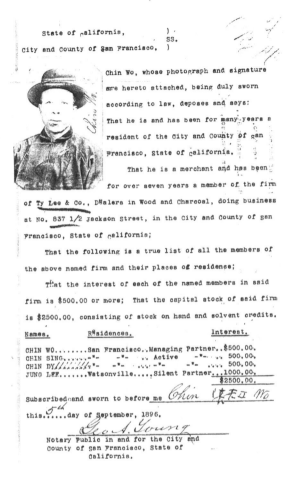

State of California,   ) .
                                 . SS.
City and County of San Francisco,)

Chin Wo, whose photograph and signature are hereto attached, being duly sworn according to law, deposes and says:

That he is and has been for many years a resident of the City and County of San Francisco, State of California.

That he is a merchant and has been for over seven years a member of the firm of Ty Lee & Co., Dealers in Wood and Charcoal, doing business at No. 837 1/2 Jackson Street, in the City and County of San Francisco, State of California;

That the following is a true list of all the members of the above named firm and their places of residence;

That the interest of each of the named members in said firm is $500.00 or more; That the capital stock of said firm is $2500.00, consisting of stock on hand and solvent credits.

Names.	Residences.		Interest.
CHIN WO	San Francisco	Managing Partner	$500.00.
CHIN SING	-"-	Active	500.00.
CHIN DY	-"-	-"-	500.00.
JUNG LEE	Watsonville	Silent Partner	1000.00.
			$2500.00.

Subscribed and sworn to before me Chin 正王玉 Wo

this ...... day of September, 1896.

Geo A. Young

Notary Public in and for the City and
County of San Francisco, State of
California.

Chin Wo had two active partners, who were kinsmen, and one silent partner, who probably was a relative in Ty Lee and Company of San Francisco, dealers in wood and charcoal. Note his signature in English and Chinese. (Courtesy of the National Archives and Records Administration)

the 1870 census, but their names might have been transliterated differently. Six Chinese woodchoppers and one Chinese cook lived and worked at the George Chubbuck timber ranch near South Lake Tahoe. Three of these woodchoppers, ages twenty-eight, thirty-four, and forty-two, were married; three, ages seventeen, twenty, and thirty-two, were single. Married workers were believed to be more stable and reliable than single men. Another sixteen Chinese woodchoppers lived in the household next door to timber rancher Chauncy Lotta and his family. They ranged in age from eighteen to fifty-one; eight were married. Saw King (age twenty-eight) and How Kong (age thirty-three), who lived in a boardinghouse with others working in lumbering, were carpenters. Both men could read, so they could follow written instructions. Although there are no records to indicate how long these men remained in the United States, there is a record of a Chinese carpenter named Ah Joe of Washington. Ah Joe (b. 1854) immigrated from Taishan in 1870, made enough money to travel to China in 1906, was able to reenter because he had loaned a friend $1,000 in gold before departing, and was still doing carpentry work in Washington in 1907.[4] Some of these workers in the woods, therefore, probably stayed in the United States for many years, but there is little documentation to substantiate this. Two of the six Chinese wood dealers in Nevada lived in Carson City.[5] The wood dealer, Hing Luck, age forty and married, lived with Kong Chi, a forty-four-year-old wood packer, and Fing Hap, a twenty-seven-year-old unmarried woman who kept house and was probably a relative or servant rather than a prostitute.[6] Kow Can (b. 1836), a married man who could read, was the only Chinese "lumberman" (a high status) in the state.

The wives of the majority of married Chinese workers during this period lived either in a large Chinatown or in China. Immigration laws prevented Chinese wives from joining their husbands (Ling 1998; Peffer 1999). It was often the case that married men never saw their wives and children again after leaving China. Although there were no recorded case studies in Nevada, the example of Jung Fong, also known as Jeong Fong, of San Francisco was typical. He had a wife seven years his junior and a son, both of whom he never saw after leaving China in 1882 to work as a salesman and porter at the Chinese hardwood and lumber company called Sing Kee Company in San Francisco's Chinatown.[7] The family in China depended on funds sent home by the husband, but, as was the case with other ethnicities, the amounts varied; often, nothing was sent.

The anti-Chinese agitation of the 1880s to 1890s probably explains why there were no listings of Chinese involved in lumbering in Ormsby County in 1900. In 1910 Chinese lumbermen returned, and five men were listed with more details. Dong Fee (b. 1858, immigrated 1881), Fong Clang (b. 1852, immigrated 1875), Kee Hung See (b. 1884, immigrated 1892), and Kee Wing Charley (b. 1888 in California) were woodcutters, and Kowan (no first name; b. 1870, immigrated 1899) was a wood packer (NVSHPO 1900 and 1910). Dong Fee and Kowan lived near each other in Chinatown and were in their twenties. The two young Kees were probably related, and, like Fong Clang, lived on 6th Street in at the edge of Chinatown, not far from Euro-American residences. Kee Wing Charley stated that his parents knew English and that he was fluent in English. One might assume that the older three men had been cutting wood for several decades, but their names, as listed with this spelling, do not show up in any other Nevada census manuscript. These were among the last known Chinese involved in lumbering in this region.

Merchants were the intermediaries between the Euro-American and Chinese communities and provided leadership for the Chinese. According to the census manuscripts, most of the Chinese merchants and grocers could read and probably write, since they had to keep records and handle communications. Therefore knowledge of reading and writing Chinese and the ability to speak English elevated a person's status in the community. Others often had to rely on these

STATE OF NEVADA
SHOWING COUNTIES

• County Seat

Chinese woodcutters
logged in the forests
throughout Nevada, but
especially in Storey, Douglas, Washoe, Ormsby, and
Elko Counties prior to
1900.

abilities. The merchants undoubtedly were part of the upper level of Chinatown
society. Carson City had three Chinese merchants in 1870: Yuo Ah, age forty-five;
Cun Cung, age forty-three; and John Sam Wan, age forty-four. By 1880 the list of
merchants, grocers, and storekeepers had grown to fourteen: Chin Ah, age forty;
Kum Ah, age sixty-four; Lodi Ah, age forty-two; Sing Ah, age twenty-five; Wo
Ah, age forty-two; Chan Chung, age thirty-four; Sing Chung, age forty-three;
Foy Good, age thirty; Kee Hing, age sixty; Young Me, age sixty-one; Wa See,
age fifty; Man Ton, age forty; Ten Wing, age twenty-eight; and Teng Wan, age
fifty-four (NVSHPO 1880). The only person whose name appears in the 1870
and 1880 lists is John Sam/Teng Wan, a married man who lived in Carson City's
Chinatown. Whether this was another name for Sam Gibson (aka Non Chong
Yee) is unknown. The average age of these merchants in 1880 was 44, indicating
some maturity was necessary to be involved in business and suggesting an earlier
occupation in order to achieve merchant status.

Chain migration of relatives strengthened the entrepreneurial goals of Chinese immigrants; the Yee clan in Nevada was an example of this phenomenon.
Once a member of the clan realized that there were profits to be made, he sent

information back to his home village, town, or larger community (Woon 1984, 282). Sometimes he would ask for funds to help establish or support his store, or he used the rotating credit method that many overseas Chinese businessmen employed (Wu 1974, 565–584; Freedman 1958; Aldrich and Waldinger 1990, 128). The rotating credit system enabled local groups to rotate funds that enabled a member to capitalize a small business. American banks did not loan money to Chinese businesses, so the funds had to come from the person, from within the community, or from connections in China. A merchant used his connections in the home district and with those who had settled in the American West to obtain supplies. Ties were maintained as those in China and in the American West supplied goods along Chinese lineage and regional lines. Mail-order centers were usually in San Francisco and Sacramento. Business owners often informed kinsmen at home about job opportunities and might help pay their passage, sometimes with substantial interest and at other times without interest. The use of relatives and personal ties for establishing business operations was common in all capitalistic societies (Aldrich and Waldinger 1990). Once the relatives arrived in the United States, lodging might be provided at the back of or on the top floors of stores, as exemplified in Kam Wah Chung and Company in John Day, Oregon, or in designated boarding rooms in association buildings. From San Francisco to the final destination, the bonds of kinship were strengthened.

Family and regional ties were important assets for any successful merchant or labor contractor in nineteenth-century Chinese America. In these traditional business organizations based on family and regional ties, responsibility to the business and family were intertwined and what was good for the family was also good for the business (Feuerwerker 1958; Cochran 1980; W. Chan 1982; McElderry 1986). After being funded, the Chinese merchants had to acquire the skills needed to operate a small business, recruit employees who were honest and inexpensive, manage relations with customers and suppliers, survive business competition, change with the industrialized society, react to the economic downturns, and protect themselves and their employees from fraud, verbal and physical attacks, and other harmful situations. Sometimes they took a smaller profit and therefore could undercut the prices of their Euro-American competitors, or, as in the case of Quong Hing and Company in Carson City, could carry large quantities of in-expensive items, like nails, and potentially dangerous items, like blasting powder. Chinese lumber contractors provided workers for various timber ranches.

In the 1882 Chinese Exclusion Act, merchants were among the few classifications of people who could travel freely to and from the United States. One of the goals of the ambitious worker was to save enough money to enter into a business partnership and thus achieve the status of merchant. Partnerships often had to expand to include in-laws, relatives of in-laws, and immigrants from the same native region, who, in China, would be viewed as "outsiders." One documented example of how this operated in California was the case of Lee Hong, also known

as Lee Kew Son.[8] Lee immigrated in 1881 and worked as a San Francisco laundryman and in the kitchen of the St. Francis Hotel for a combined income of
twenty-six dollars per month. By 1908 he had saved enough money to pay $500
for a partnership interest in the firm of Choy Jee Tong Company, 804 Dupont
Street (now Grant Avenue). He was one of twenty-eight partners and eventually
earned thirty-five dollars per year in dividends on his $500 investment. As a
merchant, he could travel to China and had saved enough for the trip in 1913, at
which time he was paid seventy dollars per month in dividend and salary while
in China. Chinese merchants (new immigrants, returning merchants, and sons
of merchants who were classified as merchants) constituted one third of the total
number of Chinese men entering the United States between 1910 and 1924 (Lee
2008, 7–8). This general pattern applied to Chinese companies throughout the
American West. As the pool of clan investors shrank and historical conditions
changed, nonrelatives assumed the managerial and influential roles. The feeling
of "family" prevailed, as "employment families," which could be based on regional
ties, had the workplace at its core.

Little is known about most of the Chinese merchants who acted as labor contractors for a variety of employers. One of the earliest known labor contractors
was Ah Sing, who advertised in the *Carson Daily Appeal* (July 3, 1868) that his
office was in Chinatown next to Dr. Ah Kee. Ah Sing brokered jobs for cooks,
servants, and workers in all fields, and was Ah Kee's "special agent."[9] Dr. Kee,
a "botanical" physician prominent in the community, was also a family man
and businessman, traveled to China frequently, and was well known among the
Chinese and non-Chinese communities alike. His name appeared on the payroll
list of the VTRR, probably as a labor contractor.[10] In the 1866 Ormsby County
Assessment of Property, he was assessed for the following: "China house no. 2,
8, and 15" situated on lots assessed to G. A. Sears; "$100, drugs and medicines
–$150, 5 hogs –$40, and 13 chickens –$10." By 1883 he owned an entire city block,
Block 19 (between Second and Third Streets), which included the "Hung Ling
Tong," probably a fraternal organization headquarters, established in 1861. He
also served as an interpreter for the court, for example, in February 1870 in the
case of *Ah Chung v. State of Nevada*.[11] His wife and children lived in Carson City,
but their names never appeared on census records.

Chinese merchants helped maintain ties with China and Chinese culture. Terry
Boswell argued, "Chinese merchants subsidized traditional Chinese cultural and
clan activities in part to maintain their trade monopoly" (Boswell 1986, 364).
Because the store managers usually had some degree of literacy in Chinese or
English or both, the stores also sent letters and money to China and received mail,
kept important papers, and provided information about American permits, laws,
taxes, customs, and other matters of interest to customers. For example, Chin
Poy (aka Chin Gay Mon) of the Leong Kee Company in San Francisco, sent his
family one hundred dollars twice a year through the Wing Tung Git Company

Table 3–1. Population of Carson City, Chinese Men and Women in Carson City, and
Chinese in State of Nevada

Census Year	Total in Carson City	Chinese Men	Chinese Women	Total Chinese in Carson City	Total Chinese
1860	1,166	21	0	21	23
1870	3,042	661	37	698 (23%)	3,162
1880	4,227	719	83	802 (19%)	5,416
1890	3,950	(not available due to fire)		670 (17%)	2,833
1900	2,689	132	14	146 (5%)	1,352
1910	3,277	103	9	112 (3%)	927

Source: U.S. Census 1860–1910

of Hong Kong.[12] There, his fellow regional Chin Park Leong sent the money onto the Kong Chung Company of Sheck Lung How market, and the merchant there, in turn, delivered it to Chin Poy's family in the village. At each stage a small fee was charged. Like those in China, merchants often sponsored important Chinese festivals, such as New Year's festivities on the lunar calendar, with some of the funds collected. Kinship bonds also operated in times of difficulties, and through their clan associations, *hui* or *fang* or *tang*, help was given for those stranded to return home, to get medical help, and to bury the dead either in a clan or Chinese cemetery, or in the village of their birth (Woon 1978; Lai 2004; Ng 1992; Chung and Wegars 2005).

By the 1880s the Chinatown consisted of five blocks that included at least seven stores, several restaurants, several opium dens, laundries, several houses of prostitution, boarding houses, and professional and trades practitioners, notably merchants, masons, doctors, cooks, builders, and wood dealers. Several associations had their own buildings, including a headquarters for the local CCBA. A fire in 1884 destroyed most of Chinatown, but the three major *tang*—Zhigongtang (Chinese Free Masons), Hehe (Hop Wo), and Yanghe (Yung Wo)—continued to dominate Chinatown (Kautz and Risse 2000, 105). The 1886 the anti-Chinese riots completed the destruction of most of Chinatown and drove most of the Chinese away.

Zhigongtang was the secret society dedicated to the overthrow of the Manchu government in China and was located in a substantial two-story building.[13] It resembled Zhigongtang buildings in Tuscarora, Monterey, and other towns. It was rebuilt after the fire but was never as grand and eventually moved to a location near the VTRR tracks on Stewart Street and Third (Smith 2000, 69). The building survived into the 1930s, but its membership declined after the success of the 1911 Revolution in China. Merchants usually served as Zhigongtang leaders and often sat on the Chinese Consolidated Benevolent Association (CCBA) board as well. The society declined further because of the Sino-Japanese War of the 1930s and the fact that the second- and third-generation Chinese Americans were not as interested in the affairs of China.

As was the case with the Chinese in several other towns in Nevada, the Chinese were not restricted to living within the boundaries of Carson City's Chinatown in the 1880s and 1890s (Kautz and Risse 2000). The same situation in this period occurred in Virginia City and other western towns and this allowed greater integration into the larger community.

Quong Hing and Company was just one of approximately seven Chinese businesses that not only sold supplies and goods to Chinese and non-Chinese alike, but the company also provided workers to emerging entrepreneurs, including Duane Leroy Bliss (1833–1906), president and general manager of CTLFC; Henry Marvin Yerington (1828–1910), later president and superintendent of the VTRR and head of sixteen companies; and Darius Ogden Mills (1825–1910), one of the founders of the Bank of California and prominent businessman on the Comstock and in San Francisco. Its manager-owner was Sam Gibson, or Non Chong Yee, a prominent Chinatown leader, labor contractor, family man, and property owner. In the newspapers, tax records, and other documents he also was called Big Sam, Ah Chung, Ah Sam, and Quong Hing, the name of his store. Yee (Yu/Yi in pinyin) was his family name. Euro-Americans called him "Sam Gibson" because he had worked at Gibson's Saloon in Carson City before becoming a manager and partner in Quong Hing and Company (also spelled Kwong Hing, Kwong Wing, Quong Sing, Kong Hing, and other variations of the name). Many "Americanized Chinese" in Nevada adopted American names for the convenience of their Euro-American associates, and many Euro-Americans often bestowed the company's name on an individual.[14] By having an American name, Sam Gibson was able to interact more easily with many of the business and community leaders.

The name Yee Non Chong or Sam Gibson or the names of his wife and three children (Ah Cum, oldest girl, Yee King, a boy, and Ah Sue, youngest girl), who were born in Carson City, never appeared in the census manuscripts (Chung 2000) Ah Cum attended the public elementary school in Carson City and continued her elementary education in Benton and Bodie, California, where she lived with friends of her parents. Ah Cum could attend public school in Carson City because in 1871 the Superintendent of Schools permitted this. Dr. Ah Kee's children were probably the test case for the superintendent's 1871 decision to allow Chinese children in public schools. The names of Sam Gibson and his wife (Mrs. Ah Sam in 1880, Mrs. Sam Gibson in 1885) appear on county tax records, and the name Quong Hing appeared in CTLFC account books.

Quong Hing and Company was prosperous. According to the Ormsby County *Assessment of Property*, in 1878 Quong Hing paid fifty-four dollars in taxes, while Wells Fargo and Company only was assessed forty-three dollars, and Episcopal-Methodist Reverend Ah For forty-six dollars. The *Assessment of Property* in 1884 (p. 122) showed that Quong Hing owned one whole block (Block 20), one store, furniture worth $100, merchandise worth $1,500, four horses worth $200, two wagons valued at $50, ten hogs worth $50, and two boarding houses that were

Sam Gibson (aka Non Chong
Yee) managed Quong Hing and
Company in Carson City, selling
products to Chinese and non-
Chinese customers as well as act-
ing as labor contractors for lum-
bering and railroad companies.
His three children were born in
Carson City and attended public
school there until 1886. (Source:
Kee family album)

operated by Mrs. Gibson to provide lodging and meals for the workers. Quong
Hing paid the poll taxes for Ah Look, Ching Kim, Albert, and Charlie Friesbie.
In order to provide additional housing for the workers, Sam Gibson owned a
stone tenement house and possessed furniture ($100), merchandise ($1,500),
and jewelry ($200) valued at a total of $1,800 for tax purposes in 1875 and 1885
(Ormsby Tax Records, 1875, 115; and 1885, 103). In 1885 Quong Hing paid poll taxes
for four individuals—"Sam Gibson, Albert, Ko You, and Ah Look" at four dollars
per person—and two dogs at one dollar each. Based on the poll tax payments,
Mrs. Gibson was probably Ah Look. From this information, it was obvious that
Sam Gibson and his store had achieved a modicum of success.

Sometime in 1885 or 1886 the family, without Ah Cum, went to China because of
the violence, but Gibson wanted his only American-born son to return to Carson
City. King Yee's immigration papers revealed more about the family.[15] Based on
Bliss's deposition for King's reentry into the United States, it became clear that
Gibson and Bliss were on familiar terms. Bliss first saw King with his father at
Quong Hing when the boy was two years old, and when Bliss was in Hong Kong
in December 1892, the Yee/Gibson family visited Bliss and his wife. According to
Bliss, Gibson and his young son often delivered "goods to his employees in the
mountains."

Ah Cum (1879–1929), Sam Gibson's oldest child, was left with friends in Benton when her parents returned to China. At age fourteen she married Chung Kee in Hawthorne; they had six children. (Source: Courtesy of Kee family album)

King (b. ca. 1879) went to China when he was about six years old. This was the same age of Hop Lee's son Mee Wat Yee of nearby Dayton, Lyon County, when Mee Wat Yee first went back to China for his Chinese education. These two young men lived between two worlds: China and the United States. King returned to Carson City in 1897 in the first of several trips between China and the United States. The transcripts of King's testimonies in 1897 and 1904 indicated that he was not fluent in English or at ease with his life in Carson City. Unlike some of the "returned" Chinese, he signed his name in Chinese rather than English on his deposition. Bliss testified on his behalf, but it was obvious from King's testimony that King did not know Bliss as well as his father did. In his 1904 testimony King named Yerington (whom the transcriber misspelled Arlington) as a Carson City individual whom he knew best. King could describe Glenbrook and Virginia City. Eventually King moved to El Paso, Texas, where the Yee clan had another store. He died there without ever contacting his oldest sister, Ah Cum Kee, who lived in Nevada most of her life.[16] This may indicate that he was a paper son rather than her real brother.

Quong Hing Company, with its partners Sam Hing, Sam Kee, Yuk Chung, and Ah Sam (aka Sam Gibson), was located on Third Street and sold imported and American-made goods to Chinese and Euro-Americans. Like Wa Chong Company of Seattle, Quong Hing was a general merchandising firm that probably made its profits from several sources, including the sales of goods, provisions, and housing, and as a labor contractor for Chinese workers in logging, the mills, and the railroads (Nomura 1989, 123). Whenever possible, kinsmen were hired and "employment families" took the place of the traditional Chinese family in China as the source of employment, recreation, and socialization. This type of living and work situation continued until the post–World War II immigration of Chinese women and the reestablishment of a normal Chinese American family society.

The labor contractor or his company also protected the occupational monopoly of its members whenever necessary (Fong 1981, 40–41; Lai 1995a). This was the underlying reason for the "tong war" in Carson City in October 1877.[17] In many ways, Quong Hing operated like a *tang*, a social or fraternal organization that managed property, coordinated labor, provided room and board, and established economic controls through rules and regulations and credit. However, social or fraternal organizations were also concerned with welfare benefits, education, religious facilities, recreation, and ties to China.

Quong Hing probably was organized like a typical Chinese family business with connections in China for the importation of traditional Asian goods. The head of the family served as the manager, and his relatives handled other positions within the company (Tsang 2002). People who were not family members who served the company for a long time could be promoted to senior positions, and this was probably the case when the Yee clan turned over the management to someone from a different clan (but probably one from the same locality in Guangdong). Close business connections between native place in China and Carson City often meant travel between the two locations for the wealthier Chinese merchants. This was not only true for Sam Gibson but also for his son. The success of the merchandising store led to the establishment of "branch" stores, one of which was located in Texas, where King Yee eventually settled and was killed.

Quong Hing was also involved in legal disputes. In 1873 the company had a contract with Hugh Porter to cut 4,177 cords of wood at $1.80 per cord, but Porter paid the company only $6,074.05.[18] In 1875 Quong Hing employed attorneys Harris and Coffin to sue Porter, who had two mills in Dog Valley, Verdi, for the difference of $1,502.56, and won the case in court. Sometimes Chinese companies functioned in a quasi-judicial capacity. In 1877 when Lum Gee murdered Ah Ping, Quong Hing prosecuted the murderer because the Euro-American courts distanced themselves from Chinatown crimes. This kind of action by a prominent Chinese company or a *tang* was common throughout the nineteenth-century West.

Quong Hing and Company owned property in Carson City's Chinatown. According to the Ormsby County *Assessment of Property* in 1884 (p. 122), Dr. Ah Kee owned the block of land between Second and Third Streets and Carson and Valley, while Quong Hing and Company owned the next whole block from East Third to Fourth Streets and Carson and South Valley. According to the 1907 Sanborn Fire and Insurance Map of Carson City, Chinatown (sheet 11) was centered on East Third Street and South Valley and covered about five blocks east of the capitol. Unfortunately, there were no earlier Sanborn maps that included Chinatown. Archaeologists Robert R. Kautz and Danielle Risse (2000, 16) described Chinatown:

> The lots at the south side of the corner of East 3rd Street and South Valley . . . include a two-story terra-cotta lined adobe structure (#431 E. 3rd) backed by several wood frame, single-story structures with an attached shed extending through the lot almost all the way to East 4th Street. Next to that building, to its east and separated by a passageway, is a single-story brick store with a tin roof extending half-way through the lot with several small out buildings at its rear that include a terra-cotta lined furnace (incinerator?).

There also were other wooden frame buildings (residences and businesses), another adobe store with a tin roof, a major tong building, several temples (in association buildings), truck gardens, a duck pen, and brothels. The VTRR tracks traversed the southern border of Chinatown (Kautz and Risse 2000, and Sanborn maps).

Quong Hing's appeal to Euro-American customers may have been the services offered—longer hours, year-round operation, easily available credit, sales of small quantities, and a ready supply of immediately needed goods—all typical of Chinese stores of that era. This dual clientele orientation allowed for economic growth and community prominence. According to CTLFC records, CTLFC, Yerington, and Bliss regularly patronized Quong Hing and Company, buying supplies and foodstuffs in the 1870s and 1880s. In December 1870 Yerington paid Quong Wing (Hing) $805.06 for hauling wood (Yerington, UCB). Yerington also purchased keg powder for blasting, axes, hatchets, onions, candles, sugar, and canned lobster from Chinese stores. Even in the 1890s Yerington continued to utilize Chinese services, such as laundry, and purchased goods from Ah Jim Song and Ah Wong Sun (Yerington, UNR, box 4). Bliss annually bought forty thousand to eighty

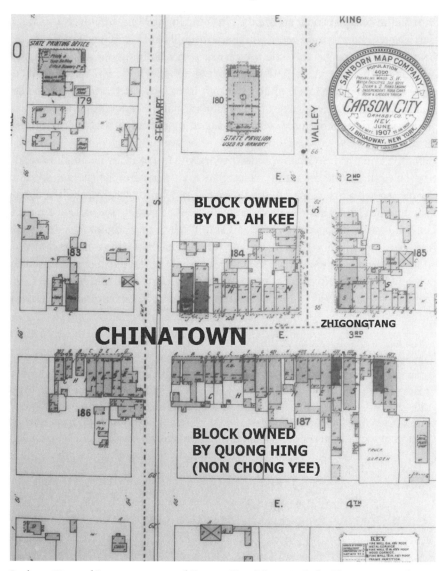

Sanborn Fire and Insurance maps of Carson City did not include Chinatown until 1907. This partial map of Chinatown indicates where the Zhigongtang and Block 3 (Quong Hing and Dr. Ah Kee's properties) were.

thousand cords of wood from Quong Hing. Walter D. Tobey, Bliss's brother-in-law, board member on the VTRR, and partner in the company Parker and Tobey, also purchased supplies from Quong Hing through the late 1880s (Tobey, Records). In March 1888, for example, he purchased $393.17 worth of supplies, and in October 1887 it was $1,420.04. The sale of goods to Euro-Americans was important to the success of Quong Hing.

Euro-Americans shopped at other Chinese owned stores as well. For example, lumberman John W. Haynie purchased goods and services from several Chinese merchandising companies, including Ty Chung, Quong Sing (perhaps Quong Hing?), Sam Sing, and Hen Lee.[19] The account books do not reveal the nature of these sales, but in at least one case it extended beyond the transaction of business.

The transition from a lineage partnership (defined by anthropologist Maurice Freedman [1966] as "sharing property") to an extended lineage partnership is exemplified in Quong Hing and Company (Freedman 1966; Sangren 1984). Sometime after Sam Gibson's departure, Albert, who was well liked by the Euro-American community, took over Quong Hing. In September 1899 the store was the most prosperous in Chinatown and paid $2,400 in taxes (Ormsby Tax List, September 1, 1889). In comparison, Chew Kee and Company, another general merchandising business involved in lumbering, paid only $900 in taxes. In sharp contrast, lumberman George Chubbuck paid only $650 that year, while E. B. Yerington, son of Henry Yerington, paid $2,600.

Because of the declining economic situation in Carson City, Albert was forced to supplement the store's income by providing food for the inmates at the jail. In 1901 he made enough money to return to China, and the *Morning Appeal* (September 18, 1901) noted,

> The leading Chinese merchant of this city . . . Albert . . . bid farewell to friends yesterday. . . . Albert was in all respeces [sic] an honorable and conscientious business man and no one ever heard a breath against the character of his business dealings during his long sojourn in this city. He did everything on the level and was regarded everywhere as a man whose word was as good as his bond and there are hundreds of our citizens who will learn of his departure with regret.

The difficulty of having "personal (nonhierarchical) management" was related to the discriminatory anti-Chinese immigration laws. The practice of hiring relatives from China was difficult, if not impossible, because of the Chinese exclusion laws, so eventually the firms like Quong Hing had to rely on "regional networks" to manage the business of a principle returning to China (Cochran 1980, intro.). In 1902 the new senior partner, Gee Kay Gong, changed the name of the company from Quong Hing to Nom Wah (or Nam Wah), located at 502 East Third Street, Carson City.[20] In 1914 the partnership papers listed seven partners, each with $1,000 invested, with last names first: Gee Kai Gong, manager; Gee Wing, Yee Sam, and Yee Ngon, general help; Yee Wo Ying, Yee Jor, and Yee Wo Tai, silent partners. In 1920 the business had a capital investment of $7,000, indicating that it maintained a prominent position. According to the 1920 census manuscript, Nam Wah, a widower, was seventy-five years old, having immigrated in 1883. He lived next door to George Sue, a fifty-three-year-old merchant in a neighborhood that was home to only four Chinese. Residential segregation had broken down. By 1924 Nom Wah's assets dropped to $4,500 and steadily declined as the Depression set in. The store sold household items, bric-a-brac, and candy during this period. In 1955 Nom Wah's beautiful stone building was one of the few buildings still standing in Chinatown. This company was one of the last Chinese businesses in Carson City and was torn down by the city in the 1960s.

Further insight into the possible activities of Quong Hing was revealed in Paul Yee's detailed study of Chang Toy (Chen Cai, also known as Chen Dao-zhi and Chen Chang-jin, d. 1920), founder of Sam Kee Company in Vancouver, British Columbia, at the turn of the twentieth century (Yee 1986). Chang Toy was one of the wealthiest Chinese merchants in Vancouver; his store sold a variety of goods and provided services such as tickets on steamships and trains, and hotel accommodations at five hotels. His charcoal manufacturing and wood yard operations allowed him to sell coal, coke, charcoal, and wood to a variety of customers, some as far away as Calgary. He was a labor contractor for a variety of businesses, including canneries, sugar mills, sawmills, shingle mills, and planing mills. Based on an examination of Chang's financial records, Paul Yee demonstrated that the average monthly wage at the sawmill in 1906 fluctuated from $14.28 to $26.69, depending on the tasks assigned. The workers received 75 percent of the original wage rate after food and supplies, ranging from 15 percent to 38 percent, were deducted. Chang Toy contracted workers for logging, cutting wood on leased land, and subcontracting logging work. He proved to be an aggressive dealer in buying and selling timber and wood products. In all probability, he was a more successful entrepreneur than Quong Hing, but his operations and practices that began after Vancouver's incorporation in 1886 probably found precedents in the Carson City's Chinatown.

The Yee clan played a significant role in other occupations in this period. CTLFC records indicated that several of the Chinese cooks belonged to the Yee clan (signatures in Chinese), keeping in the tradition of clan employment. Sam Gibson contracted for the CCRR, so it would not be surprising if he supplied the workers in 1881 to the Southern Development Company of Nevada, with Henry M. Yerington, Duane L. Bliss, Walter D. Tobey, and others as trustees, to plant trees in the public park in Hawthorne, which was billed as "China Time," according to Southern Nevada Development Company papers. After the CPRR was completed, 262 of the Chinese laborers worked on the VTRR for Sharon, Yerington, and Bliss.[21] By listing Chinese workers as "China Time," individual Chinese names were not recorded, and often anti-Chinese agitators could not see the extent to which Chinese labor was used when going through company records. In this way the captains of industry could avoid the wrath of the anti-Chinese agitators.

Meanwhile, anti-Chinese activities continued to grow and reached new heights. Anti-Chinese meetings had begun in 1876.[22] Carson City had organized an Anti-Asiatic Circle that became an anti-coolie association between April and May 1876.

At that time the anti-Chinese demonstrators drove eighty Chinese woodcutters for Yerington and Company (also called Haynie and Company) in the Carson City area from their wood camp and threatened other employers of Chinese workers that they had to get rid of their Chinese help or experience mob violence (Angel 1881, 558). These groups could not challenge the powerful business organizations that employed Chinese workers.[23] Most of the large lumber companies continued to hire Chinese workers despite the anti-Chinese movements. Reno and other towns, influenced primarily by San Francisco's labor movement, also became supporters of anti-Chinese activities. Economic stagnation was the prevailing condition during this time locally and globally (Chew 1992). This early anti-Chinese movement directed toward those in lumbering eventually contributed to driving out most of the Chinese by the mid-1880s. It also set the stage for the passage of new immigration regulations restricting the admission or reentry of Chinese laborers into the United States.

In 1881, as the anti-Chinese movement intensified, two hundred Euro-American woodchoppers working in Highland Park, just north of Walkerville near Butte, Montana, attacked the Chinese camp of forty men working for Joel Catching.[24] They drove the Chinese out and destroyed their provisions. A warrant was issued for the arrest of the men on the basis of unlawful interference with private rights and property; six men were arrested and arraigned. Public sentiment favored their release, which eventually occurred. The inability of the Chinese to find justice in American courts was common during these times of racial prejudice. Many anti-Chinese advocates felt that the passage of the 1882 Chinese Exclusion Act was not strict enough and disagreed with its ten-year limitation. In 1892 the exclusion act was extended for another ten years with more restrictions, and in 1924 the gate to America was essentially closed to the Chinese because of the national-origins policy.

After mobs tried to evict the Chinese by force, the violence reached new heights in 1885, as murder and mayhem became common. Following the lead of the 1886 Virginia City and Gold Hill Water and Flume Companies, which, under political pressure, cancelled all woodcutting contracts with Chinese labor contractors, Carson City's agitators unsuccessfully tried an economic boycott (Smith 2001, 28). They then turned to the burning of Chinatown. According to the *Morning Appeal* (August 21, 1886), the county's Chinese population dropped from 700 to 300 as a result of the movement, but these figures do not match census figures. According to the census, the population of Chinese in Carson City dropped from 802 in 1880 to 670 in 1890, and then to 146 in 1900 and 114 in 1910 (NVSHPO 1880 to 1910). By September 1886 the anti-Chinese fervor tapered off because the agitators felt that they had been successful in driving out the Chinese, and only thirty-two people attended the Anti-Chinese League meeting, where it was pointed out that the Exchange Hotel still had a Chinese cook because other cooks proved to be unreliable.[25]

The shortage of Chinese workers had begun. In November 1887, Albert, who had worked with Sam Gibson, lamented that he could not find enough Chinese woodcutters and had to hire Euro-Americans to fill his contracts.[26] The Chinese exclusion acts had prevented further mass immigration and discouraged many from remaining in the United States. This was just one case among many that convinced a good number of Euro-Americans that their anti-Chinese plank had been successful. Some variations were used elsewhere. For example, in Everett, Washington, Emory Ferguson, a former procurer for Pope and Talbot, had hired Chinese workers for his mill there, but in the 1890s the townspeople, in support of the anti-Chinese movement, drove him and his Chinese millworkers out of town and closed down the mill (Clark, 1970, 15). Their success led them to target other "undesirable" groups, including Catholics. The anti-Chinese movement even spread as far as British Columbia, where coastal sawmills struck partially in protest of the presence of Chinese workers in April 1886 (Hak, 2000, 161).

There were other Yee-controlled merchandising stores throughout Nevada at the turn of the twentieth century. Chinese partnership papers on file at the National Archives and Records Administration in San Bruno, California, indicate that Kee Chin and Company on Third Street in Carson City was wholly owned by Yee family members. This company engaged in gambling and sold lottery tickets as well as general merchandise.[27] The names of the partners were not listed in the federal census manuscript.

The Yee clan dominated Kow On and Company at 501 East Third Street in Carson City, located opposite to Quong Hing and next to See Wah's, which was also involved in lumbering.[28] As was typical in merchandising stores, when Yee Ding Chung's uncle left for China in 1906, Yee Ding Chung took over the company and, like his uncle, was known by the name Kow On. The *Morning Appeal* (January 1, 1930) described him at his death at the age of eighty-five as "one of the original merchants of this city . . . who came here when the Virginia and Truckee Railway was built." The article went on to say that he carried one of the largest stocks of "oriental goods and furnishings in the state," was head of his tang, a labor contractor for the railroads and then lumbering, but lost his fortune on stock speculations. He left a wife, probably Mrs. Au Kau On, who, at age ninety in 1941, revealed that she had been a prostitute in Virginia City prior to her marriage (Chinn 1972). Based on his occupation as merchant and his age of thirty-four in 1880, Kow On probably was Chan Chung in the federal census manuscript for 1880. In all likelihood there was no recognition in the Euro-American community that there were two individuals known by the name of the company, Kow On.

The last notable Yee in Carson City was Yee Bong (b. 1860), who was a cook and owned Yee Bong's Café on the corner of Valley and Third. He lived with eight other Yee family members in the former residence of Dr. Gee Tong, a noted herbalist who had departed with his family prior to 1920. Yee Bong claimed that he was born in Virginia City and opened his café in Carson City in 1873; in 1938,

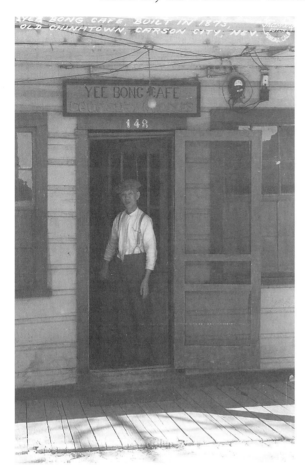

One of the last permanent residents of Carson City's Chinatown was Yee Bong (b. 1860), a café owner who was born in Virginia City and a member of influential Yee clan. (Courtesy of Robert Stoldal Collection, Las Vegas)

he was seventy-eight years old and one of the few remaining Chinese who was interviewed by historian Thomas Chinn of San Francisco.

Yee clan members could be found in other parts of Nevada as well. Yees from Taishan controlled the Bow Wah Sang Kee Company, 133 Lake Street, Reno, around the turn of the twentieth century.[29] Yee Gee Chung (aka Yee Kim Ngin and Yee Kim Gin), who arrived in 1881, had managed the general merchandising store for ten years, beginning in 1917. In 1902 there were seven Yee kinsmen controlling Wing Tang Hing Kee Company, 104 Lake Street, Reno.[30] By 1919 there were seven Yees and three others in this general merchandising store that included drugs, herbs, groceries, wearing apparel, lodging facilities, and opium bunks. Yee clan members partnered with Wong and Jee clan members to operate companies in Reno at the turn of the twentieth century, including Kwong Tai Lung and Company at 201 East Second Street. Quong Hai Lung Company at 100 Union Street (near H Street), in Virginia City, was another Yee enterprise for many decades and probably worked closely with Quong Hing.[31] Yee Coon, who could sign his name in western script, lived in Virginia City in the late 1870s and managed Quong Hi Loy.[32] In 1879 Yee's wife gave birth to his only child, a son named Yee Wing. In 1899 Yee Coon left Virginia City and moved to San Francisco to eventually become a partner in another Yee enterprise, Quong Tang Sing, 724 Commercial Street. Yee Coon's wife died in 1903, and shortly thereafter the father and son went to China, where the son married; both men returned to San Francisco in 1906. This was a very common pattern for this period. By 1888 Yee Ying had become involved in Quong Hi Loy, leaving most of the work to his relatives. In 1895 two of the partners, Yee Kew and Yee Ginn, had made enough money to go to China. Eventually by 1900 Yee Dick, Yee Lang, Yee Joe, Yee Fan, Yee Fook, and Yee Hung handled the affairs of the store and lived in Virginia City. The general merchandising firm had a capitalization of $6,000.[33] Still another store in the network was Ong Chong Lung and Company, organized in 1870 in Pioche, Lincoln County, Nevada also was dominated by Yee family members: Yee Tow King, Yee Wah Ling, Yee Soon, and Yee Lee. Yees continued to operate the store in the 1890s.[34] Yee Chong Company in Tonopah was a Yee operation under the leadership of Yee Fong.[35] The network was even larger.

The Yee clan also controlled stores in eastern Nevada, particularly in Elko and Carlin. Quong Wing and Company in Carlin was probably established because in the 1870s Carlin was a major station for the CPRR. By the 1890s the company had a capitalization of $7,000, making it the largest Chinese merchandising store in northeastern Nevada; three of the early members had retired to or were visiting in China while three others ran the store.[36] In 1871 Yee Foo Jung (b. 1851) arrived in Elko by train from San Francisco to work in Wha Lung and Company.[37] His three children, Yee Wan Hing (male, b. 1874), Yee Ling (female, b. 1876), and Yee Yut Hing (male, b. 1878) were born in Elko; in 1879 Yee Foo Jung took the entire family to China. He and his two sons returned in 1898, leaving his his wife and daughter with his younger brother in Woo Bin Village, Taishan (at that time, called Xinning/Sunning). His younger brother was a merchant in the nearby market town. After leaving Elko, Yee Foo Jung established himself in San Francisco, and by 1898 was president of the Hehe (Hop Wo) Company of the CCBA, at 751 Clay Street in San Francisco. He became a community leader in a larger Chinatown setting. In 1875 Yee Gow Jung, at age nineteen or twenty, arrived in Elko to work at his uncle's store, Wa Lung [Wah Lung] and Company, and eventually took over the business.[38] He had earned enough money to make two trips to China, one in 1890 and the other two years later. By 1896 Yee Gow Jung had moved to San Francisco to work for Kwong Wa Cheung [also spelled Quong Wah Chung] and Company at 730 Sacramento Street because business was on the decline in Elko.

Members of the Yee clan continued to own property in Carson City in the area of Third and South Valley Streets. In the 1950s Lim Yee had a residence at 421 E. Third Street, and Frank Yee of San Francisco owned land on South Valley between Third and Fourth Streets (block 22, parcels E and D). Through the clan system, they all probably helped each other in the purchase of property, shipment of goods, and other financial matters.

*   *   *

Truckee (former Coburn's Station), Nevada County, California, exemplified another strategy for ousting the Chinese and publicized the "Truckee Method" of forcing employers to fire their Chinese workers, persuading Euro-American merchants to refuse to sell to Chinese, and boycotting Chinese and non-Chinese who employed Chinese. However, violence was a part of the Truckee movement that allowed the town to claim success as the Chinese population there dropped to just two in 1900.

The discovery of gold led the Chinese to settle in Nevada County around the 1850s. The 1852 census showed 3,396 Chinese in the county, primarily in towns such as Grass Valley, French Corral, North San Juan, North Bloomfield, Washington, and Nevada City. By the early 1850s Washington (formerly called Indiana Camp) had attracted not only Chinese miners but also Chinese cordwood cutters, who sold firewood in Nevada City, the closest large town. Nevada City's Chinese Quarter, with its association houses, brothels, gambling halls, opium dens, and other recreational places, was also the main recreational area for these Chinese, but it was the town of Truckee, located near the California-Nevada border and the Tahoe Basin, that flourished as a Chinese lumbering center (Hagaman 2004). When gold was discovered in Coloma in 1848 and silver in Virginia City in 1859, a road was needed to bring miners into the area and to ship the ore out. In 1846 the infamous Donner Party had blazed the trail into the area that became known as Truckee.

Truckee was the first major stop along the CPRR after crossing the Sierra Nevada. Like Carson City, it was a commercial hub and involved in logging. In 1863 a small water sawmill was built on Coldstream Creek near Donner Lake. In 1865 logging became more widespread. By 1866 Euro-Americans settled there, and the Chinese soon followed. The Truckee Lumber Company, established in 1867 near Donner Lake, was a major supplier of railroad ties and bridge timber for the CPRR and developed one of the large lumber enterprises in the area. In October 1867 the CPRR construction team had reached the area, and because of the delay in the completion of two bridges, it probably was not until December 1867 that the workers moved into Nevada (Huffman, 1995). Other logging firms were established primarily to service the CPRR, other railroad lines, and the mines in the region.

By 1868 Truckee had 173 buildings, of which sixteen were Chinese shops, one "Oriental Restaurant," various gambling halls, brothels, opium dens, and, as was typical, twenty-five Euro-American saloons. The June 16, 1875, edition of the *Truckee Republican* claimed that all the lumber and timber used to erect homes and buildings in Nevada originated in the Truckee area. Much of the timber was used for mining and railroad and community housing as well. The town grew rapidly as a CPRR railroad station that linked east and west. According to an observer reporting to the *New York Times* (June 28, 1869), the town had two thousand people, a newspaper, and a theater.

Truckee's Chinatown attracted the Chinese working "in the mountains." About one-fourth to one-third of the men were married, but their wives lived either in China or a large Chinese community, such as nearby Wadsworth or Sacramento or San Francisco. The wealthier ones might go to Marysville, California, for entertainment in the town's larger Chinatown and three resident Chinese opera companies, or to Sacramento or San Francisco, with their large urban Chinatowns and recreational establishments. Since Truckee and Reno were closer, it was easier to travel there by train, stagecoach, or wagon.

Due to the depletion of placer gold by 1870, there were 408 Chinese and 1,179 Euro-Americans in Nevada County (Census 1870). Because they were so visible and constituted 35 percent of the population, the popular perception was that they overran the town of Truckee. According to Michael Goldstein (1988, 48, 57), in 1870 the Chinese made up 59 percent of the town's laborers, 39 percent of its total workforce, and by occupation: 93 percent of all woodchoppers, 100 percent of the vegetable gardeners and peddlers, 95 percent of its laundrymen, and 80 percent of its physicians. Although these figures decreased in the next decade, the proportion of Chinese laborers in Truckee rose from 59 to 69 percent. In 1870 only five of the seventy woodchoppers in Truckee were Euro-Americans, but by 1880 only one of 131 woodchoppers was Euro-American. The Chinese eliminated the need for "white labor," and the rallying cry against the Chinese began as Euro-American unemployment rose during the Depression.

By the 1870s Truckee's Chinatown on Front Street (originally called Main Street) near Second Street featured Fong Lee's large brick mercantile store, other stores (most notably Loon, Tang, Cheong and Company, Ah Chow's, Hi Chung's, Gee Bing's, and Quong Sing Lung), gambling dens, tailor shops, boot-making establishments, cigar and tobacco shops, opium dens, a red-light district, laundries, and a Zhigongtang.[39] When Yee Gee Peow, one of the local leaders of the Zhigongtang, died in April 1876, five hundred people, Chinese and Euro-Americans alike, from Auburn, Colfax, Reno, Carson City, and Virginia City, attended his elaborate funeral, thus demonstrating the regional ties and interethnic relations that had been established. The Zhigongtang probably was the most influential Chinese American organization in Truckee and had connections to lodges in San Francisco (Grand Lodge), Carson City, and Reno.

During the first ten years of Truckee's establishment, the Chinese played a major role in the town's development. Nevada County Assessor's records for 1868 and 1870 listed approximately thirty-five Chinese property owners, most notably store owners and herbalists.[40] Most of the buildings in Truckee were made of wood, but a few were made of brick and could withstand the numerous destructive fires. According to the *New York Times* (July 22, 1871), the loss after the May 1871 fire was "immense," but Sisson and Wallace's brick store (with the exception of the roof) escaped that fire; this led Fong Lee to decide that when he rebuilt his store, it would be of masonry on Front Street. In May 1875 fire severely damaged Chinatown, and Chinese losses were high. Loon Tung Chung and Company estimated their damages at $30,000, and like many Chinese businesses, they had been unable to purchase insurance. There was a campaign to drive the Chinese out of this prime location: anti-Chinese supporters collected money to buy up the Chinatown lots, many of which had been leased from Sisson and were uninsured (Ficklin 1997, 86).

At the same time, as soon as they collected enough funds, the Chinese bought property. They had done this for generations in China and still regarded land ownership as important. Nevada County property records indicated that Toy Hong paid Frederick Burckhalter, a banker, merchant, and fire insurance agent, $200 for lot 31 on East Main Street, and on February 1, 1876, Loon Tong Chung and Toy Hong (or Toy Wong) (not listed in the census in 1870 or 1880 as such) purchased lots on Main Street from Charles Crocker. Quong Sing Lung (b. 1840), a merchant, paid Charles Crocker $200 for two lots on Main Street West in Chinatown on September 23, 1876. Many land purchases were informally transferred in this era, so there is no accurate record of all property ownership.

Some of the Chinese leased or rented the land from E. J. Brickell (b. 1820 in Indiana), one of the major partners in the Truckee Lumber Company, who, according to Nevada County property records, had purchased a block of Chinatown from Charles Crocker in March 1879. Some leased timberland from individuals, such as Dr. William Curless, and, as was also the case in China, the trees that were to be cut were marked in an effort to prevent clear cutting or the denuding of the forests.[41] Undoubtedly, some Chinese tried to buy or lease timberland around this time.

The profile of the Chinese in Truckee indicates that they were very diverse in wealth and occupation. There were eleven grocers who were the wealthiest and most powerful Chinese men in town, with a total of $6,500 of real property (96 percent of the Chinese-owned land) and $10,200 in personal property. Four of the Chinese grocers reported their net worth: Ah Hugh (b. 1839) and Lee Sing (b. 1830) each were worth $1,000, while Sing Hong (b. 1842) was worth $2,000 to 3,000; Lee Fong, or Fong Lee, (b. 1835) was the wealthiest Chinese in town, with a worth of $3,000 in real estate and $5,000 in personal property (equivalent to some of the wealthy Euro-American lumbermen). Fong Lee was probably not his personal name but the name of his company, which had two partners. Fong Lee, a Truckee pioneer, was active in the buying and selling of property beginning in 1867 (Nevada County property records; Hagaman 2004). He provided Chinese laborers, served as an intermediary between the Chinese and non-Chinese communities, headed an association (probably the Zhigongtang), and had ties with the CCBA in San Francisco. After the 1871 fire he owned a fireproof brick house and lot on Main Street until he was forced to move. On March 18, 1873, he took advantage of a sheriff's sale to purchase more property. After the 1878 Chinatown fire, Fong Lee demanded that he be paid ten thousand dollars for his brick merchandising store and lot on the corner of Front and Second Streets, but the anti-Chinese Truckee "601" vigilantes disregarded the outrageous price tag. He also was rich enough to hire bodyguards when trouble broke out. All of these merchants and grocers undoubtedly provided merchandise and services to the large Chinese mining, logging, and railroad population in the county, and some, like Fong Lee, were labor brokers or men who hired Chinese workers for non-Chinese employers.

Truckee was also home to four physicians, two miners, eighteen laundrymen, nine cooks, one farm hand, seventy-six railroad workers, fourteen probable railroad laborers, three gardeners, one jeweler, one scavenger, two peddlers, one butcher, one maid, two women keeping house, one three-month old child, three opium house operators, twenty-two prostitutes, two gamblers, three unknown occupations, and thirty-two laborers (some might be employed in lumbering). The four doctors treated the Chinese and non-Chinese population alike, providing needed medical assistance for Chinese in the region, especially those in wood camps; two were known for their prevention and treatment of venereal diseases. Chinese doctors were often hired by Chinese associations (*tang*) to insure the good health of members, and they ranked in the upper echelons of the community. The prostitutes, gamblers, and opium houses offered recreational activities. In the 1870s there was a Chinese woodcutting operation called the Hop Who Company (probably Hehuatang) with two individual woodcutters, Ah Gao and Ah Jo, who were taxed for their property: the former for one wagon and two horses ($200) and the latter for one wagon and four horses ($200) (Lindstrom, 1993, 15).[42] These monetary figures indicated the wealth of the community leaders and their interest in "belonging" to the community through property ownership. If they had not been driven off, they might have contributed more to the development of Truckee.

Chinese laborers worked on the completion of the CPRR. Charles Crocker leased land to the Chinese, who erected Chinatowns along the railroad tracks; he later sold land to various Chinese individuals who had been successful in Truckee. In 1879 he sold some of the CPRR land to E. J. Brickell and others for $600 for a block of "Chinatown" (Nevada County property records). The largest land deal recorded was the 1883 purchase of two springs, one on seven acres of land south of the Truckee Land Association and one on seven acres of hill in back of Chinatown on the south side of the Truckee River, for a water system. The Yeck Yu Company, an organization of Chinese merchants of Truckee, paid $600 for this property. The Chinese in Truckee made enough money to invest in land and the

Truckee Republican (November 28, 1885) asserted that the Chinese owned real estate valued at more than $25,000. By 1886 they erected a water tank at the cost of several hundred dollars, but a year later, probably as part of the anti-Chinese movement, it was dynamited, the guilty party never discovered.[43]

Truckee became a supply center for the CPRR while it was under construction and remained so after the line was completed. Truckee Basin was one of the last regions in California to have the forest resources developed (Knowles 1942, 1–2). Between 1866 and 1889 the lumber industry was important to Truckee's economy. The CPRR utilized the timber resources beginning in October 1863 (Elston and Hardesty 1981, 94). In 1867 Joseph Gray and George Schaffer built a lumber mill on the Truckee River at Gray's Station, not far from Trout Creek, because they won the contract to assist in the building of the CPRR (Knowles 1942, 19). In 1868 their mill cut five million feet, providing many of the ties, telegraph poles, and snow-shed timbers for the railroad. The nearby mining community of Dutch Flat already used Chinese labor for cutting wood, so Schaffer probably hired Chinese workers from that area. Schaffer brought the first locomotive over Donner Summit on sleighs using thirty yoke of oxen, facilitating the transportation of logs. In 1871 he moved his operations to Martis Valley, three miles from Truckee, and like several other Truckee lumbermen, Schaffer became a target in the anti-Chinese movements that culminated in 1886, despite the fact that he had publicly announced that he had only seven or eight Chinese loaders working for him.[44] He was active in lumbering into the 1890s, when the short "revival" in lumbering ended as mining and railroad construction declined.[45]

Other early lumber companies, many employing Chinese, started in Truckee. The four mills of Daniel Proctor and the Excelsior Mill of Goshan and Sproul provided lumber for the construction of the CPRR until 1868.[46] In 1868 the CPRR had fifty carloads of railroad ties shipped daily from the Truckee Basin towns and 66 billion feet of timber from Truckee alone (Knowles 1942, 16; Huffman 1995; Ong 1985; Kraus 1969a; Saxton 1966; Lake 1994) Since the CPRR had employed Chinese to cut down trees and blast stumps, these men were available to other companies once construction of the railroad was completed.

As the smaller enterprises were forced to yield to the larger ones, the Chinese workers either were able to continue working or suffered from the change in ownership. The Truckee Lumber Company (TLC), the largest lumber company in the Truckee Canyon area, was an example of a large firm that took over a smaller concern with Chinese workers. At first the mines of Nevada and Utah looked to Truckee for their supply of timber, and the charcoal pits supplied fuel to smelt the ores, but then the railroads needed timbers and increased their demands by 1866, so the TLC got started with a saw-and-lumber mill near the Truckee River and became the largest lumber company in the Truckee Canyon area (Edwards and Irons 1883, 21). When Charles Crocker of the CPRR ordered approximately two million feet of bridge timbers, the company prospered. TLC had an office and warehouse in San Francisco near the freight yards, a planing mill and sash-and-door factory on the San Francisco waterfront (to supply ships), a plant in Salt Lake City near the Utah Central Railroad (providing access to Utah, Idaho, and Montana), and a warehouse and receiving yard near at the Rio Grande Western Railroad (now Denver and Rio Grande Western) terminus (thus, access to Colorado and Utah) (Goodwin 1960, 75). By 1867 TLC property holdings were extensive and included land in the Truckee area. By 1868 its lumber mill at Donner Lake had produced some ten thousand railroad ties and two million feet of bridge timber for the CPRR. In the 1870s the timber industry began to change as the demand for wood increased and larger companies arrived on the scene. Criticisms of the Chinese became more widespread.

In general, by the early 1870s Truckee's Euro-American residents regarded the Chinese with disdain. An occurrence in December 1872 was typical: Truckee's Chinatown drew the attention of the local posse when Ah Quee from North San Juan tried to recover prostitute Sin Moy for whom he had paid $500 (Ficklin, 1997, 60–61). A riot broke out in Chinatown, and Ah Quee was killed. The incident highlighted Chinese prostitution and eventually contributed to the passage of the 1875 Page Law that prohibited the immigration of prostitutes and, essentially, most Chinese women. For Euro-Americans, the incident also demonstrated that the Chinese had undesirable moral values.

In 1880 the leading citizens of Truckee's Chinatown had apparently changed. Of the 295 Chinese officially counted in the census, three were merchants, eleven were grocers, and a bookkeeper. There were two agents (probably labor contractors), sixteen cooks, eight children, one wife (the mother of four of the children), two servants, two physicians (not the same ones as a decade earlier), three laundrymen, two butchers, seventeen male railroad workers, ten female railroad workers (this may have been an error in the designation of sex or in the occupation), three peddlers, eight teamsters, nineteen laborers, twenty-three mill workers, thirty lumber pilers, and 136 wood choppers. Ah Dock (b. 1846) was an employment agent who had thirty-seven woodchoppers and twelve mill workers under his supervision (Census 1880). Based on this data, most of the workers were probably organized in groups. The Chinese constituted 69 percent of the town's manual laborers. The estimated range of the number of Chinese in Truckee in 1886 was three hundred to seven hundred, to a high of fifteen hundred, the latter estimate by the *Truckee Republican*. A merchant, possibly a relative of Fong Lee, was Yeat Fong, whose safe was robbed of $6,000, jewelry, and other valuables in 1880— another indication of the wealth of some of the inhabitants.[47] This kind of news story probably angered unemployed Euro-American workers who were jealous of the wealth the Chinese had accumulated. The recreational character of the town from the previous decade had disappeared—at least according to the census. The banking crisis of 1875–76 caused many to be delinquent in their taxes, including the formerly prosperous Ah Sing's Garden Company, but the main employment was still lumbering (Ficklin 1997, 94).

Michael Goldstein hypothesized that there was coexistence between the Chinese and Euro-Americans because jobs were plentiful in the early decade, and the *Truckee Republican* newspaper owner and editor Charles Fayette McGlashan (1847–1931), an American-born attorney and California state assemblyman, had not yet adopted his anti-Chinese stance. He advertised Chinese and Euro-American businesses in his newspaper (February 3, 1875): "Truckee's bath house is carried on by a celestial named Wah Lee, but he manages the establishment in true American style. Lovers of cleanliness, (this includes everybody) will be delighted with the arrangement of this bathing establishment if they give Wah Lee a call."

Anti-Chinese agitators became more vociferous between 1875 and 1886 as the economic situation declined. Scholars have debated the causes for the rise anti-Chinese movements, but economic competition was foremost in Truckee. New labor unions focused on "cheap Chinese labor" and stirred the passions of unemployed Euro-Americans. Racism, especially the eighteenth- and nineteenth-century pseudoscientific belief in the superiority of whites, contributed to the violence. By 1877 the Knights of Labor had unified many workers under the banner of ethnic, racial, and cultural hegemony. Since the Chinese were disenfranchised, the anti-Chinese rhetoric was an unchallenged issue binding various factions and classes in the political arena. In an era of Americans struggling to determine their own identity because of the large influx of immigrants from non–Anglo-Saxon countries, the "un-assimilating" Chinese were regarded as a prime target—people who preserved their cultural traditions and did not fit into the American "melting pot." Chinese exclusion acts and discriminatory laws that began in the 1850s demonstrated the success of these movements.[48] Chinese woodcutters were targeted as early as 1867–68 in the Carson Range.[49] Chinese were scapegoats for unemployed workers and newly formed labor unions and organizations, religious groups who resented "heathens in our midst," landowners who coveted Chinese-owned or -leased property, and politicians who knew that the Chinese could not vote and whose anti-Chinese rhetoric could rally people to their own cause. All of these factors came into play with the Chinese in lumbering and the situation in Truckee as anti-Chinese activists targeted employers of Chinese workers.

Sisson, Wallace, and Company (later Sisson, Wallace and [Clark] Crocker), a labor-contracting firm doing business at various places along the CPRR line with close contacts within the CPRR, had its headquarters in San Francisco and an office in Truckee and other major railroad stops.[50] The company, which had a brick building on Front Street as its company store, employed and supplied Chinese workers and built a "China Hotel" to house Chinese railroad workers (Nevada County property records). Sisson, Wallace, and Crocker was one of the largest operators in the Truckee River Basin in the 1870s; the company shipped, for example, between one thousand and two thousand bushels of Chinese-produced charcoal weekly to Virginia City in 1874. It also had orders for eight thousand bushels a day from mines in Utah (Knowles 1942, 23, 26). In 1872 they employed

more than 300 Chinese in the Truckee area to cut wood and make charcoal for
the CPRR and mines in Nevada and Utah (Elston and Hardesty 1981, 94–95).
They were a major West Coast dealer in Chinese goods, purchasing goods in
China and even having their teas packed in China, thus eliminating the expense
of a middleman. Their advertisement in the Truckee newspapers indicated that
in their Truckee store, they sold "a full assortment of China goods" as well as
American products and groceries, dealt in wood and charcoal, and provided
Chinese labor, even on short notice.

Sisson, Wallace, and Crocker was one of the top, if not the top, recruiter and
employer of Chinese workers for this region. By 1885 the firm had Chinese cutting thirty thousand cords of wood annually for the railroad company, employed
in "teaming," and provided services to restaurants, boardinghouses, hotels, and
laundries.[51] Sisson, acting as the Wells Fargo agent, also was a partner in the
Sisson, Egbert and Company stable in Truckee (Nevada property records). This
gave him an inroad into wagon freight transportation. By 1882 Sisson and Wallace (and later Sisson and Crocker) had extensive land holdings in the California
counties of Tulare, Nevada, Placer, Sierra, and Los Angeles; Benson in Cochise
County, Arizona Territory; Carlin in Elko County, Reno in Washoe County, and
Winnemucca in Humboldt County, Nevada; Evanston in Wyoming Territory; and
along the Southern Pacific Railroad line in Arizona, New Mexico, and Texas.[52]
Sisson's and Charles Crocker's deaths in 1888 brought an end of the firm's growth
and its large-scale employment of Chinese.

The other early large employer of Chinese in logging was German immigrant
Elle Ellen (b. 1823) (Coates, "Truckee's Notable Townspeople). In 1852 he operated a small sawmill in El Dorado County, California, but eventually moved
to Coburn's Station (renamed Truckee) in 1868. He had a young Chinese cook
working and living at his home (Census 1860–1870). This personal connection
probably contributed to his pro-Chinese laborer stance. In 1870 he had at least
fifteen Chinese woodchoppers working for him in the Trout Creek–Truckee area.
At one time he had patents on thirty-two hundred acres of timberland and ten
full sections of forestlands, and a shingle-and-planing mill (Truckee-Donner
Historical Society). He provided wood for the CPRR, Virginia City, Palisade,
Eureka, Ogden, and Salt Lake City. Like many employers, he differentiated pay
by the type of work. His woodchoppers received $1.50 per cord, and the wood
sold for $3.75 to $4.00 at the railroad station. He paid his seven Chinese loaders
$2.50 each per day for loading each carload of lumber.[53] This was much higher
than the highly publicized one-dollar-per- day average wage for Chinese labor.
According to the *Truckee Republican* (May 1, 1880), his Truckee Lumber Company
(TLC) shipped one carload of boxes to the west and four to five carloads of lumber
to the East daily. In 1883 Katz and Henry sold their mill, lumber, land, and Dog
Valley flume to Ellen's expanding TLC for $45,000 (Hummel 1969, 16). Katz then
worked for the TLC and probably brought his Chinese workers with him. The TLC

annually cut four million to six million feet of lumber and operated a seven-mile
V-flume to Verdi. In late 1886 Sisson sold part of the company's holdings to TLC,
primarily because he was getting old and troubled by the anti-Chinese agitators.
Approximately seventy Chinese worked for Elle Ellen and Sisson, Wallace, and
Company (Goldstein 1988, 17–18).

Sisson, Wallace, and Company and TLC became primary targets of Truckee's
anti-Chinese agitators. In 1886 anti-Chinese supporters in Truckee set a precedent
for how to deal with the Chinese problem, as detailed in Jean Pfaelzer's book,
Driven Out: The Forgotten War against Chinese Americans (2007). They "peace-
fully" got rid of the Chinese by boycotting Chinese employers, Chinese businesses,
Euro-American firms doing business with the Chinese, and Chinese workers.
This became known as the "Truckee Method." Although the anti-Chinese forces
claimed success, some Chinese eventually found their way back into the region,
but Chinatown was never the same as it had been. TLC was an early target, bow-
ing to anti-Chinese pressure and publicly discharging all of its Chinese workers
so that white workers could be hired.[54] Supporting the anti-Chinese movement,
the local newspaper never reported whether the Chinese workers were actually
replaced, but the company's decline began. In the 1890s the construction of the
Donner and Truckee Railroad held out some hope for the company because an
estimated 100 million feet of saw logs could be moved and made into fruit crates
(*Pacific Coast Wood and Iron* 1893, 477). The company encountered a series of
financial difficulties because of its practice of dumping sawdust and shavings
into the Truckee River. California Fish Commissioner George T. Mills ruled that
this and other lumber companies could not dump waste into the waterway any
longer.[55] By the 1890s the forests were denuded and the owners discouraged. TLC
closed its operations in the area in the early 1900s and in 1910 changed its place
of business to Oroville, Butte County, California (Nevada County property records). Eventually, the Truckee-Tahoe Lumber Company bought TLC, made its
headquarters on the site, and continues to prosper today under the management
of a fifth-generation lumberman.

There were several other notable employers of Chinese workers. Sixty Chinese
worked on the CPRR chopping wood, among other tasks. Perhaps in anticipation
of the 1886 anti-Chinese riots, the *Truckee Republican* (December 12, 1885) listed
other employers of Chinese workers: Richardson Brothers, headed by Warren
Richardson, hired twenty-five Chinese workers on a seasonal basis and in 1885
had some employed in their box factory; Pacific Lumber and Wood Company
(PLWC), under the management of E. A. Taft, employed ten Chinese loading
wood under a written contract; George Schaffer had approximately eight Chinese
loaders at his operations; and William Schaffer had four loggers and a cook at his
logging camp. In general, lumbermen with Chinese servants or workers in residence were more favorably disposed to hiring Chinese workers. As demonstrated
earlier, CTLFC was also a major employer of Chinese workers. Most employers

did not keep accurate records of their Chinese employees because anti-Chinese agitators might attack them and because they felt that Chinese names were incomprehensible. Headmen or contractors were often the only Chinese names on the books. What was important to employers was that a certain number of workers complete the tasks.

Sometimes there was a close relationship between the early lumber operators and their crews. Some of the Chinese lived next door to Euro-Americans because segregation did not take place until 1878, when a great fire resulted in the destruction of most of Chinatown, and the construction of a new Chinatown on the south side of the Truckee River was far away from the growing Euro-American population. At this time Truckee had fourteen Chinese millworkers and fifty-four woodchoppers. Only some of the woodchoppers lived in Chinatown, and those who did lived in households ranging from one to six men, while those who lived near Elle Ellen (and his family and Chinese cook) lived in one boardinghouse of nine men and a cook and another boardinghouse of twenty-one men. Lumber manufacturer James Henley from Connecticut had boardinghouses that accommodated twenty-seven Euro-American laborers, one Euro-American teamster, and thirteen Chinese laborers (who probably worked in lumbering). On a smaller scale of interracial housing, G. W. Naff, a twenty-year-old sawmill proprietor worth $2,500 in real estate and $3,000 in private property, lived with four Chinese laborers, Ah Sog (age nineteen), Ah Jim (age twenty-one), Ah Yeu (age thirty-two), and Ah Moy (age seventeen), a youthful crowd probably all involved in lumbering because they lived with a sawmill owner (Census 1870–1880). Consequently, the major occupation of the Chinese in Truckee was in lumbering and railroad construction and maintenance until the turn of the twentieth century. The ephemeral nature of the residents was not uncommon in the economic boom and bust towns of the American West. What was significant was the fact that multiethnic housing occurred, allowing the interaction among the various groups of workers, but this connection could not protect the Chinese from the anti-Chinese mobs.

The media played a prominent role in anti-Chinese agitation. The *Truckee Republican* published its first anti-Chinese editorial on January 1, 1875, which was followed by numerous other stories for the next decade or so. The main reason for the economic depression regionally was the decline of the Comstock's demand for lumber as mining began to decline in 1877 and silver production dropped to a low in 1881. Another factor: the CPRR and its spur lines were basically completed, and the railroad company had leased or sold its railroad land along the tracks to the Chinese and as towns expanded; hence, the Euro-Americans found Chinatowns on centrally located and desirable land. This was the case in Truckee.

When a suspicious fire broke out in the heart of Chinatown on May 29, 1875, causing the Chinese to incur $50,000 worth of damages, the Truckee "citizens," fearing future damages to their property, decided to try first to isolate the Chinese and advocated a forced removal of Chinatown to a location across the Truckee River.[56] The entire town was not against the Chinese, but the anti-Chinese contingent was exceedingly vociferous. The ambivalence of Truckee citizens was evident in the June 30, 1875, edition of the *Truckee Republican*, which praised the Chinese for their preparations for the Fourth of July celebration: "The spirit of generosity ever pervades the Chinese element. Ah Chow will furnish all the help that is wanted to do the work [for the celebration] and old Fong Lee will give all the Chinese confectionery that it is advisable should be eaten on this occasion."

The coexistence was too fragile to withstand the forces of racism and economic woes, however. As an economic depression of 1876 deepened, resentment against the "cheap laborers" led to more violence. By September 1876 anti-Chinese organizations, including the White Labor Club with 237 members, formed in response and demanded the expulsion of Chinese workers.[57] These were hard economic times throughout California, and the Comstock Lode in 1878 was heading toward its first major decline. Truckee's Caucasian League, organized in 1876 with three hundred members, decided to harass some Chinese woodcutters who were working for Joseph Gray by setting fire to their cabins at 1:00 A.M. and shooting the men as they escaped from the two burning cabins.[58] One Chinese man, Ah Ling, age forty-five, died; several others were wounded in what has become known as the 1876 Trout Creek Incident. The Euro-American men then set fire to other cabins, but no one else died. Seven men were involved and bound over for trial in Nevada City as a result of a reward posted by California Governor William Irwin (D, 1827–1886) and the publicity about the outrage (Pfaelzer 2007, 172–74). The *Territorial Enterprise* regarded the event as "one of the most cold-blooded and unprovoked murders ever recorded." In 1880 Gray sold his holdings to lumberman Elle Ellen and left.

Like Senator William Stewart (R-NV), McGlashan had been supportive of the Chinese presence in Truckee until he got into politics and eventually was elected president of the regional anti-Chinese organization in central California (McGlashan 1977). He represented the defendants in the Trout Creek case. There were passionate outpourings of sentiment in support of the arrested men. Public pressure developed to prevent prosecution from taking a harsh stance, and the major witnesses failed to appear. No one was found guilty, despite testimony from English-speaking eyewitness Ah Fook, a woodcutter and cabin mate of Ah Ling, who during the trial was unable to identify the culprits. The highly publicized trial in Nevada City resulted in the anticipated acquittal of the perpetrators because Chinese, although allowed to testify, usually had their testimony disregarded in cases against Euro-Americans because, as non-Christians, swearing on the Bible was regarded (by Americans) as meaningless to them. The story was carried in detail in neighboring newspapers, such as the *Gold Hill Daily News* (October 4, 1876) in Nevada and in numerous California newspapers, making this one of the most publicized criminal cases in Nevada County's history.

Anti-Chinese agitators wanted employers to fire their Chinese workers. P. Grace of Truckee, "who heretofore has always employed a large number of Chinamen," gradually fired all of his Chinese lumbermen on the premise that the trainloads of new immigrants traveling from the East Coast would replace them.[59] The idea of firing all Chinese workers was catching on and seemed to be a more peaceful way to get rid of the Chinese. Nevertheless, the Chinese continued to cut wood. The situation worsened in 1877 as the Comstock began to decline and the banking crisis spread.

Economic circumstances contributed to the growth of political movements. On August 31, 1878, the *Truckee Republican* reported that there was a 50 percent decrease in sawmilling from the previous season and that five local mills had shut down. Agitators attacked the lumber operators, including Oliver Lonkey, C. A. Bragg, G. N. Folsom, Warren and G. R. Richardson, L. A. Doan, E. Brickell, W. H. Krugger, and the Sisson, Wallace, Crocker and Company, for cutting trees on government land. The *Reno Evening Gazette* (February 21, 1878) estimated that these men had destroyed 33,045 trees valued at two dollars per tree in Nevada County alone.

The Caucasian League once again went into action; in November 1878 a mob of five hundred razed Truckee's Chinatown and ordered the Chinese to leave. The excuse they used was the threat of fire to their new businesses because of the wooden Chinatown shacks and the May 1878 Chinatown fire, which destroyed most of the buildings except Lun Yee Chung's fireproof store and cellars (K. Low; Ficklin 1997, 118; Pfaelzer 2007, 167–97). Fong Lee demanded fair payment for his brick store as the League forced Chinese to be relocated across the river and away from Front Street and the desirable center of town.

The answer, duplicated in many other towns, was to relocate Chinatown to a less desirable part of town. On November 9, 1878, the Caucasian League and five hundred supporters tore down Chinatown so that it could not be rebuilt. The Chinese were forcibly moved across the river, eastward from Bridge Street, where they remained until the mid-1880s. The Euro-American Safety Committee bought out the major stores, such as Quong Sing Lung and Wah Lee, persuaded D. H. Haskell, the land agent for the CPRR, to sell the land across the river for $600, and sweetened the deal for the Chinese by offering them free rice (K. Low).[60] The Chinese rebuilt their Chinatown on the south side of the river in compliance with these demands. Other local anti-Chinese incidents occurred, but the move toward a more significant action began to evolve.

The anti-Chinese movement began to have national support (Gold 2012). Criticisms against the Chinese ranged from their inability to assimilate, their heathen beliefs, and their sojourner mentality to their threat to the American economy (jobs, money sent to China, and other aspects). In the 1870s the labor leaders, especially Denis Kearney, called for an end to "cheap Chinese labor" (Sandmeyer 1973). His Workingmen's Party, established in 1877 on a platform of class warfare and anti-Chinese stance, and his rallying cry brought him national renown. Politicians quickly realized that this popular appeal aided in their election campaigns as well, and so they jumped on the bandwagon. Due to legal interpretations of the Constitution beginning in 1878, Chinese immigrants were ineligible to become naturalized citizens and therefore had no political power in the nineteenth century. The country was posed to adopt severe immigration restrictions, and the anti-Chinese issues were part of the planks for both political parties. The "Chinese Question" was covered in local newspapers, especially in 1880. As the *Morning Appeal* of July 16, 1880, expressed, "We cannot consent to allowing any form of servile labor to be introduced among us under the guise of immigration. . . . [It is] the duty of Congress to mitigate the evils already felt, and prevent their increase by such restrictions." President Chester A. Arthur's veto of the first Chinese exclusion bill (because—as proposed by Senator John F. Miller—it called for twenty years of exclusion) angered many people, especially those in labor and trade unions.[61] In Carson City, for example, anti-Chinese meetings were held from the beginning of March to the end of April with much fervor.[62] The *Reno Evening Gazette* (March 6, 1882) reported, "In Oakland, Stockton, Marysville, Nevada City, in fact everywhere, enthusiastic meetings were held." In April 1882 residents of San Francisco proposed a boycott of all Chinese shops, all people employing Chinese, and all patrons of Chinese businesses.[63] Newspapers in Nevada carried the story, and delegations of Nevadans attended the Anti-Chinese Convention held in San Francisco in April 1882.[64] In May 1882 Congress passed the Chinese Exclusion Act, prohibiting the immigration of Chinese labors (eventually defined as Chinese of all classes except merchants and their wives, travelers, and students) for ten years and declared Chinese ineligible for citizenship. The law went into effect in August 1882, but demands for stricter legislation with no time limits began.

The nationwide economic depression of 1884 to 1887 rekindled racial tensions. The Knights of Labor organized but found that they were unable to reach the loggers in the distant forests, so instead of calling a strike (labor's most powerful weapon), the organization adopted the anti-Chinese plank and drew wider support among workers in several occupations. Some violence continued, and the (Reno) *Nevada State Journal* (July 1, 1884) reported that a Chinese woodcutter had been killed (Schwantes 1997). In December 1885 the Knights of Labor in California, reminiscent of Unionville in January 1869, ordered all Chinese to leave San Francisco in sixty days or suffer forcible ejection.[65] This kind of activity was increasingly common in the heyday of the anti-Chinese movements. The *Morning Appeal* (December 5, 1885) argued that nonemployment of Chinese was not enough and that nonpatronization of businesses with Chinese connections should be added to the tactic. McGlashan became an ardent advocate for nonviolent anti-Chinese actions in the region for political and economic reasons.

In late November 1885 the citizens of Truckee held a mass anti-Chinese meeting. They wanted to find a legal way to be rid of the "Chinese menace." McGlashan pointed out that "white labor" had been displaced by Chinese and predicted a "showdown" if the violent members of the community had their way. He advocated the organization of a "safety committee" that would order employers to discharge their Chinese workers or face a boycott of their businesses. He reasoned that without any work, the Chinese would leave. Like several of the employers of Chinese workers, the anti-Chinese agitators of Truckee targeted Elle Ellen, along with Lewison, Day, Keiser, Schaffer, and Sisson, Crocker, and Company (formerly Sisson, Wallace, and Company). The agitators expanded their efforts beyond lumber owners and targeted hotel proprietors for employing Chinese cooks and, according to the *Truckee Republican* (December 12, 1885), received their promise to discharge their Chinese employees by January 1, 1886. They boycotted Chinese goods, particularly vegetables from Chinese gardens, and Chinese stores. The *Truckee Republican* (November 28, 1885) alleged that the CPRR had contracts for the cutting of forty thousand cords of wood that winter and that only the Chinese, who would earn $120,000, had been hired. On December 2, 1885, the anti-Chinese organization met at Hurd's Hall, above the Capitol Saloon on Front Street, to call for the total expulsions of the Chinese from the Pacific Coast. Other meetings followed, and the group decided on a peaceful, lawful boycott.

The anti-Chinese committee, reportedly with almost two hundred supporters, passed the following resolution: "Whereas; We, the citizens of Truckee, fully realize that a strong and uncontrollable current of feeling pervades this community because of the general displacement of white labor by Chinese . . . that we . . . have endeavored to [use] peaceful channels by urging the discharge of Chinese laborers, and our endeavors have been attended with abundant success."

The anti-Chinese *Truckee Republican* reported on January 30, 1886, that seven hundred Chinese were working in many positions at sawmills (except for superintendents, sawyers, and setters), factories, logging camps, restaurants, hotels and lodging houses, domestic positions, laundries, and other tasks in the Tahoe Basin—and advocated hiring Euro-Americans to replace them. They demanded that all wood contractors rescind their contracts for Chinese labor on or before January 15, 1886, and warned the Chinese to leave the woods in the vicinity of Truckee.[66]

In January 1886 the infamous "Truckee Method" was instituted in the form of boycotts of businesses that employed Chinese or traded with them, in an effort to drive the Chinese out of town without physical violence (Goldstein 1988, 49).[67] Intimidation and economic threats were used to persuade reluctant citizens to participate. Although this sort of pressure had been tried earlier in other locations, Truckee popularized the tactic. A secret committee of five led the anti-Chinese movement in Truckee. The alleged leaders, according to the *Truckee Republican* (July 3, 1886), were Dr. Harris and Mr. Atwood. The paper further stated on February 3, "Let the China lovers get on their side of the line that all may know them for what they are . . . teach little ones to abhor them. [Let] the first words that fall from a baby's lips . . . be 'Shame you China lover.'" The anti-Chinese faction also reacted to the *San Francisco Bulletin* (January 29, 1886) report that the Chinese arrivals were increasing from 3,014 in 1883 to 9,050 in 1885 because of collusion between immigration officials and Chinese immigrants using false papers. In response, Assemblyman Hugh McJunkin of California (served 1885–1886) proposed to arrest all of the Chinese for one day unless they procured passports to leave the United States—with the understanding that they would never return.[68]

Dr. William Curless of Truckee expressed public sympathy for the anti-Chinese movement, despite the fact that he employed many Chinese in his wood tracts, but he felt compelled to honor his contracts with the Chinese. In the *San Francisco Alta* (January 17, 1886), he stated that he was "so far in sympathy with the movement that if it be necessary that every stick of the timber on my land be burned in order to make the Chinese go, I shall not complain." Rhetoric and reality were at odds.

Protests by the CCBA in San Francisco, Chinese merchant organizations, Chinese American newspapers, and some American church groups had little, if any, effect. Fong Lee enlisted the support of the CCBA and its attorney, Colonel Frederick Bee, to persuade the lumbermen to honor the contracts, but Bee was ineffective. The Chinese had arms shipped to them through Tuck Chung in order to protect themselves. On January 11 the local banks called in the loans of Quong Sing Lung and Tuck Chung, thus forcing them to declare bankruptcy (Pfaelzer 2007, 184). The anti-Chinese faction in Truckee was determined to drive out the Chinese, and contrary to their "peaceful approach," they burned Quong Sing Lung's cabin at his wood camp at Donner Lake in February 1886.[69] Many of the Chinese workers were hired through Quong Sing Lung Company, a Chinese general merchandising store in Truckee that also furnished all kinds of Chinese labor to lumbermen (Edwards and Irons 1883, 180). The destruction of his cabin probably shocked many Chinese workers and convinced them not to return.

This movement had been intensified by the severity of a nationwide depression, the growth of Pacific Coast labor organizations, the 1885 act prohibiting contract labor, the denuding of forests in the Sierras, the news about the "flood" of new Chinese immigrants, and the decline of the Comstock and other mines in the West. A boycott of employers of the Chinese appeared, in the eyes of the anti-Chinese agitators, to be a peaceful way to get rid of the Chinese.

These actions drove most of the Chinese away from Truckee; McGlashan proudly heralded the actions as a victory. The reading public decided that the Truckee method of nonviolent boycotting of Chinese workers, employers of Chinese labor, and purchasers and sellers of Chinese goods had worked. By January 13, the Chinese population allegedly dropped from between five hundred and seven hundred down to ninety-seven (Goldstein 1988, ch. 5). Reno's *Weekly Nevada State Journal* (January 16, 1886) was more conservative and stated that three hundred of Truckee's Chinese lost their jobs and one hundred had left town. On

February 9, 1886, the *Morning Appeal* proudly pointed out that only one unnamed man in Truckee still hired Chinese workers. The 1886 California Anti-Chinese Non-Partisan Convention in San Jose, influenced by McGlashan, adopted the "Truckee Method" as a lawful, sensible, and fast way to drive out the Chinese.

According to the *Truckee Republican* (January 16, 1886), Sisson, Crocker, and Company and Ellen Elle decided to sign contracts with Chinese companies for the cutting of wood, most notably Quong Sing Lung, Yuen Chung Jan, Yuen Sing, Wing Hop Chuen Kee, and Tuck Chung. When the anti-Chinese agitators tried to force the Sisson, Crocker, and Company to cancel their contracts, the company responded, "We have written contracts with the railroad company which we are obliged to fill. These contracts [in writing] we sublet to the Chinamen. . . . If we were to break the contracts, we would not only lose some six thousand dollars advanced to the choppers . . . but also . . . face damages.[70] The Chinese responded in a letter to Sisson, Crocker and Company, F. Champion, Elle Ellen, and others, published in the *Truckee Republican* (January 16, 1886), that they intended to complete all contracts for wood cutting and would claim damages if the terms were violated. Elle Ellen adamantly refused to yield to the anti-Chinese agitators' demands. Chinese supporters were fighting a losing battle.

In June 1886, when the contracts ended, the boycott of Chinese workers in the logging industry was hailed as successful, but to insure the desired outcome, a fire that same month destroyed forty buildings in Chinatown, killing three individuals. The cause of the fire allegedly involved two Euro-American men smoking near the "rickety" wooden buildings in Chinatown. This, probably more than anything else, resulted in the Chinese decision to leave. The Anti-Chinese Boycotting Committee paid for the few remaining Chinese to go to San Francisco by train. In November 1886 the landlord of the remnants of Chinatown evicted all of his Chinese tenants.

By September 1886, the anti-Chinese committee pressured those who did business with the Chinese to force them to stop. This included William Carpenter and H. Monsure, who sold hogs to the Chinese; Frank Burckhalter, a grocer, leading banker, insurance broker, railroad investor, and lumber owner connected with the PLWC; the TLC's store; Mr. Wicks, and lumber baron Oliver Lonkey. Earlier, Lonkey had claimed that he employed only six Chinese at his Verdi box factory but was willing to discharge them if he could find replacements. He could not, so he continued to employ Chinese.[71]

Not all companies responded immediately to the pressure. The V. and G. H. Water and Flume Company announced in June 1886 that it would not hire any more Chinese at Lakeview.[72] The last holdout was Sisson, Crocker, and Company, so the anti-Chinese leaders called for a boycott of all of their businesses in California, Nevada, and Arizona. Sisson publicly yielded to the pressure. Sisson, Crocker, and Company eventually rescinded its contracts with Chinese agents Quong Sing Lung and Tuck Chong despite an estimated loss in excess of $6,000.[73]

In 1886 but before these developments Charles Crocker had suffered a serious head injury when his buggy overturned, a disability that eventually contributed to his death in 1888, so he was in no condition to fight the anti-Chinese boycott.

The problem was that some Chinese still remained in Truckee after the January expulsion deadline. The "Truckee Method" was not the complete success that McGlashan had reported. Harsher actions were required to drive the remaining Chinese from the area. In November 1886 William H. Kruger, representing the TLC, which owned the balance of the land where Chinatown was, decided that the Chinese would be evicted.[74] In the spring of 1887 the water tank constructed to bring water to Chinatown was blown up. In April 1887 James Van Buren allegedly assaulted Fong Lee by cutting off his queue and slashing his wrist while he was walking on Jibboom Street.[75] Van Buren pleaded innocent and, as in many court cases involving a Euro-American attacker and Chinese victim, he was acquitted and discharged. Thereafter Fong Lee hired two bodyguards to protect him, but this demonstrated that even a wealthy pioneering citizen of Truckee who was Chinese was not safe.[76] On October 1, 1888, the *Philadelphia Inquirer* reported that the Chinese in Truckee once again were ordered to leave but this time it was because one of them sold opium to an American Indian. In July 1889 Lonkey's sawmill at Prosser Creek, five miles from Truckee, was once again burned because of his continued employment of Chinese.[77] Most of the Chinese had left, and the few who remained could not get food, suffered from harassment, and could not enter stores in Truckee.

The logging industry in Truckee and the surrounding area also decline. Some of the large companies that had employed Chinese briefly prospered in the 1890s. In 1891, for example, the TLC cut 5.5 million feet of lumber; Oliver Lonkey, 3 million; and PLWC (based in Clinton, California), 5 million.[78] The CTLC still employed Chinese woodcutters in the Tahoe region. PLWC expanded its holdings into Northern California and probably sent some of its Chinese workers to these newer sites. By 1909 the seven big companies in the Truckee area ceased to cut timber in the Truckee basin because of the sluggish sales of wood and the denuded forests. In fact, one-half of the supply of virgin lumber in the continental United States had already been consumed (Compton 1906, 4). In 1910 there still were a few Euro-American lumbermen in the Truckee area, but they were not the powerful leaders of the community that the other men had been.

By 1900 only two Chinese out of a population of 2,050 residents lived in Truckee. The movement against the Chinese was now hailed as successful. The 1900 census manuscript showed that Japanese laundrymen, for example, had replaced the Chinese laundrymen, and that most of the Chinese in Nevada County, with the exception of Grass Valley and Nevada City, had moved away. The 1920 census manuscript for Nevada County listed several Chinese, who had arrived in the 1870s, scattered in small towns. The large Chinese population of the 1870s and 1880s had disappeared. By the 1910s and 1920s the once robust Chinatown of Truckee shrank, leaving a ranching population and limited job opportunities until recently.

Truckee gained national attention in its effort to solve their "Chinese problem." Between 1884 and 1886 Charles McGlashan represented Nevada County in the California Assembly, and his newspaper reflected his newly adopted anti-Chinese stance. He saw the displacement of white lumbermen and blamed the Chinese for taking away their jobs. He went up and down the state of California to rally support for his anti-Chinese cause. The significance of the "Truckee Method" was to inspire other towns to drive the Chinese out. During the first six months of his crusade many towns, including Boca, Prosser Creek, Cuba, and Clinton, organized anti-Chinese organizations. Nearby Placerville took the January 2, 1886, explosion in Chinatown as an excuse to force the Chinese from town. Other places took action to rid their towns of Chinese. Newspapers such as ones in Carson City not only criticized the Chinese employers in their towns but also in nearby towns, such as Genoa.[79] Congress was pressured to be more stringent in the nation's anti-Chinese immigration position. In response, Euro-American lumbermen rescinded their contracts with the Chinese, and employers fired their Chinese workers.

The campaign had some success and spread. Reno and Carson City citizens followed the Truckee events with great interest. Anti-Chinese organizations became very active throughout the state and targeted Chinese laborers. Carson City adopted many of the anti-Chinese policies, particularly the boycott of Chinese businesses and Euro-Americans who hired Chinese or patronized their businesses. A Carson City newspaper implied that the Chinese cook at the H. F. Dangberg Carson Valley ranch committed suicide because of the tensions resulting from the anti-Chinese movement. A *Carson Daily Independent* article (January 10, 1886) criticized the Chinese for depriving the United States of their spendable income because of their remittances to China. Shortly after the anti-Chinese meeting in Carson City, Reno started an anti-Oriental club, and the editor of the *Reno Gazette* (January 23, 1886) asserted that the Chinese in Reno were sending nearly $2,000 per month to relatives in China, thus threatening the local and national economy. Other newspapers repeated the allegation in various forms.[80] By February 1886 the charges against the Chinese in Nevada and other western states echoed each other.[81] The Knights of Labor publicized their investigation of "Chinese cheap labor" by saying that the Chinese did not have to be paid much because they had no family to support and spent only about seven dollars per month on rent and clothing and three dollars per month for food, while the Euro-American, who had a wife and children to support, spent fifty dollars per month as the average cost of living (W. W. Stone 1886, 2). They argued that the Chinese did not contribute to American development and prosperity, did not assimilate, and maintained their foreign ways, most of which were regarded as negative traits.

One of the charges against the Chinese was that they were sojourners, but how many of the ordinary workers could afford to make trips back to China, especially with the immigration laws that discriminated against Chinese workers? No records exist for Chinese workers from the Sierra Nevada, but elsewhere there were a few cases of some who could make the expensive trip back and forth. Jim Lane, a cook at Simpson's logging camp in the Olympia, Washington, area, was able to visit China for a year from May 1903 until April 1904 and could reenter on the basis of a debt of $1,000 or more owed to him.[82] Jim Boyd, aka Ng Shee Gim, was born in Taishan, had been a cook at a mill in Port Gamble, Washington, but eventually rose to the status of manager of the prosperous and influential Zee Tai Company in Port Townsend, Washington. He went to China several times, but after his departure in September 1914, he did not return within the prescribed two years, so in 1917 his Certificate of Residence (#45023) was cancelled, and he was ineligible to return to the United States.[83] Whether he intended to leave permanently cannot be determined, but since he had paid for the Certificate of Residence, he presumably intended to return to the United States. Jim Boyd and Jim Lane were fluent in English, but only Lane was readmitted to Seattle. Stories of being stranded in China were well known in the Chinese American communities.

Truckee's success was well publicized in both the *Morning Appeal* and *Reno Gazette*. Many towns in California, Nevada, Arizona, Idaho, and New Mexico, to name a few, formed anti-Chinese organizations in response to the discrimination movement and growing unemployment. The allegedly peaceful policies of the "Truckee Method" were attempted. Some places were not interested in the "Truckee Method," however; despite McGlashan's lectures in Nevada City and Grass Valley on the success in Truckee, the two towns did not support the anti-Chinese movement. The Chinese population in general declined nevertheless when stricter national exclusion acts became law. Chinese were no longer as visible nor "took away" so many jobs because of their shrinking population. After the 1890s depression, the Knights of Labor collapsed, thus silencing one of the most vociferous anti-Chinese groups, but newly formed unions picked up the banner.

Other ideas to get rid of the Chinese were circulated. In March 1886, for example, the Morrow Bill proposed that Chinese immigrants could not visit China for more than two years; otherwise, they would forfeit their right to return.[84] The Euro-American racist attitudes against the Chinese were heightened, and more anti-Chinese debates followed in regional and national newspapers and political forums.

The "Truckee Method" raised issues on a regional and national level. The controversy over the Chinese was expanded to reassess the treatment of African Americans and the limited civil rights they had gained with the passage of the Fourteenth Amendment (Maltz 1994). Additional laws were passed and discriminatory policies adopted (Hing 1993). In 1888 the Scott Act prohibited Chinese laborers from ever entering the country. In 1892 the Geary Act extended the exclusion of Chinese laborers for another ten years (renewed in 1902 and made "permanent" in 1904) and required Chinese to have certificates of residence and certificates of identification by 1894 or be subject to deportation regardless of their place of birth. Senator William M. Stewart, who had supported Chinese immigration and legal protection for all immigrants in 1870, remarked shortly before the 1892 renewal of the Chinese exclusion act: "There was a time when there was great diversity of opinion on the question of Chinese immigration to this country, but I think there is practically none now. The American people are convinced that the Chinese can not be incorporated among our citizens, can not be amalgamated, can not be absorbed, but that they will remain a distinct element" (quoted in Gyory 1998; Gold 2012).

However, newspaper reports in subsequent years indicated that some continued to prosper in the Lake Tahoe Basin's lumber industry well into the 1890s despite the anti-Chinese incidents, lack of work, social tension, and newly increased charges for services. Goldstein interpreted the boycott of Euro-American employers of Chinese workers not so much as an attack against the Chinese but as a battle between local and outside (Sisson, Crocker, Elle) business interests during a period of economic decline, with the Chinese caught in the middle (Goldstein 1988, 55).

The anti-Chinese hostility resulted in the loss of Chinese population in Carson City and Truckee, but their results differed. Carson City and its media were not as biased against the Chinese. The *Morning Appeal* published the names of the signers of the "Anti-Chinese Covenant" so that its readers knew what positions people took.[85] By August 1886 the newspaper denounced the practice of labeling people "pro-Chinese" as being similar to the sentiments surrounding the Salem witch trials. Respected Carson City business leaders supported the return of many of the Chinese, but its Chinatown was never as full of vitality as in earlier decades. Quong Hing and Company was an example of a clan business that transitioned into the early twentieth century even when the leadership changed clans. Truckee's Chinatown essentially disappeared, partly because McGlashan, his newspaper, and his supporters continued their anti-Chinese rhetoric. McGlashan's ambitions utilized the racial tensions to promote his political campaigns. Staunch supporters of Chinese workers in Truckee either died or left the area. The decline in the need for lumber contributed to the Chinese departure from these two logging centers. Only those who could find other occupations or branch out in a different direction (like Quong Hing) remained. Small companies and individual timber barons yielded to larger operations with expensive equipment, so the manual labor that the Chinese had provided was no longer needed. Newly opened forests in the Northwest and Canada attracted many who had been involved in logging in the Sierra Nevada. Mining and railroad construction concerns, the largest consumers of wood products, changed as well. The urgency for wood was simply not as great in this part of the West.

CHAPTER 4

Of Wood and Mines

The gold rush in California triggered new discoveries of mining areas in neighboring states of Nevada and Oregon. Mines needed wood products and triggered the beginning of large-scale western logging. An examination of some of the Nevada counties that were involved in mining and logging provides detailed insights into Chinese workers, the environment, timber barons and their support of the Chinese, lumber companies, and opposition to the Chinese involved in this new industry. As a result, this research dispels some popular myths, such as the antagonistic relationship between French Canadian lumbermen and the Chinese, the marital status of Chinese workers, and the unrecognized importance of those Chinese servants who were regarded as trustworthy by timber barons. As the mines declined, the need for Chinese workers in logging diminished.

Between 1850 and 1851 parts of Utah Territory that became Nevada in 1864 were settled. The newcomers quickly considered the problem of how to get wood. "The First Records of Carson Valley Utah Territory," written in 1851, acknowledged the importance of lumbering and stated in Article 11: "All timber shall be Considered *common property*, except shade trees or trees kept or planted for ornament, and all the citizens of Carson Valley Shall be free to use as they may think proper [*sic*] any timber contiguous to their claims reserving _____ acres of wood land to individuals or companies who shall erect saw mills" (J. Stone n.d.). At first lumberjacks served primarily the agricultural and ranching communities but with the advent of mining riches, "green gold" became an integral part of the gold and silver mining. Mines used most of the early wood products but houses, streets, and sidewalks, fields, and flumes and sluices also were major consumers (Hittel 1863, 306; Buckley 2000; Walker 2001, 186).

Shortly thereafter in 1853 Thomas Knott reportedly established the first sawmill on the West Fork of the Carson River in Carson Valley, and by 1859 Henry Gregory and James Riddle, both of San Francisco, established the first efficient steam-powered sawmill, which cut eight thousand to fifteen thousand board feet of lumber per day, selling at an average of seventy dollars per thousand feet, with a working force of one hundred men on their 650 acres of timberland at Mill Creek (present day Incline Village, Washoe County), some two-and-a-half miles west of Carson (Dangberg 1972, 51; *New York Times*, May 19, 1860; Thompson and West 1958, 541–42). Eventually, there were three mills on Mill Creek that cost a total $60,000 to build. Gregory's Mill was the largest. By 1860 sawmills in California, primarily around the Sierra Nevada, numbered more than three hundred and began to meet the demands of the mining industry, but more were needed. Douglas County soon had nine sawmills, operated by steam, to cut the logs harvested from the South Lake Tahoe Basin.[1] By 1866 there were fifteen sawmills north of Carson City to supply the Comstock (Hill 1987). Sawmills were moved from one place to another in order to be close to the source of timber and, if possible, near a body of water for transporting the logs. Obviously, it was expensive to build sawmills but the financial gains were great, and San Francisco–New York venture capitalists often were willing to take the risk and invest in "green gold." Other sawmills sprang up in neighboring areas to support the Comstock.

Euro-American miners were not interested in logging work until the mines declined, so in the beginning timber farmers turned to experienced French Canadians, Maine loggers, and the Chinese, who had some experience and were willing to accept almost any kind of employment. Chinese had moved into Nevada around 1851 when the Mormons hired fifty Chinese workers from San Francisco to dig irrigation ditches in Genoa, Douglas County, for farming, a centuries-old type of work that Chinese farmers knew. Soon a Chinatown, consisting of four dwellings located behind the Reese Hotel between Nixon and Fifth Streets, developed, and the Chinese sought new placer mining sites. Chinese miners were allowed to work at placers that Euro-Americans considered to be too hard to work, so they settled in nearby Dayton (originally called Chinatown) and Johntown (from the term "John Chinaman"), constituting three of the major settlements in the region at the time. The 1860 census for Carson County, part of Utah Territory, enumerated twenty-one Chinese, sixteen of whom were in the laundry business (primarily washing for clothes for miners). The 1870 census listed no Chinese miners in Storey, Douglas, Lyon, Washoe, or Ormsby Counties, but newspaper reports mention Chinese working in placer mining in the region (Chung 2011, ch. 3; "Chinese Miners in Nevada," San Francisco Bulletin, November 22, 1879; Census 1870–1880).

Genoa, located at the foot of the Sierra Nevada, was the largest town in western Utah Territory at that time and an important rest stop for travelers to and from the California gold fields. The Mormons built a sawmill to process logs; soon, rough lumber sold at one hundred dollars per thousand feet (Miller 1926, 388). Census records do not show any Chinese living in Genoa until 1880, but James W. Haines, who was born in Quebec, Ontario, in 1826 and moved to Nevada by 1863, was a long time resident of Genoa, an influential state senator serving from 1864 to 1871 and 1879 to 1883, and a timber farmer who hired Chinese workers, including Chinese cooks for his family, according to the 1880 and 1900 census (Douglas County tax records, 1860s; NVSHPO). It is probable that these early timber ranchers who had loyal and trustworthy Chinese servants used the informal Chinese network (*guanxi*) system to find Chinese workers. In 1868 Haines tried to claim that he invented the V-flume, but the court recognized that it had been used in California earlier. Haines's V-flume was 32.5 miles long and ran from Alpine County, California, to Empire City, Nevada, where the logs were loaded onto the train bound for the Comstock (Straka 2007). Local residents recall Chinese living in Genoa, but it was not until 1880 that eighteen Chinese (eight cooks, five laundrymen, one brick-and-stone mason, and four with unknown occupations) were counted (NVSHPO 1880). Some who were not counted probably worked in the isolated Daggett Creek/Heavenly Valley area, which was relatively difficult to access and where many Chinese logging camps have been discovered. Chinese merchants in Carson City provided goods to them. In 1900 Genoa still had three Chinese residents—two cooks and one laundryman—ranging in age from forty-four to fifty-seven, but no laborers or lumbermen. One of the cooks, Yat (Ya) Ah (b. 1848, immigrated 1868, married 1878), had lived in Genoa since 1880 (he had gone back to China to marry in 1878 but left his wife there). He lived alone next door to the Henry Beck family (miller) and James Campbell family (hotel business). The other cook, Les Giren (b. 1856, immigrated 1868, married 1875) worked for the Haines family, who lived next to lumberman Henry Burham and family. Both cooks were fluent in English and had saved enough money to visit China to be married before returning to the United States. In 1910 a fire destroyed Genoa's Chinatown and the downtown business district (Koval 1991). The 1910 and 1920 census did not list any Chinese. As was the case with many small, western logging towns, the Chinese had departed from the area.

By 1859 miners moved toward present-day Silver City and finally Gold Hill and Virginia City, Storey County, Nevada. The latter two towns made up the Comstock Lode, one of the richest mining discoveries in North American history. Because of the silver discovered there, Nevada was known as the Silver State, and the Chinese called it *Yinshan* (Cantonese, *Gheum shann*, Silver Mountain). California was called *Jinshan* (Cantonese, *Gum shan*, Gold Mountain). The lode ran for about four miles along the eastern slope of the Washoe Range at the foot of Mount Davidson, where the two towns of Virginia City and Gold Hill developed. The potential for "instant wealth" attracted many, but the local mining regulations forbade the Chinese from mining on the Comstock.

San Franciscans contributed to the growing anti-Chinese sentiment, and California's anti-Chinese mining resolutions and laws influenced miners in Nevada. As early as 1852 the California Legislature passed the Foreign Miners Tax for all miners who were not citizens of the United States. This law was aimed at the Chinese in an effort to discourage them from mining. Many California mining towns prohibited the Chinese from staking mining claims but did not prevent them from purchasing claims that had been previously owned and/or abandoned by non-Chinese miners or through preemption (required documents filed in county recorder's office with markers placed on boundaries of claims; purchase was not necessary). In 1852 miners in Shasta County, California, tried to drive the Chinese out; other mining communities followed suit. As the gold diminished in California, miners moved east into Nevada and brought their anti-Chinese prejudices with them (Chung 2011).

The earliest recorded anti-Chinese stance in Nevada (Utah Territory) occurred in 1859, when the Gold Hill miners adopted a resolution prohibiting the Chinese from owning a mining claim in the district (Mining Laws, 1880, 14, p. 509). Gold Hill was on the south side of Mount Davidson at the head of Gold Canyon, some six thousand feet above sea level and just one mile south of the boomtown of Virginia City. The two towns constituted a mining center that "spawned a network of almost fifty towns that promoted capitalist goals" by delivering its gold and silver to market (Moehring 1997, 362). The Gold Hill resolution prevented the Chinese from mining on the Comstock, but it did not stop them from mining in nearby areas, such as Six-Mile Canyon, near Dayton, that allowed anyone to engage in placer mining; they could seek other occupations as well.

Chinese went into the service industries as cooks, laundrymen, and servants, and into a wide variety of "professions," including physicians, dentists, and gamblers, and lumbermen. In 1870 the U.S. *Compendium of the Ninth Census* (table 9, 256) stated that there were 210 Chinese in Gold Hill and 539 in Virginia City. The larger figures differed from the 1870 federal census manuscript, which only can be regarded as symbolic rather than accurate.

The vast increased population in Nevada arose from new mineral discoveries and created a growing demand for wood—not only for the mines but also to supply the population in general.[2] The Comstock's demand for timber and lumber for underground support tunnels, fuel, equipment, dams, supports to hold up mountains, and community development seemed insatiable. In the late 1860s mining engineer Phillip Deidesheimer's invention of the square-set timbering

Table 4–1. Chinese Population in Nevada and Storey County, 1860–1890

Date	Chinese in Nevada	Chinese in Storey County	Chinese Men	Chinese Women
1860	23	0	23	0
1870	3,162	750	647	103
1875*	—	1,362	1,258	104
1880	5,416	619	577	42
1890	2,833	245	—	—

* Based on federal census manuscript data by race and birthplace; figures differ from U.S. census summary, which were usually lower, and Nevada State Historic Preservation Office database and in the 1875 Nevada (state) census.

system for underground mining to make the mines safer required pine, white fir, or (preferably) red fir logs seven feet long. Square-set timbering became a standard for the next fifty years and increased the demand for lumber.

Grant Smith (1943, 247) wrote that between 1859 and 1880, "the Sierras were devastated for a length of nearly 100 miles to provide the 600,000,000 feet of lumber that went into the Comstock mines, and 2,000,000 cords of firewood consumed by the mines and mills up to the year 1880." A single mine could use six million feet of lumber in a year (Miller 1926, 388). The famous Yellow Jacket Mine Fires of 1869 and 1873 required quick reconstruction in order to keep the mine prosperous. The 1875 Great Fire burned thirty-three city blocks of Virginia City to the ground— including four hundred businesses and one thousand homes. The prosperity in the town permitted a quick rebuilding that increased the demand for wood, and timber ranchers searched for new sources and workers. In 1876 the Comstock used an estimated 2.2 million feet of lumber per month for mining and milling.[3] At its height between 1874 and 1879, there were four thousand miners on the Comstock, and their jobs required wood products. Eight hundred million feet of lumber was used for shafts, winzes, drifts, tunnels, crosscuts, stopes, and upraises.[4]

As Dan De Quille, editor of the Virginia City's *Territorial Enterprise* and author of *The Big Bonanza*, said, "The Comstock Lode may truthfully be said to be the tomb of the forests of the Sierras. Millions on millions of feet of lumber are annually buried in the mines, nevermore to be resurrected and sixteen inches wide, thus expanding the urgent need for wood" (quoted in J. Stone n.d.). He estimated that eighty million feet of timber and lumber were annually consumed on the Comstock. Most of the timber used was yellow pine, white and red fir, and some cedar.

Established in 1873, the Carson Tahoe Lumber and Flume Company provided much of the lumber for the mines on the Comstock. This lumberyard was located just south of Carson City. The Nevada State Railroad Museum is now at this location. (Source: Nevada Historical Society)

Partnerships were sought with potential lumber barons (DeQuille 1876, 174). There was strong economic connection between San Francisco and the Comstock. Newspaper owner Allen C. Bragg (b. 1848) wrote, "San Francisco was largely built up on Comstock money" (Bragg 1911, 78). Many of the leading Nevada figures came from or settled in San Francisco and the Bay Area and would have known how to find Chinese workers. Chinese in many different occupations often visited San Francisco, the "capital" of the Chinese in America, and would have heard of the new job opportunities in the woods (Liu 1981; Chen 2000).

Chinese miners were not hesitant to cut wood when they needed it. One notable example occurred in 1857 in Coarsegold, California, and probably exemplified what took place around the mid-nineteenth century elsewhere. The miners needed wood for the sluice boxes and asked the sawmill owner, C. P. Converse in Crane Valle (present day Bass Lake), for lumber. He was unable to supply the wood because his oxen needed feed, but he allowed the Chinese miners to cut his trees and bring the logs to the mill, which they did, by hand. Once Converse had cut the logs, the Chinese shouldered the loads of wood, walked the fifteen miles to their placer site, and within a day or two were working with their new sluice boxes ("Lumber Played a Key Role"). They could have done the same in the vicinity of the mines in the Sierra Nevada.

The Chinese were among the several hundred men cutting and hauling wood. By 1862 woodchoppers stripped the area surrounding the Comstock of wood, mostly stunted pine, so the nearest source of fuel wood was in the Palmyra district in Lyon County, about eight miles southeast of Dayton, and in Washoe and Douglas Counties (Miller 1926, 388). The price of the wood varied according to the quality, available quantity, and time of year. The *Sacramento Union* (March 17, 1860) reported that lumber cost $100 per thousand board feet in March 1860 and $300 per thousand a month later. Cordwood sold for $4.25 per cord at this time (Ettinger 1995). In the summer months of 1863 the price of cedar varied from $13 to $18 per cord, while pinyon pine was $16 to $18 per cord. In the winter the price rose to $20 to $30 per cord on the Comstock.[5] On November 8, 1865, the *Gold Hill News* reported that the Comstock had spent $640,000 on timber for the mines. That year the cost of fuel wood consumed was $15 per cord.[6] The teamsters charged $200 for hauling a load to Virginia City, eighteen miles from the nearest sawmill in Carson Valley.[7] With these high prices, the "green gold" phenomenon had begun.

Prior to 1870 and the completion of the VTRR, the Chinese in Virginia City dominated the retail fuel wood market and displaced the American Indians who had played a major role in the trade earlier. In these early years, Chinese wood peddlers were a familiar sight on the streets of the Comstock just as they were in San Francisco and other western towns. They carried the wood on their backs or balanced on long shoulder poles, and when they were more prosperous, they used a mule or donkey to carry the firewood. The *Mining and Scientific Press* (November 19, 1864) observed that on a daily basis "the Chinese drivers goaded troops of donkeys over the steep slopes of the nearby Palmyra district and through El Dorado Canyon; at nightfall the little beasts were driven back to Virginia City . . . with a burden of sticks weighing from 100 to 200 pounds" (Magnaghi 2001; Blackburn 1980; James 1998; Balibrera 1965). The number of Chinese engaged in the wood trade on the Comstock dropped from 150 in 1868 to sixty-six in 1870 to only eight sawyers and four peddlers in 1880 (Magnaghi 2001, 126). The decline in Comstock mining coincided with new job opportunities in railroad construction, namely the VTRR and CCRR, and logging.

Eliot Lord (1925, 50) stated that in 1866 the 120 Chinese woodcutters sometimes earned more than $300 per day and usually sold wood at $33 to $48 per cord. During the severe winter of 1866–67, Chinese wood peddlers, who dug out roots from under six feet of snow, sold the wood for $1.75 to $2.50 per donkey load, or $60 per cord.[8] This kind of economic success was not welcome news to the unemployed or underemployed in Virginia City. Many Euro-Americans ostracized, ridiculed, tormented, and discriminated against the Chinese, but some of the powerful financial leaders of the community recognized the need for Chinese labor and afforded them some protection during the rising tide of anti-Chinese activities beginning in 1860.

Supply and demand and harsh winters could drive the prices up or down. In 1867 Storey County's Gould and Curry Mill reported producing 11,442 of cord wood at the cost of $168,830, with the average price of $14.72 per cord, and 172,857 feet of lumber at a cost of $3,725, with the average price per thousand at $42.40 (Nevada Appendix to Senate, 1867, 79). During the summer of 1869 Chinese lumberman Kwong Toa alone collected seven hundred cords of wood for future sale. A scarcity of wood closed the mines and mills on the Comstock in January 1868.[9] By the winter of 1868 the price resumed at an average of $1.50 per donkey load, which provided sufficient fuel for six fires in a common parlor stove. On September 29, 1869, the *Territorial Enterprise* credited the Chinese woodcutters for saving the Comstock's population from freezing to death.

By the 1870s Virginia City had more than seven thousand inhabitants and was a bustling mining town. The cost of hauling wood, fuel, and lumber to the Comstock Lode from the Carson and Washoe Valleys was so exorbitant that some mine owners relocated their ore mills to the Sierra foothills (Knowles 1942, 8). The famous Ophir Company relocated to the two thousand acres of woodland it owned close to its reduction mill near Washoe Lake at the foot of the Sierras. This operation employed nearly one hundred men in lumbering (cutting, hauling, preparing the wood, producing wood charcoal, and performing other related tasks).[10] During its boom years between 1860 and 1882 the Comstock produced $293 million of gold and silver. It took a lot of wood to make this possible.

Although the census takers found it difficult to count men in lumbering because of their mobile work camps, some Chinese in other occupations with their residence in Virginia City were enumerated as shown in table 4–2.

Table 4–2. Chinese Involved in Lumbering in Virginia City, Storey County, 1870

Total Number of Chinese in County: 691 (U.S. Census figure: 749)
Total Males: 589 (U.S. Census figure: 647)
Total Females: 102 (U.S. Census figure 103)

Woodchoppers	Age	
Ah Sung	30	
Si Sling	25	
Ah Gin	20	
Ah Ben	28	These four men lived at #45 with wood packers.
Sam Que	28	
Ah Jing	24	
Sam Lee	28	
Ah Foo	24	These first four men lived at #47 with wood packers.
Ah Wan	35	Lived with other Chinese in nonlumber jobs.
Fing Choo	33	
Su Eng	34	
Lee Mong	40	
Jonathan Quong	50	
Quang Lee	36	
Sam Sing	30	
Lee Yup	39	
You Fast	30	
Sam Slam	44	
Chu Muck	44	
Sa Hung	56	
Chung Wa	46	
Lee Gee	30	
Ah Look	28	
See Poon	36	
See Ying	33	These sixteen men above lived at #53 with two carpenters.
Mock Poo	30	This man lived at #56 with wood packers and two wood peddlers.
Total:	26	woodchoppers
Average age:	33.88	

This census record showed that most of the men were between age thirty-two and thirty-three and lived in groups with similar jobs. The average age of the wood packers was one year younger than woodchoppers, and all of the men lived in Chinatown with merchants, cooks, "harlots," and gamblers as neighbors. All thirty-nine wood packers could read some English and therefore could act as intermediaries between the Chinese and Euro-American communities. They lived together in groups (with only one exception), so there were twelve households of Chinese wood packers in Virginia City. No Euro-American wood packers, wood peddlers, or wood sawyers, or any Chinese wood packers lived in other locations in 1870. There were only four Euro-American woodchoppers, so the Chinese dominated this occupation in Storey County. However, there were 196 Euro-American carpenters and three Euro-American wood dealers in the county. Euro-Americans also held all of the top positions, such as supervisors, in the lumbering companies.

Table 4–2. (*continued*)

Wood packers	Age	
Chi Wing	30	
Ci Ching	28	
William Poor	24	These three men lived at #45.
Yep Lee	22	
Chock Ti	24	
Ring Chi	30	These three men lived at #46.
Ah Funk	24	
Ah Bart	28	These two men lived at #47.
Ah Foo	33	
Sam Sling	24	
H. Sling	22	
Ah Sole	20	
Lee Sing	28	
Chang Feu	29	
Ching Coo	22	
Ah Slam	30	
Lee Slam	40	
Ah Pooh	36	
Ah Hook	30	
Cum Tung	41	
Jim Humbold	29	
Ti Loy	38	These fourteen men lived at #54.
Ah Pan	48	
Ah Song	22	
Sup Geo	22	
Chung Lee	32	
Chu Mong	34	
See Lee	30	These six men lived at #55.
M. Chow	28	
Foo Choo	39	
Ah King	34	
Ah Yun	33	These four men resided together.
George China	30	
Sou Kee	30	
Gee Sip	33	
Ah Sung	30	
Gee Moo	36	
Sam App	30	
Jim China	28	These seven men lived at #56.
Total:	39	wood packers
Average age:	32	
Capenters	**Age**	
Jack Ping	39	
Bill China	34	These two men lived at unit #53.
Peddlers	**Age**	
Ah Chee	38	
Fuck Ching	28	These two men lived at unit #54.

Source: Nevada State Historic Preservation Office database; totals differ from U.S. Census figures.

Many of the Chinese who worked in the mountains returned to Virginia City between jobs because there was a large Chinatown there with an abundance of recreational facilities and activities, so these Chinese were counted in Virginia City. In the 1870s most of the Chinese lived in the main Chinatown, located in the vicinity of G, H, I, and Union Streets. A smaller, secondary Chinatown existed away from the center of town and closer to Gold Hill. The Chinatowns provided protection and recreational facilities for the residents and Chinese in neighboring areas. At the height of the Chinese population, there allegedly were more than two thousand Chinese in the Comstock area, but there are no records to substantiate this claim. There were three or four temples for worship and socializing, gambling halls, at least five association halls, houses of prostitution, and numerous businesses in the Chinatowns (Storey County, *Assessment Book*, blocks 90–91; *Book of Deeds*, vol. 28, Plat Book, 1872, 75: Wells Fargo Directory 1878).

Like many other large Chinatowns, several Chinese physicians were available to treat the Chinese and Euro-American clients; the more prominent practitioners, like Dr. Hop Lock, advertised in the local newspapers. Chinatown also separated the Chinese from the rest of the population until the economic decline began in the late 1870s. According to the 1870 census manuscript, 40 percent of the Chinese, usually servants and cooks, lived in residences with Euro-Americans; the rest lived in Chinatown. The only example of a servant in the 1870 census manuscript was the twenty-four-year old Ah Hay, who, with the thirty-year-old cook, Yup See, lived with and worked for the merchant Samuel Haas and his family of seven. John W. MacKay of the Gould and Curry Mine had a Chinese servant and lived with him at the mine offices after the great fire of October 26, 1875 (Waldorf 1968, 31). The close connections between employer and servant often benefited the servant, who could tell relatives about job opportunities and learn about American ways.

Four additional important Nevada–Virginia City–Carson City people had Chinese servants. William Sharon (1821–1885), a Bank of California agent and U.S. Senator from Nevada from 1875 to 1881, and Henry M. Yerington, a Wells Fargo agent, partner with Bliss in the CTLFC, superintendent of the VTRR, and lumber baron, had Chinese servants whose responsibilities included signing for goods sent through Wells Fargo (Wells Fargo Express ledgers, Wells Fargo History Museum; A. J. Hood Papers). Duane L. Bliss had two Chinese servants—Ah Fong, who was age thirty-five in 1880, and Ah Sing, age sixteen in 1880—at his home in Carson City (NVSHPO 1880). Governor of Nevada John H. Kincaid also had Chinese servants, including one who allegedly "ran the governor's office." There was probably a Chinese servants' network in operation for information, especially since Bliss, Yerington, and Kincaid lived in the same neighborhood in Carson City (Abraham 1996). The more enterprising servants not only learned English and American customs but also discovered how to invest money in the United States in order to make money (James 1995).

In many Chinatowns the merchants were at the top of the social and economic scale. Virginia City's Chinatown was no exception. Storey County had twenty-five Chinese merchants serving the local population (NVSHPO 1870–1880). Hy Loy (1825–1887) was the wealthiest Chinese, declaring a worth of $5,000 in 1870. He was a merchant, leading member of the Yee clan's Hehe huiguan (Hop Wo Association), and a labor contractor. Euro-Americans often called him by the name of his general merchandising company, Quong Hai Loy, which Yee Ying took over in 1888.[11] Hy Loy owned several buildings valued at $2,161 on K and Union Streets (Storey County *Map Book*, 1875). In 1879 he hired 260 Chinese to work on the Truckee Meadows irrigation project. Because of the need for men to work in the mountains cutting and gathering wood, he was also a labor contractor for some of the lumbering companies based in Virginia City. Quong Hai Loy was one of the last two Chinese stores in Virginia City's Chinatown. In Confucian China, merchants were the lowest of four classes in Chinese society, but with the advent of international trade, their prominence rose both in China and in the American West.

By the 1875 state census of Virginia City, a change in Chinese residential patterns became more obvious: 16.8 percent (107) lived with Euro-Americans, mostly

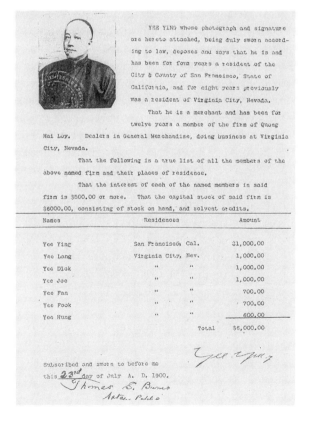

Chinese partnership papers were filed with the Bureau of Immigration and have been preserved in the National Archives and Records Administration. Yee Ying's papers for his business in Virginia City are typical of these records. (Source: NARA, San Bruno)

as servants or cooks; 35.5 percent (226) lived next door to Euro-Americans; and only 47.7 percent lived in the main Chinatown. Although anti-Chinese literature and advocates claimed that the Chinese preserved their traditional culture and values, the Chinese in Virginia City exemplified the greater adaptation to American society that occurred. Adaptation, acculturation, and assimilation were "two-way streets," and both the immigrants and majority society had to make accommodations and changes. By the 1870s this was evident in Chinese marriages. In 1875 a local judge married a Chinese couple; in 1878 a Chinese couple had an "American and Chinese" ceremony; and in 1881, a Chinese couple simply married in the local Methodist Church.[12] These Chinese had accepted American marriage practices; and the local authorities had allowed the marriages to take place in their chambers or churches.

In the 1880s the population of Chinese and non-Chinese alike had declined due to the economic depression. This was reflected in the number of men involved in lumbering. There were only six men cutting or sawing wood living in Virginia City: Ah Dung (age thirty-five), Ah Fun (age twenty-four), Ah Ho (age forty), Ah Lyn (age sixty), and Cook In (age twenty-nine). This was a much older group than those enumerated in 1870. Based on the Ormsby County assessment rolls, slightly more is known about Ah Dung. In 1884 and 1886 Ah Dung had three mules valued at $200, lumber in Kings Canyon valued at $100, and a wagon valued at $25, owing a tax of $10.38. Only one Euro-American woodchopper and two sawyers were listed in the census. Two Chinese carpenters out of more than two hundred other carpenters also served the community: Ah Foo (age thirty-six) and Ah Fouey (age thirty) (NVSHPO 1880). In all probability, these two men were not the same as the two carpenters in 1870. Of the six Chinese wood dealers in Nevada in 1880, two were in Carson City and four were in Eureka, Nevada. There was none in Virginia City, but there were four Euro-American wood dealers there. However, there were apparently Chinese still involved in the delivery of wood. Four of the nine men categorized as being in the "wood business" were Chinese doing business in Virginia City: Gun Jam (b. 1830), Way Lee (b. 1830), Koy Ma (b. 1848), and See Young (b. 1853). The first three men lived in Chinatown, while twenty-seven-year-old See Young lived on Mill Street with ten Chinese laborers who were undoubtedly involved in lumbering (NVSHPO 1880). The *Morning Appeal* (June 10, 1880) reported that there was a "Chinese wood wagon . . . drawn by a six-horse team," indicating that the Chinese still were involved in direct deliveries. Newspaper accounts were more accurate than the census in many cases.

The destruction of the 1890 census manuscript has created an unfortunate void in knowledge about this transitional period. The 1900 Virginia City census manuscript listed two Chinese wood sawyers, At Wah (age sixty, immigrated 1860) and his neighbor, Wong Lsoy (age fifty-three, immigrated 1868); in 1910 Loun Jo (age sixty-five, immigrated 1863), a woodchopper who lived alone with non-Chinese neighbors, and Jan Bock (age seventy-five, immigrated 1856), a carpenter who lived with two Chinese men who were cooks—all were "long time" residents in the American West (NVSHPO 1900). Jan Bock owned his own shop and probably had lived in Virginia City for several decades. Unfortunately, these two men were not listed in any of the other Nevada census manuscripts, but this is not surprising, since their occupations were highly mobile, and the spelling of Chinese names varied by census taker. Their advanced age and early immigration dates suggest that they had been in these professions for many years. The tremendous decline in the number of Chinese in lumbering suggests that there were fewer opportunities in Virginia City and more in neighboring areas and states. Involvement in the lumbering industry, after all, was a transient occupation.

When the Chinese arrived, many Euro-American miners opposed their presence but focused on "get rich quick" schemes, leaving the Chinese to fill jobs offered by timber owners. These employers were connected to mining but expanded their enterprises to include logging.

Several of the Euro-Americans made fortunes as a result of the increasing need for wood products in mining. At first, small, independent timber ranchers cut the wood for the mines and community. By the 1870s larger companies took over the smaller ones and began to create logging empires. Both groups used Chinese workers, but by the 1880s many logging companies in the Sierra Nevada used larger numbers of Chinese or contracted the jobs out to the Chinese. The most famous of the early timber ranchers was Mark Twain, whose campfire accidentally destroyed his trees, as he described in his book *Roughing It* (1872), but it was men like Michele Spooner, Duane L. Bliss, Henry M. Yerington, and Walter Hobart who prospered because their companies hired hundreds of Chinese laborers.

*   *   *

The Nevada counties of Douglas, Storey, Lyon, Washoe, and Ormsby, located on or near the Tahoe Basin and the Carson Range, had many Chinese employed in logging, and so Chinese communities soon developed. Similar situations occurred as new virgin forests gradually opened elsewhere. For the Chinese, the primary attractions to this labor-intensive work were familiarity with the work, the potential for higher wages (more than the average one dollar per day in other jobs), work locations away from anti-Chinese violence, and the quiet and solitude of the beautiful mountain forests. The negative aspects included the hard manual labor, the harsh winter months, wild animals, and the dangers involved in logging.

Logging developed rapidly in Douglas County. The first serious operations in logging the Tahoe area began with several independent loggers; the most famous were Michele E. Spooner, a French Canadian entrepreneur, and his partner, Simon Dubois. In 1860 they established Spooner Ranch on 640 acres, about three miles east of Lake Tahoe (J. Stone n.d.). Spooner expanded his operations with other partners, called his new company Summit Fluming, and established his headquarters in Glenbrook. By 1870 the company controlled 1,840 acres at Spooner Summit, a shingle mill, and a sawmill, which employed two Chinese cooks. That year Bliss and Company absorbed Summit Fluming (Nevada Historic Marker 225). Glenbrook was convenient because it was on a major transportation route between the mines in central California and Nevada, but its importance diminished with the completion of the CPRR in 1869. The early timber ranchers of the 1850s found Chinese workers to be reliable—some had logging experience in China, others knew how to cut trees and make ties for railroad companies. It appears that successive owners of the timber ranches continued the employment of some of the Chinese workers.

The 1880 census manuscript listed thirty-eight Chinese living in Glenbrook: twenty laborers (who lived in a boarding house next to wood contractor Michele Spooner and his family), ten cooks (two working for Spooner), six laundrymen, one gardener, and one sheepherder (NVSHPO 1880; Wrobleski 1996). Spooner's Chinese cook had a Euro-American assistant. The sheepherder did not live in a Chinese enclave as did the gardener, cooks, and laundrymen but lived instead in a Euro-American neighborhood. Glenbrook had four sawmills, a company-owned general store, two hotels, and a number of houses. Nearby were "Chinese gardens," where Ah Fung (b. ca. 1855) grew and harvested fresh produce to feed the workers and enhanced the talents of the Chinese cooks.

Archaeological evidence indicated that the Chinese might have started their own lumbering operation at Slaughterhouse Canyon, near Glenbrook, that included a mill and flume (Giles 1996). This would be in keeping with the developments of Chinese-owned lumbering operations in places like Hawaiʻi, Nicaragua, and Thailand. The "men in the mountains" could have been working for a Chinese operation. Local rumor attributed the disappearance of the site to a boating accident: it was believed that the Chinese managers were invited to cross Lake Tahoe to inspect a rival company's operations when a bomb sank the steamer, leaving the Chinese operation without leadership (Elmer Rusco, based on oral interviews.)

The connection between mining leaders and logging operations was exemplified in several lumber companies. The Pacific Wood, Lumber, and Fluming Company (PWLFC), established in 1874, was owned by two of the "Comstock Bonanza Kings," John Mackay (1831–1902, a major Comstock figure) and James Fair (1831–1894, a U.S. Senator from Nevada between 1881 and 1887). In 1875 they agreed to transport timber, lumber, and wood for the VTRR (PWLFC papers). In that same year they built two steam-powered sawmills at the cost of $250,000 and constructed a fifteen-mile flume that eventually became the largest V-flume in Nevada. The flume dropped from their mill in the mountains north of Lake Tahoe on Hunter Creek to Huffaker's Station, an active stage-stop center from 1858 to 1868 in Truckee Meadows. The trestle required two million feet of lumber and fifty-six thousand pounds of nails. It could carry five hundred cords of wood or five hundred thousand feet of lumber per day. Thousands of horses would have been needed to move the wood if the flume had not been built. Most of the flume herders were Chinese, and perhaps the trestle builders were as well they had gained their experience from working on railroad construction. The PWLFC owned more than three thousand acres of timberland in 1877 and reportedly cut twenty-five thousand feet daily between 1874 and 1877. In August 1875, responding to anti-Chinese agitators, the PWLFC announced that they had no Chinese employees, but in July 1876 there were reports of 110 to120 Chinese piling and loading wood at its flume terminus at Huffaker's Station.[13] The 1877 PWLFC payroll was $81,000 per month. In 1877 they extended the flume to total twenty-three miles. Their flume could move up to one thousand cords of firewood or a half-million board feet of construction timber daily through 1880 (Angel 1881, 191). According to the *Morning Appeal* (November 1, 1880), Fair not only employed a thousand Chinese workers at his wood ranches, but he also sent "tons of silver past the U.S. Mint daily to sell to the Chinese [in China]." The figure was likely an exaggeration, but Fair probably employed a large number of Chinese workers and, as a Comstock mine owner, was interested in the silver trade between the United States and China. One writer listed only eight hundred men working for the PWLFC, but this lower figure is understandable since the workers in the woods fluctuated seasonally (Wilson 1992, 48). Like loggers elsewhere, these men probably worked twelve hours per day, six days per week, in small groups of ten to fifteen men. The logs were then loaded onto the CPRR or the VTRR for further distribution.

In all of Douglas County that year, there were 160 Chinese, including eighty-seven Chinese laborers, fifty-two of whom were "in the mountains," and twenty-six cooks (Census 1880). In this group, the ages ranged from sixteen to sixty-five, and, according to the census taker, all were able to read. For men doing this type of hard manual labor, the ability to read among the entire group seems highly unlikely. If this were the case, literacy could be found among Chinese in lumbering. This was probably the group working in the mountains above Genoa and South Lake Tahoe or in the Spooner Summit area for CTLFC. No Euro-Americans were recorded in the same area, so it is highly probable that the Chinese were the only ones cutting wood at that particular location.

Canadian Andrew Wormsley (b. 1850, also spelled Walmsley) of Dayton, Lyon County, operated charcoal kilns in the Pine Nut Range, Douglas County, and used Chinese workers there from the 1870s to 1910s.[14] Pinenut trees were used for firewood and for making charcoal for smelting furnaces. The charcoal was shipped to Virginia City for the mines. According to the *Territorial Enterprise* (October 19, 1877) eighty Chinese men were cutting timber and making charcoal (called coal burners) in the Pine Nut Range in order to supply the Comstock. The 1880 census manuscript listed seventeen Chinese coal burners in Pine Nut Hills. In that year the other three Chinese coal burners lived elsewhere. Eight Chinese lived in a boardinghouse next door to Andrew Wormsley and probably worked for him. Two, were ages fifteen and eighteen, were just beginning their work career. The other nine lived in a separate boardinghouse. According to Wormsley's grandson Ray, the charcoal burners lived in the Pine Nut Hills in the summer but in Dayton in the winter, even into the early 1900s. The Pine Nut range was located along the East Fork of the Carson River, so men working in lumbering also could participate in placer mining. Although the census manuscripts listed no Chinese miners in Douglas County, the *Nevada State Journal* (January 16, 1886) noted that Chinese placer miners were working on the East Fork. The fact that Forest Service archaeologist Carrie E. Smith found a mining pan in one of the Chinese wood-camp sites in Daggett Creek, Douglas County, suggests that a combination of the two occupations might not have been unusual.

In nearby Lyon County, which also started as a mining community, the profile was very different. Dayton was an earlier settlement dating to around 1851, and by 1859 the town had twelve houses and two stores (Hattori 1991, 38:1–18). In the 1860s the area was a major milling center for the Comstock, with fourteen mills between Dayton and Silver City to the northwest. In the same period some 335 stamp mills operated in Dayton Valley ("History of Dayton"). The early placer miners had disappeared by the time of the 1870 census. In 1870, 116 Chinese, including two women who were "keeping house" (Mary Tahi, age 24, and Sing Ye, age 25) and nine women who were listed as "harlots," lived in Lyon County (NVSHPO 1870). The term "harlots" appeared in the 1870 census throughout the American West as a prelude to the "anti-prostitution" 1875 Page Law that essentially kept Chinese women from immigrating into the United States. Thirty-three of the 105 men were "laborers," which meant they could have worked in mining or lumbering or a multitude of other occupations, but the majority of the men (forty-two of them) were listed as cooks. The only merchant, Ah Lun (b. 1830), who was worth $400, left by 1880; two men, Hop Lee (also He Li, b. 1846) and Bon Ah (b. 1835), became the leading merchants in Chinatown. By 1880 Dayton's general population had dropped from twenty-five hundred in 1865 to two hundred, but with the construction of the Carson and Colorado Railroad (CCRR), there was a brief increase.

Wood was cut in Lyon County in the winter and early spring because of the warmer climate; between the late spring to early fall, woodsmen turned to the thick forests of the Tahoe Basin, Sierras, Truckee Meadows, Truckee River Canyon, the head waters of the East Carson River. They worked as far north as Bodie, California, and as far south as Aurora, Nevada. Johnson's Cut-Off (later known as Kings Canyon Road) connected the regions of Carson Valley, Lake Tahoe's south shore, Placerville, and Spooner Summit.

The profile of the Chinese population changed in 1880 because the CCRR was under construction, so Lyon County was the "home" of over two hundred Chinese railroad workers. Labor contractor Ah Quong, "perhaps the slipperiest Chinaman ever exiled from far Cathay," had to take the men from Reno to Wadsworth to Churchill Canyon, a very circuitous route, because the three hundred

Euro-American workers hired in June 1880 were unhappy about their low wage of $1.75 per day, and they blamed the Chinese labor force (Myrick 1962, 168; *Reno Evening Gazette*, January 24, 1879). By 1880 eight men, most in their forties, were miners; only one man, Wuei Ho (age thirty-three), worked as a wood chopper. No other Chinese was listed as being involved in lumbering. However, in 1900 three Chinese woodchoppers—Hong Ah (age fifty-five), Kee Day or Day Kee (age forty-four), and Jung Hong (age sixty-three)—lived in Dayton. The advanced ages of the men suggest that they had been in lumbering in the American West for several decades. These men made Dayton their home base but worked in wood camps throughout the region.

More information was available on Day Kee because of his application for a duplicate certificate of residence.[15] Born in 1855 in China, he immigrated in 1881, could read but not speak English. He was single. Based on his 1905 application for a duplicate certificate of residence, required by the 1892 Geary Act to prevent illegal Chinese immigration, Day Kee had lived in Nevada City, California, for eleven years before moving to Dayton, Lyon County, around 1892, where he lived for the next eighteen years. His original certificate of residence, issued in 1892, burned in a fire while he was working at a wood camp. Another woodcutter, Yee Ah You (b. 1856) testified about the fire and two Chinese merchants from Dayton supported his claim. After hiring an attorney to argue his case, the Immigration Bureau issued him a duplicate certificate. He exemplified those who worked in transient wood camps but had a base that they called "home," where they kept important papers. In many cases, this base was a fellow regional's store. By the 1910 census, Day Kee probably was no longer living in Nevada, since his name does not appear in Nevada's 1910 census manuscripts.

Workers from Washoe and Douglas Counties also logged the Sierra Nevada. As the industry developed and expanded, Chinese in the woods were active in the region. Washoe County was typical of the early lumbering development. Within Washoe County were at least one hundred thousand acres of rich timberland, whereas Douglas County had only thirty thousand to forty thousand acres, both benefiting from the Sierra Nevada. Storey County had only stunted trees after 1862 (Miller 1926, 387). Towns grew up to supply the need first for the mines and then for the railroads. In the 1860s in Washoe County there were twelve to eighteen sawmills with 30 million feet cut annually, primarily for use on the Comstock and in railroad construction. Sales reached $75,000 per month. Approximately two hundred men worked in lumbering in Washoe County, and more than five hundred animals, primarily oxen, transported the logs to central staging areas. In the 1860s through 1870s Washoe County had pioneered the extensive use of flumes. Flumes sped the transportation of the lumber, and logs could descend seventeen hundred feet in fourteen seconds, for example, in Verdi.[16] Between 1862 and 1867, Washoe County produced 193 million feet of lumber and had the greatest number of trees cut.

Washoe Valley provides one example of corporate takeover during this period. Not far from Franktown, on the west side of the Washoe Valley, Gilman N. Folsom, Charles A. Bragg, and Albert Bragg operated the Central Mill between 1861 and 1870. The men then purchased the Pacific Wood and Lumber Company (PWLC, not to be confused with the PWLFC owned by Mackay and Fair around Hunter Lake) at Camp 18, now called Clinton, California, and built a four-mile, narrow-gauge railroad to haul logs to the company's mill. According to a local history enthusiast and lumberman descendant, the late John Fulton of Tahoe City, the company hired Chinese workers, and archaeological evidence supported this. From 1868 until 1878 the company produced about forty-five thousand feet per day and owned 2,920 acres of land. Chinese artifacts were seen at many wood-camp sites. In 1878 the PWLC began operating its narrow-gauge, steam-operated railroad, making the transportation of the logs faster and safer. In 1879 the sawmill burned down and the company began to decline.

Farther south at nearby Franktown in 1855, Mormon Elder Orson Hyde built a second sawmill and improved it the next year with equipment from nearby Placerville (Knowles 1942, 4–5). Until 1859 sawmills at Franktown and Lake Valley, El Dorado County, California, were the only ones in the Truckee Basin area. By the mid-1860s there were twelve to eighteen sawmills. Franktown and vicinity probably reached its height of production by the 1860s. In 1865 the Nevada Surveyor General stated in his annual report, "How fast our beautiful pine forests are melting away before the . . . blows of the wood and lumberman" (Knowles 1942, 11–12). A small Chinatown eventually developed in Franktown, but fires, floods, and other natural calamities ravished Franktown and its Chinatown periodically. In 1880 the census manuscript listed fifty-three Chinese loading wood in Franktown: fourteen lived in one boardinghouse with one cook (Ah Jack, age thirty-six) and fifteen in another boardinghouse with one cook (Ah Fong, age forty) (Census 1800). The youngest wood loader was age eighteen, the oldest, age sixty. The census taker for the first group noted that all but one were single, and most were in their twenties, with the oldest age forty-five. They lived near the wood contractor William Fitzpatrick, age twenty-six, who operated a boardinghouse for Euro-Americans. The second group was older, with two men age sixty and several in their fifties. Three lived in another unit. An additional three Chinese wood loaders lived in Washoe Valley, and these men were older, ranging in age from sixty-two to sixty-eight. In this census group in Washoe County, five had the name Ah Fook, three Ah Pow, three Ah Sing, two Ah Yee, and two Ah Young, thus making the tracing of individuals difficult. Census takers probably had a difficult time counting individuals "in the mountains" because of the complication of reaching them—hence, minimal numbers were listed. Unskilled Chinese working at the lumber camps as flume herders, for example, were classified as "laborers" and could not be separated from those in other occupations, such as railroad maintenance, unless their names appeared next to or near a Euro-American lumberman.

One of the main centers of lumbering activity was at Crystal Peak–Verdi, Washoe County. Crystal Peak was located at the foot of the Sierra near the state line. All of the property was in Sierra County, California, but the town was listed as part of Washoe County, Nevada. Crystal Peak began as a trading post in 1854. As early as 1852 Sierra Valley had several portable sawmills to supply the local ranchers with lumber (Dixon et al. 1995, 21). The discovery of the Comstock Lode and the construction of railroads prompted the establishment of more mills in the area, such as John Dixon's Yuba Mill that cut about ten thousand feet daily between 1867 and 1879 (Knowles 1942, 16).

In the early 1860s Crystal Peak boomed as a coal, copper, and silver mining town, but as the mineral deposits diminished, Crystal Peak became an important source of lumber between 1864 and the 1920s. In 1864 the Crystal Peak Company, involved in timber and mining interests in Sunrise Basin and on the Verdi Peak, laid out the town of Crystal Peak (Thompson and West 1958). The route between Truckee and Verdi was easier through Dog Valley, which by 1864 was part of the California Emigrant Trail and the Donner Lake Wagon Toll Road (Goodwin 1960, 12; Verdi Mill Company). By July of that year there were four sawmills; by May of the next year, there were six sawmills "capable of providing each 1,000 feet of dressed lumber per hour" (Knowles 1942, 14). In 1866 the lumber industry that paid a major portion of the taxes for the county. The town peaked in 1867 because the logging operations supplied the ties, buildings, bridge timbers, and other facilities for the CPRR.

The Chinese played a role in the lumber industry in this region. In 1868 the Chinese in Crystal Peak reportedly included merchants, gamblers, butchers, freighters, woodcutters, and others (Goodwin 1960, 15). In 1868 the town had five stores, four hotels, and numerous saloons, and a Chinese population of one thousand. In 1870 Crystal Peak was shipping wood to the Comstock by train.[17] When the CPRR made Verdi its station a half-mile away, the hotel owned by James Carson, two stores, and a post office were moved to Verdi.[18] However, the two saloons and brewery of James Carson and two other businesses, the J. B. Gillhem blacksmith shop, the W. E. Squires shoemaking shop, remained in Crystal Peak. Saloons were a prominent feature in logging towns since most of the Euro-American men were males, either single or living away from their families, and drinking was a major pastime. The blacksmith shop was especially important in fabricating new metal parts or fixing broken ones for the sawmills and loggers. The shoemaker made and repaired boots that were required for working in the forests; evidence of these boots were found in Chinese work-camp sites.

In 1870 the Crystal Peak census listed eight Chinese woodchoppers whose ages ranged from twenty to forty, one Chinese laundryman, and two Chinese cooks. The reputed one thousand Chinese given in the 1868 newspaper article were either no longer there or, more likely, were not counted or permanently resided elsewhere. According to the *Nevada State Journal* (August 9, 1874), a slightly more than one hundred Chinese followed Euro-American lumbermen, scavenging remaining trees, stumps, roots, and brush in Crystal Peak and Verdi for sale as cordwood. That same article pointed out that the Chinese owned two teams to haul the cordwood to the CPRR station in Reno, but there were no individuals listed as such in the census manuscripts. Chinese freighters were on a higher economic level than laborers and had to have the capital to purchase and maintain their wagons, equipment, and animals. This indicated the different levels of work that they performed.

Crystal Peak lasted for a few more years before it declined in the mid-1870s because the CPRR had moved the train station at Verdi and because of anti-Chinese violence (Lindstrom 1993, 10). By January 1875 Euro-Americans viewed the Chinese as an economic threat in Crystal Peak. Chinese workers were assaulted and robbed, but the Chinese continued working there.[19] For the Chinese workers, natural disasters were compounded by anti-Chinese violence. In February 1875 the newspaper reported that several Chinese working near Crystal Peak once again were assaulted and robbed:

> There were twelve Chinamen in the cabin, when . . . three white men, with red shirts on, busted in the door of their cabin and demanded all the money they had in the camp . . . they commenced cutting them with knives and two of the Chinamen were wounded. . . . The would-be murderers and robbers got twenty-five dollars from the Chinamen and decamped. There seems to be prowling around that vicinity a number of petty larceny thieves and cut-throats.[20]

In 1876 the violence against the Chinese intensified and spread. In the spring of 1876 the citizens of Tybo in central Nevada publicized that Chinese woodchoppers and burners were not welcome in the town. This boycott was mild compared to later actions.[21] Members of the Caucasian League set fire to a cabin occupied by three Chinese in Crystal Peak; as the Chinese fled, one was killed and another seriously wounded.[22] Attacks on Chinese occurred in nearby areas throughout the late 1870s, and Chinese working in the woods sometimes were assaulted, robbed, or killed.[23] These kinds of violence became more common. By 1880 Chinese workers left Crystal Peak and other areas where violence frequently occurred. What began as a logging site for mining transitioned to a supplier of wood for the CPRR. This was one of many examples of the influence of the railroad on the prosperity or death of a town.

As Crystal Peak declined, Verdi grew as the lumbering center, Reno as the commercial supply center. This entire area has seen the heavy exploitation and destructive cutting of timber in order to support frontier community building projects, mining, railroad construction, and the multitude of other uses for wood. The area also was subject to frequent fires due to lightning strikes and high winds.

In 1875 the state census for Washoe County registered 250 Chinese males and seventeen Chinese females. Verdi listed three Chinese woodchoppers (Ah Tong, Aph Ho, Ah Woo), whose ages ranged from twenty-three to twenty-eight, and eleven Chinese laborers who boarded with the Chinese and Euro-American woodchoppers and undoubtedly worked in logging. A multiethnic male housing that was probably operated by the lumber company suggests that there might have been greater socialization between the groups. All male households were not unusual in the American West, where men lived without wives and family and therefore found it more convenient to live in boardinghouses (Hardesty 1988, 14–16). There were four additional Chinese laborers living nearby whose ages ranged from fourteen to fifty. This is a far cry from the estimated one-hundred-plus Chinese woodcutters reported in the *Nevada State Journal* (August 9, 1874).

The 1880 census manuscript had more details. Between Reno and Verdi there were eight Chinese residents, including Ah Jack (age forty-two), the labor contractor, and Ah Chung (age eighteen), his cook. These two individuals were the only Chinese living with non-Chinese in this locality. Otherwise, the pattern of segregated residence reemerged. The remaining six were laborers. In Verdi, ten Chinese laborers and one Chinese cook worked for John Foulkes.[24] A Chinatown had been established, but on October 21, 1890, the Chinatown burned down.[25] Below Verdi near Steamboat Dock, there were forty-seven Chinese laborers living in six residences that also probably were boardinghouses. Living in small, tight quarters was possible because the men usually only slept there. Recreational activities often were in community centers, such as association halls and what Euro-Americans popularly called "joss houses." Transient workers frequently stayed in the community centers, association houses, or temples until they could settle in more permanent facilities.

Anti-Chinese violence was often directed against employers of Chinese workers. Oliver Lonkey (Lonquille, 1832–1905), a French Canadian who moved to Nevada in 1855, had a sawmill in Grass Valley, California, in 1864, and moved to Virginia City in 1872 to provide lumber for the Comstock. Like many of the early Comstock lumbermen, both Chinese and non-Chinese, he leased the land that gave him a head start in the industry (Lee 2008).[26] Lonkey had been active in lumbering in the area since 1862 and opened several mills in the Tahoe Basin and Sierra Nevada region. He moved to the Verdi-Truckee area in 1882 and has been credited with the founding of Verdi. Lonkey and E. R. Smith, also of Virginia City, owned the Verdi Planing Mill that dressed lumber, cut shingles, and made doors, windows, and furniture with a team of eight men.[27] Although the firm's headquarters were on C and Mill Streets in Virginia City, their operations were in the Verdi area. Lonkey spent $60,000 to build several sawmills in Dog Valley. All kinds of finished lumber, some furniture, and boxes were manufactured there. The Dog Valley sawmill was in full operation in the 1870s and shipped the lumber out through Verdi (J. Lee 2008; Hummel, 1969, 15). Chinese often loaded the wood products onto the nearby trains. Lonkey branched out to Prosser Creek Station near Truckee.

Lonkey continued to employ Chinese workers even after the Truckee Secret Committee of Five in September 1886 ordered him to fire all Chinese workers.[28]

When he refused, fires broke out on his properties. Several of the mills had to be rebuilt, and in 1888 the corporation was renamed Verdi Mill Company, which produced dressed lumber of all kinds. Anti-Chinese agitators demanded that Oliver Lonkey fire his cooks in Verdi and Prosser Creek. Lonkey adamantly refused even when Euro-Americans said that they would work for the same wages as the Chinese. His personal cook changed his name to Tom Lonkey and served the Lonkey family until Oliver's death. In 1888 the agitators burned Lonkey's factory at Verdi and in 1889 destroyed his sawmill at Prosser Creek, about five miles from Truckee.[29] By 1900 Oliver Lonkey enlarged his operations, giving it a new name: Verdi Lumber Company (VLC) (Goodwin 1960, 48). Xavier, Oliver's older brother, worked as a carpenter for the VLC. In September 1905 Oliver Lonkey died; his brother Eli died in February 1919. The Lonkey brothers were well respected in the lumber industry. Without their support, Chinese who had worked for the VLC left the area. A few may have followed their Verdi supervisor to Oregon to work in lumbering.

Another influential lumberman was John P. Foulkes (also spelled Foulks). Foulkes built the toll bridge over the Truckee River in 1862, owned the "Snug" Saloon in Crystal Peak in 1867, and became interested in lumbering (Goodwin 1960, 12–13). In 1874 Foulkes and Company purchased the Old Excelsior sawmill, built in 1864, southwest of Crystal Peak. John P. Jones built a shingle mill nearby at Verdi. During the 1874 season Foulkes cut eight hundred thousand feet of lumber for the Nevada market. He expanded his operations by building several mills, including the Essex Mill that did planing and produced shingles. He used a horse chute (horses tow the logs along the chute) to transport logs to the mill because it was cheaper than the recently introduced Dolbeer steam donkey (Dixon et al. 1995, 24). Nearby Dog Valley also had a sawmill in full operation with daily supplies to Verdi. According to the *Reno Evening Gazette* (October 26, 1878), both Foulkes and Jones portrayed themselves as supporters of Denis Kearney's anti-Chinese movement and argued politically that California should keep the Chinese and not send them elsewhere, but this did not deter them from hiring Chinese workers.

According to the 1880 census for Verdi, Foulkes employed ten Chinese in his lumber mill (Goodwin 1960, 33–38). The "laborers" lived next door to Foulkes and his family. Their employment was contrary to his earlier anti-Chinese stance but the need for workers probably led him to change his mind. By the 1880s, because of the mining bust on the Comstock and the diminishing wood requirement of the railroads, Foulkes produced box shooks (slats to make fruit boxes for shipping) and shipped his lumber to California (Waechter et al. 1995, III-27). The contradictory public statements of lumber barons against Chinese labor while continuing to hire Chinese to work in lumbering appeared to be a common practice. Foulkes continued to issue contracts to Chinese to cut wood. The public rhetoric helped the lumber barons avoid attacks by anti-Chinese zealots. The attacks against Lonkey, though, prompted Foulkes to dismiss his Chinese workers. In 1890 the

Chinatown in Verdi burned down and the Chinese workers no longer worked or gravitated to that area.[30] Neither Foulkes nor his children were listed in the 1900 to 1920 census manuscripts for Nevada, so apparently they also moved elsewhere. Verdi experienced a revival when the VLC built a logging train beginning in 1900 that had feeder lines in several directions. The line eventually totaled thirty-two miles by 1924, allowing more access to the forests (Myrick 1962, 412).

According to the 1870 federal census manuscript, Washoe County had the following population: Clark's Station 16, including 1 Chinese; Crystal Peak 120, including 11 Chinese; Franktown 271, including 7 Chinese; Geiger Grade 55, including 4 Chinese; Glendale 129, including 4 Chinese; Mill Station 129, including 2 Chinese; Ophir 110, including 1 Chinese; Red Rock 6, all Chinese; Reno 1,035, including 81 Chinese; Truckee Meadows 320, including 26 Chinese; Wadsworth 253, including 36 Chinese, and Washoe City 552, including 42 Chinese. The small and scattered residences of the Chinese population in Washoe County meant that for supplies and recreation, the Chinese went either to Truckee, California, Carson City, Nevada, or Reno, Nevada. Reno, with the largest Chinese population in Washoe County, had the following occupational profile: cooks and restaurant workers, twenty-four; laundry, fourteen; laborers, thirteen; prostitutes, eleven; gamblers, six; grocers, three; physician one; apothecary, one; domestic, one; unknown, three. While some of the laborers may have been involved in lumbering, they could also have been working for the railroad. What was more evident was that Reno was a recreational center for Chinese workers in the region. The three grocers, Ah Pat, Ah Kit, and Lee Fook, were the suppliers of food and other imported products. Medical care was available from Ah Chung, age thirty-nine, the apothecary, and Ah Wah, age thirty-nine, the physician. Truckee, California, located in the opposite direction, had a larger Chinatown and a greater number of Chinese recreational facilities, including gambling and opium houses and a red light district.

Between 1875 and 1890 Washoe Country replaced Storey County as the most populous county. Storey's population began to fall from 19,528 people in 1875 to only 3,673 people at the turn of the century because of the 1881–1900 Depression. At the same time Washoe County's population rose from 3,953 people in 1875 to 9,141 in 1890, and it remained the most populous county in Nevada from 1890 until 1950. The train town of Reno (formerly Lake's Crossing) became the state's center of commercial activities.

Nearby was Empire City, Ormsby County, which began as a logging town in 1855 and cut mining timber until 1910. Fifty-one Chinese were listed in the census as laborers, and most of these men worked in some aspect of logging, especially in millwork. Empire City also had one doctor, thirteen cooks, one waiter, and one servant constituting the rest of the Chinese community (NVSHPO 1860–1910). In 1862 the Carson River Lumbering Company organized a wood drive down the East Fork of the Carson River from Markleeville, California, to Empire City, Nevada, in order to provide the Comstock with wood. This was the first time the

East Carson River was used for this purpose, and the technique made Empire City a major lumbering center. One of the best and largest sawmills in the state at that time was the Empire Mill, owned by Hobbs, Russell and Company (Miller 1926, 391). Most of the timber came from Silver Mountain, Alpine County, California (on the western side of the Sierra Nevada and the east fork of the Carson). The lumber had to be driven down the Carson River over eighty miles, requiring forty days in the usual drive. The mill employed twenty men who worked twelve-hour days. At its height, an average of five million cords were produced annually.[31] From Empire some of the "saw logs" (1' by 1' by 8') went directly to the Comstock mines. In 1863 the state legislature granted the company an exclusive franchise for five years to use the Carson River to transport the wood. Other lumbering companies sprang up. Eventually there was a controversy between the Carson Valley farmers and the mill men over the use of the limited waters of the Carson River as dams were constructed to hold back the water until a log drive occurred. For the next thirty years Empire supplied wood for the mines, mills, and railroads, but the supply of timber diminished. By 1881 many of the lumbermen had moved to the virgin forests of the Wood River country.[32] In 1895 the last cordwood drive down the Carson River originated in Empire (Smith 2000, 26). The prosperity of the town declined thereafter.

*   *   *

Mining was a great impetus to logging. Early timber barons became wealthy by providing the mines with wood, and some of the major timber ranchers hired Chinese workers. Most Euro-Americans dreamed of getting rich quickly and did not seek work in the young lumber industry in the American West. The logging industry prospered even more when railroad construction and maintenance increased the demand for wood products, but the character of the industry changed as large logging companies took over the smaller, independent timber ranchers who had originally supplied the mines. Some of the timber owners supported their Chinese employees through difficult times of anti-Chinese movements. Only a few of the many stories have survived. By the 1880s three lumbering companies dominated the Sierra Nevada and Carson Range forests, and all had connections to the Comstock and railroad construction: CTLFC, PWLFC and Sierra Nevada Wood and Lumber Company (SNWLC) built on earlier smaller companies. Company and district court records, census data, and newspaper reports showed that all three employed Chinese workers well into the 1890s. With the decline of the mines came the decline in logging, especially since the Sierra Nevada had been severely denuded of its rich forests, technological advances required less wood for the railroads, and the Chinese exclusion acts from 1882 through 1902 limited the availability of Chinese workers.

CHAPTER 5

Of Wood and Trains

The frenzy of western railroad construction that began in California around 1854 stimulated the rapid growth of logging. By the 1870s railroad companies were among the leaders in developing principles of forest management, establishing forest plantations, and promoting forest research, especially wood preservation, something that the Chinese had done centuries earlier (Cox 1981b, 190). Both the mining and railroad companies received a great incentive to be involved in logging with the passage of the Timber and Stone Act of 1878 that gave anyone the ability to claim up to 160 acres of timberland in Washington, Oregon, California, and Nevada for $2.50 per acre for mining and domestic purposes (Zimmerman 1998; Ricks 1915; Frederick 1993, 9). This opened the door for more intense cutting and led to the transition from small, independent owners to the development of larger, better-capitalized companies, often with ties to California and/or New York, merchandising, mining, and railroad companies.

One historian estimated that between the late 1870s and 1900, railroads used twenty to thirty percent of the annual American timber production, with the largest purchases between 1880 and 1900 (Pisani 1985, 344). An 1890 issue of the *Scientific American* estimated that 73 million ties were needed annually for new roads and the maintenance of old ones (Olson 1971, 11). The vast quantity of wood needed led to development of large lumbering firms. Three companies in the Sierra Nevada absorbed the earlier independent timber ranchers to provide wood not only for the Comstock and nearby mines but also for interstate and intrastate standard- and narrow-gauge railroads: the Carson Tahoe Lumber and Flume Company (CTLFC), Pacific Wood Lumber and Flume Company (PWLFC), and Sierra Nevada Wood and Lumber Company (SNWLC). They all employed Chinese workers until the 1890s to early 1900s. At least one, the CTLFC, was directly connected with the construction of railroads. They and others in the Sierra Nevada undoubtedly participated in the growing American lumber trade with Hawai'i and Asia. These and other logging companies were also targets for anti-Chinese movements. These companies, their Chinese employees, and the events surrounding their rise to prominence demonstrated the importance of wood products in this era of the 1870s to early 1900s and the role of the Chinese in the building of the American West.

Utilizing their experience in China and on railroad construction, the Chinese worked in logging and helped to build standard- and narrow-gauge railway lines that connected the forests, rural areas, and transportation centers in the West. This allowed towns like Carson City, Nevada, and Olympia, Washington, both state capitals, to prosper and for the frontier to be settled and industrialized.

The early railroads in California included an 1854 logging train, which ran for twenty miles in Humboldt County, had wooden rails, and was pulled by animals to transport logs to a body of water (Carranco and Fountain, 1964; Karshner 1995, 13). In 1854 Chinese workers were added to the construction team of the Panama Railroad, completed in 1855, through a contractor who received $25 per month per man (Cohen 1971). Several early railroad companies in California employed Chinese workers, including the Sacramento Valley Railroad (SVRR, 1852–1877), an early rival to the CPRR. The use of Chinese in railroad construction was known prior to the 1860s, when the CPRR sought railroad workers, but it was the construction of the CPRR that highlighted Chinese workers who scouted for the best path to lay tracks, cut down trees, cleared and graded the roads, blasted the tunnels, used nitroglycerin for the first time, built the snow sheds, cut and laid the ties, and performed numerous other tasks. Because the CPRR kept few records of individual employees but listed the headman, the number of workers is not known; the estimate has been fifteen thousand Chinese workers, or approximately 90 percent of the workforce. Despite their overwhelming participation, the Chinese are seldom mentioned in books and articles about the CPRR and western railroad construction.

The connections between logging, mining, and railroading began with the constructions of the SVRR (designed to help transport ore from the Comstock) and its rival, the CPRR (until the CPRR and its new parent company, the Southern Pacific Railroad (SPRR), gained dominance in the western railroad construction projects). In 1854 the SVRR employed at least 150 Chinese workers, who might later have worked for the CPRR. In 1861 Theodore Dehone Judah (1826–1863) succeeded in incorporating the Central Pacific Rail Road Company of California and obtaining the financial support and talents of Collis Potter Huntington (1821–1900), Mark Hopkins Jr. (1813–1878), Leland Stanford (1824–1893), and Charles Crocker (1822–1888), known as "The Big Four" of Sacramento (Myrick 1962–2007; Bain 1999; White 2011). The CPRR and the UPRR, the first transcontinental railroad, transformed the landscape of the American West as it linked the east with the west in 1869. For example, prior to the CPRR's completion, in order to reach the Comstock, passengers and freight traveled on steamships or riverboats from San Francisco to Sacramento, then by stage or wagon to Nevada City, Grass Valley, and Dutch Flat, then onto Verdi, Reno, and finally the Comstock. After the two lines were connected, freight and passengers moved easily between east and west; a feeder line, the VTRR, linked the CPRR to the Comstock.

The Big Four knew that they had a rich resource of timber in the virgin forests of the Sierra Nevada, with its northern Carson Range spur. The Pacific Railway Act of 1862 (U.S. Statutes at Large, vol. 12, p. 489) gave the railroad company the right to take timber from public lands two hundred feet in width on each side of the railroad line for the use of the railroad. Loggers that the railroad hired were not particularly concerned with state boundary lines in this region, so California and Nevada public lands were viewed as a single source. However, the ability to transport the lumber played a major role in deciding which forests could be harvested (Greeley 1923, 353). Because lumber imported from the northeast was very expensive, by the early 1850s production was well underway in the Sierra Nevada and Tahoe Basin. From Truckee to the East Carson River, there were sixty miles of prime virgin forests, but the most valuable of trees, the Douglas fir, could be found in abundance only in the Lake Tahoe region. Once the wood was cut and processed, it was shipped to San Francisco, Sacramento, and the Mother Lode in California, as well as to mines and railroad projects in Nevada, Utah, and Arizona. According to CPRR General Freight Agent Richard Gray, in his report dated January 1883, the top six items (in pounds) sent from San Francisco eastward were: tea—992,450; wood—459,650; sugar—769,540; silk—399,830; wood scoured—459,650; and wine—2,480. On the SPRR: tea—7,900; wood—358,310; sugar—420,160; silk—0; wood, scoured—6,890; wine—491,810 (Locke, Scrapbook). By the early 1900s lumber from the West Coast was one of the largest single items of railway tonnage (Johnson 1910, 256). The completion of the transcontinental railroads made it easier to sell lumber to Hawaiʻi and Asia, which became very important in helping to balance the lumber companies books during times of American economic depressions. It also freed the American West from dependence on eastern, mid-western, southern, and European wood supplies, and opened new marketplaces.

The Big Four needed workers to build the railroad and to work in logging. C. Crocker and Company, a general merchandising firm in Sacramento that later became the Contract and Finance Company, played a major role in the construction of the CPRR and the hiring of laborers (Carman and Mueller 1927; Bain 1999, 205, 209). Initially, CPRR Supervisor Crocker hired approximately fifty Chinese men, reasoning that if the Chinese could build the Great Wall of China, they could build the CPRR (Garraty and Carnes 1999, 5:746–47). Crocker later stated, "We got some Cornish miners from Virginia City and paid them extra wages. We put them on one side [of the job] and the Chinamen on the other side. We measured the work every Sunday morning, and the Chinamen without fail, always outmeasured the Cornish miners. The Chinese are skilled in using the hammer and drill; they proved themselves equal to the best Cornish miners in the work" (quoted in Takaki, 1989, 6–7). His co-directors reluctantly agreed to hire them.

By 1864 or 1865 the Chinese accounted for four thousand of the five thousand workers on the CPRR (Chiu 1963, 42–43; W. Chew 2004). According to Paul Ong (1985), at the peak of work they were exploited because their wages were one-third of the prevailing wage rate, thus allowing the CPRR about $130,000 higher profits. Labor contractors, both Chinese and Euro-American, were the source of manpower for all of these endeavors These middlemen made railroad construction and increased production in logging possible. At first the CPRR hired many of the workers through Chinese labor-contracting companies that also sold general merchandise in San Francisco and Sacramento. This was evident in the CPRR payroll records (California State Railroad Museum, Sacramento). The first Chinese railroad workers to be listed by name (probably headmen) were Hung Wah and Ah Toy, who supervised a crew of twenty-three unnamed workers for the CPRR in January and February 1864. In June 1866 the Hung Wah Company, the largest Chinese labor contractor, had 506 men working three shifts around the clock for the CPRR. Only three men were listed on one early payroll roster as being involved in lumbering: Ah Foo, woodchopper, and Ah Ting and Ah Tong, packers (W. Chew 2004, 70). Like Hung Wah, these probably were names of labor contractors or headmen rather than individuals because of the large number of choppers and packers needed. In October 1866 some of the names of the Chinese contracting companies were Hop Sing Hong (perhaps Hop Sing Tong?), Ah Coon, Ah Fong, and Ah Cum (CPRR payroll no. 311, California Railroad Museum). By 1868 there were ten thousand to fifteen thousand Chinese working for the CPRR. When the CPRR reached Lake's Crossing (Reno), only about five thousand workers were retained because the most difficult and hardest work of crossing the Sierra Nevada was complete (W. Chew, 2004; Huang 2006 and 2010).

Discouraged Chinese miners from Dutch Flat, Nevada City, Grass Valley, and other Mother Lode towns in California were among the early CPRR workers, making up about fifty percent of the new employees. One of the reasons for their recruitment was that seven of the thirty-one incorporators of the CPRR lived in the Gold Country and could easily find unemployed Chinese miners. Some Chinese traveled from Downieville and other towns in California into Nevada to work on the railroad or had experience working on other California lines (W. Chew 2004; Olson 1971). According to the *Reese River Reveille* (July 26, 1866), the CCBA reported in 1866 that of the fifty-eight thousand Chinese registered with them, 25 percent (2,320) worked for the CPRR. In 1867 Collis Huntington wrote that he wanted a half-million more Chinese workers by 1868 (Huntington to E. B. Crocker, October 3, 1867; Deverell 1994, 40–44). Like many logging firms, the CPRR used a system of paying headmen or labor contractors instead of individual Chinese workers, so an accurate count of workers is unknown.

The working conditions in railroad companies were similar to those in the woods. Generally, Chinese were paid an average of thirty dollars to thirty-five dollars monthly for twelve-hour days, six days a week. They purchased their food and supplies at the company store. According to the *Railroad Gazette* (September 10, 1870), the rations for Chinese workers per day per man were: two pounds of rice; one-third ounce of tea; one pound of beef, pork, or fish; one-third pound of vegetables; and a small quantity of lard or oil. The Chinese furnished their own bedding. Contractors provided their quarters and all tools. Medicines and medical attention, which was important to Chinese workers, were free and usually under the direction of the Chinese district association (*huiguan*) that provided the physician, since medical care by the company was offered only to Euro-American workers. A tin of opium was twelve dollars and a pipe load was twenty-five cents in 1875 (Wrobleski 1996, 18, 20). Opium was not yet illegal, and a small amount often was used as a painkiller. Gregory Mark (1995) believed that opium addiction was not as widespread among the Chinese as most Americans thought, and dangerous work, as often was the case in railroad construction, required a clear mind.

The food, especially freshly killed chickens—available in China only on special occasions—was included in the standard railroad workers' diet. Food was part of the attraction to the job. Chinese working in the woods often worked under the same arrangements. In some cases, friendships developed between the Chinese and Euro-American workers, as seen in the case of the telegraph operator named Cook, who mourned the tragic death of his Chinese friend, Jim, who died accidentally while working on a tunnel crew for the SPRR extension across Yuma, Arizona, in 1878 (MacGregor 2003, 536). In many cases, Euro-Americans regarded the Chinese with disdain or viewed them as nameless and unimportant beings, and these men were the most vociferous when in the company of anti-Chinese agitators.

Like workers at the lumber camps, the railroad construction crews often used milled lumber for part of their temporary housing (Wrobleski 1996, 34). Traversing through the hot deserts of Nevada in the late spring, tents were substituted. After 1869 some Chinese railroad maintenance men lived in railroad cars converted into semi-permanent housing. In San Francisco, because of the shortage of housing materials, redesigned railroad cars with a Victorian flare were popular among Euro-Americans, so the practice of living in railroad cars was not regarded as strange. Once the lines were completed, Chinese workers continued the upkeep the roadbeds, maintenance work, ties replacement, and work on modifications to the line. Railroad ties lasted only five to ten years in the 1870s to 1880s, so lumber crews were in high demand during this era (Pisani 1997, 25). As late as 1876 the CPRR was still working on road construction and replacing ties, trestles, and iron rails with Chinese workers.[1] The more skilled workers became section men who took care of the tracks. Charles Crocker went on to build the Southern Pacific and continued to employ Chinese not only in railroad construction but also for logging work.

The CPRR had trained many of the Chinese workers to cut down trees in order to clear roads and to assist in the construction of a variety of structures, such as the picturesque Secret Town Trestle in California near the Nevada border. Many similar wooden trestles on a smaller scale were built for railroad lines.[2] In general, workers took a week to construct a large trestle. Trestles were also needed for flumes. Wooden structures, such as bridges, sidewalks, railroad ties, and buildings, required continual maintenance. Around the turn of the century chemical treatments were developed to preserve the wood, so fewer loggers were employed or contracted for logs.

Opinions about the capabilities of the Chinese workers changed from laudatory to mildly critical. According to James Strobridge, superintendent of construction for the CPRR, the Chinese were steady workers and performed all sorts of jobs, including as teamsters and carpenters (Senate Report 689, 32 of 36). Although he was originally against the hiring of Chinese workers, in the end Strobridge developed a positive opinion about their contributions and rewarded his Chinese "bosses" with a party in his private car at Promontory, Utah, after the "Golden Spike" ceremony. In 1882 he came out of retirement to work with the Chinese on the Tehachapi and Mohave lines. Leland Stanford defended the use of Chinese in a report to President Andrew Johnson on October 10, 1865 (Kraus 1969a, 111). He felt that they were quiet, peaceable, patient, industrious, economical, and able to learn all different kinds of work. He emphasized that they were not slaves but were organized by societies that were primarily concerned with mutual aid and assistance. These societies also handled their wages, supplied their foods, and provided other necessities through American or Chinese merchants, who deducted food expenses from their monthly wages. Logging companies used this same system.

In an era of increasing national railroad strikes, in July 1867 about two thousand of Stanford's "docile" Chinese eventually felt that they were underpaid and went on strike for ten days, demanding a forty-dollar monthly wage and a ten-hour work day. The bold action was precipitated by the horrific deaths of five of their countrymen in an explosion in a tunnel a mile above Cisco that accentuated the dangers involved in their work.[3] After withholding food deliveries, the strike was settled on the old basis of thirty dollars per month with twelve-hour work days with the quiet understanding that their pay would be increased.[4] A month later, they received thirty-five dollars for a twenty-six-day month, and the Chinese felt that they had helped James Strobridge "save face" (an old Chinese concept) by delaying the raise and, in the traditional Confucian manner, accepting a compromise figure.

Between 1863 and 1869 the construction of the CPRR had an advantage over the UPRR because of the readily available supplies of lumber from the Sierras. Cutting was done on a small scale between 1856 and 1867, but with the construction of narrow-gauge logging railroads and development of the V-flume, remote forests became accessible to the CPRR and supporting rail lines, as well as the growing logging companies. As a result, logging increased, and some of the owners cut all of the trees on their land without any thought of the future or of forest management.

Construction of the CPRR made "the State of Nevada a nucleus . . . of a Pacific railroad" because of the riches of the Comstock Lode.[5] Between 1850 and 1880 the railroads had been granted approximately four million acres of land in Nevada by the federal government in an effort to encourage railroad construction, and some of this was timberland that could be sold to private parties (Miller 1926, 385). In 1864 Nevada achieved statehood, and interest in the acquisition of timberland was reaching new heights, fueled by the resource demands of mining and railroads. As a first order of business, the state of Nevada had all timberland in the state inventoried. Next, the state secured a patent for the whole inventory from the United States, so whoever wanted any of the land had to purchase it from the state (see Bliss mss). The average price of the land varied from $1.25 to $10 per acre, with a tax of 25 cents per acre for land denuded of trees. The exception was the railroad-owned land. According to the Controller of Nevada in 1879, the CPRR owned 11 million acres of land, 5 million of which was in Nevada at a value of $30 million, or $6 per acre (Nevada 1881, "Annual Report of the Controller," 13–19). In 1877 Secretary of Interior Carl Schurz warned that at the existing rate of lumber use, the forests were being depleted nationally such that within twenty years there would be an insufficient supply for domestic needs (Pisani 1997, 18). The dismal national prediction reiterated by Schurz in 1889 was evident in the nearly denuded Tahoe/Truckee River Basin.

The CPRR-contracted firms could cut the trees on federal land under the railroad construction contract and on land given to the company by the federal government. In the Sierra Nevada the CPRR and its contractors logged extensively, using Chinese workers for a variety of jobs. Chinese worked as advance scouters to determine the route of the CPRR ("History of Carlin"). Chinese loggers cut the trees with handsaws and axes and blasted the stumps to clear the way for the graders. They created roadbeds and leveled roads, built tunnels, snow sheds, and bridges, and eventually laid ties and sometimes even heavy tracks (Huffman 1995). They used picks, shovels, and wheelbarrows—no machinery. Unskilled workers often became skilled in logging and the use of equipment like saws and axes. Manual labor performed in China was similar to these tasks in the American West.

Some new types of work were introduced. Blasting powder was used for removing tree stumps and tunneling through the mountains. As many as four hundred kegs of powder at four dollars per keg were used daily (Fleming 1971, 16–17). The Chinese became experts at using the recently introduced but highly unstable nitroglycerin, which was eight times more powerful than powder, for blasting. Many Chinese died building tunnels, and the pay was relatively low

(77½ cents per day), but they nevertheless went on to build tunnels for other rail lines (MacGregor 2003, 541–47). Later Euro-American supervisors had crews of Chinese who specialized in tunneling and took them from one railroad or road construction job location to another. The Euro-American rationale was that since the Chinese had invented gunpowder, they could handle dangerous explosives, but many died from working with nitroglycerin.

On May 10, 1869, the first transcontinental railroad line was completed as the UPRR met the CPRR at Promontory Point, Utah (Yen 1977). According to Ward McAfee (1974), the CPRR could have gone farther than Promontory Point, but various communities, including San Francisco, blocked or delayed its construction in 1863 and 1864. Euro-American laborers erroneously believed that the completion of the line meant that the now-unemployed, lower-paid Chinese laborers threatened their jobs. Labor leaders tried to organize the Euro-American workers to join the anti-Chinese movement. They were supported by the growing popular presses and rising politicians. However, several hundred Chinese continued to work for the CPRR doing maintenance, roadwork, and other tasks, including working in station restaurants so that passengers and crewmen could eat. Some of the released workers performed other work for the CPRR, such as making wood charcoal, replacing ties regularly, and maintaining the rail lines, while others worked on the construction and maintenance of other rail lines, especially feeder lines to the CPRR. Nevertheless, the general population believed that "swarms" of Chinese were about to take their jobs or cause their salaries to be lowered. The phrase "cheap Chinese labor" became a popular rallying cry for union leaders and politicians.

Some of the Chinese began to work in lumbering, and one of the significant firms hiring them was the CTLFC, which began in 1870 as Yerington, Bliss, and Company to provide wood for the Comstock and the construction of the VTRR. Large logging companies often moved their base of operations near or next to railroad lines instead of being concerned with the location of bodies of water. The company soon bought out Michele E. Spooner and his partners, Oliver (b. 1832) and John Lonkey, the Elliot Brothers, Henry M. Yerington, William Fairburn, and Simon Dubois' Summit Fluming Company for $80,000, or $300 per acre, for the timberland in Douglas, Ormsby, and El Dorado Counties. This gave them more forestland, a shingle mill, and a sawmill. This was yet another example of how small timber ranchers yielded to larger corporations.

Between 1871 and 1873 Yerington and Bliss established the CTLFC with Bliss as president and general manager (Bliss 2013). The CTLFC continued to expand, purchasing August Pray's 1861 Summit Mill and Fluming Company and Glenbrook mill, barn, blacksmith shop, and other buildings for $5,025 in 1874 and timberland from the Elliott brothers at $6 per acre (Nevada 1875, 13–19). CTLFC now owned some seven thousand acres of timberland and the Summit Mill, making improvements and extending its V-flume so that logs could be transported more easily. The distance from Tahoe to Carson is fourteen miles, and the V-flume could carry seven hundred cords of wood, or a half-million board feet of mining timber, in one day, whereupon it could be transported to Virginia City or elsewhere (Straka 2008, 3). The Chinese tended their eleven-mile Clear Creek Flume (formerly Summit Flume), which at one point had a fairly terrifying trestle one hundred feet off the ground, and its numerous feeder flumes. The CTLFC continued to buy up smaller timber owners.

The Hobart acquisition was an important one for the CTLFC. Hobart was a small but significant company using Chinese workers and providing wood for mines and trains. In 1873 Nevada State Controller Walter Hobart joined with former Nevada and California Surveyor General Seneca Marlette to begin operating a small sawmill in Little Valley, near Incline Village, in order to provide wood for the Comstock. Hobart was the first and youngest Comstock millionaire. In 1878 they incorporated their company as the Sierra Nevada Wood and Lumber Company (SNWLC) and eventually owned sixty-five thousand acres of timberland on the east side of the Tahoe Basin in the Carson Range. They employed 150 French Canadians and 250 Chinese. They produced seventy-five thousand board feet of lumber per day at their height of production. With its later subsidiary, the Nevada Lumber Company, both headquartered at first in Virginia City, then Incline Village, SNWLC became one of the largest companies in the region and competed with the CTLFC (Richards). Along with the Donner Lumber and Boom Company and PWLFC, the SNWLC dominated the northern half of the Tahoe Basin, while the CTLFC and El Dorado Wood and Fluming Company (EDWFC) controlled much of the southern half (Smith 2001). These men realized the great profits to be had. The SNWLC only paid one dollar per acre for eighty acres near the Little Truckee River and went on to harvest the timberland (Wilson 1992, 71). Some of the newly purchased land was part of the CPRR land grants. Eventually, the company owned almost eight thousand acres of timberland and Crystal Bay, another main office, as well as a large milling complex in the area (Petersen, Seldomridge, and Stearns 1993, 1:32).

The Chinese logged most of the wood in and around Crystal Bay. The wood was shipped on their logging train, the Incline Railroad, built in 1881 and consisting of four cars that were hauled uphill some four thousand feet with a fourteen-hundred-foot gain in elevation. At the top, the logs, about one-and-a-half cords of wood, were emptied into a V-flume and carried south to the Comstock via a water tunnel, traveling some 3,994 feet on another V-flume until the load reached Little Valley and the VTRR station at Lakeview. By 1883 the company owned seventy thousand acres north of Truckee. A company town, Overton, located 6½ miles north of Truckee on Prosser Creek, developed and eventually was renamed Hobart Mills (Rowley and Rowley 1992). A reporter visiting the area in June 1891 noted that there was a camp of some two hundred men at work. The eventual reception point for the logs from the Tahoe Basin was at present-day Sand Harbor on Lake Tahoe (Myrick 1962, 425–29).

Hobart's primary residence was in San Francisco, and he probably knew some Chinese labor bosses.[6] He patronized the Chinese store Quong Hing and Company in Carson City, which also provided supplies to many of the workers in the Tahoe Basin. Ledgers dated 1880–1882 of the SNWLC noted payments to Quong Hing for goods and services, such as repairs on the company's dump. SNWLC employed the Chinese in lumbering as well as those working in the construction of their rail line. The discovery of two Chinese camps at the flumes in the West Portal indicated that Chinese worked as flume herders and tended the tunnel (Arthur Koeber report in J. Stone). After the death of Walter Hobart Sr. in June 1892, the operations declined; in 1894 the flume and some timberland acres were sold to the CTLFC and the Truckee Lumber Company (TLC). The SNWLC Chinese employees probably continued to work for the CTLFC and TLC.

Yerington, Bliss, and Company subcontracted independent operators like M. C. Gardner to saw logs for the construction of railways and for use in the mines. Gardner had a four-year contract for 50 million feet of logs from his ranch on the west side of Lake Tahoe.[7] Gradually, Yerington and Bliss expanded their holdings with more sawmills and forestland, and in 1873 the Gardner holdings became part of the CLTFC (Douglas County, *Book of Deeds*; CTLFC papers).[8] They continued to buy up small timber ranchers and made Glenbrook the center of their operations.

In 1875 Yerington also operated a subsidiary—or "shadowy"—firm, the El Dorado Wood and Fluming Company (EDWFC), headed by Yerington, A. J. Ralston, and Captain John W. Haynie (Lindstrom and Hall 1994). EDWFC operated in California around the Lake Tahoe Basin and cut lumber in Washoe, Ormsby, and Douglas Counties in Nevada, in El Dorado County, California, and other locations (EDWFC records). EDWFC also purchased land for mineral and water rights (Douglas County, book F (A12), 623–24 is one example). The primary purpose of the company was to provide wood to the Comstock mines by transporting it on the VTRR. The CTLFC and EDWFC dominated the lumber industry in the Tahoe Basin.

Haynie had connections with the Chinese community in Carson City. He not only was a customer of Chinese merchandising companies, such as Sam Sing Company, Quong Sing Company, and Kwong Wo Lung, but he also donated funds to the Chinese Methodist minister Ah For when he attempted to build a Chinese Chapel for the Episcopal Church in 1875 (Haynie, ledger). Haynie was active in purchasing timber ranches and mills from smaller owners, such as James W. Haines, between 1875 and 1880 in the East Peak and Daggett Pass area near the Kingsbury Grade. He probably continued using Haines's Chinese workers; as well, his partnership with Yerington in the EDWFC likely allowed him to support the employment of Chinese workers.

In 1880 EDWFC was in financial trouble and owed the government $87,000.[9] Bliss was summoned but disavowed any connection with Haynie and Yerington. In 1881, after cutting almost all of the wood in the area near Brown's Station (about twenty-two miles west of Carson City), the EDWFC closed its operations there. An estimated eighty-six thousand cords of wood had been harvested from that area at a low average estimate of $602,000 (at $7 per cord) and shipped via the VTRR to the Comstock.[10]

In order to go deeper into the Sierra Nevada, CTLFC constructed the Carson Tahoe Railroad from April 19 to August 21, 1875, employing some 150 to 250 men, most of whom were Chinese.[11] The Carson Tahoe Railroad traversed steep grades; once it was completed, trains made six daily trips to Spooner Summit carrying an estimated daily total of three hundred thousand board feet of lumber and eventually totaled ten miles in length (Myrick 1962, 422). The logging train was much more efficient than the older method of using animals for hauling. Another train at Lake Valley was added to link the logging camps, flumes, roads, ditches, and trains. Roads had to be leveled and trestles of wood built in the steep mountains. Fantastic wood trestles carried the trains over valleys and ravines. At its height in the late 1870s through 1880s, CTLFC owned approximately fifty thousand acres of timber at Lake Tahoe and Lake Valley (south of Lake Tahoe), covering all five counties adjacent to the Tahoe Basin; they cut 14 million feet annually, transported the logs by rail and flumes to Carson City, and employed as many as five hundred men in milling and logging (Nevada *Appendix* 1887). Most of the company's activities took place in Glenbrook, Spooner Summit, and Clear Creek Canyon. In February and March of 1885 the entire crew at Lakeview was Chinese, and other records showed Chinese employment at the Summit Flume and Mill No. 2 in 1886 and 1888 (CTLFC, box 5). Within twenty years of operations, CTLFC probably logged one-fifth of the entire Lake Tahoe Basin (Goodwin 1960, 75). Without Chinese labor, this feat may not have been possible.

Another major addition to CTLFC was the property of George Washington Chubbuck, a sole proprietor and manager of timberland in the Tahoe Valley just east of present-day Camp Richardson on the south shore of Lake Tahoe. His brother, S. W. Chubbuck, the state senator from Storey County in 1875, probably provided an early link between politics and lumber interests in the Nevada legislature. Chubbuck employed French Canadian lumberjacks and more than one hundred Chinese and Portuguese cordwood cutters on his Lake View logging ranch (Scott 1975, 1:212, 2:13; Petersen, Seldomridge, and Stearns 1994, 42). He also had a Chinese cook, who probably helped him recruit Chinese workers. The South Lake Tahoe Museum has a photograph of three Chinese "trimmers" watching the felling of a tree on the Sierra House ranch at Lake View (see chapter 2). In 1884 he concluded a contract with CTLFC and EDWFC to provide timber from his own lands. In 1886 Chubbuck built a narrow-gauge railroad from Bijou to Sierra House (a mile away from Cold Creek Canyon) called the Lake Valley

Railroad (Myrick 1962, 424–25). By 1893 there were 10.5 miles of track. It is probable that Chubbuck employed Chinese laborers to do the grading, since they were
experienced and available (Vatter 1985, 245). By 1886 Chubbuck was bankrupt.

Eventually, CTLFC bought the ranch and the Lake Valley Railroad. The CTLFC
expanded the rail line to Meyers, thus allowing more timberland to be cut. Log
chutes and ox wagons moved the timber to the Lake Valley Railroad. The pier
at Bijou allowed the logs to be dumped into Lake Tahoe so that they could be
transported by steamer across the lake to sawmills at Glenbrook and then taken
to Carson City and Virginia City. In 1898 the Lake Valley forests were denuded,
and the Bijou operation ceased. As with numerous other narrow-gauge railroads,
the tracks and rolling stock of the Lake Valley Railroad were removed and reused
in Tahoe City for the Lake Tahoe Railway and Transportation Company (Smith
2001, 14).

In 1879 Bliss moved his wife and five children from Gold Hill to Carson City
and into their new eighty-five-hundred-square-foot mansion on Mountain Street
across from the governor's mansion. Personal, top-level, informal communications between the governor and Bliss became easier with this relocation. Networking between the servants in the governor's mansion and the Bliss mansion
probably also became more frequent.

In the 1880s production at the Glenbrook mills, the industrial center of the
CTLFC, had dropped by 50 percent due the economic depression on the Comstock, but Bliss and Yerington were determined to expand their empire. By 1887
the CTLFC brought in 14 million feet of wood annually from adjacent counties
in California across Lake Tahoe to Glenbrook and eventually by rail and flumes
to Carson City (Nevada 1887, Douglas County, 56). The financial situation was
not improving. In 1888 Bliss and Yerington had a multimillion-dollar business.
Bliss discovered a new interest and turned his attention to tourism in the Tahoe
Basin. The CTLFC continued to purchase more forestland. In 1894 they bought
the Sierra Lumber Company's business from Hobart and Marlett for about a half-
million dollars.[12] The CTLFC also acquired the Nevada Lumber Company and
Sierra Nevada Wood and Flume Company around the Tahoe Basin. Trees could
be cut on the east, south, and west shores of Lake Tahoe. Within twenty years
they owned or leased approximately one-fifth of the land in the Tahoe Basin with
three mills at Glenbrook, a box and planing mill at Carson City, three logging
railroads and one freighting railroad, two steamers to transport the logs across
Lake Tahoe, logging camps, a box factory in Carson City, and a large lumberyard
at Spooner Summit and another near Carson City, to name the major holdings
(CLTFC papers; Smith 2001). At its peak the CTLFC owned fifty thousand acres
or more in all five counties in the Tahoe Basin, harvested 750 million board feet
of lumber, and a half-million cords of wood (CTLFC Records; "Carson Tahoe").
Most of the independent and small timber ranchers no longer existed. In 1895
Bliss withdrew from his involvement with the lumbering industry because of his

interest in tourism, turning instead to development of the Glenbrook Hotel and Tahoe recreational sites.

Logging operations ceased in 1896 due to the depletion of timber on their lands and the decline of mining on the Comstock. In 1898 the mills and the Lake Tahoe Railroad that the Chinese had built were dismantled. In 1899 Bliss moved his family to a mansion in Pacific Heights, San Francisco, near the home of Darius Mills. Both Bliss and Yerington became very wealthy from their investments in "green gold." The partners spent an estimated $1 million on the lands, plants, and business, with an additional $300,000 for the Lake Tahoe Railroad to present-day Spooner Summit (Goodwin 1960, 4). The CTLFC had taken advantage of the state lands and expanded further by buying out the small lumbermen. Bliss died at age of seventy-four in 1907, Yerington in 1910. They were succeeded by their sons, William S. Bliss and E. B. Yerington, who remained with the company until the late 1920s, yet the sons probably had few or no Chinese employees, as the Chinese exclusion acts drastically reduced the number of Chinese laborers available for hire. Fortunately, both the CTLFC and EDWFC were involved in real estate. This enabled the EDWFC to survive until 1940. In 1947 William S. Bliss dissolved the CTLFC.

Duane Bliss also got his brother-in-law, Walter Tobey, involved in the lumbering business. Parker and Tobey Lumber Company, a firm that eventually worked closely with Bliss, also supplied "China labor" as subcontractors who paid their workers through Chinese agents (the only names on the payroll) (W. Bliss papers; Parker and Tobey; Tobey: CLTFC boxes 7 to 9). The CTLFC paid Parker and Tobey from April 1879 through May 1882 (only scattered records available) for "China Time," lumbering work. Subcontracting was a method employed to circumvent the law adopted in California, Nevada, and other western states, prohibiting corporations from employing Chinese, a statute that was not overturned until 1880.[13] In 1875 Tobey sold 296 acres to CTLFC (Parker and Tobey, box 3, 179). In 1878, Parker and Tobey received and processed wood at a flume dump along the VTRR tracks at Franktown. They contracted with Hobart and Marlette to flume, dump, and pile lumber and wood onto the VTRR. For this and other tasks, they used Chinese workers through the 1890s (Hill 1987, 24–26). The firm was also involved with the Lakeview dump. Canceled checks from Parker and Tobey at the University of Nevada, Reno, Special Collections Library showed that the Chinese employees were paid $1.24 to $1.50 per day in 1883–84 and $2.00 per day in 1885. They were paid in groups, once a month, with the labor boss receiving the funds. The Chinese headman kept the difference between the wages he paid to the actual workers and the payments made by the company for the work, thus acting as a middleman subcontractor (Boswell 1986, 358). Often, the labor contractor did not take a profit from the workers in this manner but, as a merchant, made his income instead from selling goods to the workers. Parker and Tobey paid Euro-American laborers three dollars to four dollars per day individually on a regular basis throughout the month, but the type of job, which may have been more skilled, was not specified (Smith 2001, 27; Parker and Tobey; Tobey). The average monthly salary had to take into consideration the one to five days off that the Chinese took during Chinese New Year when the usual amount of work could not be conducted. Yerington was aware of the importance of Chinese New Year and complained about the fact that the output was less than normal, but he learned to expect their absence at that time of year (Yerington UNR, Letter to Mills, January 27, 1876. Parker and Tobey and others also experienced this annual drop in production.

Employers of Chinese workers often patronized Chinese general stores. Bliss and Tobey were regular patrons of Quong Hing and Company in Carson City; one canceled check showed that Parker and Tobey had purchased $1,420.04 from Quong Hing in 1887 and $393.17 in 1888 (Tobey). One can assume that there were positive relations, especially with the Chinese manager of Quong Hing, Sam Gibson (Non Chong Yee).

The CTLFC and Yerington and Company bought goods from other Chinese merchants and used other Chinese labor contractors, including Ahi Tate and Ah Jack, for hiring men to cut and haul wood (CTLFC; Yerington, UNR, journal entries, 1872–1873, on Ah Jack). Like the railroad contractors, the lumber contractors provided living quarters, food, tools, medicine, and medical attention (Wrobleski, 1996, 18).[14] In 1870 Ahi Tate (b. 1830) lived in Carson City near two doctors, Tung Tong Sung (b. 1820) and See Hope (b. 1840), and the woodchopper See See (b. 1835). The presence of the Chinese doctors was important to treat the injuries that the men sometimes sustained; often, the provision of a doctor and medical care was a clause in Chinese employment contracts (Liu 1998, 173–91). The Chinese felt that Eastern medical treatments were more effective and centuries older than Western medicine (Hinrichs and Barnes, 2013). Labor contractors could recruit more workers if they informed their prospective employees that a Chinese physician was available.

At CTLFC Chinese workers were paid according to their type and location of the job. CTLFC payroll records for 1876–1879, 1882–1883, 1886, and the 1890s showed that at the flume camps on Spooner Summit, the Chinese worked as cooks, dishwashers, and flume herders. Others worked at the mills at Glenbrook, on the railroad section crew camps in Lake Valley, and on the steamer *Meteor*, which Bliss bought from Lucky Baldwin in order to traverse Lake Tahoe (CTLFC papers; W. Bliss papers, boxes 5–6). The Chinese also worked at the Carson Dump and Saxton's Camp. On average, the Chinese received lower wages than Euro-Americans but did not have to pay the required fifty cents deducted from Euro-American wages as the monthly medical fee. There was a "glass ceiling," even in the camps: the Chinese were generally not allowed to rise above a certain level. Euro-Americans held all supervisory positions, thereby earning more money, but in certain positions the Chinese made more money than their Euro-American counterpart.

Archaeologists Susan G. Lindstrom and Jeffrey T. Hall (1994) provided a detailed analysis based on payroll information on the production rates and pay scale of Chinese and Euro-American camps at Lake Valley. Their study indicated that the Chinese had the highest production rates (perhaps because of larger crew size) but were paid less than Euro-Americans for the same type of work. This contradicts the findings that compared job type pay scales and court records involving lawsuits over wages.

The pay records illustrated this. In 1876 the payroll record indicated that, on average, the Chinese received $1 per day for their work while other Chinese received $14 for twelve days of work (W. Bliss papers, box 5), and few earned more. In the early 1870s at the Markleeville Flume Company with Yerington as president, China Charley was paid $44.28 as his regular thirty-day salary, or about $1.48 per day (Markleeville records). In 1878 Ah Gee cooked for a month and received $40, while Ah Sam, another cook, only received $30 in the same pay period. Ah Sam was probably an assistant cook. This was the same pay range for non-Chinese cooks. Location and number of meals or customers likely determined the exact wages. For example, a cook at the Glenbrook House between 1868 and 1869 received $38 per month (Glenbrook House). In the 1890s Chinese cooks Ah Charley and China Charlie earned $40 to $50 per month (July 1891), which was the rate if they worked in San Francisco, for example. Non-Chinese cooks received $30 to $40 per month (CTLFC; W. Bliss papers, box 6). Cooks at the Summit Flume earned $10 more than those cooking for the railroad crew. The top salary at the Summit Flume for October 1891 was $53.84; most other workers received $50 per month, equal to Ah Charley's $50 in his role as cook. Dishwashers earned $25 per month (thirty days). The higher salary paid to the Chinese added fuel to the anti-Chinese movement.

CTLFC payroll records in June and July 1883 listed fifty-five names of Chinese workers, and the signatures on the documents were all in the same hand, indicating that an agent or labor contractor signed for the wages. Although many of the Chinese on the CTLFC payroll signed their names in English (Charley Tong in 1882, for example) or in Chinese to match their given American name (such as Ah Sam in 1878), many of the cooks and workers signed their real Chinese names. For example, Ah Charley in the 1890s, making $50 per month, signed Yu Ci (Cantonese pronunciation of last name was Yee, first name probably Gee). Throughout this period, many were members of the Yee clan, which was indicated in Chinese only: Ah Sam (1879), Ah Joe and Ah Jean (1891), Ah Ling, Ah Charley, China helper (1890s).

The surname Yee in Chinese appeared frequently. The Yee merchants of Carson City, especially Sam Gibson (Yee Non Chong), probably got these men their jobs. A networking system arose among them. For instance, Yee Fong was a major supplier of vegetables from 1888 to 1891 and raised his produce at Glenbrook, where "Chinese gardens" were located on the south side of Lower Pray Meadow.

He undoubtedly was the same Ah Fung (b. 1855) in the 1880 census manuscript who was single, could read, and lived by himself. Next door on both sides were Chinese laundrymen, who in turn lived next door on both sides to Euro-Americans. Yee Fong provided goods to Chinese cooks so that the food was more tasty and healthy. Housing integration in many parts of rural Nevada was in evidence during the late nineteenth century, so it would not be surprising if Yee Fong also sold his neighbors fresh produce.

On the other hand, those who signed their name in English, like Ah Lee, did not indicate their real surname because "Ah" is a familiar term of address, not a surname or first name. Ah Lee earned three dollars per day and had the more difficult job of loading wood for the *Meteor*, the steamship used to move lumber across Lake Tahoe (CTLFC payroll, October 1879). Sam Tong, a watchman at the mill, earned sixty dollars per a month, the same salary as the mill watchman John Matatal (CTLFC, payroll, September and November 1891 are examples). Thus, contrary to labor union allegations of lowers wages, the CTLFC Chinese workers were paid at the same rate as the non-Chinese workers in certain jobs. Equality in salaries and higher salaries than Euro-American workers occurred elsewhere. At Port Townsend, Washington, the Admiralty Hotel paid some of its Chinese employees as much as sixty dollars per month—twenty dollars more than the average Euro-American monthly wage—and others only fifteen dollars per month, depending upon the job (Liestman 1994). In general, the Chinese were never in the top echelon of wage earners.

The CTLFC responded to anti-Chinese movements of the 1880s by discontinuing payroll lists of individual Chinese workers. Instead, the labor contractors, including Quong Hing and Company and Parker and Tobey Lumber Company, were paid for "China Time" in the 1890s. Chinese workers loaded the cordwood and lumber onto the VTRR cars at Lakeview, King's Canyon, and Carson City (Wurm and Demoro 1983, 48). The VTRR paid the Chinese labor contractor, such as Dr. Ah Kee of Carson City, and also avoided problems with individual payroll names (Nevada State Museum, Carson City). The CTLFC and VTRR circumvented criticism and potential violence from anti-Chinese agitators in this way, and the books were easier to keep by subcontracting work to middlemen instead of individuals. The CPRR had also used this system.

The popular but erroneous belief was that all the wood cut from the surrounding areas, in both Nevada and California counties, was used on the Comstock. Actually, shipments of wood and wood products went to the East and West on the CPRR. It is not inconceivable that some of these logs eventually were shipped to Asia from San Francisco because there was an active timber trade at this time.

Several Chinese wood camps in Lake Valley, South Lake Tahoe, California, appeared to be controlled by Chinese labor contractors (Smith 2001, 20–30). The Sue Kee Camp had as many as twenty wood camps and a store that was located in 1889 in block 21 of Carson City's Chinatown, while Ah Pow had fifteen camps and a store (Kautz 2006, 32). Ching Sing had five camps; Ah Lim had four. These were probably company names, so they did not appear in the census records. As with the CPRR, payroll distributions often were made to the labor boss so that in July 1891 the CTLFC paid Ah Lim $1,176.73 for wood, $47.78 for lumber, and $19.20 to deliver the wood to the LVRR, for a total of $2,224.51, while Fong Yee was paid $17.16 for mill work, $13.75 for fluming, and $2.25 for the shop bill for a total of $30.91 (CTLFC payroll, July 1891).

By the 1880s in some areas, such as Truckee, California, the Chinese constituted almost 100 percent of the loggers. Unemployed or underemployed men wanted their jobs, but few of them wanted to match them in their productivity. The Chinese were hired to do other work. The skills acquired during railroad construction provided them with experience for logging and road construction, including the amazing feat of creating the steep and winding Tioga Road through Yosemite, California, and the nationally recognized complex Tehachapi Railroad route.

More than one thousand of the released Chinese CPRR workers joined the CTLFC and the construction of the VTRR, subsidiary rail lines, as well as other projects. The VTRR was the handiwork of Bliss and Yerington, the principles in the CTLFC who provided much of the lumber for the Comstock. Both men favored hiring Chinese workers. In his memoirs, Duane L. Bliss stated that he moved to Carson City in 1860 and then relocated to Gold Hill in 1862 (Bliss mss; Wheeler 1992).[15] A year later he started to work in a bank, which was later renamed the Bank of California. In 1867–68 William Sharon (1821–1885), who headed the Bank of California's Virginia City branch beginning in 1864 and had all of the mines and mills on the Comstock connected with the bank within two years, selected Yerington to be the superintendent of the proposed VTRR from the Carson City end and Bliss from the Virginia City end (Virginia and Truckee, *Papers*, Huntington, UNR).[16] Sharon and Darius Ogden Mills, president of the Bank of California, who were both millionaires, backed numerous enterprises during the 1870s, including the CTLFC.[17] J. A. Rigby, who, in 1874 built the first store in Glenbrook, was a major stockholder in the CTLFC and other lumber companies. The Comstock–San Francisco business connections were important to these enterprises.

Yerington was a part of the Crocker inner circle because he had dated and in 1877 married Charles Crocker's niece, who had been raised by Judge Edwin B. Crocker (1818–1875) and his wife. Edwin Crocker was also the attorney for the CPRR. Yerington later became president of the VTRR and emulated Charles Crocker on a smaller scale in his expansion of business activities. Eventually, Yerington served as president of sixteen companies, including the CCRR, Bodie and Benton Railroad (BBRR), the Bodie Hydraulic Mining and Water Company, and the SNWLC, to name just a few (Yerington Papers, UCB). In many ventures he employed Chinese, especially in those with Bliss in the Tahoe Basin.

In 1868 plans were developed for the construction of the VTRR connecting Virginia City to Carson City and later Carson City to Reno. A year later the first spike was hammered in. Between February 18, 1869, and April 1, 1869, twelve hundred men, most of whom were Chinese, worked on the grading and surveying of the VTRR. They lived in thirty-eight camps between Virginia City and Carson City. "Most of the laborers . . . [were] brought over from the nearly completed Central Pacific. Agitations and demonstrations against the 'Celestial[s]' were fomented by elements in the miners' unions, but they were soon quieted" because the employers promised not to employ the Chinese in the mines. In order to further appease the anti-Chinese agitators, the last segment of track into Virginia City was completed by an all Euro-American crew (Wurm and Demoro 1983, 37; Myrick 1962, 137–38).

The big challenge of VTRR construction was the elevation change, as Virginia City was 1,575 feet above the mills along the Carson River. This was solved by wrapping the tracks around the hills for 13½ miles at a 2.2 percent grade to total twenty-one miles. Based on their experience on the CPRR, Chinese workers cleared and graded the roads and, through teamwork, laid the rails weighing between forty-five and fifty-six pounds (Wrobleski 1996, 8–9). Yerington shifted his Chinese workers between railroad construction and logging work for the CTLFC. One case may be representative of others. Ah Chow had worked on the VTRR while residing permanently in Virginia City, but after the line was completed he went to work as a woodchopper at the CTLFC wood yard at Clear Creek, south of Carson City.[18] One can assume that his job for the VTRR involved cutting trees, so his new position in 1870 at Clear Creek was really a continuation of the old one. Like Bliss in his relationship with Sam Gibson, Yerington also had longstanding friendships with a number of Chinese individuals, as exemplified in the case of G. Ah Chew, who had worked for him on the VTRR from Carson City to Reno before he returned to China. When Ah Chew returned to Nevada in January 1876, he wrote to Yerington asking for a job, which Yerington granted, owing to his power and influence (Yerington papers, UNR). The line was completed between Virginia City and Carson City in 1870, but not without trouble.

In September some 350 Comstock miners who were afraid of losing their jobs marched to a nearby Chinese railroad camp, drove the Chinese workers out, and destroyed their living quarters at one of the several camps.[19] The local newspapers covered the uproar. Sharon met with representatives from the miner's union and worked out a compromise so that construction could continue with the last leg, from the American Mine to Virginia City, being completed by Euro-American workers. Sharon's use of Chinese workers, his work policies, and his irresponsible service as Nevada's United States Senator (1874–1880) earned him the enmity of the editor of Carson City's *Morning Appeal* (October 10, 1880), who also charged that Sharon "takes all the money made [by the VTRR] to San Francisco, where he lives." Sharon seldom spent time in Nevada or Washington, D.C. The completion of the VTRR in 1870 had a negative effect on Chinese wood peddlers, since the line now delivered coal and cordwood to the Comstock. It also boosted the prosperity of the Comstock, since wood easily and reasonably could be transported.

By 1871 the Comstock was connected to the state capital, Carson City, where quartz reduction mills were located along the Carson River. Feeder lines to the standard gauge VTRR were built to Yerington's wood flume at the south of Kings Canyon near Carson City and to the lumberyards at Clear Creek Canyon in Carson City. In 1872 the VTRR extended north through Franktown, Washoe City, and Steamboat Springs to Reno, some thirty-one miles, where it connected with the CPRR. This allowed the lumber from the Sierra Nevada to be sold at a reasonable price to the Comstock mines and for the ore to be transported to the CPRR station in Reno, as well as facilitating the shipment of lumber and charcoal east and west of Reno.

The Chinese workforce on the Reno extension varied in size from eighty to one thousand and many lived in Carson City or Reno (Rogers 1997, 17–18). In 1872 the *Nevada State Journal* (July 20) reported that three hundred Chinese were working on the VTRR and had paid their poll taxes in Reno. Additional men were hired to work on the grading between Steamboat and Carson City, bringing the total to six hundred Chinese workers by June 1872.[20] Labor contractor James Burke of Bell and Burke provided most, if not all, of the Chinese workers for the VTRR. According to the *Nevada State Journal* (May 18, 1872), Burke paid the three hundred Chinese workers just over $5,000 (after deducting expenses for provisions). The average figure of less than $17 was probably for two weeks' work and did not indicate salary by different jobs or time spent on the job (some probably did not work a full two weeks). The newspaper article also pointed out that the Chinese paid for their own food and personal supplies, ordered through their agents, which was how the Chinese merchants made their profits. After their experience building the CPRR and the VTRR, Chinese workers were hired for many of the standard and narrow gauge railroads that continued to be built in the American West.

The VTRR hauled wood to the mines, ore to the mills, and supplies to the communities. Between 1873 and 1877, the VTRR had the following shipments of lumber and wood:

Year	Lumber shipments (in feet)	Cords of Wood
1873 (first half)	23,938,624	43,468
1874	52,220,801	139,808
1875	72,536,465	179,295
1876	71,633,072	212,278.5
1877	39,981,967	221,496.75

In 1875 the VTRR had thirty-five trains per day traveling from Carson to Virginia City with a weekly load of ten thousand cords of wood (*Carson Valley News*, March 13, 1875). Bliss estimated that at its peak, forty-four to forty-six VTRR trains per day traveled between Carson and the Comstock; in 1876 it operated thirty-four trains each day from Carson to Reno.[21] Each trip used three to four cords of wood just to fuel the locomotives (Knowles 1942, 3). A typical Comstock mine could burn twenty-five cords of wood each day at the height of operations, wood cut primarily from the forests around Lake Tahoe. According to Bliss, in one year, from August 1, 1875 to August 1, 1876, 72 million feet of lumber and 320,000 cords of wood went to the Comstock from Carson City. The two famous mines, the Bonanza Mines and Consolidated Virginia, alone took 2.5 million feet of lumber per month and 10,000 to 13,000 cords of wood in their operation (Knowles 1942, 3). At its height in 1876 the VTRR hauled 260,000 tons of ore going in the opposite direction and had eighteen locomotives. In the 1870s and 1880s Chinese labor crews out of Carson City loaded cordwood and lumber onto the VTRR cars at Lakeview, King's Canyon, and south Carson (Wurm 1983, 48). The cordwood was critical to fuel the train engines of the VTRR as well as the smelters and buildings in Virginia City and Gold Hill. The lumber was especially important after the 1875 fire in Virginia City, since most of the town had to be rebuilt.

Bliss and Yerington were discouraged by the anti-Chinese violence as well as the loss of production between 1876 and 1886. In November 1877 there was a great fire at the wood dump in Carson City resulting in the loss of 11,250 cords of wood, 6,250 of which belonged to them, 3,000 to the VTRR. The estimated loss was $47,000. Fortunately, they had insurance (Smith 2000, 1:63–64). Yerington and Bliss continued to establish other supporting and interlocking companies, many of which employed Chinese. Earlier rival logging companies, several with Chinese employees, eventually were subsumed under the CTLFC and other large corporations. This was possible because demand for lumber in mining and railroad construction and maintenance was still strong.

In general, Bliss and Yerington regarded the Chinese workers as reliable and therefore hired them for various jobs. In 1880–1883 Yerington made the VTRR the parent company of the CCRR (sold in 1900 to Crocker's Southern Pacific Company) from Mound House, Nevada, to Keeler, California, operating from April 18, 1881, until 1934. Yerington held the titles of president and superintendent. Five hundred Chinese worked on the construction of the CCRR. Some of the land for the railroad was purchased from Chinese landowners who lived in Dayton (Dayton Historical Society Museum, land deeds). Yerington probably followed many of the same practices of employment that he had used for the VTRR workers. Yerington used another infamous labor contractor for the CCRR. Like the other labor contractors, Ah Quong (b. 1847), who lived in Reno and had been the Chinese labor contractor for the building of the CCRR, and Sam

Thayer (Chinese), who had worked for the CPRR, could read English and were fluent in several dialects of Chinese, very important skills for labor supervisors, headmen, and contractors. Ah Quong did not have the financial success or stability that some Chinese and several Euro-American labor contractors enjoyed. Poor business practices, gambling, and speculation in the stock market may have contributed to his downfall. Yerington then headed another railroad construction project.

In 1881–82 Yerington used Chinese workers to construct the BBRR in Mono County, California, primarily to serve the mines in between the towns of Bodie and Benton. As the Comstock declined, new mining areas opened, and by 1877 mines at Bodie, California, began to prosper. Bodie, at an elevation of 8,374 feet, was a rough and lawless town, and in 1881 the only man hanged for a crime to that date was Chinese (Wedertz 1969). Yerington invested in mining and a sawmill in the region. Bliss and Yerington turned to the forests of eastern California to supply Bodie with lumber and used Chinese workers to build the narrow gauge BBRR and work in the wood camps (Wedertz 1969, 155; Myrick 1962, 296–313).

As on the VTRR, the Chinese construction crew on the BBRR also was attacked. Thomas Holt, the superintendent, hired about two hundred Euro-Americans and a growing number of Chinese to work on the line. According to the prevailing rumors, timber teamsters incited the Bodie miners, many of whom came from the Comstock, to attack the Chinese workers. Upon hearing the rumors, Holt wisely moved his crew of forty to fifty Chinese to the solitary Paoho Island in Mono Lake. The only way to reach them was on the one Mono Lake steamer that was not available to the agitators, so the Chinese were safe on the island. Chinese merchants in Bodie raised $300 to help support the railroad workers on Paoho Island with food and other necessities until the uproar was over. Eventually, the Chinese completed the line. When the supporting Chinese woodcutters in a nearby area were about to be attacked, the sheriff from Bodie intervened and the miners' two-day protest ended. Violence against the Chinese was all too common.

The tremendous need of the railroads for lumber led to the growth of numerous mills at Truckee Meadows, Crystal Peak, and Verdi, located on the California-Nevada border not far from the Carson Range and Reno. In Truckee Meadows (near Truckee), Washoe County, there were sixteen Chinese woodchoppers whose ages ranged from fourteen to forty-one, one Chinese laborer who was involved in lumbering, five Chinese cooks, and three Chinese laborers working in agriculture. All of the Chinese woodchoppers in Truckee Meadows lived in two dwellings that were probably boardinghouses. Most of the Euro-Americans engaged in the logging in the area lived in boardinghouses of ten people.

As the various railway lines were completed, the released workers found jobs on other interstate and intrastate lines and road construction. In 1870s steam engines and iron rails replaced horsepower and wooden rails of the previous era. Many narrow-gauge railroads, which cost half the price of standard-gauge lines, were built. This brought down the price of shipping goods (Floyd 1985). Resentment eventually had built up about the rates set by the railroad monopolies, especially the CPRR, so narrow gauges came into vogue. Chinese workers often were hired as part of the construction crew for narrow gauges. These railroad lines and others transformed the lumber industry, opening new forests and making it easier to ship the logs.

Ken Drushka, in his book *Working in the Woods*, wrote:

> The extensive development of railway logging created a need for a variety of related tasks and equipment. The most basic of these was the construction of road grades. Throughout the West, from the late 1800s, contractors employed a large, transient population of railway labourers building main lines as well as industrial lines for logging and mining companies. In many cases these crews were Chinese, unorganized, underpaid, and discriminated against by exclusionary laws preventing them from engaging in higher-paying work or acquiring logging rights. Most of the work on logging lines was done by hand, using picks and shovels to level out a roadbed on which the ties and steel rails were laid. Commonly, labourers contracted to build "stations" consisting of 100 feet of roadbed for an agreed upon rate. Blasting powder, packed in hand-drilled holes, was used on rock cuts when they could not be avoided. The primary objective was to keep grades on main lines below two and a half to three percent, and spur lines below about six percent. (152–53)

An 1883 description of a California logging train stated:

> The track is of the usual gauge, but the cars are platforms of only half the ordinary length, and are fastened together by ropes, shortened up when the train is empty, but lengthened so as to separate loaded cars by six or eight feet, in order that the protruding ends of the logs shall not interfere. The track is rudely built and rickety, the rails being heavy strap-iron bolted upon string-pieces. It [the train] runs shakily through tunnels of infinitely varied verdue, curves along ledges blasted out of the brown and fern-hung rocks of the creek shores, traverses low ground upon causeways of ties and stringers . . . ventures out upon some precarious bracket-trestle whence it might plunge directly into the stream. (Anonymous 1883)

Between 1869 and 1920 other Chinese worked on standard- and narrow-gauge lines, intrastate and interstate, as well as logging and short lines. Narrow gauge lines also served the agricultural community by bringing products to major transportation centers. By the 1920s narrow-gauge logging trains that once been popular operated seasonally, and because many were privately owned, they often were dismantled and the parts reused whenever possible as logging declined.

Chinese worked on other lines. The Nevada census records indicated that in 1870, 246 Chinese worked on the railroads; in 1880 the figure increased to 576, a result of the CCRR construction. Once the rail line was completed, additional

A logging train is about to deposit logs in the river to send to the nearby mill. Animals were no longer needed to transport the logs, and the logging trains made new forest areas accessible. (Walter Chung, photographer, author's collection)

work and maintenance still was required, so, for example, in 1875 twenty Chinese were hired to maintain the Eureka-Palisade Railroad built in 1873 in Nevada.[22] In 1873 the residents of Olympia, Washington, decided to build their own narrow-gauge spur line because they had been bypassed by the Northern Pacific Railroad. Records identified a Chinese labor contractor named Jimmia, who recruited forty Chinese to construct the Thurston County Railroad, completed in 1878, which saved Olympia "from economic oblivion and preserved it as the capital" of Washington ("Olympia's Historic Chinese Community"). By the mid-1880s narrow gauge railroads were used to move saw logs through the mountains. The Madera Sugar Pine Lumber Company, which was established in 1874 in California, built the Yosemite Mountain Sugar Pine Railroad, a narrow-gauge (3 ft.) railway located near Fish Camp, California, that had seven locomotives, more than 100 log cars, and 140 miles of track—along with a 54-mile flume. The company logged more than thirty thousand acres until the operations closed in 1931, and because it practiced clear-cutting, almost no trees remained by the tracks at the time of its closure (Yosemite Mountain Sugar Pine). Approximately one-third of its workers were Chinese. There were many other train lines built in the mountains and forests of the American West.

Chinese worked elsewhere. In 1874 the California Lumber Company began building its fifty-mile-mile V-flume from the mountains near present-day Oakhurst to Madera, the county seat of Madera, in California; by 1942 the southern Sierra had more than 500 miles of railroad track, 170 miles of lumber flumes, 28 locomotives, 16 sawmills, and hundreds of lumber camps scattered throughout the mountains (Johnston 1984, 7). In 1881 Ephraim Shay patented his geared locomotive and logging trains driven by the powerful Pacific Coast Shay engine—or one of its competitors, such as the geared Climax and Heisler engines—which could transport the heavy logs to the connecting main railways through the steep hillsides, thus eliminating many manual laborers (Koch 1971). At first, logging engines burned cordwood, but eventually some burned fuel oil, which was more expensive to obtain. If the Chinese did not work on the laying of ties and tracks, they often were employed to cut the cordwood or work on loading and unloading the logging trains, which meant riding on trains that had a high accident rate, as cows or other animals wandered onto the tracks, or curves were too sharp for the speeding train going downhill.

In 1868 Chinese workers were brought to Portland to help in railroad construction in that region (Cox 1974, 139). Others went to Washington state, where they constituted two-thirds of the railroad workers in that state between 1870 and 1900 and thus helped to open new markets for the shipment of wood and agricultural products to the East (Hildebrand 1977). About six hundred workers, now experienced in railroad construction, moved to build portions of the Alabama and Chattanooga Railroad; another 250 worked for General John G. Walter for the Houston and Texas Railroad. In 1875 approximately 150 Euro-Americans and 300 Chinese were employed to work on the twenty-two-mile-long railroad running through Nevada and Placer Counties, California, called the Nevada County Narrow Gauge (Locke 1962).[23] At the Colfax, California, station, the narrow gauge came in from the east and the CPRR from the west, thus creating an important connection for the movement of goods. The railroad superintendents had worked on the construction of the CPRR and paid the Euro-American workers thirty dollars per month, the Chinese twenty-six dollars per month. This was probably the base salary and did not take into account any extras. The Chinese worked an eleven-hour day and were regarded as better workers, so they became the predominant ethnic group.

The abilities of the Chinese were demonstrated when Thomas Durant (1820–1886), with his UPRR's Euro-American crew, challenged Crocker's predominantly Chinese crew with eight Irishmen to see which team could lay the most track in one day. On April 10, 1869, a CPRR train of sixteen cars loaded with rails and materials for two miles of track was unloaded, backed out, and followed by another sixteen cars. That was repeated five times until ten miles and fifty-six feet of track were laid (a record that still has not been broken in modern times). The Chinese handled a total of 4,462,000 pounds of materials. Crocker won and Durant hired some Chinese as section crews and, in 1873, as coal miners in southern Wyoming for the UPRR. By 1880 about two hundred Chinese worked at the UPRR mines at Almy; another six hundred or seven hundred worked in the coal mines in Rock Springs, Wyoming, one hundred miles to the east, under the contractors Beckwith and Quinn, with Ah Say as the middleman (Evanston Urban Renewal 1996, 2–3; Storti 1991). Records of the names of Chinese workers at fifty-eight different camps at Rock Springs, Wyoming, showed that many of the men were kinsmen with the same family names (House Report 1886, 33–45). Undoubtedly, some of the older men had worked on railroad projects.

Former CPRR workers went into other jobs. Even within Nevada there were railroad jobs, and the 1870 and 1880 federal census manuscripts and 1875 Nevada state census listed many Chinese working for the railroad and settling in station towns like Lovelock, Winnemucca, and Elko. In 1876 the Chinese worked on the construction of the Southern Pacific Railroad (SPRR) connecting San Francisco and Los Angeles, creating the second major railroad line in the country. In December 1878 a crew of nine hundred Chinese worked on the South Pacific Coast Railroad, another three hundred to four hundred on a narrow gauge in Santa Clara, California (MacGregor 2003, 89). In the early 1880s the Chinese worked on the challenging construction of the steep and mountainous Tehachapi Railroad for the SPRR. In 1885 the CPRR merged with the SPRR, and the latter controlled freight in and out of San Francisco. Along these lines new towns rose up and new jobs opened up. By the 1880s lumber from the forests of the American West was the largest single item of early railroad tonnage (Johnson 1910, 256). This coincided with the dominance of Chinese working in the woods in the 1880s and 1890s.

Eventually, more Euro-Americans found labor contracting profitable. The tremendous amount of money involved may be exemplified by the Mills and Onderdonk Company, which, according to the *San Francisco Examiner* (April 11, 1882) had two contracts totaling $20 million to hire Chinese workers to perform road construction for the Canadian Pacific Railroad in 1882. The agents of the firm offered twenty-eight dollars per month with free passage and food across the Pacific for unskilled Chinese workers, with an increase of $1.25 per day after three months of work. For their recruiting efforts, labor contractors received approximately one dollar per person. Such large-scale recruitment undoubtedly lent support to the union's agitations and others who supported Chinese exclusion. These kinds of reports in the news media contributed to the anti-Chinese frenzy.

Anti-Chinese violence in Nevada directed toward Chinese in lumbering during the era of railroad construction arose in 1867 in Nevada. Colonel R. R. Johnson, an attorney, employed eight or nine Chinese, who were supervised by Cyrus Griffith on Johnson's wood ranch near Washoe City in June 1867.[24] Their presence at his ranch and the report in the *Gold Hill Daily News* (June 3, 1867) that there were about two hundred other Chinese woodchoppers working the hills around El Dorado Canyon gave rise to an anti-Chinese movement to drive the Chinese out of the business. The agitators organized an "anti-coolieism" club that connected with the one in San Francisco. The local newspaper, the *Eastern Slope* (June 3,

1867) took the stance that since the Chinese were permitted to immigrate, they should be permitted to labor. For newspapers supporting industrialization, this was a common editorial position throughout the West. The newspaper's ultimate aim was to prevent further Chinese immigration, not defend the ability to hire Chinese workers. Moreover, Johnson's wood ranch provided the CPRR with the needed lumber, and westerners recognized the importance of a transcontinental railroad. On June 22, 1867, the same newspaper published a long editorial defending the Chinese as providers of a service to the development of the Pacific Coast, freeing it from the domination of the manufacturers of the East Coast. In the concluding remarks, the editorial stated: "Chinese labor has thus far on this coast had the same effect to raise wages of labor, inasmuch as through their labor the resources of the State have been developed as they could not have been developed except for that labor." However, this was not a popular opinion.

Unfortunately, the presence of the Chinese coincided with the beginning of the labor movement in the American West. In the 1870s Denis Kearney's sandlot speeches in San Francisco and throughout the country turned disgruntled workers against "cheap Chinese labor," and this spread into Nevada. Labor unions were trying to get organized and gain support and this anti-Chinese rallying cry was one of the most successful organizing tools in the American West. Politicians and popular media, especially newspapers, joined in the movement. Unable to protect themselves because of their inability to become naturalized citizens or to vote and thus have political clout, coupled with their unfamiliarity with American customs, the Chinese became the scapegoats and victims of many hostile and even violent acts. After the successful passage of the 1875 Page Law, anti-Chinese agitators targeted Chinese laborers, including those engaged in lumbering.

In June 1876 one hundred anti-Chinese agitators drove the Chinese off the VTRR roundhouse in Carson City, where they had been working on the gravel train. The agitators decided to make the Chinese in Chinatown gather all of their belongings and drove them over the Ormsby County line.[25] In July 1876 another killing occurred at Huffaker's Station at the cabin of ten Chinese lumber workers.[26] Another incident in 1876 focused on driving eighty Chinese woodcutters from the Yerington–Haynie and Company wood camp located in Empire.[27] The anti-Chinese mob threatened other employers with the same action if they did not fire their Chinese workers. This may have resulted in the quick departure of the Chinese from a wood camp in Spooner Summit, leaving numerous stacks of cordwood that were found nearby. A *Reno Evening Gazette* editorial (April 6, 1876) stated, "The Chinese may be a nuisance, but they are here in answer to our invitations, and under treaty, must be protected." Nevertheless, when the Euro-Americans were arrested and tried, they almost always were acquitted and freed. American criminal law did not protect the Chinese victims from these acts of violence throughout the West. The lack of protection often forced the Chinese to relocate.

The federal government also participated in the discrimination against the Chinese by passing unfair laws and regulations. Between 1882 and 1900 immigration officials severely limited the number of Chinese who could enter the United States by adding restrictions and unnecessary paperwork. They believed that they had found a way to reduce the numbers of Chinese in the United States, but their effectiveness was questionable. In a report to J. D. Power of the U.S. Treasury, Chinese Bureau Inspector James Dunn at the Port of San Francisco reported on November 28, 1899, that from June 1, 1898, to October 31, 1898, 556 Chinese laborers departed with return certificates, and 752 were admitted because they had return certificates.[28] During the same period a year later, 323 laborers departed with return certificates and 630 were admitted with return certificates. Consequently, more laborers returned than departed. However, the required return certifications, in Dunn's opinion, solved the problem of Chinese laborers, but the Chinese in the merchant and native-born (that is, born in the United States) categories were becoming increasingly problematic because the Chinese were using these to gain admission. In 1898, 638 Chinese merchants were admitted and 16 were denied admission. A year later, 801 were admitted and 91 were denied. Finally, of those claiming to be born in the United States, in 1898, 418 were admitted, 202 were denied, and a year later, 300 were admitted and 69 were denied. Immigration officials were troubled by their inability to deny more Chinese admissions, and eventually this led to the idea of counting all of the Chinese in the United States between 1904 and 1905 to check on their papers. Those without proper government papers were to be deported immediately (House Report 1906).

With the decreasing number of available workers and community leaders (merchants), the Chinese reevaluated their situation and chose occupations that were more service oriented. They also had to adjust to the decreasing number of kinsmen entering the country by expanding their "employment families" to include men from the same or neighboring villages or to be more accepting of any Chinese immigrant, regardless of his place of birth.

The memory of the opposition to Chinese labor persisted, and the Nevada state legislature became involved in attempt to ban the Chinese from working on railroad construction. Despite an 1879 law prohibiting the use of Chinese labor on all railroad construction projects chartered by the state, the Chinese continued to work on railroad projects, probably as subcontractors under the approved Euro-American contractors (Carter 1975, 85–86). Such discriminatory laws and policies led to shadowy recordkeeping such that payrolls often showed no Chinese names despite newspaper accounts of Chinese workers employed by a particular company or on a project.

The Comstock economic decline that began in 1879 negatively affected the VTRR and CCRR as well as other railway lines. In 1890 the VTRR stopped paying dividends until mining revived briefly. In 1907, when Virginia City was experiencing a critical fuel shortage and four feet of snow, The *Territorial Enterprise*

(January 17, 1907) reported that Yerington, as president of the VTRR, ordered men to destroy the historic bridge known as the Union Bridge, which had cost more than $75,000 when constructed, in order to have the two hundred cords of wood cut up for fuel. The VTRR ceased to operate in 1924 and was dismantled in 1950. By early years of the twentieth century the entire phenomenon of mining, trains, and lumber prosperity became a thing of the past, but fond memories of the VTRR led to its resurrection as a tourist attraction in 2010.

Charles Crocker built other railroad lines as well. In July 1882 Crocker, with A.C. Bassett, N.T. Smith, and Jospeh L. Willcutt of the SPRR along with Alvin Sanborn, president of Watsonville Mill and Lumber Company, filed articles of incorporation for Loma Prieta Company, and by 1882 they began to build the Loma Prieta Railroad in Central California that ended in Monte Visa (Hamman 1980, 33–43). In 1883 the *Sacramento Bee* reported that there were two hundred Chinese graders working with Swedish woodchoppers. W. F. Knox of Sacramento brought in his two Chinese track teams, one clearing and grading and the second laying ties and spiking down rails. The Chinese also built most or all of the eleven wooden bridges on this line. The five-mile-long track took one year to complete, and its last section of 1.3 miles had a grueling grade of 108 feet, or 2 percent grade, which has been regarded as a great construction feat even by today's standard. In 1899 the railroad closed due to landslides and other problems.

New occupations opened for the Chinese. By 1900 a few Chinese worked primarily as domestics on the eastern side of the Tahoe Basin (Koval 1991, 7). Some were probably working in the Glenbrook hotels, since Glenbrook had become a tourist town. The majority of Chinese had moved away to San Francisco or found new employment opportunities elsewhere, including the Midwest, South, and East.

In 1920 some Chinese still worked for the railroad lines and into the twenty-first century in a variety of capacities, including an individual who rose to the position of railroad agent.[29] They often worked as cooks for railroad crews or as restaurant owners catering to the twenty-four-hour needs of railroad crews. In 1999 according to John Fong, restaurant owner in the railroad town of Carlin, Nevada, the railroad paid him a fee to remain open twenty-four hours a day to serve crew members and passengers, and this was just enough to make ends meet when the economy was tight.

The building of the CPRR and several railroads created another boom in the lumber industry and the establishment of new towns. During and shortly after the CPRR construction period, several railroad towns developed. Auburn and Colfax in California and Verdi and Reno in Nevada were just two of many examples. Other towns, like Dutch Flat and Crystal Peak, declined because the railroad bypassed them. Chinese workers for the railroad companies and supporting logging industries settled in the new towns, but like Euro-American lumbermen, they moved around until they found a satisfactory job and place to live, or they returned to China.

* * *

The increased demand in lumber saw the growth of large corporations taking over smaller companies. Bliss and Yerington were among the new lumber barons who expanded their property and entered into the growing railroad construction business as well as other related enterprises. Like many others, they used Chinese workers whenever they could and protected them against anti-Chinese violence. Railroad construction and maintenance required more wood. Working in the woods allowed some of the able Chinese to earn better wages, which allowed them a higher standard of living than their counterparts in the railroad and mining industries. This was evident in the higher quality of everyday dishware found in archaeological sites discussed in chapter 3. By the beginning of the twentieth century, the mining, railroad, and logging industries had changed with the decline in profitable mines, completion of railway lines, and the rising demand for forest conservation. The Chinese no longer played an important role in the business of the logging industry, and their contributions were forgotten.

CONCLUSION

The Chinese played a significant role in the development of the West through their work in mining, railroad construction, and logging. The Comstock, for example, would not have attained its incredible level of development and sophistication without lumber from the Sierra Nevada and Carson Range. The migration of kinsmen and fellow regionals provided a substitute family environment, since women and children seldom were allowed to enter the United States, but this situation, created by federal immigration laws, tied the men to their homeland and strengthened their identity as Chinese. They came with high expectations of becoming wealthy, but the majority never achieved that goal. Many obtained jobs through regional and kinship organizations or through Euro-American or Chinese labor contractors. For mutual aid, they joined family and regional associations and/or secret societies, which helped them preserve their Chinese cultural traditions and ties to the homeland (*qiaoxing*).

In the 1880s most of the men working in lumbering in the Sierra Nevada were Chinese—a fact that has not been recognized in most immigrant histories. They undertook a variety of jobs: wood transportation; mill operation; cutting, packing, splitting, stacking, fluming, loading/unloading, scaling, and marketing wood; digging ditches, grading roads, building and maintaining flumes; making land surveys; cooking and cleaning; raising fresh produce and providing fresh fish; and caring for the animals (mules, oxen, horses) were just some of the types of the actual and support work involved. Some of their jobs were very dangerous, especially flume tending. Due to prejudice, they were seldom given the higher status of "lumberjack," but they may have performed the task of felling the big trees and doing the work of lumberjacks. They certainly were involved with all of the other work. Their salaries may not have been much different from their Euro-American counterparts. However, instead of receiving their pay individually, they often worked under a labor boss (Chinese or American) who held the contract with the lumber companies and paid the workers after the labor boss took a percentage. Some were able to earn more than the "dollar a day" salary that was commonly believed to be the salary of the Chinese. They earned wages according to the type of job they did. The men who were wood-camp cooks were an example of those earning wages similar to or more than non-Chinese cooks. When they realized they could own timberland and had the funds to buy property, they went to court to secure that right of property ownership. The great need for their services was attributable to the booming mining communities and the construction of railroads. Both ephemeral and permanent communities rose and desperately needed wood products. They contributed to the growth and settling of the American West by providing this essential commodity.

While the mines had utilized much of the early logged wood, the railroads consumed wood products for railroad ties, bridges, stations, and fences, and mines and trains alike used wood for fuel. One historian calculated that the railroads used 20 percent to 25 percent of the annual timber production between the 1870s and 1900 (Pisani 1985, 344). In the 1890s an estimated 73 million railroad ties were needed annually for the construction of new roads and the maintenance of old ones. Railroads also enabled the loggers to go deeper into the forests. Undoubtedly, like the Roseburg–Coos Bay railroad in Douglas County, Oregon, in 1893, Chinese workers were used to construct the narrow-gauge railroads and often to work on the logging trains (Vatter 1985, 254). Railroad owners and lumber companies treated the forests as private property, so some engaged in clear-cutting. Few were cognizant of the importance of conservation.

Working in the woods was fraught with danger from natural disasters (Prouty 1985). Flooding, lightning, and forest fires often destroyed wood camps and their inhabitants in the mountains. In 1875 eleven Chinese woodcutters were killed by a snow slide near Genoa.[1] In 1876 there were two logging camps in the mountains of Diamond Range near Eureka, Humboldt County, California, and a cloud burst caused the death of thirteen Chinese woodchoppers. Only one survived to tell the story, while all of the Italian woodchoppers, whose camp was higher, drowned.[2] An 1881 avalanche buried eight Chinese woodcutters working for Doughtery's Mill Company on their narrow-gauge line, the South Pacific Coast Railroad near Santa Cruz, California, but ten others were able to escape.[3] In 1881 Nam Yaing, a Chinese wood seller, was struck by lightning and killed instantly near the Carson River on his way home to Virginia City.[4] These were just a few of the numerous examples.

Other tragedies occurred as well. In 1888 in Hayward, California, fifty Chinese and almost twenty-five Euro-Americans were logging together; about one Chinese logger a week was seriously injured by falling trees, while none of the Euro-Americans seemed to have that problem.[5] Flume tenders and others were often hit by heavy logs or drowned transporting logs in ponds or rivers to the mill site. A logjam on the V-flume system could result in injury or death as the logs piled up and spilled onto the herder's position. Moving machinery, sharp saw blades, axes, and other equipment often caused accidents that resulted in the loss of life or limb. Logs rolled and injured workers trying to grease log carriages or roads. According to the *Idaho Tri-Weekly Statesman* (February 22, 1879), rolling logs caused two-thirds of all fatal accidents at the wood camps.

Equipment breakdowns were frequent. Fragments of wood splintered and caused bodily damage. Logging trains crashed or brakes failed or the trains derailed after hitting an animal or other object. In 1891 the derailing of the Lake Valley Railroad train near Glenbrook, part of the CTLFC, resulted in the death of four Chinese woodcutters and only slightly injured the engineers and fireman, who were the only other people on the train.[6] Wooden bridges and trestles collapsed because they had been hastily built or were anchored on unstable ground. Injuries from falling trees or other accidents were common and led to demands for better safety measures (Lawson 2010). Isolated in the mountains, workers were subject to attacks by wild animals. These situations discouraged many potential lumbermen.

The Chinese workers faced dangers that most loggers never encountered. Ethnic antagonisms and economic competition led to numerous confrontations with Euro-Americans, new immigrants, and American Indians who raided Chinese camps or drove them out of the area, burned their cabins, or used them as target practice. It is not surprising that many of the Chinese wood-camp sites contained spent ammunition, probably as a result of the need to protect themselves and to hunt for food. Archaeologist Theresa Solury (2004), looking at a site in Spooner Summit in 2004, found spent ammunition accounting for nearly 5 percent of the total artifact assemblage from a late-nineteenth-century Chinese work camp. In 1879 American Indians raided the camp of Chinese woodchoppers in Independence Valley near the mining town of Tuscarora, Nevada. Fortunately, the Chinese found safety and protection in Tuscarora because the town's founders supported Chinese workers. In another case that same year, Euro-Americans provided liquor to some American Indians and incited them to kill and scalp some Chinese in Mason Valley, Nevada. The result was the imprisonment of the American Indians in Aurora, Nevada, and each Euro-American was fined $300 for furnishing the liquor (*Evening News* December 5, 1888). The Chinese learned to endure the prejudice, hostility, violence, and negative stereotypes from the majority community.

Woodchopper wars and personal attacks were not uncommon. Robbers were a threat in all walks of life, but in the isolated wood camps, it was more commonplace. In 1889 a group of robbers attacked a Chinese wood camp; one robber was killed, while a Chinese worker was fatally shot (*Philadelphia Inquirer*, November 15, 1889). In 1890 Ah Chung and Ah Toy were axed to death in their isolated cabin on a ranch in Colusa County, near Chico, California. Their partially eaten bodies were not discovered for several days (*Duluth News-Tribune*, May 12, 1890). As the newspaper story implied, this was another case of eliminating the economic competition and racism. The inability of the Chinese to testify in American courts against Euro-Americans made them easy victims.

At the turn of the twentieth century, the Chinese began to leave the forests of the Sierra Nevada. Many factors contributed to this situation. The Chinese exclusion acts, federal discriminatory regulations, the rise of anti-Chinese movements that were often violent, the activities of labor unions, and racism led to a shortage of Chinese workers. The loneliness of the lifestyle for men who traditionally were tied to home and family, as well as the aging of the first generation of immigrants, caused them to turn to other, less strenuous occupations. The deaths of the major Chinese labor employers, such as Bliss, Yerington, and Crocker, who were supportive of the Chinese, also played a role. At the end of the nineteenth century the logging industry had transitioned from small companies to large corporations that often were involved in several types of industries, not just logging. Men like Yerington employed the Chinese in mining, railroad construction, and other enterprises, often shifting the workers to perform different jobs. Some businesses were involved in international trade, especially in fulfilling the economic demand that China (and Asia) had for wood and wood products, which declined during World War I. In addition, the denuding of the forests from clear-cutting, insect infestations, fires, lightning, and other natural disasters, the introduction of new technologies in logging resulted in fewer jobs. Due to the fluctuation of domestic prices in the lumber market as mining and railroad construction declined, the new federal and regional conservation programs, mergers and industrial restructuring, labor and government investigations of the dangers of the occupation, and opening of new timberlands elsewhere, the Chinese left the Sierra Nevada logging industry.

The federal government's legislative arm and widespread economic changes contributed to a decrease in the Chinese population and availability of Chinese workers. The 1882 Chinese exclusion act and subsequent discriminatory legislation led to demands for further restrictions until the 1924 Reed Johnson Immigration Act established a quota of one hundred Chinese admissions annually. This decreased the number of available workers and opened the door for other immigrants to work in logging. The Bureau of Immigration under Commissioner General of Immigration Terrence Powderly began to establish rules for stricter enforcement of Chinese immigration from 1900 to 1902 and his successor, anti-Chinese labor leader Frank Sargent, harassed the Chinese in the United States by conducting a special Chinese census that allowed the government to deport any Chinese without proper identification papers (House Report 1906). Many Chinese lost these documents in fires or robberies and had to apply for duplicates at great expense. The Crash of 1893 that affected railroad, mining, and lumber probably drove many Chinese to seek other types of employment. Virginia City, which at one time was reputed to have a total population of twenty thousand, had dwindled to only seven thousand residents by the early 1890s, and the mines, once paying magnificent dividends, were lucky if they were paying anything at all to stockholders (*New York Times*, December 10, 1892). The decline meant that the need for wood by the Comstock and other regional mines was no longer urgent. By the turn of the century there were fewer jobs open to the Chinese in logging and fewer Chinese workers who wanted to work in lumbering.

A rise in European immigration in the period from 1880 to 1924 also contributed to an increase in ethnic/racial competition in the labor markets because these new immigrants could provide the needed unskilled labor. This coincided with the rise of labor unions that fought the influx of low-paid immigrant workers (Olzak 1989). Between 1880 and 1915, the number of labor unions in the United States rose from 31 to 183 (Olzak 1989, 1318). Labor leaders spoke out against the Chinese and turned their attention to other groups, including Catholics. Sometimes the new immigrant groups ranked lower than the Chinese: for example, in 1884 the leader of the Knights of Labor, Terrence V. Powderly, remarked that the new Hungarian immigrants "work for little or nothing, live on fare which a Chinaman would not touch (Powderly papers) Racism and discrimination increased with the influx of new, different-looking immigrants from Europe.

There were hints about a change in attitude regarding the Chinese. The *Pacific Coast Wood and Iron* (San Francisco, November 1892, 241) actually found the Chinese more desirable than the turn-of-the-twentieth-century European groups—Russians, Poles, and Italians—and advocated restriction of these groups:

> We have put up bars against the incoming of the Chinese, but we have put none up against the not less undesirable multitudes from parts of continental Europe. The Chinese are seldom criminals or paupers, but the prisons and poor houses are filled with other foreigners of the lowest, vilest classes . . . the Russians, the Poles, the Huns and the Italians of the most ignorant and undesirable classes [still continue to immigrate in large numbers]. (Reprinted in the *Philadelphia Evening Telegraph*)

Discrimination and prejudice now focused on new victims rather than only the Chinese, owing in part to the effectiveness of the Chinese exclusion laws.

Success in logging, as in mining and railroad construction, often depended on the fluctuations of markets, corporate decisions, resources, consumer demands, and local, regional, and national politics. There also was a great variation in prices for lumber as the industry experienced continual booms and busts (Warf 1988, 331). With economic depressions and the decline of mining and railroad construction, the nature of the industry changed by the turn of the twentieth century. In 1891, for example, the Chinese constituted 35.3 percent of the labor force in the coastal region of British Columbia, where logging was a major occupation but declined thereafter (Hak 2000, 151). In the 1920s Chinese were working in the lumber industry in British Columbia along with Japanese and Asian Indians (Creese 1988).

The same phenomenon was seen in Washington Territory. Between 1860 and 1880, eight out of every ten dollars invested in manufacturing went to the timber industry, but it was not until the advent of the railroad that timber production grew. In 1880 Washington Territory ranked thirty-first among all states and territories in timber production, but by 1890 it was fifth, and in 1905 it ranked first, a position held until 1930 ("Evergreen State"). Much of the success was due to

German immigrant Frederick Weyerhaeuser (1834–1914), whose company was headquartered there beginning in 1900 and whose primary focus has been the growing and harvesting of timber, and the production, distribution, and sale of wood and wood fiber products (De Lorme 1986).

In the 1890s, in order to fill the void created by a shortage of Chinese workers, employers turned to the Japanese. The Japanese immigrants, who were more highly educated because of Western educational reforms undertaken by the Meiji government beginning in 1868, did not inherit all of the prejudices and stereotypes that had been created during the anti-Chinese movements of the late 1870s through 1890s. Americans were proud of how they helped the Japanese modernize and be victorious over the Chinese in the Sino-Japanese War of 1894–1895 and Russo-Japanese War of 1904–1905. Many Japanese were experienced woodcutters because of the Japanese love for wood products. When they arrived as laborers, they lived in segregated sections of the wood camps (Dubrow 2002, ch. 1). Unlike the Chinese, they were allowed to bring their wives and to establish families and social communities. They worked in the Pacific Northwest, especially Washington, and in California towns like Truckee, and thus they replaced the Chinese. They did not have labor contractors but used a numbering system, rather than their names, for American payroll records. Consequently, their experiences were different from those of the Chinese in late-nineteenth-century Nevada and eastern California.

The lumber industry saw great technological improvements, and the labor-intensive nature of the business, with reliance on unskilled or semiskilled workers, became less dependent on the unskilled. By the 1880s, animal and human power was greatly assisted by machinery: steam donkeys yanked the logs off the mountains, steam engines hauled them to the mill, steam-powered sawmills cut them into lumber, and the steam locomotives transported the lumber to the market (Sierra Logging Museum). Logging railroads and high-speed cable yarders used between 1900 and 1920 were replaced by tractor-truck logging. Manual labor and draft animals were seldom needed. The machinery was expensive, and large corporations bought up smaller ones that could not afford such equipment necessary to survive in this competitive market. After 1905 the per-capita consumption of wood declined as new building materials, especially brick, cement, iron, and stone, began to be used instead of wood (Pisani 1985).

It would be erroneous to assume that all Chinese woodcutters began and remained in this occupation. The Chinese had to be adaptable, so they moved either into other occupations or to work in other forests. Although there are no known examples in California or Nevada, there is the history of Yuen Chiu Duck (Yai Nam), who left Zhongshan county, Guangdong, for Hawaiʻi at the age of twenty-five (Yuen, 1994, 11). He worked as an herbalist and sugar cane plantation worker, saved enough money to return to China to marry, and fathered a daughter. In 1892 he brought his family to Hawaiʻi; he then had four other children before his wife died in 1904. He operated a laundry, which was destroyed by fire in 1900. For the next twenty years until his retirement, he worked as a woodcutter and taro grower. In 1932 he died at the age seventy-two. The diversity of his occupations was likely not uncommon in the late nineteenth to early twentieth century as the Chinese struggled to earn a decent living and provide for the family.

The original Chinese lumbermen who had immigrated in the 1870s and 1880s or earlier and worked in the Sierra Nevada were now older. Some had died or returned to China. Some found new, less strenuous occupations such as cooking, farming, laundering, or merchandising. Wong Sam was one such person.[7] Married to a woman with bound feet and leaving three children in China, he immigrated in 1882 and became a partner in the Yuen Fook Lumber Yard, 741 Pacific Street in San Francisco. He made enough money to visit China once in 1890. When the lumber company closed in the early 1900s, he moved to Ogden, Utah, where he became a vegetable peddler making a profit of seventy to eighty dollars per month. Eventually he retired around 1916 to San Francisco. Another, Jung Young (b. 1854, immigrated 1872), was a carpenter in San Francisco.[8] He made enough money to make two trips to China, but when business declined he became a musician. In 1901 he lost all hearing and turned to paper hanging as his occupation around 1911. Unfortunately, there were few documents that revealed the livelihood and history of Chinese workers whose names were known and were only briefly featured in this study.

Logging moved to other locations and many of the practices established in the Sierra Nevada continued, including the hiring of a headmen to supervise and be responsible for twenty to forty Chinese, attracting Chinese cooks to work in the lumber camps with higher salaries, and requiring the workers to buy at company stores. By 1900 most of the Chinese who remained in lumbering had moved to other locations—California, Idaho, Oregon, Washington, or British Columbia, where the lumber industry was growing and new forests opened. For instance, by the turn of the twentieth century, Chas R. McCormick and Company of San Diego, California, an employer of Chinese workers, was providing mining timbers to Nevada and Arizona (Coman and Gibbs 1968, 271). Timber production from the public timberlands of the Pacific Northwest rose dramatically after the turn of the century and attracted new immigrant workers, including the Japanese, to recently established wood camps (Liecap and Johnson 1979). When the Canadian government adopted new timber allocations in 1905, Americans turned to British Columbia's resources, and by 1910 the American investment in that province's logging industry was estimated at $65 million (Rajala 1993, 78).

The conservation movement was prompted by the vast deforestation that had been occurring. According to Edward Ewing Pratt (1918, 7), former chief of the Bureau of Foreign and Domestic Commerce, the original forest of the United States was estimated at 850 million acres; by 1918 only some 545 million acres remained. The government was aware of the urgent need to save the forests and passed a forest reserve act in March 1891 (Defebaugh 1906–1907, 1:420). Archaeologist Susan G. Lindstrom summarized the situation:

> Evidence suggests that logging interests did little to conserve the natural environment, and for the first several decades, logging practices were unregulated. Yet the entire Tahoe basin was not clear-cut. At least 38 old-growth stands have been located within Tahoe's upper and lower Montane forests. Inaccessible stands, excessively large trees, and deformed trees were left due to difficulty in transport or milling. Stands around resorts were preserved for aesthetic reasons. (Lindstrom, 2001)

Part of the deforestation was due to forest fires, insect infestations, and the natural life cycle of trees. Then, as now, lightning strikes led to serious forest fires. Additional blame has been placed on the sheepherders in the Sierra Nevada because they were accused of failing to douse their campfires completely, which led to devastating forest fires (Magee 1892, 658).

Deforestation also coincided with a decreased domestic demand for lumber resulting from the increased use of substitutes in construction, but overseas markets grew. The lumber industry revived somewhat when Congress opened unreserved government timberland to lumbermen (Robbins 1982, 24). American trade with China had increased considerably from $20,150,000 gold in 1894 to $253,890,000 gold in 1895. (U.S. Dept. of State 1897, Statistics, 1:163). Part of this trade was in timber. In 1897 Hong Kong, for example, imported 26,389 tons of timber (U.S. Dept. of State 1898, Commercial Relations, 1:1036). That year Americans believed Senator Albert Beveridge's statement that "China's trade is the mightiest commercial fact in our future."[9] American exports of lumber tripled in sales between 1869 ($2,817,906) and 1888 ($7,515,719) and continued to grow into the first part of the twentieth century.[10] China was one of the countries importing American lumber during this period because most of the country's own accessible timberland had been cut or destroyed and because there were trains to move logs. For example, in 1917 China imported 21,348 million board feet of fir alone, valued at $271,397 (U.S. Dept. of Commerce 1919, 255). World War I adversely affected the export lumber market, resulting in more closures of western lumber companies. Assistant Forester of the United States William B. Greeley pointed out that in 1907, when 46 billion feet of lumber was cut, the market quickly declined to less than 38 billion feet in 1915). This led to a decrease in price, since only 40 percent of the trees were sold at market. Numerous lumber and sawmill companies closed (Pratt 1918, 8, 10).

In 1910 the Southern Pacific Railroad, successor to the CPRR, was the largest timber holder in the United States (Todes 1975, 15). In the southern Sierras, V-shaped wooden flumes, chutes, and inclines transported the lumber from the mills to the railroad stations until 1931, when the depressed market led to their abandonment. Overseas sales also declined. By the time of this slowdown most Chinese workers had changed to other occupations or had passed from the scene.

Some early firms hired many Chinese, and some of these kept their workers, despite mounting anti-Chinese agitation and violent acts of racism. The CTLFC and EDWFC, which employed upwards of five hundred men, did much of their work on a contract basis and had many Chinese workers. According to the *San Francisco Examiner* (February 27, 1900), the two lumber companies owned fifty thousand acres of timberland that had been denuded. By this time, the CTLFC land was valued at fifty cents per acre and the EDWFC land at twenty-five cents per acre (Yerington papers, UCB, carton 3). Little is known about the individual workers, but some of the sketches provided in the previous chapters give some insight to their lives and experiences.

Some Chinese workers returned to China. Historian Erika Lee (2006, 9) has shown that between 1884 and 1941 only 4 percent of the Chinese were able to make two visits to China, and 9 percent could make only one visit. Pressure from family members was a primary motivation to return. The little money that they had made and the remittances that they had sent to their families in China might have been sufficient for these workers to retire in relative comfort (Woon 1983–1984, 689–90). Those who had not been financially successful could not return because of a "loss of face." Relatives in China expected them to lavish gifts upon them and to live in relative splendor. Contributions had to be made to the clan coffers for public works, festivals, schools, and other community affairs. One could not return without the trappings of success. Some also had no desire to return to an "unchanging China," with its rigid traditions and stratified society. Perhaps many simply realized that they had adjusted to life in America and preferred to spend their last years in the United States. One example was Quong Kee, who had immigrated to Virginia City as a cook's apprentice and then found a job as a cook for the railroad construction crew in Elko, Nevada, where he specialized in making Irish stew. He made enough money to go back to China several times, but in the end he settled in Tombstone, Arizona; he opened the famous Can Can Restaurant there and was famous for his pheasant under glass served on white tablecloths (Burgess 1949; Cheek 1989). The Earps and Claytons, whom he knew from Virginia City, were regular customers. He retired to nearby Bisbee, Arizona, a town that prohibited Chinese from living there but made an exception for him. When he died in 1933, his body was brought back to Tombstone, where a fancy and well-attended funeral was held. He was buried in Boot Hill Cemetery near his long-time friend, local *tang* leader and "madam," Mrs. Ah Lum. He, like many others, preferred living in the United States.

Finally, the United States government's growing concern over the conservation and management of the forests led to the creation of the Forest Service. The forest conservation movement was gaining momentum, so loggers were forced to find new woodlands elsewhere. Forest fires and diseases took their toll on the trees. Clear-cutting had denuded many of the forests. The Forest Reserve Act of 1891 allowed the president to establish forest reserves from timber-covered land in the public domain. Several early leaders and visionaries, along with far-sighted presidents (especially Theodore Roosevelt), scientific and conservation organizations, and newly trained forestry professionals led the successful effort to retain millions of acres of federal forest land. In 1905 the U.S. Department of Agriculture created a new bureau, the Forest Service, and in 1907 the forest reserves were renamed as national forests. In those early days, the Forest Service was responsible for the conservation and the protection of the forests. The denuding of the forests as done during the heyday of logging was restricted. Fortunately, enough forests remained for regeneration so that large tracts of beautiful woodlands now cover much of the Sierra Nevada and Carson Range.

The Chinese came to the United States in search of work and thousands found employment in working with wood often in isolated forests. Labor contractors, regional associations, newspaper advertisements, and networking led them to these jobs. Whenever possible, they worked with extended family members, clansmen, and fellow regionals. They contributed to the growth of the western lumber industry and watched large corporations like the CTLFC absorb the small independent timber ranchers and smaller corporations. They participated in many aspects of lumbering, including the construction of narrow-gauge railroads and logging trains, often based on their experience working on the CPRR. They helped open new timberland for the needed wood products. These Chinese made a significant contribution to the building of the American West that should now be recognized in studies of American immigration. Based on a closer examination of the historical record, old stereotypes do not hold true. It remains for future generations of researchers to fill in the gaps presented in this work in order to complete this interesting chapter of American history.

NOTES

Introduction

1. As mentioned in the preface, place names and terms referring to China are rendered in pinyin, but Cantonese is used for the people who originate in the vicinity of Guangzhou (Canton).

2. Yong Chen (2000, 14) described the prosperity in Shunde based on the local gazetteer, but in Taishan and Kaiping there was flood, drought, and famine in the early to mid-nineteenth century.

3. During the period of free migration (1848–1882), 317,023 immigrated to the United States and 150,886 (about 48 percent) returned; there was no information about multiple returns (Yang 2002, 237).

Chapter 1. Early Contact and Migration

1. *Biloxi Daily Herald*, September 15, 1900.

2. A China house, erected at the Double Springs Ranch in 1849, was the second courthouse of Calaveras County, California, and was photographed by Richard O. Everett for Thomas Layton around 2000. The original building measured thirteen feet by twenty-six feet, has Chinese characters on the rafters, was made of Chinese camphor wood, and (since 2010) can be seen at the Calaveras County Museum, San Andres, California. The *San Francisco Sun*, November 15, 1849, said the buildings could be one-story or two-story structures. The frame and covering sold for $1,500. These "China houses" were found throughout California, Nevada, Idaho, Oregon, and Washington, even at the end of the nineteenth century.

3. *San Francisco Bulletin*, July 25, 1858, and October 11, 1878.

4. *Sanyi* are immigrants from generally the three counties of Panyu, Nanhai, and Shunde in the southern and western regions of Guangdong, part of the Pearl River Delta region.

5. Oral interview with descendant Andrea Yee, 2013.

6. INS RG 86, entry 132, box 107, file 13928, no. 26.

7. *Baltimore Sun*, December 5, 1848.

8. INS RG 85, entry 132, box 107, file 13928, exhibit 25; author's translation.

9. *Joss* is a Chinese pidgin English word derived from Portuguese *deus/deos*, "god."

10. *San Francisco Bulletin*, September 1, 1880; December 22, 1887.

11. "Letter of Chinamen to Governor Bigler," *Alta California*, April 29, 1852.

12. *San Joaquin Republican*, June 16, 1860.

13. *San Joaquin Republican*, March 15, 1858. Census recorders often did not bother with "men in the mountains," since it was so difficult to reach them. The Chinese were able

to buy claims second hand, and in once example in Calaveras, Amador County, their purchase in 1857 of the "Jordan claim" netted them $20,000 two years later. *San Joaquin Republican*, November 5, 1859.

14. *Winnemucca [Nevada] Silver State*, May 12, 1894.

15. Oral interview with Frank Chang about his father's "news" sessions in Lovelock, Nevada, 2000.

16. *San Francisco Bulletin*, November 19, 1873.

17. INS RG 85, box 14, file 1355, Washington, D.C.

18. INS, Bus. Partnership, File 1356/310, San Bruno.

19. VTRR payroll records, 1878, Nevada State Railroad Museum, Carson City.

20. *California Express*, Marysville, October 22, 1859.

21. *San Francisco Bulletin*, February 2, 1870.

22. *San Francisco Bulletin*, November 23, 1888.

23. See, for example, California Supreme Court, *[Joseph] Sisson v. [Emerline] Wallace, 1896,* 114 Cal. 42, 43 [45P 10000]. These are two of the heirs of Albert Sisson and William H. Wallace involved in an important lawsuit that involved Chinese workers.

24. Also see *San Francisco Bulletin*, May 29, 1881, and March 22, 1864; and *New York Times*, July 18, 1869; July 21, 1869; September 22, 1869; October 12, 1869; November 1, 1869; September 21, 1870; March 20, 1880.

25. *Baltimore Sun*, August 27, 1875; *San Francisco Bulletin*, February 29, 1860; July 28, 1869; April 24, 1882.

26. *Georgia Weekly Telegraph*, July 23, 1869; *Columbus Daily Enquirer*, September 28, 1869; *Macon Weekly Telegraph*, November 5, 1869; *New York Herald*, December 31, 1869; *Baltimore Sun*, March 27, 1875 (supplement); *San Francisco Bulletin*, April 24, 1882; and obituary note with quote, *Macon Telegraph*, October 1, 1882.

27. Washoe District Court, *Ah Jack v. Stephen Cornsen*, April 21, 1881, case 1791, box 118.

28. *Ah Jack v. Tide Land Reclamation Company*, case 7126, Supreme Court of California, 61 Cal. 56; 1882 Cal. LEXIS 537, June 30, 1882.

29. Washoe County District Court, *A. Lindley and Company v. Ah Jack*, August 26, 1885, case 2321, box 397. See also Cole and Chin 1999.

30. INS RG 85, file 9623/56, NARA, San Bruno.

31. *Chae Chan Ping v. United States*, 130 US 581 (1889) was a case involving a China-born laborer who had a return certificate but was denied reentry due to the Scott Act, which was passed while he was in China. Lee Gee's situation was different because he was an American citizen by birth but still denied reentry. For a broader perspective, see Weiner 2006, 96–97.

32. INS RG 85, box 17, 2270, NARA, Washington, D.C.

Chapter 2. Work and Workers

1. *San Francisco Bulletin*, September 25, 1889.

2. *San Jose Mercury*, April 21, 1907.

3. See also *Silver State*, January 10, 1894.

4. *Carson City Morning Appeal*, August 13, 1873.

5. See also *Truckee Republican*, May 23, 1872 and June 1, 1872; *Territorial Enterprise*, May 25, 1872.

6. See also *Sierra Sun*, September 12–18, 2002; Reno 1996.

7. *San Francisco Bulletin*, April 19, 1879; *Duluth Daily News*, January 1, 1887; U.S. Labor Statistics 1913, 1–178.

8. *San Francisco Bulletin*, November 22, 1878.

9. *Territorial Enterprise*, July 29, 1876.

10. Oral interview with daughter Ynez Lisa Chan Jung.

11. A sunken boat was discovered in Lake Tahoe around 2000 and had a boulder with the Chinese number 5 written in red on it. The significance of this is unknown.

12. INS RG 85, files 13500/823 and 13500/839, NARA, San Bruno.

13. INS RG 85, 13504/837, NARA, San Bruno; see also Christoff 2001.

14. *San Francisco Bulletin*, May 10, 1889.

15. INS RG 85, 9777/38 and 1356/145, NARA, San Bruno.

16. Supreme Court 0129, February 6, 1883.

17. *Nevada State Journal*, September 4, 1883, and February 21, 1884.

18. *Reno Savings Bank v. Wing Hing Sung and Company*, November 28 1879, case 1631, Washoe County, 2nd Judicial District Court, box 80, on microfilm at the Washoe County Recorder's Office.

19. This may be the same See Wah who was a member of the Hop Sing tong in Virginia City in 1876. See "The Chinese War," *Territorial Enterprise*, February 26, 1876.

20. Washoe District Court Records, Washoe County Recorder's Office, *Duncan McRae v. His Creditors*, December 1880, case 1833, box 120.

21. *Territorial Enterprise*, obituary, February 4, 1894.

22. Ormsby District Court, *Sierra Wood v. Wah Hi*, February 19, 1881, case 1824, Nevada State Archives and Library, Carson City. The case was very convoluted. Yerington and Company also hired Hi Wah for services and goods. See Yerington and Company Papers, NC 738, University of Nevada, Reno, Special Collections Library, Day Book entry for 1873. Duncan McRae, who appears in other lawsuits, was not counted in the 1870 or 1880 census for Nevada. The Sierra Wood and Lumber Company Wood Records, 1899–1900, can be found at the University of California, Berkeley, Bancroft Library, C-G 132, box 1. The main offices moved from Virginia City, Storey County, Nevada, to Overton, Nevada County, California, by the 1890s.

23. Washoe County Recorder's Office, District Court Records, *Ah Lue v. M. Hogan*, case 2110, box 138.

24. Sparks Heritage Museum, Nevada; Robert Morrill, oral interview, 2010, on China Camp stove.

25. Personal communication with Lindstrom.

Chapter 3. Carson City and Truckee

1. *Silver State*, October 17, 1878.

2. *Reno Crescent*, February 27, 1869.

3. *Silver State*, January 20, 1902.

4. INS RG 85, RS1518, box 34, file 43926, NARA Seattle.

5. The other four wood dealers lived in Eureka, Eureka County, where five Chinese woodchoppers also lived. The construction of railroad lines made the expansion of available timberland possible.

6. In anticipation of the 1875 Page Law, most Chinese women in Nevada were listed as prostitutes or harlots in the 1870 census.

7. INS RG 85, file 144048/5295/9, NARA, Washington, D.C.

8. INS RG 85, file 14315/14-2.

9. *Ye Wan Tong v. Ah Kee*, September 5, 1885, box 16, case 785.

10. *Carson Daily Appeal*, July 18, 1869; VTRR payroll, Nevada State Railroad Museum.

11. Ormsby District Court, box 4, case 144.

12. INS RG 85, file 12580/16-3, NARA, San Bruno.

13. Photograph, Nevada Historical Society.

14. INS RG 85, file 9998/184, box 95, NARA, San Bruno.

15. INS RG 85, file 9998/184, box 95, dated 1902.

16. Oral interview with great-granddaughter Shirlaine Kee Baldwin.

17. *Territorial Enterprise*, October 21 1nd 25, 1877.

18. Ormsby District Court, *Sam Kee v. Hugh Porter*, case 831, July 7, 1875.

19. John Haynie Papers.

20. INS RG 85, file 13360/117, box 86, San Bruno.

21. *Carson City Morning Appeal*, December 16, 1880.

22. *Carson City Morning Appeal*, May 13, June 14, June 16, June 24, June 26, and July 1, 1878.

23. See, for example, *Carson City Morning Appeal*, April 5 and May 14, 1876.

24. *Salt Lake Tribune*, December 31, 1881.

25. *Carson Daily Independent*, September 12, 1886.

26. *Carson City Morning Appeal*, November 16, 1887.

27. INS RG 85, file 13561/83, NARA, San Bruno; five partners including men in El Paso, Texas.

28. INS RG 85, file 12889/4-14, NARA, San Bruno; Assessor's Map Book, 1883–1884.

29. INS RG 85, files 13561/332 and 19817/11-3, NARA, San Bruno.

30. INS RG 85, files 13561/244 and 16351/3-3, NARA, San Bruno.

31. INS RG 85, files 13561/92, 141, and 127, NARA, San Bruno.

32. INS RG 85, file 10132/17 box 17, NARA, San Bruno.

33. INS RG 85, file 12561/141, NARA, San Bruno.

34. INS RG 85, file 13561/122, NARA, San Bruno.

35. INS RG 85, file 13561/260, NARA, San Bruno.

36. INS RG 85, file 13561/305, NARA, San Bruno.

37. INS RG 85, files 13561/224 and 9649/203, box 49, NARA, San Bruno.

38. INS RG 85, files 9649/203, box 49, and 13561/224, NARA, San Bruno.

39. *Truckee Republican*, April 19 and November 14, 1876.

40. Quang Sing Chang, Hin Chin, Hi Chung, Ah Coon (Donner Lake), Gin Wo Hang, Ye Hang, Ah Him, Loon Hop, Hung Qwan, Ah How, Ah Pawn, Quang Kee, Fong Lee, Hong Lee, Yee Sing, Tang Lee, Hing Toy, Ah Lock, Ah Moy, Loon Sing, Hong Quam, Hong Sing, Ye Sung, Lee Tang, One Wau, Quong Wo, Wo Hop and Kee, Wright and Kee, Billy Yang (Donner Lake), Fun Ye, Hang Ye, Sung Ye, Hi Young, Lee Yu, Hi Yung, Yu Fun, Jim Yung, and Ah Howe are the names listed (Nevada County Assessor). Some may be a variation of the same person's name or a reversal of first and last names.

41. *Truckee Republican*, October 30, 1878.

42. See also *Truckee Republican*, September 30, 1876.

43. *Sacramento Union*, April 8, 1887.

44. *Truckee Republican*, Decemnber 12, 1885.

45. *Nevada State Journal*, August 1, 1893.

46. *Buissonet Journal*, October 1868 to January 1869.

47. *Truckee Republican*, October 30, 1880.

48. These laws include the 1875 Page Law that essentially made it very difficult for Chinese women to immigrate, the first national racist 1882 prohibition of Chinese laborers, the 1892 expansion of the meaning of laborers to include physicians and religious leaders, the 1893 requirement for certificates of identity and residence, and the 1924 immigration act that essentially limited Chinese immigration to 105 per year. See Salyer, 1995, and McClain, 1994.

49. *Territorial Enterprise*, January 9, 1868; *Carson Daily Independent*, May 1, 1868.

50. *Truckee Republican*, November 17, 1880.

51. *Daily Transcript*, January 1, 1886.

52. *Los Angeles Times*, September 9, 1882.

53. Thompson and West 1958, 168; *Truckee Republican*, December 12, 1885.

54. *Carson Daily Independent*, January 6, 1886.

55. *Nevada State Journal*, August 27, 1893.

56. *Truckee Republican*, June 2 and June 30, 1875.

57. *Truckee Republican*, September 30, 1876.

58. *Nevada State Journal*, June 20, 1876; see also Coates; and Pfaelzer 2007.

59. *Truckee Republican*, May 3, 1876.

60. *Truckee Republican*, November 6, 13, 16, 20, and 23, 1878. J. F. Moody (hotel, lumber), Schaffer (lumber), Cruthers (furniture), Richardson (lumber, doors), Irwin (livery and feed stables), D. J. Crowley (newspaper, lawyer), Greely (variety store, post office), J. Marzen (meat market), J. Gray (lawyer), Burckhalter (banker, grocery, hardware, cigar, stage lines, fire insurance), Brickwell (lumber), and Keiser (judge) were the merchants. The group wanted Chinatown rebuilt across the river near Indian Camp. See K. Low.

61. *Carson City Morning Appeal*, April 11, 1882.

62. *Carson Daily Independent*, March 8, March 9, April 18, April 19, April 20, and April 22, 1882.

63. *Carson City Morning Appeal*, April 12, 1882.

64. *Carson City Morning Appeal*, April 21–23, 1882.

65. *Carson City Morning Appeal*, December 5, 1885.

66. *Truckee Republican*, January 2, 1886, and continuing through the year.

67. *Sacramento Record Union*, January 2, January 7, January 15, and January 18, 1882.

68. *Carson Daily Appeal*, January 1, 1886.

69. *Truckee Republican*, February 3, 1886.

70. INS RG 85, box 7, file 12511/513; box 35, file 13508/7376;bBox 15, file 13502/819, NARA, San Bruno.

71. *Truckee Republican*, September 8 and December 12, 1886.

72. *Nevada State Journal*, June 5, 1886.

73. *Sacramento Record Union*, February 2 and February 12, 1886.

74. *Nevada City Transcript*, November 9, 1886.

75. *Truckee Republican*, April 6 and June 16, 1887.

76. *Nevada City Transcript*, November 8, 1887; *Truckee Republican*, November 23, 1887.

77. *San Francisco Bulletin*, July 22, 1889.

78. The list of lumber cut in feet was as follows: Boca Mill Company—6.5 million, Truckee Lumber Company—5.5 million, Pacific Lumber and Wood Company—5 million, George Schaffer—5 million, Elle Ellen—4 million, Doan and Hamlen—3.5 million,

Richardson Brothers—3.5 million, Oliver Lonkey—3 million, Peck and Lewis—3 million, Lewison and Smith—2 million, Kidder and Mason—1 million, for a total of 42 million feet of lumber (*Pacific Coast Wood and Iron* 16:5 [November 1891], 227, later renamed *Pioneer Western Lumberman* [San Francisco], Bancroft FSD1.P5).

79. *Carson Daily Independent*, January 10, 1886.

80. *Carson Daily Independent*, January 26, 1886, for example.

81. *Reno Evening Gazette*, February 2 and February 9, 1886.

82. INS RS 497, box 15, CR 43941, NARA, Seattle.

83. INS RS 1281 box 34, CR 45022, NARA, Seattle.

84. *Nevada State Journal*, March 20, 1886.

85. March 24, March 26, and March 27, 1886.

Chapter 4. Of Wood and Mines

1. *Carson Valley News*, March 6 and March 13, 1875.

2. *New York Times*, January 11, 1868.

3. *Territorial Enterprise*, October 1, 1878.

4. *Truckee Republican*, September 8, 1886.

5. *Gold Hill Daily News*, October 20, 1863. One cord equaled 1,536 board feet of wood.

6. *Gold Hill Daily News*, December 9, 1865.

7. *New York Times*, May 19, 1860.

8. *Gold Hill Daily News*, March 1, March 2, March 25, 1867; *Territorial Enterprise*, March 2 and March 25, 1867.

9. *Territorial Enterprise*, February 28, 1868.

10. *San Francisco Bulletin*, June 3, 1861; and October 24 and October 30, 1862.

11. INS RG 85, Partnership Records, RG83, file 13561/141, NARA, San Bruno.

12. *Territorial Enterprise*, May 20, 1875, and January 12, 1878; *Virginia Evening Chronicle*, June 23, 1881.

13. *Nevada State Journal*, August 25, 1875, and July 28, 1876.

14. Interview with grandson Ray Walmsley, 2004.

15. INS, box 107 entry 132, #13965, NARA, Washington, D.C.

16. *Territorial Enterprise*, October 26, 1878.

17. *Reno Crescent*, June 11, 1870.

18. *Nevada State Journal*, January 21 and January 23, 1875.

19. *Nevada State Journal*, February 5, 1875.

20. *Nevada State Journal*, February 5, 1875.

21. *Territorial Enterprise*, May 3, 1876; *Eureka Sentinel*, April 29, 1876.

22. *Nevada State Journal*, June 20, 1876.

23. *Nevada State Journal*, February 4, 1875; July 21 and July 22, 1876.

24. *Nevada State Journal*, August 9, 1874.

25. *Reno Evening Gazette*, October 21, 1890.

26. Storey County Recorder's Office, *Book of Deeds*, Miscellaneous Index v. 2, I 119, dated February 12, 1877 is just one of many examples of Lonkey's leases. For a Chinese example, see Sue Shong Yuen and George Mann lease, J160, dated January 24, 1880.

27. *Nevada State Journal*, August 9, 1874.

28. *Truckee Republican*, November 10, 1886)

29. *Nevada State Journal*, July 25, 1889.

30. *Reno Evening Gazette*, October 21, 1890.

31. *Territorial Enterprise*, August 16, 1866.

32. *Carson Daily Independent*, April 6, 1881.

Chapter 5. Of Wood and Trains

1. *New York Times*, May 12, 1876; *San Francisco Chronicle*, June 11, 1881. There were charges of fraud against the CPRR, alleging that the Big Four were skimming from the profits and cutting the costs of repairs so that the railroad was unsafe for the transportation of passengers.

2. White Pine County Museum Photograph Collection and A. J. Russell's "Big Trestle," 1869 photograph on east slope of Promontories.

3. *San Francisco Bulletin*, June 28, 1867.

4. *San Francisco Bulletin*, July 5, 1867.

5. *New York Times*, September 22, 1873; Henry mss; Daggett 1881.

6. *Reno Evening Gazette*, November 10, 1933, obituary.

7. *Carson Valley News*, April 10, 1875.

8. Douglas County Recorder's Office, *Book of Deeds*, book D (A10), 452–54 (John P. Elliot to H. M. Yerington and D. L. Bliss); 518–19 (Hillard Dunning to J. W. Haynie, H. M. Yerington, A. J. Ralston); 523–24 (John Lyon to H. M. Yerington and D. L. Bliss); 525–26 (Augustus W. Pray to H. M. Yerington and D. L. Bliss): these are just some examples of the land transfers. The records of the Carson and Tahoe Lumber and Fluming Company are in the University of Nevada, Reno, Special Collections Library, NC72, and are supplemented by the William W. Bliss papers, collection 96-53.

9. NARA RG21, *United States v. El Dorado Wood and Flume Company*, October 1, 1880, case 318, box 42, San Bruno.

10. *Carson Daily Independent*, April 6, 1881.

11. *Genoa Valley News*, May 8, 1875; Myrick 1962, 422, does not mention Chinese workers.

12. *Tacoma Daily News*, October 4, 1894.

13. California Conststitution, article 19, sec. 2, overturned in *In re Tiburcio Parrott* 1 F. 481; 1880 U.S. App. Lexis 2017; 6 Sawy, 349).

14. See also *Reno Evening Gazette*, September 10, 1870.

15. Duane L. Bliss, "Data Concerning the Virginia and Truckee Railroad, and Those Who Planned and Carried Out That Work," mss, University of California, Berkeley, Bancroft Library, BANC mss P-G 38, p. 1. Duane Leroy Bliss (1833–1907). Bliss left Savoy, Massachusetts, at age sixteen in 1849. He went to San Francisco, then Marysville and Trinity Center, California. In 1860 he moved to Gold Hill and eventually became a partner in a Gold Hill banking firm (later the Bank of California). In 1863 he married Elizabeth T. Tobey of South Wareham, Massachusetts, and they had five children. In 1872 he moved to Carson City, built a summer home in Glenbrook, then in 1873 formed the CTLFC. William W. Bliss, *Papers*, file 96-53 with inventory, University of Nevada, Reno, Special Collections Library. Bliss's obituary is located in box 3. The Pacific Wood, Lumber, and Flume Company was incorporated in California because the primary place of business was San Francisco. In 1875 the directors were James Flood, William O'Brien, Edward Barron, and George Wallace, all of San Francisco, and John W. MacKay of Virginia City, Nevada, with a capital stock of $500,000. California State Archives, Articles of Incorporation,

7372, D1720 box 1 RD. This company should not be confused with the Pacific Wood and Lumber Company based in Clinton, California, on the Truckee River, which was owned by Charles A. Bragg and Gilman N. Folsom in the 1870s.

16. The papers of the Virginia and Truckee Railroad are in the University of Nevada, Reno, Special Collections NC427. Additional material can be found at the University of California, Berkeley, Bancroft Library; Hunting Library, San Marino, California; Nevada Historical Society, Reno; Nevada State Railroad Museum, Carson City; and the California State Railroad Museum Library, Sacramento. See also, Myrick 1962, 1:137–61.

17. *New York Times*, October 11, 1874.

18. Ormsby District Court, *Ah Tone v. State of Nevada*, March 12, 1872, case 147, Nevada State Archives.

19. *Truckee Republican*, October 2, 1869; *Gold Hill Daily News*, September 30 and October 1, 1869; *Territorial Enterprise*, September 30 and October 1, 1869; L. Chan 2001, 107–9; James 1998, 81.

20. *Nevada State Journal*, February 20, April 20 and June 1, 1872.

21. Bliss UCB; *New York Times*, March 20, 1881, and September 24, 1876.

22. *Sacramento Record Union*, July 31, 1875.

23. See also the *Nevada City Transcript*, February 18 and 27, 1875, and May 24, 1876.

24. *Eastern Slope*, June 8, 1867.

25. *Humboldt Register*, June 7 and 8, 1876)

26. *Reno Evening Gazette*, July 21, 1876; *Nevada State Journal*, July 21 and 22, 1876.

27. According to the Ormsby County assessment roll for 1876, Yerington's company at Empire cut forty-five thousand cords of wood and was taxed $5,670.00; his Carson City location had two thousand cords of wood valued at $9,000 and one thousand cords of old limb wood valued at $2,000. Nevada State Library and Archives.

28. INS RG 85, Inspector of the Chinese Bureau James Dunn to the Honorable J. D. Power, U.S. Treasury, letter dated November 28, 1899, file 532, NARA, Washington, D.C.).

29. Ong J. Hoy (b. 1864, immigrated 1873) was an agent in Wells, Nevada, for the Western Pacific Railroad in 1900. See "NVSHPO."

Conclusion

1. *Territorial Enterprise*, January 19, 22, and 26, 1875.

2. *Hartford Daily Courant*, July 24, 1879.

3. *San Francisco Bulletin*, January 21, 1881.

4. *San Francisco Bulletin*, May 25, 1881.

5. *Evening News*, December 5, 1888.

6. *San Diego Union*, July 18, 1891.

7. INS RG85, box 27, file 54116/4, and Certificate of Residence 144660, NARA, Washington, D.C.

8. INS RG85, file 53335/125, Certificate of Residence 144301, NARA, Washington, D.C.

9. U.S. *Congressional Record*, Senate, January 9, 1900, 704–11.

10. U.S. *Congressional Record*, Senate, January 9, 1900, 704–11.

SELECT BIBLIOGRAPHY

Newspapers

Alta California (San Francisco)
Baltimore Sun (Baltimore, Maryland)
Biloxi Daily Herald (Biloxi, Mississippi)
Carson City Morning Appeal (Carson City, Nevada)
Carson Daily Appeal (Carson City, Nevada)
Carson Daily Independent (Carson City, Nevada)
Carson Valley News (Douglas County, Nevada)
Columbus Daily Enquirer (Columbus, Georgia)
Daily Transcript (Nevada City, California)
Duluth Daily News (Duluth, Minnesota)
Duluth News-Tribune (Duluth, Minnesota)
Eastern Slope (Washoe City, Nevada)
Evening News (San Jose, California)
Genoa Valley News (Genoa, Nevada)
Georgia Weekly Telegraph (Macon, Georgia)
Gold Hill Daily News (Gold Hill, Nevada)
Hartford Daily Courant (Hartford, Connecticut)
Humboldt Register (Winnemucca, Nevada)
Los Angeles Times (Los Angeles, California)
Macon Weekly Telegraph (Macon, Georgia)
Nevada City Transcript (Nevada City, California)
Nevada State Journal (Reno, Nevada)
New York Herald (New York, New York)
New York Times (New York, New York)
Philadelphia Inquirer (Philadelphia, Pennsylvania)
Reno Crescent (Reno, Nevada)
Reno Evening Gazette (Reno, Nevada)
Sacramento Record Union (Sacramento, California)
Salt Lake Tribune (Salt Lake City, Utah)
San Diego Union (San Diego, California)
San Francisco Bulletin (San Francisco, California)
San Francisco Examiner (San Francisco, California)
San Joaquin Republican (Stockton, California)
San Jose Mercury News (San Jose, California)
Sierra Sun (Truckee, California)

Silver State (Winnemucca, Nevada)
Sun (Baltimore, Maryland)
Tacoma Daily News (Tacoma, Washington)
Territorial Enterprise (Virginia City, Nevada)
Transcript (Nevada City, California)
Truckee Republican (Truckee, California)
Virginia Evening Chronicle (Virginia City, Nevada)

Archival Materials

Bancroft Scraps [a collection of miscellaneous items on microfilm], Bancroft Library, University of California, Berkeley.

Bliss, Duane L. "Data Concerning the Virginia and Truckee Railroad, and Those Who Planned and Carried out That Work." Typewritten manuscript. BANC manuscripts P-G 38. Bancroft Library, University of California, Berkeley [abbr. Bliss mss].

Bliss, William. Papers. NC96.53. Special Collections, Getchell Library, University of Nevada, Reno.

Buissonet, Eugene. 1868–1869. Journal, October 1868 to January 1869. P-W 36. Bancroft Library University of California, Berkeley.

Carson and Tahoe Lumber and Fluming Company. Documents, 1883–1885. MS197. California State Railroad Museum, Sacramento.

Carson and Tahoe Lumber and Fluming Company. Records, 1854–1946. NC72. Special Collections, Getchell Library, University of Nevada, Reno.

Central Pacific Railroad Company. 1877. Records. NC1175. Special Collections, Getchell Library, University of Nevada, Reno.

Crocker, Charles. 1881–1883. Correspondence with Collis Huntington. Manuscripts, Crocker–Huntington. Huntington Library, San Marino, California.

Daggett, Rollin Mallory. 1881. *Railroad Wrongs in Nevada: Speech of Hon. Rollin M. Daggett, of Nevada, in the House of Representatives, February 25, 1881.* Washington, D.C.: s.n. Special Collections, University of Nevada, Las Vegas.

El Dorado Wood and Flume Company. Records. NC76. Special Collections, Getchell Library, University of Nevada, Reno.

Giles, Ralph. 1996. "Carson and Tahoe Lumber and Fluming Company Records and Initial Investigation Focused on Its Relationship with Chinese Nationals." Manuscript for Prof. William D. Rowley, University of Nevada, Reno, History 725. Author's collection.

Glenbrook House. 1868–1869. Accounts. NC1190. Special Collections, Getchell Library, University of Nevada, Reno.

Gompers, Samuel. 1902. "Meat vs. Rice: American Manhood against Asiatic Coolieism; Which Will Survive?" San Francisco: American Federation of Labor. Bancroft Library, University of California, Berkeley.

Goodwin, Victor O. 1967. "Verdi and Dog Valley—A Story of Land Abuse and Restoration." Manuscript on file, Tahoe National Forest, Nevada City, California.

Gottschalk, Louis, and Eve Unsell. 1923. "Ching Ching Chinaman." Musical score. New York: Jerome H. Remick.

Haynie, John W. 1860–1884. Papers. NC999. Special Collections, Getchell Library, University of Nevada, Reno.

Henry, Harold A. n.d. *The Comstock Lode and Its Impact upon the History of California.* Manuscripts printed between 1934–1970. Special Collections, University of Nevada, Las Vegas.

Hood, A. J. Papers, 1851–1894. Receipts from transportation businesses of Wells, Fargo, and Company. NC619. Special Collections, Getchell Library, University of Nevada, Reno.

Huntington, Collis. Papers. Huntington Library, San Marino, California.

Locke, William L. (1883–1913). Scrapbook and Papers [manuscript with news clippings]. Bancroft Manuscripts, University of California, Berkeley.

Low, Kenneth. n.d. "The Anti-Chinese Movement in Truckee, 1878–1886." Undated manuscript. Vertical File F870C5L68. Ethnic Studies Library, University of California, Berkeley.

Marker, P. Plat of Flumes, 1864–1876. NC1185. Special Collections, Getchell Library, University of Nevada, Reno.

Markleeville Flume Company. 1872–1875. Records. NC120. Special Collections, Getchell Library, University of Nevada, Reno.

"The Merry Makers' Chinese cook holding a fan and a rifle, 1886" [caption]. Photograph. Frank B. Rudolph Photograph Collection, Bancroft Library, University of California, Berkeley.

Nevada Railroads Collection, 1862–1950. Manuscripts: Nevada railroads. Huntington Library, San Marino, California.

Pacific Coast Wood and Iron. Later renamed *Pioneer Western Lumberman* (San Francisco). FSD1.P5. Bancroft Library, University of California, Berkeley.

Pacific Mail Steamship Company. (1867) 1975. *A Sketch of the New Route to China and Japan by the Pacific Mail Steamship Company's Through Line of Steamships.* San Francisco: Turnbull and Smith. Microfilm 4094: New Haven, Conn.: Research Pub.

Pacific Wood, Lumber, and Flume Company. 1869–1904. Records. NC90. Collection box 2, folder 2. Correspondence. Special Collections, Getchell Library, University of Nevada, Reno.

Parker and Tobey. Records, 1878–1896. NC1176. Special Collections Getchell Library, University of Nevada, Reno.

Powderly, Terrence V. "Record of the Proceedings of the Eighth Regular Session of the General Assembly, September 1–10, 1884." In Terence Vincent Powderly Papers, "Proceedings: General Assembly, 1878–1902." Catherwood Library Collection, School of Industrial Relations, Cornell University, Ithaca, New York.

Sando, Ruth Ann, and David L. Felton. "Inventory Records of Ceramics and Opium from a Nineteenth-Century Overseas Chinese Store." Undated manuscript in vertical file F869.M37S36. Ethnic Studies Library, University of California, Berkeley.

Sierra Nevada Wood and Lumber Company. 1880–1882. Ledger. NC1187. Special Collections, Getchell Library, University of Nevada, Reno.

Sierra Wood and Lumber Company. 1899–1900. Wood Records. C-G 132, box 1. Bancroft Library, University of California, Berkeley.

Southern Development Company of Nevada. 1880–1957. Records. NC74. Special Collections, Getchell Library, University of Nevada, Reno.

Sprague, Clare Roy. Sprague Collection in the Alfred "Cap" Collier Collection, Shaw Historical Library, Oregon Institute of Technology, Klamath Falls.

Sutro, Adolph. Papers. Box 4. Huntington Library, San Marino, California.

204   *Select Bibliography*

Tobey, W. D. 1884–1888. Records. NC1181. Special Collections, Getchell Library, University Nevada, Reno.

Trimmer, Arnold. 1984. Transcript of oral interview. Special Collections, Getchell Library, University of Nevada, Reno.

Utica Bullion Mining Company. 1864–1911. Records #98-32, Special Collections, Getchell Library, University of Nevada, Reno.

Verdi Mill Company. 1889–1890, 1892. Scrapbook and Letters #88-35, Special Collections, Getchell Library, University of Nevada, Reno.

Virginia and Truckee Railroad. 1865–1906. Papers. Manuscripts, HM66142-66181. Huntington Library, San Marino, California.

Virginia and Truckee Railroad. NC427, box 76. Special Collections, Getchell Library, University of Nevada, Reno.

Wells Fargo Ledger Sheets. Wells Fargo History Museum, San Francisco, California.

Yerington, Henry M. Papers. BANC manuscripts P-G 239, container 1. Bancroft Library, University of California, Berkeley [abbr. Yerington, UCB].

Yerington, Henry M. Papers. NC738, box 1, folder 1. Correspondence and journal. Special Collections, Getchell Library, University of Nevada, Reno [abbr. Yerington, UNR].

Archaeological Reports and Government Documents and Reports

California Supreme Court. 1896. *Reports of Cases Determined in the Supreme Court of the State of California*. San Francisco: Bancroft-Whitney.

California Surveyor General. 1861. *Annual Report of the Surveyor General for the Year 1860*. Sacramento: State Printing Office.

Canada. Parliament. 1902. "Report of the Commissioners Appointed to Inquire into the Subject of Chinese and Japanese Immigration into the Province of British Columbia." *Sessional Papers* 54, no. 36, vol. 13, (1902). Ottawa: King's Printer. Available online at https/archive.org/details/cu31024023463965 from Cornell University. Accessed December 1, 2014 [abbr. Canada Parliament 1902].

CH2M Hill. 2005. "Kam Wah Chung and Co. Museum, John Day, Oregon Report." Oregon State Parks and Recreation Department.

Dillingham, Eric. 2001. "Tuscarora Greenstrip Cultural Resources Survey." BLM Report 1-2035(p), BLM office, Elko, Nevada.

Dixon, Kelly J., E. Floyd Aranyosi, Richard W. Deis, and Harry W. Leeman. 1995. "Heritage Resource Inventory of the Crystal Fire Restoration Project, 1995." Toiyabe National Forest Report TY-94-1059 and Tahoe National Forest Report 05-17-1125. Tahoe National Forest, Nevada City, California.

Douglas County (Nevada). *Book of Deeds*. Recorder's Office, Minden, Nevada.

Drews, Michael P., and David C. Mathiesen. 1996. "A Class III Archaeological Survey of West Carson, V&T Bicycle Path, Carson City County, Nevada." Report for Nevada Department of Transportation.

Elston, Robert G., and Donald Hardesty. With Sheryl Clerico. 1981. "Archaeological Investigations on the Hopkins Land Exchange." Report for the USDA Forest Service. Vol. 1. Tahoe National Forest, Nevada City.

Fernow, B. E. 1894. "Report of the Chief of the Division of Forestry." In United States Secretary of Agriculture, *Report 1893*. Washington: GPO.

Goodwin, Victor O. 1960. *Verdi and Dog Valley: A Story of Land Abuse and Restoration*. U.S. Forest Service Report, Elko, Nevada.

Kautz, Robert R., and Danielle Risse. 2006. "Carson City's 'China Town': The Archaeology of Urban Nevada." Report for State of Nevada Public Works Board, KEC Project 477.

Knowles, Constance Darrow. 1942. "A History of Lumbering in the Truckee Basin from 1856 to 1936." Report available from the U.S. Forest Service and in Manuscripts, Bancroft Library, University of California, Berkeley.

Koeber, Arthur R. n.d. "Field Exploration and Documentation of 100 Sites—Cabins, Mills, Waystations (K14 with addenda #1–3)." Report on file, U.S. Forest Service, Lake Tahoe Basin Management Unit, South Lake Tahoe, California.

Koval, Ana. 1991. "The Chinese in the Lake Tahoe Basin: An Overview Resulting from a Literature Search Relating to the Chinese in the Tahoe Basin." Report for the U.S. Forest Service, Lake Tahoe Basin Management Unit, South Lake Tahoe, California.

Lindstrom, Susan G. 1993. "Archaeological Evaluation and Data Recovery at CA-NV-572-H: A Chinese Cabin Site at Juniper Flat, Cambridge Estates Subdivision, Truckee, California." Report prepared for CRB Development.

———. 1995. "North Shore Ecosystems Project Heritage Resource Inventory." Vol. 1: Report. HRR 05-19-297. U.S. Forest Service, Lake Tahoe.

———. 2001. "Archaeological Survey of 1,830 Acres between Spooner and Marlette Lakes, Lake Tahoe Nevada State Park." Vol. 1: Results. Report for Nevada Department of Conservation and Natural Resources.

———, and Crystal Range Associates. 1996. "Fueling the Comstock: The Chinese Experience at Lake Tahoe." Report prepared for the Lake Tahoe Basin Management Unit, South Lake Tahoe, California.

———, and Jeffrey T. Hall. 1994. "Final Report: Cultural Resources Inventory and Evaluation Report for the Proposed Spooner Summit and East Shore Project (Big Gulp) Timber Sales." Prepared for Carson Ranger District, USDA Toiyabe National Forest and Lake Tahoe Basin Management Unit.

———, Laura Leach-Palm, and Sharon A. Waechter. 2002. "Archaeological Survey of 2,489 Acres in Lake Tahoe Nevada State Park, Nevada, Volume 1." Report for Nevada Department of Conservation and Natural Resources.

———, and Sharon A. Waechter. 2007. "Archaeological Investigations at Alder Hill for the Gray's Crossing Development, Nevada County, California: Volume II: Historic-Era Sites; Part A: Report," Report for East West Partners, Truckee.

Mattes, Merrill J. 1970. "Charcoal Kilns." Historic Structures Report. National Park Service, San Francisco, California. National Park Service Library, Denver, Colorado.

Mires, Peter B., and Margaret E. Bullock. 1995. "The Farmer and the Gatekeeper: Historical Archaeology and Agriculture in Early Carson City, Nevada." Report for the Nevada Department of Transportation.

National Archives and Records Administration. 1866–1938. Records of the District Courts of the United States, United States Circuit Court, Ninth Circuit Court Northern District of California, United States Commissioner, Common Law and Equity Case Files, RG 21. San Bruno, California.

National Archives and Records Administration. *Census Manuscripts (Population Schedules), 1860–1940*. Microfilm [abbr."Census"].

Neuenschwander, Leon F., James W. Byler, Alan E. Harvey, Geral I. McDonald, Denise S. Ortiz, Harold L. Osborne, Gerry C. Snyder, and Arthur Zack. 1999. "White Pine in the American West: A Vanishing Species—Can We Save It?" *SIRS Government Reporter*. SuDoc No. A 13.88:RMRS-GTR-35, 1–21.

"Nevada County Assessor's Records, 1868, 1870." Accessed in 2011 at http://webpages.cwia.com/
~mflicklin/tax.recs.html [no longer available]. See http://www.mynevadacounty.com.

"Nevada County Selected Property Records/Truckee, 1864–1920." Available at http://
westerly-journeys.com/Truckee/propralt.html (accessed December 1, 2014).

Nevada Division of Water Planning. "Truckee River Chronology, Part 2." Available at
http://water.nv.gov/mapping/chronologies/truckee/part2cfm.

Nevada State Archives and Library. State Census 1875. Microfilm. Carson City.

Nevada State Historic Preservation Office (NVSHPO). 1850–1920. Data based on Census
Manuscript [abbr. NVSHPO]. Formerly available at http://dmla.clan.lib.nv.us/docs/
shpo/NVCensus/FindPeople (removed from Web site September 2013); updated to 1950
at http://recordsproject.com/census/Nevada.asp; does not contain the same format.

Nevada State Legislature. 1867. *Appendix to Senate Proceedings, 3rd Session.*

———. 1875. *Appendix to the Journal of the Assembly, 7th Session.* Carson City: State Printing Office.

———. 1879. *Statutes Passed in the 9th Session.* Carson City: State Printing Office.

———. 1881. "Annual Report of the Controller." *Appendix to the Journal of the Senate and
Assembly, 10th Session.* Carson City: Maddrill.

———. 1885. "Report of the Surveyor-General and State Land Register of the State of
Nevada for 1883 and 1884." *Appendix to the Journals of the Senate and Assembly, 12th
Session.* Carson City: State Printing Office.

———. 1887. "Report of the Surveyor-General and the State Land Register of the State of
Nevada for the Year 1887." Assessor's Report for Douglas County. *Appendix to the Journals of the Senate and Assembly of the 13th Session.* Carson City: State Printing Office.

Ormsby County. *Assessment of Property* and *Assessment Rolls.* Nevada State Archives and
Library, Carson City.

———. Assessor's Office. *Tax Lists.*

———. Assessor's Office. *Tax Records.*

———. *Mortality List.* Avaialble at http://www.us-census.org/pub/usgenweb/census/nv/
ormsby/1870/mortality.txt (accessed December 1, 2014).

———. *Ormsby District Court Records.* Nevada State Archives and Library, Carson City.

Petersen, Frederic F., Jeffry S. Seldomridge, and Steven M. Stearns. 1994. "Cultural Resources Inventory of the Heavenly Ski Resort, Nevada and California." Report prepared
for Harland Bartholomew and Associates and the U.S. Forest Service, Lake Tahoe Basin
Management Unit.

Rogers, C. Lynn. 1997. "Making Camp Chinese Style: The Archaeology of a V&T Railroad Graders' Camp, Carson City, Nevada." ARS Project 865. Report for Silver Oak
Development Company.

Shaw, Clifford. 2013. "Chinese Woodcutter Camps in the Rough Creek and Table Mountain
Area of Western Mineral County, Nevada: A Collection of Notes." privately printed
and previously distributed through amazon.com.

Silver, Sue. 2012. "China Camp and Chinese Camp." Research Notes. U.S. Forest Service
Office, Sparks, Nevada.

Smith, Carrie E. 2001. "An Evaluation Plan and Research Design for 14 Historic Properties
within the Heavenly Ski Resort Expansion, Douglas County, Nevada." Report for the
U.S. Forest Service, South Lake Tahoe.

———, and Kelly J. Dixon. 2005. "Determination of Eligibility for Inclusion in the National
Register of Historic Places of 19 Historic Sites within the Heavenly Ski Resort, Douglas
County, Nevada." Report for the U.S. Forest Service, South Lake Tahoe.

State of Nevada. 1871. "Report of the Surveyor-General." *Journal of the Proceedings of the Senate, 5th Session.* Carson City: State Printing Office.

———. 1885–1889. "Report of the Assessor's Office." *Appendix to the Journal of Senate and Assembly, 12th session [1885], 13th session [1887], and 14th session [1889].* Carson City: State Printing Office.

Storey County [Nevada]. *Book of Deeds.* 1860–1890.

———. County Recorder's Office. *Assessment Book.*

———. 1875. *Map Book.*

U.S. Bureau of Labor Statistics. 1913. "Wages and Hours of Labor in the Lumber, Millwork, and Furniture Industries, 1890–1912." *Bulletin* 129:1–178.

U.S. Congress. 1877. "Report of the Joint Special Committee to Investigate Chinese Immigration." 44th Cong, 2nd Sess., Senate Report 689, dated February 27, 1877 [cited as "Senate Report 689"].

———. 1886. House of Representatives, "Providing Indemnity to Certain Chinese Subjects." 49th Cong, 1st Sess., House Report 2044, May [cited as "House Report 1886"].

———. 1906. House of Representatives. "Facts Concerning the Enforcement of Chinese Exclusion Laws." 59th Cong., 1st Sess., Doc. 847, May [cited as "House Report 1906"].

U.S. Department of Commerce. 1870–1910. Bureau of the Census. *Ninth Census (1870) of the United States* through *Fourteenth Census (1910) of the United States.* Washington, D.C.

———. 1870. *Compendium of the Ninth Census (1870).* Washington, D.C.: Government Printing Office [cited as U.S. Compendium 1870].

———. 1880. Bureau of the Census. *Tenth Census of the United State: 1880, Mining Laws.* Vol. 14. Washington, D.C. [cited as Mining Laws].

———. 1919. Bureau of Foreign and Domestic Commerce. *Trade of the United States with the World, 1917–1918.*Washington, D.C.: GPO.

U.S. Department of State. 1894. Bureau of Statistics. *American Lumber in Foreign Markets.* Special Consular Report. Vol. 40. Washington, D.C.: GPO.

———. 1897. Bureau of Statistics. *Commercial Relations of the United States with Foreign Countries during the Years 1895 and 1896.* Vol. 1. Washington, D.C.: GPO.

———. 1898. *Commercial Relations of the United States with Foreign Countries during the Years 1896 and 1897.* Vol. 1. Washington, D.C.: GPO.

U.S. Immigration and Naturalization Service. National Archives and Records Administration. Record Group 85. Riverside and San Bruno, California; Seattle, Washington; and Washington, D.C. [abbr. INS, RG 85, NARA, location].

U.S. Secretary of the Interior. 1872. *A Compendium of the Ninth Census (June 1, 1870).* Washington, D.C.: GPO.

Waechter, Sharon, Julia G. Castello, Susan G. Lindstrom, and William Bloomer. 1995. "Final Report on the Assessment of Damages from the Cottonwood, Crystal, and Hirschdale Fires at 10 Sites on the Tahoe and Toiyabe National Forests." Cultural Resources Report 05-17-1129. Nevada City, California: Tahoe National Forest. University of Nevada, Reno Library.

Washoe County [Nevada] Recorder's Office. *Washoe District Court Records.* Microfilm.

Books, Dissertations, Theses, and Articles

Aarim-Heriot, Najia. 2003. *Chinese Immigrants, African Americans, and Racial Anxiety in the United States, 1848–82.* Urbana: University of Illinois Press.

"About City Mill." Available at www.citymill.com/about.HISTORY.html (accessed December 1, 2014).

Abraham, Terry. 1996. "Class, Gender, and Race: Chinese Servants in the North American West." Paper presented at the Joint Regional Conference Hawai'i/Pacific and Pacific Northwest Association for Asian American Studies, Honolulu, March 26, 1996. Available at http://webpageswww.uidaho.edu/special-collections/papers/chservnt.htm.

Abrams, Kerry. 2005. "Polygamy, Prostitution, and the Federalization of Immigration Law." *Columbia Law Review* 105 (3): 641–716.

Adams, Kramer A. 1961. *Logging Railroads of the West*. New York: Bonanza.

Akin, Marjorie, James Bard, and Gary Weisz. 2015. "Asian Coins Recovered from Chinese Railroad Labor Camps: Evidence of Cultural Practices and Transnational Exchange." *Historical Archaeology* 49 (February): 110–21.

Aldrich, Howard E., and Roger Waldinger. 1990. "Ethnicity and Entrepreneurship." *Annual Review of Sociology* 16:111–35.

Allerfeldt, Kristofer. 2003. "Race and Restriction: Anti-Asian Immigration Pressures in the Pacific North-west of America during the Progressive Era, 1885–1924." *History* 88 (January): 53–73.

Anderson, Kay. 1991. *Vancouver's Chinatown: Racial Discourse in Canada, 1875–1980*. Montreal: McGill-Queen's University Press.

Andrews, Ralph W. 1954. *"This Was Logging!" Selected Photographs of Darius Kinsey*. Seattle, Wash.: Superior.

Angel, Myron, ed. 1881. *History of Nevada with Illustrations and Biographical Sketches of Its Prominent Men and Pioneers*. Oakland, Calif.: Thompson and West.

Anonymous. 1884. "Lumber Trade of the United States." *Journal of the Society of Arts* (December 26): 152.

Anonymous. 1967. "Railroads and Lumber Marketing 1858–78: The Relationship between an Iowa Sawmill Firm and the Chicago & Northwestern Railroad." *Annals of Iowa* 39 (Summer): 33–46.

Anonymous. 1994. "Japanese Canadians and the Racialization of Labour in the British Columbia Sawmill Industry." *BC Studies* 103 (Fall): 33–59.

Anonymous. 2000. "The History of Chinese Immigration." *Brown Quarterly* 3 (Spring): 2.

Anonymous. 2001. "Through the Eyes of the Emigrants and Miners: The Look of the Sierra Nevada, 1841–1860." *Overland Journal* 19 (4): 136–45.

Anslinger, Harry J., and William F. Tompkins. 1953. *The Traffic in Narcotics*. New York: Funk and Wagnalls.

Antony, Robert J. 1989. "Peasants, Heroes, and Brigands: The Problems of Social Banditry in Early Nineteenth-Century South China." *Modern China* 15 (April): 123–48.

"Archaeologists Find Evidence of Chinese Camp in Sierra." 2003. *Tahoe Daily Tribune*, September 26, available at http://www.tahoedailytribune.com/article/20030926/NEWS/309260101.

Arkush, R. David, and Leo O. Lee, eds. 1989. *Land without Ghosts: Chinese Impressions of America from the Mid-Nineteenth Century to the Present*. Berkeley: University of California Press.

Armentrout Ma, L. Eve. 1984. "Fellow-Regional Associations in the Ch'ing Dynasty: Organizations in Flux for Mobile People; A Preliminary Survey." *Modern Asian Studies* 18 (2): 307–30.

Aurin, Marcus. 2000. "Chasing the Dragon: The Cultural Metamorphosis of Opium in the United States, 1825–1935." *Medical Anthropology Quarterly* 14 (September): 414–41. New series.

Axsom, Jessica. 2009. "Yeong Wo Mercantile on the Comstock." Master's thesis. University of Nevada, Reno.

Bachman, Ben. 2002. "Logging in the West." *Trains* 62 (April): 42–44.

Bahre, Conrad J., and Charles F. Hutchinson. 1985. "The Impact of Historic Fuelwood Cutting on the Semidesert Woodlands of Southeastern Arizona." *Journal of Forest History* 29 (October): 175–86.

Bain, David Howard. 1999. *Empire Express: Building the First Transcontinental Railroad.* New York: Viking.

Balibrera, Dana Evans. 1965. "Virginia City and the Immigrant." Master's thesis. University of Nevada, Reno.

Bancroft, Hubert Howe. 1890. *History of California.* 7 vols. San Francisco: History Co., 1884–1890.

Barde, Robert, and Gustavo J. Bobonis. 2006. "Detention at Angel Island: First Empirical Evidence." *Social Science History* 30 (Spring): 103–36.

Barrett, Doug. 1980. "Truckee's Chinatown: Historic Home of Schemers and Rascals," *Truckee Republican* (February 1). Reprinted by the Truckee Historical Society.

Barry, James P. 2008. "Robert Dollar—Logging Boss." *Inland Seas* 64 (Fall): 219–25.

Barth, Gunther. 1964. *Bitter Strength: A History of the Chinese in the United States, 1850–1870.* Cambridge, Mass.: Harvard University Press.

Bauer, K. Jack. 1981. "Pacific Coast Commerce in the American Period." *Journal of the West* 20 (July): 11–20.

BeDunnah, Gary P. 1973. *A History of the Chinese in Nevada 1855–1904.* San Francisco: R and E.

Beesley, David. 1991. "More Than *People v. Hall*: Chinese Immigrants and American Law in a Sierra Nevada County, 1850–1920." *Locus* 3 (Spring): 123–39.

Belsky, Richard. 2005. *Localities at the Center: Native Place, Space, and Power in Late Imperial Beijing.* Cambridge, Mass.: Harvard University Asia Center.

Berner, Richard C. 1958. "Source Materials for Pacific Northwest History: The Port Blakely Mill Company Records." *Pacific Northwest Quarterly* 49 (Summer): 82–83.

———. 1966. "The Port Blakely Mill Company, 1876–89." *Pacific Northwest Quarterly* 57 (4): 158–71.

Blackburn, George M., and Sherman L. Ricards. 1980. "The Chinese of Virginia City, Nevada, 1870," *Amerasia* 7 (1): 51–71.

Bliss, William S. 1992. *Tahoe Heritage.* Reno: University of Nevada Press.

———. 2013. "Duane L. Bliss." Available at http://www.duanelbliss.com (accessed December 1, 2014).

Bodnar, John. 1985. *The Transplanted: A History of Immigrants in Urban America.* Bloomington: Indiana University Press.

Boswell, Terry E. 1986. "A Split Labor Market Analysis of Discrimination against Chinese Immigrants, 1850–1882." *American Sociological Review* 51 (June): 352–71.

Bowden, Jack. 2002. "Land, Lumber Companies and Mills in the Klamath Basin—1864–1950." *Journal of the Shaw Historical Library* 16 (16): 4–41.

Bragg, Allen C. 1911. "Pioneer Days in Nevada." In *Second Biennial Report, Nevada Historical Society 1909–1910*, 72–81. Carson City: State Printing Office.

Brecher, Edward M., and the Editors of *Consumer Reports* Magazine. 1972. "Opium Smoking is Outlawed." Available at http://www.druglibrary.org/Schaffer/Library/studies/cu/cu6.htm (accessed December 1, 2014).

Brook, Timothy. 2010. *The Troubled Empire: China in the Yuan and Ming Dynasties*. Cambridge, Mass.: Harvard University Press.

Buckley, J. 2000. "Building the Redwood Region: The Redwood Lumber Industry and the Landscape of Northern California, 1850–1929." PhD dissertation. University of California, Berkeley.

Bunker, Mike. 1881. "Early Biographies from White Pine." In *History of Nevada with Illustrations and Biographical Sketches of Its Prominent Men and Pioneers*, edited by Myron Angel. Oakland, Calif.: Thompson and West.

Bunting, Robert. 1994. "Abundance and the Forests of the Douglas-Fir Bioregion, 1840–1920." *Environmental History Review* 18 (Winter): 41–62.

Burgess, Opie Rundle. 1949. "Quong Kee: Pioneer of Tombstone." *Arizona Highways* 27 (July): 14–16.

Cabezas, Amado, and Gary Kawaguchi. 1988. "Empirical Evidence for Continuing Asian American Income Inequality: The Human Capital Model and Labor Market Segmentation." In *Reflections on Shattered Windows: Promises and Prospects for Asian American Studies*, edited by Gary Y. Okihiro, Shirley Hune, A. A. Hansen, and John M. Liu, 144–64. Pullman: Washington State University Press.

Cannon, W. J., Ernest B. Price, and T. C. McConnell. 1925. "Forestry, Mining, and Fisheries." In *Fukien: A Study of a Province in China*, edited by the Anti-Cobweb Club. Shanghai: Presbyterian Mission Press.

Carman, Harry J., and Charles H. Mueller. 1927. "The Contract and Finance Company and the Central Pacific Railroad." *Mississippi Valley Historical Review* 14 (December): 326-41.

Carranco, Lynwood. 1961. "Chinese Expulsion from Humboldt County." *Pacific Historical Review* 30 (November): 329–40.

———. 1962. "Logging Railroad Language in the Redwood Country." *American Speech* 37 (May): 130–36.

———. 1973. "The Chinese in Humboldt County, California: A Study in Prejudice." *Journal of the West* 12 (January): 139–62.

———, and Mrs. Eugene Fountain. 1964. "California's First Railroad: The Union Plank Walk, Rail Track, and Wharf Company Railroad." *Journal of the West* 3 (2): 243–56.

"Carson Tahoe Lumber and Fluming Company." Available at http://www.truckeedonner railroadsociety.com (accessed December 1, 2014).

Carson, Scott Alan. 2005. "Chinese Sojourn Labor and the American Transcontinental Railroad." *Journal of Institutional and Theoretical Economics* 161 (March): 80–102.

Carter, Gregg Lee. 1975. "Social Demography of the Chinese in Nevada; 1870–1880." *Nevada Historical Society Quarterly* 18 (2): 73–89.

Cassel, Susie Lan, ed. 2002. *The Chinese in America: A History from Gold Mountain to the New Millennium*. Walnut Creek, Calif.: Altamira.

Chan, Anthony B. 1981. "Orientalism and Image Making: The Sojourner in Canadian History." *Journal of Ethnic Studies* 9:37–46.

Chan, Loren B. 2001. "The Chinese in Nevada: An Historical Survey, 1856–1970." In *Chinese on the American Frontier*, edited by Arif Dirlik, 85–122. Lanham, Md.: Rowman and Littlefield.

Chan, Sucheng. 1984. "Chinese Livelihood in Rural California: The Impact of Economic Change, 1860–1880." *Pacific Historical Review* 53 (August): 273–307.

———. 1986. *This Bittersweet Soil: The Chinese in California Agriculture, 1860–1910*. Berkeley: University of California Press, 1986.

———. 1991a. *Asian Americans: An Interpretive History*. Boston, Mass.: Twayne.

———, ed. 1991b. *Entry Denied: Exclusion and the Chinese Community in America, 1882-1943*. Philadelphia: Temple University Press.

———. 1996a. "Asian American Historiography." *Pacific Historical Review* 65 (August): 363–99.

———. 1996b. "The Writing of Asian American History." *OAH Magazine of History* 10 (Summer): 8–17.

———. 2000. "A People of Exceptional Character: Ethnic Diversity, Nativism, and Racism in California Gold Rush." *California History* 79 (Summer): 44–85.

Chan, Wellington K. K. 1982. "The Organizational Structure of the Traditional Chinese Business Firm and Its Modern Reform." *Business History Review* 41 (2): 218–35.

Chan, Yenyen. 2011. "Chinese History in Yosemite." Available at www.nps.gov/yose/photosmultimedia/chinese.htm (accessed December 1, 2014).

Chandler, Robert J. 1984. "'Anti-Coolie Rabies': The Chinese Issue in California Politics in the 1860s." *Pacific Historian* 28 (Spring): 29–41.

———, and Stephen J. Potash. 2007. *Gold, Silk, Pioneers and Mail: The Story of the Pacific Mail Steamship Company*. San Francisco: Friends of the San Francisco Maritime Museum Library.

Cheek, Lawrence W. 1989. "A Place Called Bisbee." *Arizona Highways* 65 (February): 4–11.

Chen, Guoqing, and Zhang Keping, eds. 1994. *Zeng Guofan Quanji* [The Complete Works of Zeng Guofan]. Xian: Xibei Daixue Chubanshe.

Chen, Shehong. 2002. *Being Chinese, Becoming Chinese American*. Urbana: University of Illinois Press.

Chen, Wen-hsien, 1940. "Chinese under Both Exclusion and Immigration Laws." PhD dissertation. University of Chicago.

Chen, Yong. 1997. "The Internal Origins of Chinese Emigration to California Reconsidered." *Western Historical Quarterly* 28 (Winter): 520–46.

———. 2000. *Chinese San Francisco, 1850–1943: A Trans-Pacific Community*. Stanford, Calif.: Stanford University Press.

Chen Da [Chen Ta]. 1923. *Chinese Migrations, with Special Reference to Labor Conditions*. Bulletin 340. United States Bureau of Labor Statistics. Washington, D.C.: GPO.

———. 1940. *Emigrant Communities in South China*. New York: Institute for Pacific Relations.

Chester, Robert Neil. 2009. "Comstock Creations: An Environmental History of an Industrial Watershed." PhD dissertation. University of California, Davis.

Chew, Kenneth S. Y., and John M. Liu. 2004. "Hidden in Plain Sight: Global Labor Force Exchange in the Chinese American Population, 1880–1940." *Population and Development Review* 30 (March): 57–78.

Chew, Sing C. 1992. *Logs for Capital: The Timber Industry and Capitalist Enterprise in the Nineteenth Century*. Westport, Conn.: Greenwood.

Chew, William F. 2004. *Nameless Builders of the Transcontinental: The Chinese Workers of the Central Pacific Railroad*. Victoria, B.C.: Trafford.

Chin, Tung Pok, and Winifred C. Chin. 2000. *Paper Son: One Man's Story*. Philadelphia: Temple University Press.

Chinn, Thomas. 1972. "Observations 1935–1942." *Chinese Historical Society of America* 7:6–8.

Chiu, Ping. 1963. *Chinese Labor in California, 1850–1880: An Economic Study*. Madison: State Historical Society of Wisconsin, University of Wisconsin.

Christoff, Peggy Spitzer. 2001. *Tracing the "Yellow Peril": The INS and Chinese Immigrants in the Midwest*. Rockport, Maine: Picton.

Chu, Yung-Deh Richard. 1973. "Chinese Secret Societies in America: A Historical Survey." *Asian Profile* 1 (1): 21–38.

Chung, Sue Fawn. 1987. "The Chinese Experience in Nevada: Success Despite Discrimination." *Nevada Public Affairs Review* 2:43–51. Special Issue: Ethnicity and Race in Nevada, edited by Elmer Rusco and Sue Fawn Chung.

———. 1994. "Destination: Nevada, the Silver Mountain." In *Origins and Destinations: 1992 Conference on Chinese Americans*, 111–39. Los Angeles: Chinese Historical Society of Southern California and UCLA Asian American Studies.

———. 1997. "Their Changing World: Chinese Women of the Comstock." In *Women on the Comstock: The Making of a Mining Community*, edited by Ronald James and C. Elizabeth Raymond, 203–28. Reno: University of Nevada Press.

———. 1998. "Fighting for Their American Rights: A History of the Chinese American Citizens Alliance." In *Claiming America: Constructing Chinese American Identities during the Exclusion Era*, edited by K. Scott Wong and Sucheng Chan, 95–126. Philadelphia: Temple University Press.

———. 2000. "Between Two Worlds: Ah Cum Kee (1876–1929) and Loy Lee Ford (1882–1921)." In *Ordinary Women, Extraordinary Lives: A History of Women in America*, edited by Kriste Lindenmeyer, 179–95. Delaware: Scholarly Resources.

———. 2011. *In Pursuit of Gold: Chinese American Miners and Merchants in the American West*. Urbana: University of Illinois Press.

———. 2006. "The Zhigongtang in the United States, 1860–1949." In *Empire, Nation, and Beyond: Chinese History in Late Imperial and Modern Times*, edited by Wen-hsin Yeh and Joseph Eshrick, 231–49. Berkeley: University of California Press.

———, and Priscilla Wegars, eds. 2005. *Chinese American Death Rituals: Respecting the Ancestors*. Walnut Creek, Calif.: AltaMira.

Clark, Lew, and Ginny Clark. 1978. *High Mountains and Deep Valleys: The Gold Bonanza Days*. San Luis Obispo, Calif.: Western Trails.

Clark, Mark. 2002. "Logging Technology: An Introduction." *Journal of the Shaw Historical Library* 16 (16): 78–98.

Clark, Norman H. 1970. *Mill Town: A Social History of Everett, Washington, from the Earliest Beginnings on the Shores of Puget Sound to the Tragic and Infamous Event Known as the Everett Massacre*. Seattle: University of Washington Press.

Clement, Ralph. 1938. *Lumber, Its Manufacture and Distribution*. 2nd edition. New York: Wiley.

Cloud, Patricia, and David W. Galenson. 1987. "Chinese Immigration and Contract Labor in the Late Nineteenth Century." *Explorations in Economic History* 24 (January): 22–42.

Coate, Bill. 2010. "Lumber Kept Madera County Alive." *Sierra Star*, October 28. Available at http://www.sierrastar.com.

Coates, Guy H. n.d. "The Richardson Brothers: A Truckee Legacy." Manuscript on file with the author. Truckee, California.

———. n.d. "The Trout Creek Outrage." Available at http://truckeehistory.org/history Articles/history6.htm (accessed December 1, 2014).

———. n.d. "Truckee's Notable Townspeople and Memorable Characters." Available at http://truckeehistory.org/historyArticles/history11.htm (accessed December 1, 2014).

Cochran, Sherman. 1980. *Big Business in China*. Cambridge, Mass.: Harvard University Press.

———. 2000. *Encountering Chinese Networks: Western, Japanese, and Chinese Corporations in China, 1880–1937*. Berkeley: University of California Press.

Cohen, Lucy M. 1971. "The Chinese of the Panama Railroad: Preliminary Notes on the Migrants of 1854 Who 'Failed.'" *Ethnohistory* 8 (4): 309–20.

———. 1995. "George W. Gift, Chinese Labor Agent in the Post–Civil War South." In *Chinese America: History and Perspective*, 157–78. San Francisco: Chinese Historical Society of America.

Cohen, Myron L. 1968. "The Hakka or 'Guest People': Dialect as a Sociocultural Variable in Southeast China." *Ethnohistory* 15 (3): 237–92.

Cole, Richard P., and Gabriel J. Chin. 1999. "Emerging from the Margins of Historical Consciousness: Chinese Immigrants and the History of American Law." *Law and History Review* 17 (Summer): 325–64.

Colin, Joseph R. 1979. "'Old Boy, Did You Get Enough of Pie?' A Social History of Food in Logging Camps." *Journal of Forest History* 23 (October): 164–85.

———. 1989. "Grub and Chow: Food, Foodways, Class, and Occupation on the Western Frontier." *European Contributions to American Studies* 16 (March): 128–31.

Colton, L. J. 1967. "Early Day Timber Cutting along the Upper Bear River." *Utah Historical Quarterly* 35 (Summer): 202–8.

Coman, Edwin T., Jr., and Helen M. Gibbs. 1968. *Time, Tide, and Timber: A Century of Pope and Talbot*. New York: Greenwood.

Compton, Wilson. 1906. *The Organization of the Lumber Industry: With Special References to the Influences Determining the Prices of Lumber in the United States*. PhD dissertation. Princeton University, Princeton, N.J. Published by American Lumberman, Chicago, 1916.

Conner Prairie Interactive History Park. 1994. "Fuel for the Fires: Charcoal Making in the Nineteenth Century." *Chronicle of the Early American Industries Association*. Available at http://www.connerprairie.org/learn-and-do/indiana-history/america-1800-1860/19th -century-charcoal-making.aspx (accessed December 1, 2014).

Coolidge, Mary Roberts. 1909. *Chinese Immigration*. New York: Holt.

Cornford, Daniel Allardyce. 1983. "Lumber, Labor, and Community in Humboldt County, California." PhD dissertation. University of California, Santa Barbara.

———. 1987a. "To Save the Republic: The California Workingmen's Party in Humboldt County." *California History* 66 (June): 130–42.

———. 1987b. *Workers and Dissent in the Redwood Empire*. Philadelphia: Temple University Press.

Cox, John H. 1950. "Trade Associations in the Lumber Industry of the Pacific Northwest, 1899- 1914." *Pacific Historical Quarterly* 41 (October): 285–311.

Cox, Thomas R. 1970. "Lumber and Ships: The Business Empires of Asa Mead Simpson." *Forest History* 14 (July): 16–26.

———. 1974. *Mills and Markets: A History of the Pacific Coast Lumber Industry to 1900*. Seattle: University of Washington Press.

———. 1981a. "Single Decks and Flat Bottoms: Building the West Coast's Lumber Fleet, 1850–1929." *Journal of the West* 20 (July): 65–74.

———. 1981b. "The Stewardship of Private Forests: The Evolution of a Concept in the United States, 1864–1850." *Journal of Forest History* 25 (October): 188–96.

———. 2010. *The Lumberman's Frontier: Three Centuries of Land Use, Society, and Change in America's Forests*. Corvallis: Oregon State University Press.

————, Robert S. Maxwell, Phillip Drennon Thomas, and Joseph J. Malone. 1985. *This Well- Wooded Land: Americans and Their Forests from Colonial Times to the Present.* Lincoln: University of Nebraska Press.

Creese, Gillian. 1988. "Class, Ethnicity, and Conflict: The Case of Chinese and Japanese Immigrants, 1880–1923." In *Workers, Capital, and the State in British Columbia*, edited by Rennie Warburton and David Coburn, 55–85. Vancouver: University of British Columbia Press.

Currier, Viola Noon, 1928. "The Chinese Web in Oregon History." Master's thesis. University of Oregon, Eugene.

Dangberg, Grace. 1972. *Carson Valley—Historical Sketches of Nevada's First Settlement.* Minden, Nev.: Carson Valley Historical Society.

————. 1975. *Conflict on the Carson.* Minden, Nev.: Carson Valley Historical Society.

Daniels, Roger. 1988. *Asian America: Chinese and Japanese in the United States since 1850.* Seattle: University of Washington Press.

————. 1997a. "No Lamps Were Lit for Them: Angel Island and the Historiography of Asian American Immigration." *Journal of American Ethnic History* 17 (1): 10–17.

————. 1997b. *The Politics of Prejudice: The Anti-Japanese Movement in California and the Struggle for Japanese Exclusion.* Berkeley: University of California Press.

"Dare to Shoot the Flume." Available at http://www.thestormking.com/Products/Books/ The_Flume/the_flume.html (accessed December 1, 2014).

Davis, David H. 1996. "Log Chutes of the Pacific Northwest Coast: A Fast, Efficient, Yet Dangerous Method Used by Early Loggers to Transport Fresh-Cut Timber." *Columbia: Magazine of Northwest History* 10 (September): 14–18.

Dearinger, Ryan L. 2009. "Frontiers of Progress and Paradox: Building Canals, Railroads, and Manhood in the American West." PhD dissertation. University of Utah, Salt Lake City.

Defebaugh, James E. 1906–1907. *History of the Lumber Industry of America.* Chicago: American Lumberman.

Delgado, James P. 2009. *Gold Rush Port: The Maritime Archaeology of San Francisco's Waterfront.* Berkeley: University of California Press.

De Lorme, Roland L. 1986. "Rational Management Takes to the Woods: Frederick Weyerhaeuser and the Pacific Northwest Wood Products Industry." *Journal of the West* 25 (1): 39–43.

Deng Yibing. 2005. "Qingdai qianqi zhushu yunyuliang" [The volume of bamboo and lumber transported in the early Qing dynasty]. *Qingshi yanjiu* [Research in Qing history] 2 (May): 32–43.

Denny, Owen Nickerson. 1880. *Oregon Lumber in China.* Washington, n.p.

De Quille, Dan. 1876. *The Big Bonanza: An Authentic Account of the Discovery, History, and Working of the World-Renowned Comstock Lode of Nevada.* Hartford, Conn.: American.

Dettman, Jeffrey Alan. 2002. "Anti-Chinese Violence in the American Northwest: From Community Politics to International Diplomacy, 1885–1888." PhD dissertation. University of Texas, Austin.

Deverell, William. 1994. *Railroad Crossing: Californians and the Railroad, 1850–1910.* Berkeley: University of California Press.

Ding, Jianmin, and Tingbi Xu. 1995. *Zhongguo de senlin* [China's Forests]. Beijing: Shangwu yinshu guan.

"Dollar Steamship Company." Available at http://www.theshipslist.com/ships/lines/dollar .htm (accessed December 1, 2014).

Dou Jiliang. 1943. *Tongxiang zushi zi yanjiu* [The study of regional institutions]. Chong-qing: Zheng zhong shu ju.

Douglas, Lawrence, and Taylor Hansen. 2006. "The Chinese Six Companies of San Francisco and the Smuggling of Chinese Immigrants across the U.S.–Mexico border, 1882–1930." *Journal of the Southwest* 48 (Spring): 37–62.

Drushka, Ken. 1992. *Working in the Woods: A History of Logging on the West Coast*. Madeira Park, B.C.: Harbour.

———, and Hannu Konttinen. 1997. *Tracks in the Forest: The Evolution of Logging Machinery*. Helsinki: Timberjack.

Dubrow, Gail. With Donna Graves. 2002. *Sento at Sixth and Main: Preserving Landmarks of Japanese American Heritage*. Seattle, Wash.: Seattle Arts Commission.

Due, John F. 1951. "The Carson and Colorado Railroad." *Economic Geography* 27 (July): 251- 67.

Edwards, W. F., and Charles D. Irons. 1883. *W. F. Edwards' Tourists' Guide and Directory of the Truckee Basin*. Truckee, Calif.: Republican.

Elliott, Russell R. 1973. *History of Nevada*. Lincoln: University of Nebraska Press.

Ettinger, L. 1995. *The Best of Virginia City and the Comstock*. Reno: Ettinger.

Evanston Urban Renewal Agency. 1996. "The Chinese in Evanston, Wyoming, 1870–1939." Evanston, Wyo.: Evanston Urban Renewal Agency.

"Evergreen State: Exploring the History of Washington's Forests." Available at http://www.washington.edu/uwired/outreach/cspn/Website/Classroom%20Materials/Curriculum%20Packets/Evergreen%20State/Evergreen%20Main.html (accessed December 1, 2014).

Fairbank, John K., and Merle Goldman. (1992) 2000. *China: A New History*. Revised edition. Cambridge, Mass.: Belknap.

Feagin, Joe R. 2014. *Racist America: Roots, Current Realities, and Future Reparations*. 3rd edition. New York: Routledge.

Ferrell, Mallory Hope. 1967. *Rails, Sagebrush, and Pine: A Garland of Railroad and Logging Days in Oregon's Sumpter Valley*. San Marino, Calif.: Golden West.

Feuerwerker, Albert. 1958. *China's Early Industrialization: Sheng Hsuan-huai (1844–1916) and Mandarin Enterprise*. Cambridge, Mass.: Harvard University Press.

Ficken, Robert E. 1979. "Weyerhaeuser and the Pacific Northwest Timber Industry, 1899–1903," *Pacific Northwest Quarterly* 70 (October): 146–54.

———. 1987. *The Forested Land: A History of Lumbering in Western Washington*. Seattle: University of Washington Press.

Ficklin, Marilou West. 1997. *Showdown at Truckee*. Reno: Western.

Finges, John R. 1972. "Seattle's First Sawmill, 1853–1869: A Study of Frontier Enterprise." *Forest History Newsletter* 15 (January): 24–31.

Fleming, Thomas J. 1971. "The Race to Promontory." *American History Illustrated* 6 (3): 10–25.

Floyd, Donald R. 1985. "A Surge of Hope: Public Reactions to Arguments for Construction of Narrow-Gauge Railroads in California, 1870–1873." *California Geographer* 25:65–84.

Fong, Eric W., and William T. Markham. 2002. "Anti-Chinese Politics in California in the 1870s: An Intercounty Analysis." *Sociological Perspectives* 45 (Summer): 183–210.

Fong, Mak Lau. 1981. *The Sociology of Secret Societies: A Study of Chinese Secret Societies in Singapore and Peninsular Malaysia*. Kuala Lumpur: Oxford University Press.

Frederick, David C. 1993. "The Ninth Circuit and Natural-Resource Development in the Early Twentieth Century." *Western Legal History* 6 (2): 183–215.

Freedman, Maruice. 1958. "The Handling of Money: A Note on the Background to the Economic Sophistication of the Overseas Chinese." *Man* 59:64–65.

———. 1966. *Chinese Lineage and Society: Fukien and Kwangtung.* London: Athlone.

Fremont, Jessie Benton. 1878. *A Year of American Travel.* New York: Harper.

Fussell, Elizabeth, and Douglas S. Massey. 2004. "The Limits to Cumulative Causation: International Migration from Mexican Urban Areas." *Demography* 41:151–72.

Garraty, John A., and Mark C. Carnes. 1999. *American National Biography.* New York: Oxford University Press.

"Genoa Peak Road and Slaughterhouse Canyon." Available athttp://memory.loc.gov/egi-bin/ampage?co111d-hhdatapage&fileName (accessed February 4, 2009; no longer available online).

Glick, Clarence E. 1980. *Sojourners and Settlers: Chinese Migrants in Hawaii.* Honolulu: Hawaiʻi Chinese History Center and the University Press of Hawaiʻi.

Godley, Michael R. 1975. "The Late Chʻing Courtship of the Chinese in Southeast Asia." *Journal of Asian Studies* 34:361–85.

Gold, Martin. 2012. *Forbidden Citizens: Chinese Exclusion and the U.S. Congress: A Legislative History.* Alexandria, Va.: TheCapitol.Net.

Goldstein, Michael A. 1988. "Truckee's Chinese Community: From Coexistence to Disintegration, 1870–1890." Master's thesis. University of California, Los Angeles.

Gordon, Gregory Llewellyn. 2010. "Money Does Grow on Trees: A. B. Hammond and the Age of the Lumber Baron." Ph.D. dissertation. University of Montana, Missoula.

Gottschalk, Louis, and Eve Unsell. 1923. "Ching Ching Chinaman." Musical score. New York: Remick.

Gracomazzi, Sharon. 2004. *Trails and Tails of Yosemite and Central Nevada.* Mendocino, Calif.: Bored Feet.

Greeley, William B. 1923. "Economic Aspects of Our Timber Supply." *Scientific Monthly* 16 (April): 352–62.

Grider, John T. 2010. "'I Espied a Chinaman': Chinese Sailors and the Fracturing of the Nineteenth-Century Pacific Maritime Labour Force." *Slavery and Abolition* 31 (September): 467–81.

Guangdong Sheng zhi. 1998. *Lin ye zhi* [Records on Forestry]. Guangzhou: Guangdong renmin chu ban she.

Gyory, Andrew. 1998. *Closing the Gate: Race, Politics, and the Chinese Exclusion Act.* Chapel Hill: University of North Carolina Press.

Hagaman, Wallace. 2004. *The Chinese Must Go: The Anti-Chinese Boycott in Truckee, California, 1886.* With Steve F. Cottrell. Nevada City: Cowboy.

———, and Hank Meals. "The Nevada City, California Chinese Quarter." Available at http://www.historichwy49.com/ethnic/chinese.html (accessed December 1, 2014).

Hak, Gordon. 2000. *Turning Trees into Dollars: The British Columbia Coastal Lumber Industry, 1858–1913.* Toronto: University of Toronto Press.

Hamilton, Gary G. 1979. "Regional Associations and the Chinese City: A Comparative Perspective." *Comparative Studies in Society and History* 21 (July): 346–61.

Hamman, Rick. 1980. *California Central Coast Railways.* Boulder, Colo.: Pruett.

Handlin, Oscar. 1951. *The Uprooted: The Epic Story of the Great Migration that Made the American People.* Boston: Little, Brown.

Hanzlik, Edward John. 1928. *Trees and Forests of the Western United States.* 2 vols. Portland, Ore.: Dunham.

Hardesty, Donald L. 1988. *The Archaeology of Mining and Miners: A View from the Silver State.* Pleasant Hill, Calif.: Society for Historical Archaeology.

———. 2003. "Archaeology and the Chinese Experience in Nevada." *South Dakota History* 33 (4): 363–79.

Hattori, Eugene. 1991. "Chinese and Japanese." In *Nevada Comprehensive Preservation Plan*, edited by W. G. White, R. M. James, and R. Bernstein. Carson City: Nevada Division of Historic Preservation and Archaeology.

———, Marna Ares Thompson, and Alvin R. McLane. 1987. *Historic Pinyon Pine Utilization in the Cortez Mining District in Central Nevada: The Use of Dendrochronology in Historical Archaeology and Historical Reconstruction.* Reno: Desert Research Institute.

Heidhues, Mary Somers. 2003. *Golddiggers, Farmers, and Traders in the "Chinese Districts" of West Kalimantan, Indonesia.* Ithaca, N.Y.: Cornell University Southeast Asia Program.

Heizer, Robert F. 1947. "Archaeological Investigation of Sutter Sawmill Site in 1947." *California Historical Society Quarterly* 26 (2): 144 and 152.

Henning, G. R., and Mary Henning. 1990. "Technological Change from Sail to Steamer: Export Lumber Shipments from the Pacific Northwest, 1898–1913." *International Journal of Maritime History* 2 (December): 133–45.

Hidy, R., F. Hill, and A. Nevins. 1963. *Timber and Men: The Weyerhaeuser Story.* New York: Macmillan.

Higham, John. 1981. "Integrating America: The Problem of Assimilating in the Nineteenth Century." *Journal of American Ethnic History* 1 (Fall): 7–25.

Hildebrand, Lorraine Barker. 1977. *Straw Hats, Sandals, and Steel: The Chinese in Washington State.* Tacoma: Washington State American Revolution Bicentennial Commission.

Hill, Leslie, 1987. "The Historical Archaeology of Ethnic Woodcutters in the Carson Range." Master's thesis. University of Nevada, Reno.

Hing, Bill Ong. 1993. *Making and Remaking Asian America through Immigration Policy, 1850- 1990.* Stanford, Calif.: Stanford University Press.

Hinrichs, T. J., and Linda L. Barnes. 2013. *Chinese Medicine and Healing: An Illustrated History.* Cambridge, Mass.: Harvard University Press.

"History of Carlin." Available at http//www.rootsweb.ancestry.com/~nvelko/elko-histCarlin2_html (accessed December 1, 2014).

"History of Logging in Oregon." Available at http://www.opb.org/programs/oregonstory/logging/timeline.html (accessed December 1, 2014).

Hittell, J. 1863. *The Resources of California, Comprising Agriculture, Mining, Geography, Climate, Commerce, etc.* San Francisco: Roman.

Hsu, Francis L. K. (1948) 1967. *Under the Ancestors' Shadow.* Garden City, N.Y.: Doubleday.

———. (1953) 1970. *Americans and Chinese: Purpose and Fulfillment in Great Civilizations.* Garden City, N.Y.: Doubleday.

Hsu, Madeline Y. 2000a. *Dreaming of Gold, Dreaming of Home: Transnationalism and Migration between the United States and South China, 1882–1943.* Stanford, Calif.: Stanford University Press.

———. 2000b. "Migration and Native Place: Qiaokan and the Imagined Community of Taishan County, Guangdong, 1893–1993." *Journal of Asian Studies* 59 (May): 307–31.

Huang, Annian. 2006. *Chen mo de suo dao ding: Jian she Bei Mei tie lu de hua gong* [The Silent Spikes: Chinese Laborers and the Construction of the North American Railways]. Translated by Zhang Juguo. Beijing: Wu zhou chuan bo chu pan she.

———. 2010. *The Silent Spikes No Longer Keep Silent: Chinese Laborers and the Construction of North American Railroads.* Beijing: Shenyang Baishan.

Huang Jianchun. 1993. *Wan Qing Xin Ma huaqiao dui guojia rentong zhi yanjiu* [A study of Overseas Chinese nationalism among the Malaya Chinese in the late Qing Dynasty]. Taibei: Society of Overseas Chinese Studies.

Huffman, Wendell. 1995. "Iron Horse along the Truckee: The Central Pacific Reaches Nevada." *Nevada Historical Society Quarterly* 38 (1): 19–36.

———. 2007. "Silver and Iron: How the Comstock Determined the Course of the Central Pacific Railroad." *Nevada Historical Society Quarterly* 50 (March), 3–35.

Hummel, N. A. 1969. *General History and Resources of Washoe County, Nevada*. Verdi, Nev.: Sagebrush.

Hurt, Bert. *A Sawmill History of the Sierra National Forest, 1852–1940*. Available at http://snlm.files.wordpress.com/2009/10/usfs-sawmill-history.pdf (accessed December 1, 2014).

Hutchinson, W. H. 1973. "The Sierra Flume and Lumber Company of California, 1875–1878." *Forest History* 17 (October): 14–20.

Ingersoll, Ernest. 1883. *In a Redwood Logging Camp*. New York, n.p. Excerpted in *Harper's New Monthly Magazine*, 193–210.

Irick, Robert L. 1982. *Ch'ing Policy toward the Collie Trade, 1847–1878*. Taipei: Chinese Materials Center.

Isaacs, Harold. 1958. *Scratches on Our Minds: American Images of China and India*. New York: Day.

Iwai, Yoshiya, ed. 2002. *Forestry and the Forest Industry in Japan*. Vancouver: University of British Columbia.

Jager, Ronald. 1999. "Tool and Symbol: The Success of the Double-Bitted Axe in North America." *Technology and Culture* 40 (4): 833–60.

James, John. 1995. "Lake Tahoe and the Sierra Nevada." In *The Mountainous West: Explorations in Historical Geography*, edited by William Wyckoff and Lary M. Dilsaver, 331–48. Lincoln: University of Nebraska Press.

James, Ronald M. 1998. *The Roar and the Silence: A History of Virginia City and the Comstock Lode*. Reno.: University of Nevada Press.

James, Walter. 1995. "Water James: Reminiscences of My Younger Days." In *Chinese America: History and Perspectives*, edited by Marlon K. Hom, 75–86. San Francisco: Chinese Historical Society of America.

Jew, Victor. 2003. "'Chinese Demons': The Violent Articulation of Chinese Otherness and Interracial Sexuality in the U.S. Midwest, 1885–1889." *Journal of Social History* 37 (Winter): 389–410.

Jim, C. Y., and H. T. Liu. 2001. "Patterns and Dynamics of Urban Forests in Relation to Land Use and Development in Guangzhou City, China." *Geographical Journal* 167 (December): 358–75.

Johnson, Emory R. 1910. "Sources of American Railway Freight Traffic." *Bulletin of the American Geographical Society* 42 (4): 243–60.

Johnson, Graham E., and Glen D. Peterson. 1999. *Historical Dictionary of Guangzhou (Canton) and Guangdong*. Lanham, Md.: Scarecrow.

Johnson, Judith M. 1960. "Source Materials for Pacific Northwest History: Washington Mill Company Papers." *Pacific Northwest Quarterly* 51 (July): 136–38.

Johnston, Andrew. 2004. "Quicksilver Landscapes: The Mercury Mining Boom, Chinese Labor, and the California Constitution of 1879." *Journal of the West* 43 (Winter): 21–29.

Johnston, Hank. 1984. *The Whistles Blow No More: Railroad Logging in the Sierra Nevada, 1874–1942*. Glendale, Calif.: Trans-Anglo.

Judd, Richard W. 1984. "Lumbering and the Farming Frontier in Aroostook County, Maine, 1840–1880." *Journal of Forest History* 28 (April): 56–67.

Jue, Willard G. 1983. "Chin Gee-Hee, Chinese Pioneer Entrepreneur in Seattle and Toishan." *Annals of the Chinese Historical Society of the Pacific Northwest* 1:31–38.

Kanazawa, Mark. 2005. "Immigration, Exclusion, and Taxation: Anti-Chinese Legislation in Gold Rush California." *Journal of Economic History* 65 (3): 779–805.

Kane, June Mary. 1908. "Verdi: Its Growth and Development." Thesis. University of Nevada, Reno.

Karlin, Jules Alexander. 1948. "The Anti-Chinese Outbreaks in Seattle, 1885–1886." *Pacific Northwest Quarterly* 39 (April): 103–30.

Karshner, Gayle. 1995. "Wooden Rails." *Humboldt Historian* (Winter): 13–15.

Kersten, Earl W., Jr. 1964. "The Early Settlement of Aurora, Nevada, and Nearby Mining Camps." *Annals of the Association of American Geographers* 54 (December): 490–507.

King, Haitung, and Frances B. Locke, 1980. "Chinese in the United States: A Century of Occupational Transition." *International Migration Review* 14 (Spring): 15–42.

Koch, Michael. 1971. *Shay Locomotive, Titan of the Timber*. Denver: World.

Kohlmeyer, Fred W. 1983. "Lumber Distribution and Marketing in the United States." *Journal of Forest History* 27 (April): 86–91.

Kraus, George. 1969a. "Chinese Laborers and the Construction of the Central Pacific." *Utah Historical Quarterly* 37 (1): 41–57.

———. 1969b. *High Road to Promontory: Building the Central Pacific (now Southern Pacific) Across the High Sierra*. Palo Alto, Calif.: American West.

Lai, Chuen-yan David. 1975. "Home County and Clan Origins of Overseas Chinese in Canada in the Early 1880s." *BC Studies* 27:3–29.

———. 2010. *Chinese Community Leadership: Case Study of Victoria in Canada*. Singapore: World Scientific.

Lai, Him Mark. 1995a. "Chinese Regional Solidarity: Case Study of the Hua Xian (Fa Yuen) Community in California." In *Chinese America: History and Perspectives*, 19–60. San Francisco: Chinese Historical Society of America.

———. 1995b. "Historical Development of the Chinese Consolidated Benevolent Association/'Huiguan' System." In *Chinese America: History & Perspectives*, 13–51. San Francisco: Chinese Historical Society of America.

———. 2004. *Becoming Chinese American*. Walnut Creek, Calif.: AltaMira.

———, Genny Lim, and Judy Yung, eds. 1991. *Island: Poetry and History of Chinese Immigrants on Angel Island, 1910–1940*. Reprint edition. Seattle: University of Washington Press.

Lake, Holly. 1994. "Construction of the CPRR: Chinese Immigrant Contribution." *Northeastern Nevada Historical Society Quarterly* 94 (4): 188–99.

LaLande, Jeffrey M. 1979. *Medford Corporation: A History of an Oregon Logging and Lumber Company*. Medford, Ore.: Klocker.

Lanner, Ronald M. 1981. *The Pinon Pine: A Natural and Cultural History*. Reno: University of Nevada Press.

Lau, Estelle T. 2006. *Paper Families: Identity, Immigration Administration, and Chinese Exclusion*. Durham, N.C.: Duke University Press.

Lawson, James. 2009/2010. "Explaining Workplace Injuries among BC Loggers: Cultures of Risk and of Desperation." *BC Studies* 164 (Winter): 51–74.

Layton, Thomas N. 2002. *Gifts from the Celestial Kingdom: A Shipwrecked Cargo for Gold Rush California*. Stanford, Calif.: Stanford University Press.

Lee, Erika. 2003. *At America's Gates: Chinese Immigration During the Exclusion Era, 1882-1943*. Chapel Hill: University of North Carolina Press.

——. 2006. "Defying Exclusion: Chinese Immigrants and Their Strategies during the Exclusionary Era." In *Chinese American Transnationalism: The Flow of People, Resources, and Ideas between China and America during the Exclusion Era*, edited by Sucheng Chan, 1–21. Philadelphia: Temple University Press.

Lee, Jane. 2008. "'Fidelity and Industry': The Archaeology of a Late-Nineteenth-Century Chinese Woodcutter Camp in Dog Valley, California." Master's thesis. University of Nevada, Reno.

Lee, Vivien F. 1983. "New Markets: People's Republic of China." In *World Trade in Forest Products*, edited by James S. Bethel, 416–17. Seattle: University of Washington Press.

"The Legends and Lore of Dayton's History." Available at http://daytonnvhistory.org/history.htm (accessed December 1, 2014).

Leitner, Jonathan. 2003. "North American Timber Economy: Log Transport, Regional Capitalist Conflict, and Corporate Formation in Wisconsin's Chippewa Basin, 1860–1900." *Review—Fernand Braudel Center for the Study of Economies, Historical Systems, and Civilizations* 26 (2): 173–219.

Leland, Charles Godfrey. 1975. *Fusang; or, The Discovery of America by Chinese Buddhist Priests in the Fifth Century*. New York: Curzon.

Leong, Sow-Theng. 1997. *Migration and Ethnicity in Chinese History: Hakkas, Pengmin, and Their Neighbors*. Stanford: Stanford University Press.

Lewis, Oscar. (1938) 1966. *The Big Four: The Story of Huntington, Stanford, Hopkins, and Crocker, and the Building of the Central Pacific Railroad*. New York: Knopf.

Li, Peter S. 1988. *The Chinese in Canada*. Toronto: Oxford University Press.

Liang, Zai, Miao David Chunyu, Guotu Zhuang, and Wenzhen Ye. 2008. "Cumulative Causation, Market Transition, and Emigration from China." *American Journal of Sociology* 114 (November); 706–37.

Liecap, Gary D., and Ronald N. Johnson. 1979. "Property Rights, Nineteenth-Century Federal Timber Policy, and the Conservation Movement." *Journal of Economic History* 39 (March), 129–42.

Liestman, Daniel. 1994. "'The Various Celestial among Our Town': Euro-American Response to Port Townsend's Chinese Colony." *Pacific Northeastern Quarterly* 85 (July): 93–104.

Light, Ivan. 1972. *Ethnic Enterprise in America*. Berkeley: University of California Press.

Ling, Huping. 1998. *Surviving on the Gold Mountain: A History of Chinese American Women and Their Lives*. Albany: SUNY Press.

——. 2012. *Chinese Chicago: Race, Transnational Migration, and Community Since 1870*. Stanford, Calif.: Stanford University Press.

Liu, Boji. 1981. *Meiguo huaqiao shi* [A History of the Chinese in the United States]. New edition. Taibei, Taiwan: Li ming wen hua shi ye gongsi.

Liu, Dachang. 2001. "Tenure and Management of Non-State Forests in China since 1950: A Historical Review." *Environmental History* 6 (April): 239–63.

Liu, Haiming. 1998. "The Resilience of Ethnic Culture: Chinese Herbalists in the American Medical Profession," *Journal of Asian American Studies* 1 (2): 173–91.

———. 2002. "The Social Origins of Early Chinese Immigrants: A Revisionist Perspective." In *The Chinese in America: A History from Gold Mountain to the New Millennium*, edited by Susie Lan Cassel, 21–26. Walnut Creek, Calif.: AltaMira.

———. 2005. *The Transnational History of a Chinese Family: Immigrant Letters, Family Business, and Reverse Migration*. New Brunswick, N.J.: Rutgers University Press.

Locke, Marvin Elliott. 1962. "A History of the Nevada County Narrow Gauge Railroad." Master's thesis. University of California, Los Angeles.

Loomis, Erik. 2008. "The Battle for the Body: Work and Environment in the Pacific Northwest Lumber Industry, 1800–1940." PhD dissertation. University of New Mexico, Albuquerque.

Lord, Eliot. 1925. *The Drama of Virginia City*. N.p.: Nevada Branch of the American Association of University Women.

Louie, Andrea. 2004. *Chineseness across Borders: Renegotiating Chinese Identities in China and the United States*. Durham, N.C.: Duke University Press.

Louie, Emma Woo. 1985–1986. "New Perspectives on Surnames among Chinese Americans." *Amerasia Journal* 12 (1): 1–22.

———. 1991. "Name Styles and Structure of Chinese American Names." *Names* 39 (3): 225–37.

Lowe, Sharon. 1993. "Pipe Dreams and Reality: Opium in Comstock Society, 1860–1887." *Nevada Historical Society Quarterly* 36 (3): 178–93.

"Lumber Played a Key Role in Keeping Madera Alive," http://www.cityofmadera.org/web/guest/our-history.

Lydon, Sandy. 1985. *Chinese Gold: The Chinese in the Monterey Bay Region*. Capitola, Calif.: Capitola Book Co.

MacGregor, Bruce. 2003. *The Birth of California Narrow Gauge: A Regional Study of the Technology of Thomas and Martin Carter*. Stanford, Calif.: Stanford University Press.

MacKay, Donald. 1978. *The Lumberjacks*. Toronto: McGraw-Hill Ryerson.

MacKenzie, Donald, and Elwood R. Maunder. 1972. "Logging Equipment Development in the West." *Forest History* 16 (October): 30–33.

Mackie, Richard Somerset. 2000. *Island Timber: A Social History of the Comos Logging Company, Vancouver Island*. Victoria, B.C.: Sono Nis.

Magee, Thomas. 1892. "The Preservation of Our Forests." *Overland Monthly* 29 (June): 658-62.

Magnaghi, Russell M. 2001. "Virginia City's Chinese Community, 1860–1880." In *Chinese on the American Frontier*, edited by Arif Dirlik, 123–48. Lanham, Md.: Rowman and Littlefield.

Maltz, Earl M. 1994. "The Federal Government and the Problem of Chinese Rights in the Era of the Fourteenth Amendment." *Harvard Journal of Law and Public Policy* 17 (Winter): 223–52.

Mark, Gregory Yee. 1995. "Opium in America and the Chinese." In *Chinese America: History and Perspectives*, 61–74. San Francisco: Chinese Historical Society of America.

Marks, Robert B. 1996. "Commercialization without Capitalism: Processes of Environmental Change in South China, 1550–1850." *Environmental History* 1 (January): 56–82.

———. 1997. *Tigers, Rice, Silk, and Silt: Environment and Economy in Late Imperial South China*. Cambridge: Cambridge University Press.

May, Ernest R., and John K. Fairbank, eds. 1986. *America's China Trade in Historical Perspective: The Chinese and American Performance*. Cambridge, Mass.: Committee on American-East Asian Relations of the Department of History, Harvard University.

Mazumdar, Sucheta. 1991. "Asian American Studies and Asian Studies: Rethinking Roots." In *Asian Americans: Comparative and Global Perspectives*, edited by Shirley Hume, et al., 29–30, 41. Pullman: Washington State University Press.

McAfee, Ward. 1975. *California's Railroad Era, 1850–1911*. San Marino, Calif.: Golden West.

McClain, Charles J. 1994. *In Search of Equality: The Chinese Struggle against Discrimination in Nineteenth-Century America*. Berkeley: University of California Press.

McClelland, Robert. 1971. *The Heathen Chinee: A Study of American Attitudes toward China, 1890–1905*. Columbus: Ohio State University Press.

McDonald, Philip M., and Lona F. Lahore. 1984. "Lumbering in the Northern Sierra Nevada: Andrew Martin Leach of Challenge Mills." *Pacific Historian* 29 (Summer): 18–31.

McElderry, Andrea. 1986. "Confucian Capitalism? Corporate Values in Republican Banking." *Modern China* 12 (July): 401–16.

McGlashan, Nona M. 1977. *Give Me a Mountain Meadow: The Life of Charles Fayette McGlashan (1847–1931); Imaginative Lawyer-Editor of the High Sierra, Who Saved the Donner Story from Oblivion and Launched Winter Sports in the West*. Fresno, Calif.: Valley.

McKeown, Adam. 1999. "Conceptualizing Chinese Diasporas, 1842 to 1949." *Journal of Asian Studies* 58 (May): 306–37.

———. 2001. *Chinese Migrant Networks and Cultural Change: Peru, Chicago, Hawaii, 1900–1936*. Chicago: University of Chicago Press.

———. 2003. "Ritualization of Regulation: The Enforcement of Chinese Exclusion in the United States and China." *American Historical Review* 108 (2): 377–403.

Mead, Walter J. 1966. *Competition and Oligopsony in the Douglas Fir Lumber Industry*. Berkeley: University of California Press.

Mei, June. 1979. "Socioeconomic Origins of Emigration: Guangdong to California, 1850–1882." *Modern China* 54 (October): 463–501.

Mengzi [Mencius]. *Liang hui wang*. Translated by James Legge as *The Works of Mencius*. New York: Paragon. Reprint of 1923 Shanghai edition, vol. 3.

Menzies, Nicholas Kay. 1988a. "Trees, Fields, and People: The Forests of China from the Seventeenth to the Nineteenth Centuries." PhD dissertation. University of California, Berkeley.

———. 1988b. "Three Hundred Years of Taungya: A Sustainable System of Forestry in South China." *Human Ecology* 16 (4): 361–76.

———. 1994a. *Forest and Land Management in Imperial China*. New York: St. Martin's.

———. 1994b. "Forestry." In *Science and Civilisation in China*, edited by Joseph Needham, 541–667. Vol. 6: Biology and Biological Technology, Part 3. Cambridge: Cambridge University Press.

———. 2007. *Our Forest, Your Ecosystem, Their Timber: Communities, Conservation, and the State in Community-Based Forest Management*. New York: Columbia University Press.

Miller, Char, ed. 1997. *American Forests: Nature, Culture, and Politics*. Lawrence: University Press of Kansas.

Miller, Eunice. 1926. "The Timber Resources of Nevada." *Nevada State Historical Society Papers, 1925–1926*, 385–89. Reno: Nevada State Historical Society.

Miller, Stuart Creighton. 1969. *The Unwelcomed Immigrant: The American Image of the Chinese, 1785–1882*. Berkeley: University of California Press.

Moehring, Eugene P. 1997. "The Comstock Urban Network." *Pacific Historical Review* 66 (3): 337–62.

Moore, Catherine. 2005. "Ties that Bind: The Hahn Brothers of Hardy County." *Goldenseal* 31 (2): 22–27.

Mosley, Stephen. 2010. *The Environment in World History.* New York: Routledge.

Myrick, David F. 1962–2007. *Railroads of Nevada and Eastern California.* Berkeley, Calif.: Howell-North, 1962–1963 (vols. 1–2); Reno: University of Nevada Press, 2007 (vol. 3).

Newbold, K. Bruce. 2004. "Chinese Assimilation across America: Spatial and Cohort Variations." *Growth and Change* 35 (Spring): 198–219.

Newell, Gordon R., and Joe Williamson. 1960. *Pacific Lumber Ships.* New York: Bonanza.

Newman, R. K. 1995. "Opium Smoking in Late Imperial China: A Reconsideration." *Modern Asian Studies* 29 (October): 765–94.

Ng, Franklin. 1987. "The Sojourner, Return Migration, and Immigration History." In *Chinese America: History and Perspectives,* 53–71. San Francisco: Chinese Historical Society of America.

Ng, Wing Chung. 1992. "Urban Chinese Social Organization: Some Unexplored Aspects in Huiguan Development in Singapore, 1900–1941." *Modern Asian Studies* 26 (July): 469–94.

Nomura, Gail M. 1989. "Washington's Asian/Pacific American Communities" In *Peoples of Washington: Perspectives on Cultural Diversity,* edited by Sid White and S. E. Solberg, 113–56. Pullman: Washington State University Press.

Olson, Sherry H. 1966. "Commerce and Conservation: The Railroad Experience. *Forest History* 9 (January): 2–15.

———. 1971. *The Depletion Myth: A History of Railroad Use of Timber.* Cambridge, Mass.: Harvard University Press.

Olzak, Susan. 1989. "Labor Unrest, Immigration, and Ethnic Conflict in Urban America, 1880- 1914." *American Journal of Sociology* 94 (May): 1303–33.

Ong, Paul M. 1985. "The Central Pacific Railroad and Exploitation of Chinese Labor." *Journal of Ethnic Studies* 13 (2): 119–24.

Orser, Charles E., Jr. 2004. *Race and Practice in Archaeological Interpretation.* Philadelphia: University of Pennsylvania Press.

Paden, Irene D., and Margaret E. Schlictmann. 1959. *The Big Oak Flat Road: An Account of Freighting from Stockton to Yosemite Valley.* Yosemite National Park, Calif.: Yosemite Natural History Association.

Park, Seung Ho, and Yadong Luo. 2001. "Guanxi and Organizational Dynamics: Organization Networking in Chinese Firms." *Strategic Management Journal* 22 (May): 455–77.

Peffer, George Anthony. 1999. *If They Don't Bring Their Women Here: Chinese Female Immigration Before Exclusion.* Urbana: University of Illinois Press.

Pendleton, Robert L. 1937. "Forestry in Kwangtung [Guangdong] Province, South China." *Lingnan Science Journal* 16 (3): 473–80.

Peng, Yusheng. 2004. "Kinship Networks and Entrepreneurs in China's Transitional Economy." *American Journal of Sociology* 109 (March): 1045–74.

Petersen, Keith C. 1987. *Company Town: Potlatch, Idaho, and the Potlatch Lumber Company.* Pullman: Washington State University Press; Moscow, Idaho: Latah County Historical Society.

Peterson, Charles E. 1965. "Prefabs in the California Gold Rush, 1849." *Journal of the Society of Architectural Historians* 24 (December): 318–24.

Pfaelzer, Jean. 2007. *Driven Out: The Forgotten War against Chinese Americans.* New York: Random House.

Pineda, Baron. 2001. "The Chinese Creoles of Nicaragua: Identity, Economy, and Revolution in a Caribbean Port City." *Journal of Asian American Studies* 4 (3): 209–33.

Pisani, Donald J. 1985. "Forests and Conservation, 1865–1890." *Journal of American History* 72 (September): 340–59.

———. 1997. "Forests and Conservation, 1865–1890." In *American Forests: Nature, Culture, and Politics*, edited by Char Miller. Lawrence: University Press of Kansas.

Polkinghorn, Robert Stephen. 1984. *Pino Grande: Logging Railroads of the Michigan–California Lumber Company*. Glendale, Calif.: Trans-Anglo.

Polk's Spokane City Directory, 1913. Vol. 22. Spokane, Wash.: Polk.

Pomeroy, Earl. 2003. *The Pacific Slope: A History of California, Oregon, Washington, Idaho, Utah, and Nevada*. Reno: University of Nevada Press.

Porter, Robert P. 1882. *The West from the Census of 1880: A History of the Industrial, Commercial, Social, and Political Development of the States and Territories of the West from 1800 to 1880*. Chicago: Rand McNally.

Portes, A., and J. Borocz. 1989. "Contemporary Immigration: Theoretical Perspectives on Its Determinants and Modes of Incorporation." *International Migration Review* 23 (3): 606–30.

Pratt, Edward Ewing. 1918. *The Export Lumber Trade of the United States*. Miscellaneous Series 67. Washington, D.C.: Department of Commerce, Bureau of Foreign and Domestic Commerce.

Prouty, Andrew M. 1985. *More Deadly Than War! Pacific Coast Logging, 1827–1983*. New York: Garland.

Qin, Yucheng. 2003. "A Century-Old 'Puzzle': The Six Companies' Role in Chinese Labor Importation in the Nineteenth Century." *Journal of American–East Asian Relations* 12 (3/4): 225–54.

———. 2009. *The Diplomacy of Nationalism: The Six Companies and China's Policy toward Exclusion*. Honolulu: University of Hawai'i Press.

Quimby, George I. 1948. "Culture Contact on the Northwest Coast, 1785–1795." *American Anthropologist* 50 (April–June): 247–55. New series.

Rajala, Richard A. 1989. "Bill and the Boss: Labor Protest, Technological Change, and the Transformation of the West Coast Logging Camp, 1890–1930." *Journal of Forest History* 33 (October): 168–79.

———. 1993. "The Forest as Factory: Technological Change and Worker Control in the West Coast Logging Industry, 1880–1930." *Labour/Le Travailleur* 32:73–104.

———. 1997. "The Evolution of West Coast Logging." *Legion Magazine* [Canada] 1.

Rapoport, Roger. 1983. "Port Gamble: The Company Town That's Still Working." *American West* 20 (2): 30–36.

Regehr, T. D. 1984. "Letters from End of Track." In *The CPR West: The Iron Road and the Making of a Nation*, edited by Hugh A. Dempsey, 37–54. Vancouver, B.C.: Douglas and McIntyre.

Reimers, David M. 2005. *Other Immigrants: The Global Origins of the American People*. New York: New York University Press.

Reno, Ronald L. 1996. "Fuel for the Frontier: Industrial Archaeology of Charcoal Production in the Eureka Mining District, Nevada, 1869–1891." PhD dissertation. University of Nevada, Reno.

Richards, Gordon. "Sierra Nevada Wood and Lumber Company." Available at http://truckeehistory.org/historyArticles/history33.htm (accessed December 1, 2014).

Richardson, S. D. 1990. *Forests and Forestry in China: Changing Patterns of Resource Development*. Washington, D.C.: Island.

Richmond, Al. 1988. "Apex: A Vanished Arizona Logging Community." *Journal of Arizona History* 29 (Spring): 75–88.

Select Bibliography

Ricks, Hiram Lambert. 1915. "The Timber and Stone Act of 1878 as Adjudicated by the Courts." J. D. dissertation. University of California, Berkeley.

Robbins, Willliam G. 1982. *Lumberjacks and Legislators: Political Economy of the U.S. Lumber Industry, 1890–1941*. College Station: Texas A&M University Press.

Robertson, Donald B. 1986. *Encyclopedia of Western Railroad History: The Desert States— Arizona, Nevada, New Mexico, Utah*. Caldwell, Idaho: Caxton.

Rohe, Randall. 1986. "The Evolution of the Great Lakes Logging Camp, 1830–1930." *Journal of Forest History* 30 (January): 17–28.

———. 2002. "Chinese Camps and Chinatowns: Chinese Mining Settlements in the North American West." In *Re/collecting Early Asian America: Essays in Cultural History* edited by Josephine Lee, Imogene L. Lim, and Yuko Matsukawa, 31–53. Philadelphia: Temple University Press.

Ross, Douglas E. 2013. *An Archaeology of Asian Transnationalism*. Gainesville: University Press of Florida.

Rowe, William T. 1990. "Modern Chinese Social History." In *Heritage of China: Contemporary Perspectives on Chinese Civilization*, edited by Paul S. Ropp, 256–59. Berkeley: University of California Press.

Rowley, William D., and Patricia Rowley. 1992. "Lumbering and Logging at Hobart Mills." *Nevada Historical Society Quarterly* 35 (Fall): 195–201.

Roy, Patricia E. 1984. "A Choice between Evils: The Chinese and the Construction of the Canadian Pacific Railway in British Columbia." In *The CPR West: The Iron Road and the Making of a Nation*, edited by Hugh A. Dempsey, 13–16. Vancouver, B.C.: Douglas and McIntyre.

———. 1989. *A White Man's Province: British Columbia Politicians and Chinese and Japanese Immigrants, 1858–1914*. Vancouver: University of British Columbia Press.

Rusco, Elmer R. 2001. "Riot in Unionville, Nevada: A Turning Point." In *The Chinese in America: A History from Gold Mountain to the New Millennium*, edited by Susie Lan Cassel, 91–105. Walnut Creek, Calif.: AltaMira.

Rusco, Mary K. 1981a. "Chinese in Lovelock, Nevada: History and Archaeology." *Halcyon*, 141–51.

———. 1981b. "Counting the Lovelock Chinese," *Nevada Historical Society Quarterly* 24 (4): 319–28.

Ryan, Terrence. 2009. "The Pacific Coast Lumber Trade." *California Territorial Quarterly* 79:24–35.

Salyer, Lucy E. 1995. *Laws Harsh as Tigers: Chinese Immigrants and the Shaping of Modern Immigration Law*. Chapel Hill: University of North Carolina Press.

Sandmeyer, Elmer C. (1939) 1973. *The Anti-Chinese Movement in California*. Urbana: University of Illinois Press.

Sangren, P. Steven. 1984. "Traditional Chinese Corporations: Beyond Kinship." *Journal of Asian Studies* 43 (May): 391–415.

Saxton, Alexander. 1966. "The Army of Canton in the High Sierra." *Pacific Historical Review* 35 (2): 141–51.

———. 1971. *The Indispensable Enemy: Labor and the Anti-Chinese Movement in California*. Berkeley: University of California Press.

Schmidt, Ryan. 2006. "The Forgotten Chinese Cemetery of Carlin, Nevada: A Bioanthropological Assessment." PhD dissertation. University of Nevada, Las Vegas.

Schuppert, Thomas. 1993. *Central Arizona Railroad and the Railroads of Arizona's Central Timber Region*. San Marino, Calif.: Golden West.

Schwantes, Carlos. 1982. "Protest in a Promised Land: Unemployment, Disinheritance, and the Origin of Labor Militancy in the Pacific Northwest, 1885–1886." *Western Historical Quarterly* 13 (October): 373–90.

———. 1997. "From Anti-Chinese Agitation to Reform Politics: The Legacy of the Knights of Labor in Washington and the Pacific Northwest." *Pacific Northwest Quarterly* 88 (Fall): 174–84.

Schwendinger, Robert J. 1978. "Chinese Sailors: America's Invisible Merchant Marine, 1876- 1905." *California History* 57 (1): 58–69.

———. 1988. *Ocean of Bitter Dreams: Maritime Relations between China and the United States, 1850–1915*. Tucson, Ariz.: Westernlore.

Scott, Edward B. 1957. *The Saga of Lake Tahoe: A Complete Documentation of Lake Tahoe's Development Over the Last One Hundred Years*. 2 vols. Crystal Bay, Nev.: Sierra-Tahoe.

See, Lisa. 1995. *On Gold Mountain: The 100-Year Odyssey of a Chinese American Family*. New York: St. Martin's.

Seward, George. 1881. *Chinese Immigration, its Social and Economic Aspects*. New York: Scribner's.

Shah, Nayan. 2001. *Contagious Divides: Epidemics and Race in San Francisco's Chinatown*. Berkeley: University of California Press.

Shaw, Norman. 1914. *Chinese Forest Trees and Timber Supply*. London: Unwin.

Sieber, George Wesley. 1971. "Lumbermen at Clinton: Nineteenth Century Sawmill Center." *Annals of Iowa* 41 (2): 779–802.

Sierra Logging Museum. "Logging History." Available at http://www.sierraloggingmuseum .org/History/history.htm (accessed December 1, 2014).

Simmel, Georg. 1955a. *Conflict*. Translated by Kurt H. Wolff. Glencoe, Ill.: Free Press.

———. 1955b. *The Web of Group Affiliations*. Translated by Reinhard Bendix. Glencoe, Ill.: Free Press.

Sinn, Elizabeth. 1997. "Xin Xi Guxiang: A Study of Regional Associations as a Bonding Mechanism in the Chinese Diaspora: The Hong Kong Experience." *Modern Asian Studies* 31 (May): 375–97.

———. 2013. *Pacific Crossing: California Gold, Chinese Migration, and the Making of Hong Kong*. Hong Kong: Hong Kong University Press.

Smith, Grant H. 1943. "The History of the Comstock Lode, 1850–1920." *University of Nevada Bulletin* 37 (July 1). Geology and Mining Series. Reno: University of Nevada Press.

Smith, Lindsay M. 2003. "Identifying Chinese Ethnicity through Material Culture: Archaeological Excavations at Kiandra, NSW." *Historical Archaeology* 21:18–29.

Smith, Raymond. 2000. *Carson City Yesterdays*. Minden, Nev.: Smith.

Soennichsen, John. 2011. *The Chinese Exclusion Act of 1882*. Santa Barbara, Calif.: Greenwood.

Solury, Theresa E. 2004. "'Everlasting Remembrance: The Archaeology of 19th-Century Chinese Labor in the Western Lumber Industry." Master's thesis. University of Nevada, Reno.

Songster, E. Elena. 2003. "Cultivating the Nation in Fujian's Forests: Forest Policies and Afforestation Efforts in China, 1911–1937." *Environmental History* 8 (July): 452–73.

Steiner, Stan. 1979. *Fusang, the Chinese Who Built America*. New York: Harper and Row.

Stephens, John W. 1976. "A Quantitative History of Chinatown, San Francisco, 1870 and 1880." In *The Life, Influence, and Role of the Chinese in the United States, 1776–1960*:

Proceedings, Papers of the National Conference Held at the University of San Francisco, July 10, 11, 12, 1975, 71–88. San Francisco, Calif.: Chinese Historical Society of America.

Stewart, Robert E. 2008. "Sam Clemens and the Wildland Fire at Lake Tahoe." *Nevada Historical Society Quarterly* 51 (Summer): 103–15.

Stoddard, Charles H. 1978. *Essential of Forestry Practice*. 3rd ed. New York: Wiley.

Stone, Julie R. "Lumber Industry at Lake Tahoe." Available at http://www.nevadaheritage.com (accessed June 12, 2011).

Stone, W. W. 1886. "The Knights of Labor on the Chinese Labor Situation." *Overland Monthly* 7 (March): 1–6.

Storti, Craig. 1991. *Incident at Bitter Creek: The Story of the Rock Springs Chinese Massacre*. Ames: Iowa State University Press.

Straka, Thomas J. 2006. "On Chris Kreider's 'Ward Charcoal Ovens' and Nevada's Carbonari." *Environmental History* 11 (April): 344–49.

———. 2007. "Timber for the Comstock." *Forest History Today* (Spring/Fall): 4–15.

———. 2008. "Ghost of a Western Logging Era." *Journal of the West* 47 (4): 3–9.

———. 2010. "Forests of Northeastern Nevada." *Northeastern Nevada Historical Society Quarterly* (September 1): 46–50.

———, and Robert H. Wynn. 2008. "History on the Road: Charcoal and Nevada's Early Mining Industry." *Forest History Today* (Fall): 63–66.

Strong, Douglas H. 1981. "Preservation Efforts at Lake Tahoe, 1880–1980." *Journal of Forest History* 25 (April): 78–97.

Sung Ying-hsing [b. 1587]. 1966. *T'ien-kung k'ai-wu: Chinese Technology in the Seventeenth Century*. Translated by E-tu Zen Sun and Shiou-chuan Sun. University Park: Pennsylvania State University.

Takaki, Ronald T. 1989. *Strangers from a Different Shore: A History of Asian Americans*. Boston: Little and Brown.

Tam, Shirley Sui Ling. 2002. "The Recurrent Image of the Coolie: Representations of Chinese American Labor in American Periodicals, 1900–1924." In *The Chinese in America: A History from Gold Mountain to the New Millennium*, edited by Susie Lan Cassel, 124–39. Walnut Creek, Calif.: Altamira.

Tappeiner, J. C., II. 1986. "Silviculture: The Next 30 Years, the Past 30 Years." Part 2: The Pacific Coast. *Journal of Forestry* 84 (5): 37–46.

Taylor, Bayard. 1988. *El Dorado; or, Adventures in the Path of Empire*. Lincoln: University of Nebraska Press.

Thompson, Judy Ann. 1992. "Historical Archaeology in Virginia City, Nevada: A Case Study of the 90-H Block." Master's thesis. 3 vols. University of Nevada, Reno.

Thompson, Thomas, and Albert West. 1958. *Thompson and West's History of Nevada, 1881*. Introduction by David F. Myrick. Berkeley, Calif.: Howell-North.

Tinkham, E. R. 1937. "Studies in Chinese Mantidae (Orthoptera)." *Lingnan Science Journal* 16 (3): 482.

Todes, Charlotte. (1931) 1975. *Labor and Lumber*. New York: Arno. Reprint of the 1931 edition.

Totman, Conrad. 1987. "Lumbering Provisioning in Early Modern Japan, 1580–1850." *Journal of Forest History* 31 (April): 56–70.

———. 1989. *The Green Archipelago*. Berkeley: University of California Press.

———. 1995. *The Lumber Industry in Early Modern Japan*. Honolulu: University of Hawai'i Press.

Tsai, Shih-shan Henry. 1979. "Preserving the Dragon Seeds: The Evolution of Ch'ing Emigration Policy." *Asian Profile* 7 (6):497–506.

Tsang, Eric W. K. 2002. "Learning from Overseas Venturing Experience: The Case of Chinese Family Businesses." *Journal of Business Venturing* 17:21–40.

Tutorow, Norman E. 1971. "Leland Stanford, President of the Occidental and Oriental Steamship Company: A Study in the Rhetoric and Reality of Competition." *American Neptune* 31 (2): 120–29.

Unwin, Peter. 2004. "A Brief History of Trees." *Beaver* 84 (June/July): 20–27.

Valentine, David W. 1999. "Historical and Archaeological Investigations at 26PE2137: American Canyon, Pershing County, Nevada." Master's thesis. University of Nevada, Las Vegas.

Vatter, Barbara A. 1985. *A Forest History of Douglas County, Oregon to 1900*. New York: Garland.

Vermeer, Eduard B. 1991. "The Mountain Frontier in Late Imperial China: Economic and Social Developments in the Bashan." 2nd series. *T'oung Pao* 77 (4/5): 300–329.

Vimalassery, Manu Mathew. 2011. "Skew Tracks: Racial Capitalism and the Transcontinental Railroad." PhD dissertation. New York: New York University.

Voss, Barbara L. 2005. "The Archaeology of Overseas Chinese Communities." *World Archaeology* 37 (3): 424–39.

Waldorf, John Taylor. 1968. *A Kid on the Comstock*. Berkeley, Calif.: Friends of the Bancroft Library.

Walker, Richard A. 2001. "California's Golden Road to Riches: Natural Resources and Regional Capitalism, 1848–1940." *Annals of the Association of American Geographers* 91 (March): 167–99.

Wang, Chi-chen. 1930. "Notes on Chinese Ink." *Metropolitan Museum Studies* 3 (December): 114–33.

Wang Gungwu. 1998. "Introduction: Migration and New National Identities." In *The Last Half-Century of Chinese Overseas*, edited by Elizabeth Sinn, 1–12. Hong Kong: Hong Kong University Press.

Wang Tai Peng, 1994. *The Origins of Chinese Kongsi*. Selangor Darul Ehsan, Malaysia: Pelanduk.

Warf, Barney. 1988. "Regional Transformation, Everyday Life, and Pacific Northwest Lumber Production." *Annals of the Association of American Geographers* 8 (June): 326–46.

Watson, James L. 1975. *Emigration and the Chinese Lineage: The Mans in Hong Kong and London*. Berkeley: University of California Press.

———. 1977. "The Chinese: Hong Kong Villagers in the British Catering Trade." In *Between Two Cultures: Migrants and Minorities in Britain*, edited by James L. Watson, 180–213. Oxford: Blackwell.

———. 1982. "Chinese Kinship Reconsidered: Anthropological Perspectives on Historical Research." *China Quarterly* 92 (December): 589–622.

Wedertz, Frank S. 1969. *Bodie 1859–1900*. Bishop, Calif.: Chalfant.

Weiner, Mark S. 2006. *Americans without Law: The Racial Boundaries of Citizenship*. New York: New York University Press.

Wells Fargo. 1878. *Directory of Chinese Business Houses*. San Francisco: Wells Fargo.

Wen, Zhengde. 1995. "Breaking Racial Barriers: Wo Kee Company, a Collaboration between a Chinese Immigrant and White American in Nineteenth-Century America." In *Chinese America: History and Perspectives*, edited by Laurene Wu McClain, 13–17. San Francisco: Chinese Historical Society of America.

Whalley, Robert. 2007. "The Sociotechnical History of the Verdi Lumber Company." Available at verdihistory.org/docs/verdilumber.pdf (accessed December 1, 2014).

Whatford, J. Charles. 2000. "Fuel for the Fire: Charcoal Making in Sonoma County: An Overview of the Archaeology and History of a Local Industry." Fresno, Calif.: Society for California Archeology.

Wheeler, Session S. 1992. *Tahoe Heritage: The Bliss Family of Glenbrook, Nevada*. Reno: University of Nevada Press.

White, Richard. 2011. *Railroaded: The Transcontinentals and the Making of Modern America*. New York: Norton.

Williams, Bryn. 2011. "The Archaeology of Objects and Identities at the Point Alones Chinese Village, Pacific Grove, California (1860–1906)." PhD dissertation. Stanford University, Stanford, California.

Williams, Michael. 1989. *Americans and Their Forests: A Historical Geography*. Cambridge: Cambridge University Press.

Willson, Margaret, and Jeffery L. MacDonald. 1983. "Racial Tension at Port Townsend and Bellingham Bay, 1870–1886." In *Annals of the Chinese Historical Society of the Pacific Northwest*, 1–15. Seattle: Chinese Historical Society of the Pacific Northwest.

Wilson, Dick. 1992. *Sawdust Trails in the Truckee Basin: A History of Lumbering Operations 1856–1936*. Nevada City, Calif.: Nevada County Historical Society.

Winant, Howard. 2001. *The World is a Ghetto: Race and Democracy Since World War II*. New York: Basic.

"A Winter Night's Ride in the Sierra." 1870. *Overland Monthly* 4 (June): 512–17.

Woirol, Gregory. 2011a. "An Investigation of the Working and Living Conditions of Migratory Laborers in the Pacific Northwest, 1914." *Pacific Northwest Quarterly* 102 (3): 117–31.

———. 2011b. "Men of the Woods: Life in a Sierra Lumber Camp." *Californians* 5 (5): 32–45.

Wolf, Eric. 1982. *Europe and the People without History*. Cambridge: Cambridge University Press.

Wong, Bernard. 1998. "The Chinese in New York City: Kinship and Immigration." In *The Overseas Chinese: Ethnicity in National Context*, edited by Francis L. K. Hsu and Hendrick Serrie, 143–73. Lanham, Md.: University Press of America.

Woon, Yuen-fong. 1978. "Social Discontinuities in North American Chinese Communities: The Case of the Kuan in Vancouver and Victoria, 1850–1960." *Canadian Review of Sociology and Anthropology* 15 (November): 143–51.

———. 1983–1984. "The Voluntary Sojourner among the Overseas Chinese: Myth or Reality?" *Pacific Affairs* 56 (Winter): 673–90.

———. 1984. "An Emigrant Community in the Ssu-yi [Siyi] Area, Southeastern China, 1855–1949." *Modern Asian Studies* 18 (2): 273–308.

———. 1989. "Social Change and Continuity in South China: Overseas Chinese and Guan Lineage of Kaiping County, 1948–87." *China Quarterly* 118 (June): 324–44.

Wrobleski, David Eugene. 1996. "The Archaeology of the Chinese Work Camps on the Virginia and Truckee Railroad." Master's thesis. University of Nevada, Reno.

Wu, David Y. Hu. 1974. "To Kill Three Birds with One Stone: The Rotating Credit Associations of the Papua New Guinea Chinese." *American Ethnologist* 1 (August): 565–84.

Wunder, John R. 1983. "The Chinese and the Courts in the Pacific Northwest: Justice Denied?" *Pacific Historical Review* 52 (May): 191–211.

———. 1986. "Chinese in Trouble: Criminal Law and Race on the Trans-Mississippi West Frontier." *Western Historical Quarterly* 17 (January): 25–41.

Wurm, Ted, and Harre W. Demoro. 1983. *The Silver Short Line: A History of the Virginia and Truckee Railroad*. Glendale, Calif.: Trans-Anglo.

Wynn, Graeme. 1981. *Timber Colony: A Historical Geography of Early Nineteenth Century New Brunswick*. Toronto: University of Toronto Press.

Yang, Philip Q. 2002. "The 'Sojourner Hypothesis' Revisited." *Diaspora* 9 (Fall): 235–58.

Yee, Paul. 1986. "Sam Kee: A Chinese Business in Early Vancouver." *BC Studies* 69–70 (Spring-Summer): 70–96.

Yen, C. H. 1981. "Ch'ing's Changing Images of the Overseas Chinese (1644–1912)." *Modern Asian Studies* 15:261–85.

Yen Tzu-kuei. 1977. "Chinese Workers and the First Transcontinental Railroad of the United States of America." PhD dissertation. St. John's University, New York.

Ye Xian'en. 1981. "Guanyu Huizhoudi dianpu zhi [On the Bondservant System of Huizhou]. *Zhongguo Shehui Kexue* 1:181–96.

Young, James A. and Jerry D. Budy. 1979. "Historical Use of Nevada's Pinyon-Juniper Woodlands." *Journal of Forest History* 23 (July): 112–21.

Yu, Henry. 2001. *Thinking Orientals: Migration, Contact, and Exoticism in Modern America*. New York: Oxford University Press.

Yuen, Jack K. 1994. *Chuck Hum Village: A Photographic Essay*. Honolulu: Harbor Graphics.

Yung, Judy, and Erika Lee. 2010. *Angel Island: Immigrant Gateway to America*. New York: Oxford University Press.

Zackey, Justin. 2007. "Peasant Perspectives on Deforestation in Southwest China: Social Discontent and Environmental Mismanagement." *Mountain Research and Development* 27 (May): 153–61.

Zeier, Charles D. 1987. "Historic Charcoal Production Near Eureka, Nevada: An Archaeological Perspective." *Historical Archaeology* 21 (1): 81–101.

Zhu Guohong. 1994. *Zhonguo Haiqai Yimin: Yixiang Qianyi de Lizhi Yanjiu* [Chinese Emigration: A Historical Study of the International Migration]. Shanghai: Fudan University Press.

Zhu, Liping. 1996. "How the Other Half Lived: Chinese Daily Life in Boise Basin Mining Camps." *Idaho Yesterdays* 38 (4): 20–28.

———. 2013. *The Road to Chinese Exclusion: The Denver Riot, 1880 Election, and the Rise of the West*. Lawrence: University Press of Kansas.

Zimmerman, Robert. 1998. "Log Flume." *American Heritage of Invention and Technology* 14 (2): 58–63.

Zo Kil Young. 1971. *Chinese Emigration to the United States, 1850–1880*. New York: Arno.

———. 1975. "Chinese Emigration: The Means of Obtaining Passage to America." *Journal of Asiatic Studies* [Korea] 28 (2): 215–29.

Zurndorfer, Harriet. 1985. "Local Lineages and Local Development: A Case Study of the Fan Lineage, Hsiu-ning Hsien, Hui-chou, 800–1500." *T'oung Pao* 70:18–52.

———. 1989. *Change and Continuity in Chinese Local History: The Development of Hui-chou Prefecture 800 to 1800*. Leiden: Brill.

INDEX

Some Chinese individuals are listed with their first name and then last name because their last names could not be determined without the Chinese characters. "Ah" is not a last name but a term of address for a familiar person. These names do not designate a single individual because several men, for example, were called Ah Sing.

SUE FAWN CHUNG is Professor Emerita of history at the University of Nevada, Las Vegas, and author of *In Pursuit of Gold: Chinese American Miners and Merchants in the American West*, an honor book selection for the Caroline Bancroft History Prize.

THE ASIAN AMERICAN EXPERIENCE

The University of Illinois Press
is a founding member of the
Association of American University Presses.

———————————————————————

Typeset in 10.5/13 Adobe Minion
Composed by Lisa Connery
at the University of Illinois Press
Manufactured by Cushing-Malloy, Inc.

University of Illinois Press
1325 South Oak Street
Champaign, IL 61820-6903
www.press.uillinois.edu